1789

1789

1789

GEORGE WASHINGTON
AND
THE FOUNDERS
CREATE AMERICA

Thomas B. Allen

ROWMAN & LITTLEFIELD
Lanham • Boulder • New York • London

Published by Rowman & Littlefield
An imprint of The Rowman & Littlefield Publishing Group, Inc.
4501 Forbes Boulevard, Suite 200, Lanham, Maryland 20706
www.rowman.com

86-90 Paul Street, London EC2A 4NE

Distributed by NATIONAL BOOK NETWORK

British Library Cataloguing in Publication Information Available

Library of Congress Cataloging-in-Publication Data Available

ISBN 9781538183090 (cloth)
ISBN 9781538197851 (paperback)
ISBN 9781538183106 (electronic)

♾™ The paper used in this publication meets the minimum requirements of American National
Standard for Information Sciences—Permanence of Paper for Printed Library Materials, ANSI/
NISO Z39.48-1992

For Phil Spitzer

Books by Thomas B. Allen

Fiction

The Last Inmate

A Short Life

(with Norman Polmar)

Ship of Gold

(with William S. Cohen)

Murder in the Senate

Non-Fiction

The Quest

War Games

Possessed: The True Story of an Exorcism

CNN's Guide to the 1992 Election

The Washington Monument: It Stands For All

Shark Attacks

The Shark Almanac

George Washington, Spymaster

Harriet Tubman, Secret Agent

Remember Pearl Harbor

Remember Valley Forge

Declassified

Guardians of the Wild

The Blue and the Gray

Vanishing Wildlife of North America

Offerings at the Wall

America from Space

Animals of Africa

Tories: Fighting for The King

The First Mormon Candidate

Acts of Congress

Intelligence in the Civil War

1789: The Founders Create America

(with Harold W. McCormick and William E. Young)

Shadows In the Sea

(with Scottie Allen, Joel Garbus and Theresa Garbus)

Living in Washington: A Moving Experience

(with Norman Polmar)

Rickover : Controversy and Genius

Merchants of Treason

World War II: Americans at War 1941-1945

Code-name: Downfall

Spy Book

(with Paul Dickson)

The Bonus Army: An American Epic

(with Todd Braisted)

The Loyalist Corps

(with Roger MacBride Allen)

Mr. Lincoln's High Tech War

Time Capsule: The Book of Record

Contents

PROLOGUE: ELEVEN STATES CREATE A NATION 9

1 THE GREAT CAUSE 17

2 THE SPECTER OF A KING 29

3 THE RELUCTANT PRESIDENT 47

4 OUT WITH THE OLD 55

5 A NEW GOVERNMENT AWAKENS 63

6 "NOW A KING" 71

7 ETIQUETTE ADVICE FOR THE PRESIDENT 87

8 "ALL IS BARE CREATION" 99

9 THE CONSTITUTION AS BLUEPRINT 105

10 COUNTING WE THE PEOPLE 115

11 AMERICA'S "OTHER PERSONS" 127

12 A TUB FULL OF RIGHTS 137

13 "HE SHALL HAVE POWER" 147

14 STRICKEN WASHINGTON, FEARFUL NATION 157

15 WASHINGTON GETS A BASTILLE KEY 163

16 SEEING AMERICA'S FARMS AND FACTORIES 169

17 MANY PIRATES—AND NO NAVY 183

18 THE SECOND SESSION: HOPE AND ANGST 191

19 ON THE FRONTIER, SPIES AND PLOTS 203

20 TOWARD AN AMERICAN LANGUAGE.......................... 217

    EPILOGUE: IN RISING GLORY 231

Appendices

1 THE "CORRECT"
   CONSTITUTION OF THE UNITED STATES 247

2 INSIDE THE DOZEN: THE BILL OF RIGHTS 261

3 A TIMELINE OF THE FOUNDING OF
   THE UNITED STATES AND
   THE FEDERAL GOVERNMENT 265

   ACKNOWLEDGMENTS 275

   NOTES 277

   BIBLIOGRAPHY 325

   BIBLIOGRAPHIC SOURCES 326

   INDEX 377

   ABOUT THE AUTHOR... 395

PROLOGUE

ELEVEN STATES CREATE A NATION

ere is a moment in the swift passage of time toward 1789: On September 17, 1787, in the old Pennsylvania State House in Philadelphia, the Constitutional Convention was ending, and members were signing the Constitution they had created. Ben Franklin looked toward the "President's Chair," where Washington had sat, presiding over the convention. Painted on the back of the chair was a sun. Often, amid "the vicissitudes of my hopes and fears," Franklin had looked at that sun, unable to tell whether it was rising or setting: "But now," he said, "I have the happiness to know that it is a rising and not a setting Sun."[1]

Imagine the year 1789 to be the rising sun, its beams reaching out beyond time, because America's founding story cannot be told strictly in terms of time. Much of the 1789 narrative flows from people. Seven future Presidents were people of 1789: Washington, John Adams, Jefferson, Madison, Monroe, John Quincy Adams—and Andrew Jackson, who would emerge from the Tennessee frontier and, in a new century, preside over a rapidly expanding nation.

Why 1789? The Constitution came to life in that mighty year, wielding new powers and transforming eleven independent states into the United States of America. The first presidential election was held in that year, and the first Federal Congress began its first session of lawmaking. Not all that made America happened in 1789, but everything that happened in that epochal year would shape and empower the history that has followed it.

Although the country celebrates 1776 for our independence and 1781 for our revolutionary victory, we can see in 1789 not only the true birth of the nation but also its destiny: Threads of unification would bind the states together in a powerful transcontinental nation. The emergence of political parties would challenge the idea of national unity. And the beginning of the long struggle over slavery would sunder North from South.

America's road toward nationhood, and toward the pivotal year of 1789, began as merely a faint trail blazed by both what John Adams called the opinions of colonists—"their wishes and passions, their hopes and fears"—and the era's "strange oscillation between love and hatred, between war and peace."[2] The government was the First Continental Congress, comprised of delegates from the colonies who met briefly in 1774 to protest what they called the Coercive Acts—attempts by the British to tame colonists who were resisting new taxes. In 1775, the Second Continental Congress convened and in 1776 declared independence from Britain. In 1781, Congress ratified the first national constitution, the Articles of Confederation, which would ineptly govern until it was superseded by the U.S. Constitution in 1789.

Adams wrote about that "strange oscillation" three months after about seven hundred British troops had clashed with some seventy Massachusetts Minutemen on the Lexington Green in April 1775. In a panicky burst of British muskets and slashing bayonets, eight Americans fell, mortally wounded. The Revolutionary War, a milestone on the road to nationhood, had begun.[3]

Yet even at this point, Adams and many other delegates to the Second Continental Congress believed there still was a chance for peace with Britain. A cessation of conflict, rather than a severing of ties, was uppermost in their minds. A clear drive toward independence did not yet seem to be in the air in the American colonies. In March 1775, Adams had written, "That there are any who pant after 'independence' . . . is as great a slander on the province [of Massachusetts] as was ever committed to writing,"[4] and on July 5 he and forty-seven other members of Congress passed what came to be called the Olive Branch Petition, urging King George III to ignore the "delusive pretenses, fruitless terrors, and unavailing severities" unleashed by the king's ministers to punish the restive colonies. George refused even to read the petition.

Dissenting voices soon began to be heard in the colonies. On June 3, 1776, Congressman Richard Henry Lee, scion of Virginia's most distinguished family, suggested that independence was necessary because it was "the only means by which foreign alliance can be obtained."[5] Four days later, he stood in Congress and raised his left hand, on which he wore a black silk glove. In a hunting accident in 1768 he had blown off the fingers of his left hand. The black glove concealed the injury, drew attention when he raised his hand in debate—and became a sign of his grit.[6] In his booming voice, he spoke: "Resolved: that these United Colonies are, and of right ought to be, free and independent States, that they are absolved from all allegiance to the British Crown, and that all political connection between them and the state of Great Britain is, and ought to be totally dissolved."[7] Note "free and independence states." Lee—like most Americans—envisioned a string of nation-states, each one clinging to its sovereignty. In the debate that followed, one of the great undercurrents of American history can be clearly discerned: the tension between identification with one's state and one's country.

Congressmen from the colonies of New York, New Jersey, Pennsylvania, Delaware, Maryland, and South Carolina wanted to ensure that their homelands would remain free and independent states should they break with Britain. Some members, before voting on Lee's resolution, asked for more time to get advice from their state legislatures. That was easy enough for the Pennsylvania delegation because of the arrangement in the State House (now called Independence Hall): the Pennsylvania state assembly met on the second floor and the Continental Congress convened on the first.[8] North Carolina's delegates had been told by their own state legislature that they could vote for Lee's independence resolution as long as the legislature wrote a constitution preserving North Carolina's status as an independent state, and other state legislatures made similar demands.

Back in 1775, each member of the Continental Congress had pledged, "under the ties of virtue, honour, and love of his country," not to divulge "any matter or thing agitated or debated . . . without leave."[9] Continuing that rule, Congress voted for secrecy to delay the independence debate and at the same time appointed a committee—composed of Adams, Thomas Jefferson, Benjamin Franklin, Roger Sherman of Connecticut, and Robert R. Livingston of New York—"to prepare a declaration" in case Congress eventually did vote for independence.[10]

Secrecy was an acceptable legislative rule, even for the creation of the Declaration of Independence. Some of the desire for secrecy stemmed from a natural distrust of strangers and realization that Loyalists were among the delegates. Each of them carried his own apprehensions about the temporary colleagues he was to meet and deal with. "Here is a diversity of religions, educations, manners, interests, such as it would seem impossible to unite in one plan of conduct," John Adams wrote.[11] Secrecy—a form of self-protection for distrustful delegates—was so thorough that defeated motions and votes were expunged from the record lest dissenting information leak to the outside world.[12]

Thanks mostly to Jefferson, we know the timeline of the Declaration of Independence. He was selected by the committee to do the writing, and he submitted a draft of the declaration on June 27, 1776, soon after Lee's proposal. It was presented to Congress the next day as debate continued. To Jefferson's annoyance, members voted to strike out some of his words and phrases. The most contentious deletion was a long passage on slavery—ironic in retrospect, for Jefferson himself was a slave owner—which began with these words: "He has waged cruel war against human nature itself, violating its most sacred rights of life and liberty in the persons of a distant people who never offended him, captivating & carrying them into slavery."[13] The inherent contradiction between a nation demanding freedom for itself while preserving the enslavement of others was literally written out of the draft, a deletion whose consequences would be felt for centuries afterward.

Finally, on July 2, Congress nearly unanimously adopted Lee's resolution for independence (with the New York delegation abstaining until July 9 because of outdated instructions from the New York Provincial Congress.[14]). The delegates, who had showered devotion upon King George only a year before, now denounced him and his "long train of abuses and usurpations." On the same day, in a foreshadowing of the conflict to come, a British fleet carrying thirty-two thousand British Army troops sailed into New York Harbor.[15]

On July 4, Congress ordered that the declaration be printed, and suddenly there it was for all to see: independence. But not yet nationhood; the declaration ended with a reminder that the former colonies were "free and independent states"—thirteen little countries, each with "full power to levy war, conclude peace, contract alliances, establish commerce, and to do all other acts and things which independent states may of right do."

The proclamation of independence did not reflect the turbulent political realities beyond the walls of Congress, where tens of thousands of Americans opposed the Revolution. They called themselves Loyalists. Supporters of independence called them Tories. Americans in favor of the Revolution, who saw themselves as sympathizers with the British Whigs—who tried to curb royal authority and boost the power of Parliament—became known as Whigs themselves, or Patriots, the more acceptable label. Every able-bodied white American man had to make one of the seminal choices that would confront the citizenry of a country not yet completely born: Would he take up arms against King George III? Would he support the rebellion and, in the eyes of many, become a traitor? Or would he remain loyal to the Crown? Every state, too, had to wage a war within itself.

Thousands of Loyalists armed themselves and formed battalion- and regiment-size military units, launching a civil war whose savagery—including lynchings, house burnings, and tar and featherings—shocked even the battle-hardened redcoats and Hessians (Britain's hired German soldiers). As the Patriots' debates and protests evolved into war, many Loyalists fled to Canada, Britain, or the Caribbean. On March 17, 1776 (remembered now as Evacuation Day), hundreds of Loyalists sailed away from Boston with the armada that evacuated British troops, a Patriot chant taunting them as they left their homes and farms behind: "The Tories with their brats and wives / Have fled to save their wretched lives."[16] The internal conflict persisted throughout the war; Brigadier General Nathanael Greene, taking command of the Continental Army of the South in 1781, wrote to Colonel Alexander Hamilton: "The division among the people is much greater than I imagined." The Tories and the Whigs, Greene said, "persecute each other, with little less than savage fury. There is nothing but murders and devastation in every quarter."[17]

Again and again in these years, Americans were asked to prove which side they were on by taking oaths of allegiance. Congress ordered all Continental officers to declare their loyalty to the United States; meanwhile, many enlisted men, unpaid and despairing, deserted the Continental Army and joined Loyalist forces. The Revolutionary War would last nearly seven years, but it would take two more years before peace was declared. On the rebels' side, 4,435 would be killed and 6,188 wounded.[18] About 24,000 British soldiers would be killed.[19] No one knows how many Loyalist Americans died fighting for the king.

Even when the war began to subside, the states, each demanding its sovereignty, were distrustful of the central authority that had been needed to fight a war. Even as one committee of the Continental Congress was writing the Declaration of Independence, another committee began working on what would be called the Articles of Confederation.

Congress approved the plan for government in November 1777, but the bickering of states over competing land claims delayed ratification. It was not until March 1, 1781 that they agreed to accept a weak federal government by ratifying the Articles of Confederation.

Although the document has been sometimes labeled America's first constitution, it was more a treaty among the states, joined into a "firm league of friendship." Each state "retains its sovereignty, freedom, and independence, and every power, jurisdiction, and right" not delegated to Congress, "the primary organ of the new national government."

Under the Articles, Congress could make alliances, manage relations with Indians, and declare war but could not draft soldiers. Delegates to Congress were chosen by the state legislatures, not by voters. Although each state was nominally still sovereign and independent, the states of the Confederation gave to the Second Continental Congress (thereafter known as the Congress of the Confederation) the right to maintain armed forces, but not the power to levy the taxes that would give General Washington the funds he needed for his army. The states—not Congress—had the power to tax.

Beyond the debating in Philadelphia, a war was still being fought—and being chronicled.

In May 1780, when the British captured Charleston and began their Loyalist-aided conquest of South Carolina, more than 2,500 American soldiers became prisoners. One was David Ramsay, a military surgeon. To pass the time, he began writing a history of the war he was living through. When he was released, after eleven months, he kept writing, eventually covering the Revolution from its origins in the 1760s to the peace treaty that ended it in 1783.

It was not until 1789 that Ramsay felt he could finally publish the work he had labored over for all those years, *The History of the American Revolution.* It was not until 1789 that he felt able to declare that the Revolution truly had ended. He wrote, "The old Congress and confederation, like the continental money, expired without a sigh or groan. A new Congress, with more ample powers and a new constitution; partly national and partly federal, succeeded in their place to the great joy of all who wished for the happiness of the United States."

Ramsay's book was itself one of the events that made 1789 a year studded with American firsts: it was the first history of the Revolutionary War written by an American combat veteran and printed on an American press by an American publisher. As *The History* says, "The experience of former ages has given many melancholy proofs that popular governments have seldom answered in practice to the theories and warm wishes of their admirers. The present inhabitants of independent America now have an opportunity to wipe off this aspersion, to assert the dignity of human nature, and the capacity of mankind for self-government."[20]

1

THE GREAT CAUSE

*I*n a niche above the west entrance of the golden-domed Connecticut capitol, in Hartford, is a statue of Lieutenant Colonel David Humphreys, a poet and a soldier who was emblematic of the men who had waged the Revolutionary War and returned home to wage the peace.[1] Humphreys served as an aide to General Washington in the Revolution; among his other wartime accomplishments, he enlisted the first black troops into the Continental Army. He is believed to be America's first sonneteer, and the statue honors his contribution to Connecticut history as not only a warrior but also a writer. One of his sonnets, written in July 1776 and focusing on men going off to war, ends with these lines:

> *Though certain death to threaten'd chains be join'd.*
> *Though fails this flesh devote to freedom's cause,*
> *Can death subdue th' unconquerable mind?*
> *Or adamantine chains ethereal substance bind?*[2]

Freedom's cause—or simply "the Cause"—was a rallying phrase for many Patriots besides Humphreys during the war. It was spoken of reverentially, and it evoked a vague vision of a future America unyoked from British control. As Thomas Paine wrote in *Common Sense*, "Everything that is right or reasonable pleads for separation. The blood of the slain, the weeping voice of nature cries, 'TIS TIME TO PART."[3] Yet it is important to note that in 1776, when both *Common Sense* and the sonnet were written, the Cause meant independence from Great Britain and the sovereignty of states, not nationhood. Nevertheless, a nation was beginning to emerge.

Before any thought could be given to how to shape the new nation—how, essentially, to invent a new form of governance from the ground up—the Revolution first had to be securely won. In 1781, Humphreys bore witness to a landmark battle that many mistakenly believed spelled the end of the war and thus the end of the major work of the Cause. On October 19 of that year, a combined American and French force defeated General Charles Cornwallis at Yorktown. Afterward, Humphreys was given the honor to carry to the Congress of the Confederation in Philadelphia tokens of the Yorktown victory: the regimental flags that the British had surrendered to the Continental Army. [4] Many Americans—including members of the Confederation Congress—concluded that the war itself had just ended at Yorktown and that the disbanding of the army was nigh. After all, as a major general in that battle, the Marquis de Lafayette, exulted soon afterward in a letter from Yorktown to Jean-Frédéric Phélypeaux, Count of Maurepas and the French secretary of state: "The play is over, the fifth act has just ended." [5]

But the truth was more complex. Both continuing conflicts with the British Army and tensions within the Continental Army continued after Yorktown. General Washington, soon after accepting the British surrender, expressed a far more sober view than Lafayette's. In a November 1781 letter to an aide-de-camp Washington said that although the victory "is an interesting event . . . if it should be the means of relaxation, and sink us into supineness and security, it had better not have happened. . . . Peace may be further removed from us than we expect." [6] Indeed, men on both sides went on fighting and dying even into the spring of 1782, when Benjamin Franklin was in Paris to lead peace talks with British negotiators. From the victory at Yorktown through the end of 1783, there were more than seventy skirmishes between Loyalists and Patriots. [7] During this period, the British still occupied New York City and manned six forts along a vast northern frontier stretching from present-day Maumee, Ohio, to Lake Ontario. The end of the war seemed to be both in sight and frustratingly elusive.

Washington, concerned about the large British forces in New York and in Charleston, South Carolina, sent reinforcements both south and north. On April 1, 1782, the general himself arrived with about seven thousand men at the encampment along the Hudson River highlands near Newburgh, about sixty miles north of New York. Although Washington faced internal threats from his officer corps, which was then seething with grievances because they had not received their promised salary and bonuses, his primary concern centered on the twenty thousand British troops downriver in the city.[8] Should the Paris peace talks break down, Washington believed, the British might suddenly resume warfare by sailing up the Hudson and landing an invasion force.

He ordered the renewal of the General Alarm warning system, which had been built in 1776 after the British captured New York City. His men erected bonfire beacons—pyramidal piles of wood and brush about twenty feet high and spaced fifteen to twenty miles apart—along the Hudson from the city north to their camp at Newburgh. They could be set afire, one by one, relaying a signal northward to warn of the upriver advance of a British armada. Tests have shown that one beacon, set atop what was later called Mount Beacon, 1,530 feet high and directly across the river from Washington's encampment, could have been seen as far north as Poughkeepsie. The beacons, which were not used in combat, would have been spectacularly effective at night. Daytime riverside warnings relied on billowing smoke or men waving huge red-and-white striped flags.[9]

Humphreys, an aide on the military staff collectively known as "Washington's family," welcomed the general, soon after his arrival, with an ambitious idea: Humphreys believed that the Continental Army was strong enough not only to repel a British attack but also to thrust into Canada. "It is unnecessary to dwell upon the glory that would result," he wrote in a report to Washington on April 7, pointing out that Continental possession of Canadian land might be a useful bargaining chip in the Paris peace talks.[10] But Humphreys dropped that idea after talking to officers whose men had begun to desert for lack of pay, and soon he warned Washington of "the daily diminution" of his army. The "loss of discipline," Humphreys predicted, "will certainly succeed, & a train of Evils will be induced."[11]

The discontent among officers and enlisted men alike had deep roots. In 1778, Congress had promised officers that once the war ended, they would receive half-pay for seven years thereafter and that each soldier would receive a postwar bonus worth about $1,900 in today's dollars. (See footnote on page 52 for an explanation of 18th century American money.) The bonus was later extended to soldiers' widows and orphan children. Many soldiers and their officers, however, believed that Congress had no intention of paying them what they were owed; after all, the Articles of Confederation enabled Congress to establish an army but not to levy the taxes to pay for it.

The army's doubts were amplified when, in an embarrassing display of Congress's empty treasury, the express rider who delivered the official news of the Yorktown victory reached Philadelphia only to find that Congress did not have enough money to pay his expenses. Instead, Congress members chipped in and paid him out of their own pockets.[12] The men of the Continental Army at Newburgh were beginning to realize that peace would not be a gift; ahead lay uncertainty, a postwar nation whose only status was that it consisted of thirteen sovereign states that were no longer under British rule. They were potentially a nation, but during those tense days at Newburgh, they were still a nation unborn.

The unrest over the army's pay began, interestingly, to reveal differing visions of the country's governance that would not be wholly reconciled until 1789. As the new nation began to envision the end of the war and look toward its future, many were grappling with concepts of a government for the new nation: Hew to the Old World model of a monarchy? Forge a new executive form of government? Turn to the army and place the young nation under military rule? Or could it become a nation based on newly minted laws? One incident in the struggles over army compensation richly illustrates the complexities of these questions.

On May 22, 1782, General Washington, at his headquarters in a fieldstone farmhouse near Newburgh, received another warning about discontent among the soldiers, this one in the form of a letter from Colonel Lewis Nicola, commanding officer of the Corps of Invalids. Early in the war, Congress, at Nicola's suggestion, had created the corps, composed of men unfit for combat, "to be employed in garrisons, and for guards in cities and other places, where magazines or arsenals, or hospitals are placed."[13] Nicola, born in Ireland in 1717, once had been an officer in the British Army. After spending most of his military career in Ireland, he quit in 1766 and sailed to Philadelphia with his wife and children. Three years later, he began publishing the *American Magazine and General Repository,* believed to be America's first scientific journal, and he became a member of the American Philosophical Society, founded by Benjamin Franklin. When the Revolutionary War began, he served in military posts in and around Philadelphia and in 1777 took command of the Corps of Invalids.[14] Nicola wrote to Washington in a kind of detached, scholarly dialect, beginning: "The injuries the troops have received in their pecuniary rights have been, & still continue to be too obvious to require a particular detail, or to have escaped your Excellencies notice, tho your exalted station must have deprived you of opportunity of information relative to the severe distresses occasioned thereby."[15]

What has come to be known as the Newburgh Letter went on for 2,335 words. Had it been shorter and clearer, perhaps Nicola would not have erroneously gone down in history as the man who "offered Washington a crown." He did not do that. But despite his opaque prose, he did convey a critique of republicanism and a military bias toward monarchy. Nicola said he was writing to Washington in response to "several conversations I have had with officers, & some I have overheard among soldiers." Then he got to his point: The war had "shown to all, but especially to military men . . . the weakness of republics." Congress, he wrote, should procure "a sufficient tract in some of the best of those fruitful & extensive countries to the west of our frontiers." These lands, which Nicola saw as a sort of potential new nation beyond the Ohio River, would presumably be ruled by former army officers who would be given the territory by Congress. It could be "formed into a distinct State under such mode of government as those military who choose to remove to it may agree on . . . [and] it may . . . be requisite to give the head of such a constitution as I propose, some title apparently more moderate, but if all other things were once adjusted I believe strong argument might be produced for admitting the title of king." (Nicola seemed to be using "State" in the sense of a sovereign nation.)[16]

Washington's reaction was shocked and swift. He replied within hours: "Be assured Sir, no occurrence in the course of the War, has given me more painful sensations than your information of there being such ideas existing in the Army . . . banish these thoughts from your Mind, and never communicate, as from yourself, or any one else, a sentiment of the like Nature." Rather than dictate his reply to a copyist, Washington wrote it in his own hand and made a file copy, providing evidence that he never had wanted anything to do with a monarchy. Humphreys, as the general's aide, and Jonathan Trumbull, as his secretary, both signed "an exact copy" of the letter, "which we sealed and sent off."

The chastised Nicola seems to have obeyed Washington. But military mutterings about monarchy continued. Little more than a month after receiving the letter from Nicola, Washington received one from Major General James Mitchell Varnum of the Rhode Island militia. Because "Avarice, Jealously & Luxury" controlled the people of the failing republic, Varnum wrote, "absolute Monarchy, or a military State, can alone rescue them from all the Horrors of Subjugation."[17]

In reply Washington wrote, "The conduct of the people at large is truly alarming," but he did not go on to express outrage over the idea of monarchy as he had before. Instead he wearily conceded that "destructive passions . . . too generally pervade all Ranks," and he expressed hope that they "shall give place to that love of Freedom which first animated us in this Contest."[18]

Officers such as Nicola and Varnum seemed to foresee a postwar government in which the officer corps would aid in the establishment of a monarchy, if Washington desired them to do so. Peace finally came, yet it brought only more frustration and more anger in the Continental Army, and more despair in the fieldstone farmhouse at Newburgh, where Washington sensed the "dark side of our affairs . . . the discontents which, at this moment, prevail universally throughout the Army."[19] By that time the soldiers had not been paid for months. Congress was wrangling over the promised half-pay and even considering disbanding the army to solve the soldiers' grievances. And some in the ranks, too, began to speculate whether the new country should operate under military control or civilian law.

In October 1782 Washington ordered his Continental Army troops to set up a winter cantonment in a forested area at New Windsor, about six miles southwest of his Newburgh headquarters. Here there were enough trees for the men to build shelters and harvest firewood. The soldiers chopped down thousands of trees to build nearly six hundred log huts of uniform size and shape, all neatly arrayed regiment by regiment. At the suggestion of a chaplain, the soldiers also erected the centerpiece of the cantonment, a 110-foot-long log building with a vaulted ceiling, windows, and plaster walls. It was dubbed the Temple of Virtue, in a fashion whose relevance would soon become evident.[20]

In January 1783, several Continental Army officers—including some facing debtors' prison—sent three representatives to Philadelphia to present to Congress a petition that warned, "The uneasiness of the soldiers, for want of pay is great and dangerous; any further experiments on their patience may have fatal effects."[21] Congress rebuffed them two months later, and other officers—apparently led by Major General Horatio Gates and his twenty-four-year-old aide de camp, Major John Armstrong Jr.—decided on a bolder move. On March 10, they began to circulate in the Newburgh camp an anonymous letter that disregarded the chain of command by inviting officers to a defiant meeting. The writer, calling himself a "fellow soldier," asked whom peace would bless: "A country willing to redress your wrongs [or] a country that tramples upon your rights, disdains your cries and insults your distresses?" The 1,200-word missive urged the officers to meet the following day and "come to some final opinion" about what to do next.[22]

Washington obtained a copy of the letter and foresaw another dark event, perhaps even a mutiny. It had happened before. In January 1781, Continental Army troops, starving and freezing, had mutinied in their winter quarters near Morristown, New Jersey. Shortly after officers and a board of sergeants negotiated an end to that uprising, hundreds of other troops had begun a mutiny at Pompton Camp, twenty miles away.[23] That time, there was no negotiation. Washington ordered a special force of more than five hundred men under Major General Robert Howe "to bring the Mutineers to unconditional submission and, their principal leaders to instant & condign punishment."[24] Howe's men encircled the troops' huts and aimed two fieldpieces at them. Howe ordered the mutineers to parade unarmed before him. He had three men identified as ringleaders pulled out of the ranks, and, after trying them on the spot, he sentenced them to death. "Finding themselves closely encircled and unable to resist," wrote James Thacher, a surgeon in the Continental Army, "they quietly submitted to the fate which awaited them": execution by a firing squad made up of other mutineers, who were ordered to fire three shots into the head and three into the chest of each of their comrades. Two of the three condemned men were duly executed; the third, "being less criminal," was pardoned.[25]

The mutinies made Washington fear that the army was self-destructing. In 1781, he wrote an uncharacteristically emotional circular letter to northern state governors, with a copy to Congress: "The aggravated calamities and distresses that have resulted from the total want of pay for nearly twelve Months, for want of cloathing at a severe season, and not unfrequently the want of provisions, are beyond description . . . . It is in vain to think an Army can be kept together much longer."[26]

Thus Washington, likely with the events of 1781 in mind, responded to the anonymous 1783 letter by ordering the officers to postpone their meeting for four days and assemble at the Temple of Virtue on March 15. He was enough of a scholar of the classics to know this day was the Ides of March, the date of the assassination of Julius Caesar. Surprising the audience, Washington walked into the temple and stood on its raised platform. "By an anonymous summons," he began, "an attempt has been made to convene you together—how inconsistent with the rules of propriety! how unmilitary! and how subversive of all order and discipline—let the good sense of the Army decide." After sarcastically admiring the "great art" of the anonymous letter, he reduced it to its basic threat: "If Peace takes place, never sheath your Sword says he untill you have obtained full and ample Justice—this dreadful alternative, of either deserting our Country in the extremest hour of her distress, or turning our Army against it." He asked the officers "to express your utmost horror and detestation of the Man who . . . wickedly attempts to open the flood Gates of Civil discord, and deluge our rising Empire in Blood."[27]

After he finished his speech, Washington started to read a letter from a congressman but faltered over its small, cramped words. From his pocket he took out his new spectacles, which the officers had never seen him wear. "Gentlemen," he said, "you will permit me to put on my spectacles, for I have not only grown gray, but almost blind, in the service of my country."[28] Many men began to weep.

Washington finished reading the letter and walked out. The officers, however, stayed in the temple and voted to denounce "the infamous propositions" in the anonymous letter and reaffirm their loyalty to Congress. The moment still endures in the U.S. Army's *Field Manual 1,* which cites Washington's action at Newburgh, when the "future of the Republic was in doubt," as a lesson to instill in American soldiers the indisputable fact that the military is under civilian control.[29] Within the space of less than a year, then, Washington had exemplified two guiding principles of the newborn nation: it would have no king, and its army would not govern.

After the meeting, Washington followed his masterful handling of the fuming officers with a pivot to Congress. "I fix it as an indispensable Measure," he told one congressman, "that previous to the Disbanding of the Army, all their accounts should be completely liquidated and settled."[30] That was no easy task: as a modern analyst of the 1783 crisis has pointed out, "Settlement involved the different laws and procedures of the states, Congress, and various departments within the Army. In addition to back pay and cash bounties, the government of the United States and the several states had to consider tax free land titles, clothing allowances, and other rations in the computations. Each soldier needed to be treated individually."[31]

Also working to defuse the officer crisis was Alexander Hamilton, who had resigned his commission as lieutenant colonel after heroically leading his men against a key British rampart at Yorktown. He had plunged into New York politics, becoming a member of the Congress of the Confederation, and now, at the height of the crisis, he produced a congressional compromise: soldiers who had enlisted for the duration of the war would be furloughed and could return to their homes. Men with enlistments of three years or less would not get furloughs, and settlement of their wages would be delayed. Washington, with congressional approval, instead proclaimed to his troops that each soldier could decide whether to accept a furlough. Momentarily, this looked like another successful Washington move to calm his soldiers. But once again the threat of mutiny was ticking away, this time among Pennsylvanian troops.

About eighty Pennsylvanian officers and militiamen marched into Philadelphia on June 20, 1783. They did not plan to confront the Congress of the Confederation on the first floor of the State House, but to complain to the Supreme Executive Council of Pennsylvania and its president, John Dickinson, on the second floor. The soldiers—

displaying, as many did in the new country, a preference for state authority over congressional—demanded that their states pay them.

Congress was not in session on this Saturday, but Hamilton and
others convinced the congressional president, Elias Boudinot, to call
an emergency meeting. By the next morning, the mutineers numbered
some four hundred. Many were drunk and all looked like a collective
threat to the congressmen who shouldered their way through them
into the State House. From their first-floor chamber, the congressmen
looked out their windows to see bayoneted muskets and soldiers shaking their fists, and believed they were being threatened, even though
the soldiers were demanding action not from Congress but from their
state. Congress promptly passed a resolution informing Dickinson and
the Supreme Executive Council of Pennsylvania that "the authority
of the United States" had been "grossly insulted by the disorderly and
menacing appearance of a body of armed soldiers about the place in
which Congress were assembled." The resolution was duly entered in
the records of the council.[32]

Dickinson and other state officials claimed that the mutineers were
not truly threatening Congress and so refused to provide security to its
nervous members. Negotiations with Hamilton and other congressional officials broke down, and on June 22, Dickinson announced that
Congress would abandon Philadelphia and reconvene in Princeton,
New Jersey, on June 26.[33]

The flight from Philadelphia began the itinerant wandering of
Congress, from Princeton to Annapolis, then to Trenton and to New
York City, and back to Philadelphia in 1787 for the Constitutional
Convention, then to New York again in 1789, and back one more time
to Philadelphia in 1790. In that same year Congress passed a statute
to establish a permanent home for itself via creation of the District
of Columbia, on the Potomac River, at a site chosen by President
Washington. Congress, allowing a decade for planning and construction, would move one last time in 1800.

The uproar that had chased Congress out of Philadelphia in 1783,
and the earlier mutinies following chaotic battles of the Revolution,
not only expressed the dissatisfaction of the country's nascent army but
also began the long struggle—at last concluded in 1789—to create a

nation with a strong central government. That government would replace the one in which, as historian Kenneth R. Bowling put it in his
masterful article on the Philadelphia mutiny: "Continental soldiers
under the command and control of Congress [had] ignored the federal
government and sought instead to settle their accounts with the State
of Pennsylvania. . . . the mutiny and subsequent removal of Congress
[from Philadelphia] is an appropriate symbol of the lack of power and
prestige of the federal government in 1783."[34]

As the mutinies and the ominous days at Newburgh show, the end
of the war did not mean the beginning of peace, or of nationhood. At
this point, six years before the seminal year of 1789, America had, in
essence, fourteen separate governments: each of the thirteen states plus
one created by the Congress of the Confederation. All were blockades
on the road toward the hazy idea of federalism, yet no one was quite
sure how to clear the way.

That the path to federalism was eventually found was made clear
by the poet-soldier David Humphreys, who accompanied George
Washington to Annapolis when the general resigned his commission
as commander-in-chief to Congress in December 1783, thus under-
lining his commitment to civilian rule. Humphreys also accompanied
Washington in New York on April 30, 1789, when the former general
took the oath of office as the new country's first president.

Speaking to fellow veterans on the Fourth of July of that auspicious
year, Humphreys used his poet's voice to celebrate what the Cause had
given the country: "the complete establishment of a new general government." He continued, "I feel a confidence, from the sensations of my
own heart, that every bosom in this assembly beats high at the thought
of our country's happiness."[35] Speaking as a witness to history, to war
and peace, to a failed Congress and to the First Federal Congress, to
Washington as general and to Washington as president, Humphreys
had been, over a tumultuous decade, one of the countless fighters for
the Cause who had recognized its true purpose—not mere freedom,
but the building of a nation.

Incredibly, however, there still were Americans who envisioned a
nation that would be a monarchy with George Washington as the king.

2
———

THE SPECTER OF A KING

On March 12, 1783—even as General Washington, the Continental Army, and the Congress were contending with the fraught issue of soldier pay, and while sporadic fighting continued—the packet boat *George Washington*, her trans-Atlantic voyage nearing an end, sailed up the Delaware River to Philadelphia harbor. She had once been the Royal Navy warship *General Monk*, but she was captured during the Revolution and given her illustrious new name.[1] Under the command of a former privateer, the ship had left France with papers, signed by American and British negotiators, containing the outline of a peace treaty destined to end the Revolutionary War. Work on the treaty had begun almost a year earlier, in April 1782; British representatives at the talks included David Hartley and Richard Oswald, and speaking for America were, among others, Benjamin Franklin, John Adams, John Jay, and Henry Laurens. As soon as the ship arrived in Philadelphia, the documents were taken to the State House, where members of Congress learned the final terms of the treaty.

After examining the papers upon their arrival at the Congress, James Madison wrote to Edmund Randolph (who would later serve with him in the Constitutional Convention in 1787): "The tenor of them is that the United States shall be acknowledged and treated with as free, sovereign, and independent." [2] He went on to describe the agreed-upon boundaries delineated by the Treaty of Paris: Great Britain ceded to the United States all territory between the Allegheny Mountains on the east and the Mississippi River on the west, thereby doubling the size of America. He also noted that American fishermen would retain the same Newfoundland fishing rights that they had possessed before the war. Separately, Britain ceded the territories of East Florida and West

29

Florida to Spain, which would claim exclusive navigation rights on the Mississippi River.

The treaty also contained an American agreement to end the persecution of Loyalists by state and local governments and restore confiscated property to their Loyalist owners. Or, more accurately, the treaty instructed Congress to ask the states to end the persecution. Congress did not have the power—or the inclination—to rehabilitate Loyalists, and did not do so, despite the treaty agreement. The states mainly ignored the request in the treaty. Some state legislatures assumed the right to give parcels of confiscated Loyalist land to people that the legislatures judged worthy. Georgia, for example, bestowed plantations on Brigadier General Nathanael Greene[3] and Brigadier General Anthony Wayne.[4] New York gave Tom Paine a New Rochelle farm that had been owned by a Loyalist.[5]

At the same time, in the log cabins at the cantonment near Newburgh, and in a small garrison downriver at West Point, unpaid soldiers were wondering whether the rumors of peace would prove true. Then, on April 19, 1783—the eighth anniversary of the battle of Lexington— Congress approved the preliminary articles of peace. (Congress would ratify the final version of the treaty on January 14, 1784.) As Private Joseph Plumb Martin later wrote, on that day "we had general orders read which satisfied the most skeptical, that the war was over." It had been a long war for Martin, who had enlisted for a six-month hitch in a Connecticut militia at the age of fifteen in 1775 and later joined the Continental Army. In early June 1783, he wrote that his captain "handed us our discharges, or rather furloughs, permission to return home, but, [we had] to return to the army again, if required." Martin saw through Congress's plan to avoid completely disbanding the army. The so-called home furlough, he wrote, "was policy in government." He understood that official discharges would have cut the soldiers off from the army permanently and denied them their overdue pay. The result would have been the creation of an army of angry veterans. And, as he says in a sample of New England understatement, that such a government move "might cause some difficulties."[6] Given the atmosphere of distrust and conspiracy, rumors about a military coup inevitably circulated even as the Treaty of Paris was negotiated and sent to the United

States. Ordinary soldiers began to drift off to civilian lives, technically on home furlough—actually, sent back to civilian life without the back pay owed them. Ex-soldier Martin, like many enlistees, had been promised one hundred acres of land when the war ended. Congress was planning to get the land parcels from the vast lands north of the Ohio River.

"When the country had drained the last drop of service it could screw out of the poor soldiers, they were turned out like old worn out horses, and nothing said about land to pasture them upon," Martin wrote.[7] Congress did appropriate what were called "Soldier lands" in what would become Ohio. But Congress did not set up a system to make sure that ex-soldiers—rather than speculators—got the Soldier lands.[8]

At Newburgh, some unpaid officers began to form the Society of the Cincinnati, a fraternal society that soon would prove both controversial and influential. The Society was founded in 1783 by Continental Army officers and French supporters who had fought together in the Revolution. At first, the group did not appear especially remarkable: the originator of the idea, Major General Henry Knox, did not seem to be a mutineer. Quite the opposite: a hero of the Revolution and a close comrade of Washington, Knox started out wanting only to preserve the officers' wartime comradeship via a fraternal organization honoring Lucius Quinctius Cincinnatus, the Roman statesman who, according to legend, had been summoned from his farm by the Roman Senate in about 460 BCE when enemy armies threatened Rome. Cincinnatus, made dictator ("Master of the People") by the Senate, led his troops to a swift, victorious defense of the city, then refused any reward and returned to his farm.[9]

Knox, a rotund Boston bookseller turned brave and brilliant artillery officer, had told John Adams in 1776 that once the war was over, he wished simply for "some ribbon to wear in his hat or in his button-hole, to be transmitted to his descendants as a badge and proof that he had fought in defence of their liberties."[10] By 1783, anticipating the end of the war, Knox was discussing his idea with other officers, including the Prussian-born Baron Friedrich Wilhelm Von Steuben, who, as the drill-master of Valley Forge, had transformed the Continental Army into a disciplined fighting force. Washington himself, though not a founder of the society, soon joined it and accepted when its members chose him as their president general, a role he served in from 1783 to 1799. The society quickly added to its membership more than two thousand past and present officers, including Alexander Hamilton, along with more controversial figures such the discontented Lewis Nicola and James Mitchell Varnum, as well as the conspiring Horatio Gates and John Armstrong Jr.

In May 1783, at Newburgh, in their first informal meeting, the society's founders announced that their primary goals were to "preserve inviolate those exalted rights and liberties of human nature for which they have fought and bled" and to "promote and cherish, between the respective States, that union and national honor so essentially necessary to their happiness, and the future dignity of the American Empire." Members would also care for fellow officers and their families when they were in need. To reflect states' political sovereignty, the society was divided into autonomous state societies. The first general meeting of the Society convened in Philadelphia on May 4, 1784, and lasted two weeks.[11]

Authority came from each member, not from a hierarchy. Decorations were decided upon; founding member Pierre L'Enfant, a French engineering officer wounded in the war, designed "a Medal of Gold, of a proper size to receive the emblems, and suspended by a deep blue ribbon two inches wide, edged with white, descriptive of the Union of France and America."[12] L'Enfant later sailed to France to supervise the manufacture of the medal, which displayed an eagle on its face and Cincinnatus receiving his sword from the Roman Senate on its reverse.[13]

Despite its innocuous beginnings, the society soon began to be looked at suspiciously; its ranks were, after all, a concentration of the country's men of means and political influence. And all its members were officers, including French officers who had served in the Continental Army or Navy for at least three years of the war. Officers of the state militias, however, were ineligible for membership, as were enlisted men. The rules of the Continental Army, modeled on those of the British Army, forbade fraternization between officers and their men, and the society decided to follow that quasi-aristocratic structure.

The society's founders also declared it a hereditary organization, with membership passing to the eldest male heir.

The Society of the Cincinnati thus presented to America one of its first conspiracy theories: was the group trying to encourage royal rule? Thomas Jefferson, a onetime colonel in the Virginia Militia, was not qualified for membership, and he was among those who wondered whether the Cincinnatians favored an American drift toward rule by a king. "Some officers of the army," he wrote years later, are "trained to monarchy by military habits."[14] He named Steuben and Knox, founders of the society, as being among "the leading agents" of pro-monarchy intentions.[15] Critics pounced on the idea of this hereditary society, citing as further evidence of its monarchical intentions its decorative medallion, which looked suspiciously like those worn by members of foreign pro-monarchy orders. On his trip to France to supervise the making of the "Medal of Gold," L'Enfant fueled apprehensions about foreign cavaliers when he obtained permission from King Louis XVI for French officers to join the society and wear its insignia—thus bestowing an actual royal endorsement on the society.[16] This is as close as the society came to being affiliated with foreign royalty.

"What is to be done with the Cincinnati?" John Adams (not qualified to be a member) asked in a 1785 letter to Congressman Elbridge Gerry. "Is that order of chivalry, that inroad upon our first principle, equality, to be connived at? It is the deepest piece of cunning yet attempted. It is sowing the seeds of all that European courts wish to grow up among us."[17] Samuel Adams, as a Founding Father and igniter of the Revolution, added his voice to the growing clamor, saying the society was rapidly striding "towards an hereditary Military Nobility as was ever made in so short a time."[18] In 1784, a joint Massachusetts legislative committee condemned the society as "unjustifiable, and if not properly discountenanced, may be dangerous to the peace, liberty and safety of the United States in general, and this Commonwealth in particular."[19]

Another leading critic was South Carolina judge and politician Aedanus Burke (who had served in the Continental Army, but not long enough to qualify for Cincinnati membership). In 1783, soon after the society's founding, he issued a pamphlet whose title declared its thesis:

"Considerations on the Society or Order of Cincinnati; Lately Instituted by the Major-Generals, Brigadier-Generals, and Other Officers of the American Army. Proving That It Creates a Race of Hereditary Patricians, or Nobility."[20] It was reprinted throughout the country, and resolutions denouncing the Cincinnati were introduced into several state legislatures besides that of Massachusetts. Critics of the society saw the creating of a hereditary class as a step toward a monarchy.[21]

Washington was well aware of the distrust of the society and, as Jefferson would later recall, Washington was "determined to use all his endeavors for its total suppression." But "he found it so firmly riveted in the affections of the members, that . . . he could effect no more than the abolition of its hereditary principle," Jefferson noted.[22] But even that would prove impossible. Washington seemed to see the society as a patriotic organization that bound together the band of brothers who had fought in the war, and during his presidency, he directly and indirectly appointed many members to government jobs.

At the first national meeting of the Society in Philadelphia in 1784, Washington suggested the abolition of the principal target of critics' attacks: the hereditary descent rule. Although delegates at the meeting had agreed to keep their discussions secret for fear outsiders might seize upon their remarks, Washington's words were covertly copied and encrypted by one delegate and published many years later. Despite Washington's plea, the state-sovereignty laws meant that most state chapters of the society could quietly reject Washington's suggestion and continue the heredity practice.[23]

Benjamin Franklin and John Jay both denounced the society for creating an American nobility that could lead to a country ruled by a man on a throne. In a 1784 letter to his daughter, Franklin mused, "I only wonder that, when the united Wisdom of our Nation had, in the Articles of Confederation, manifested their Dislike of establishing Ranks of Nobility, by Authority either of the Congress or of any particular State, a Number of private persons should think proper to distinguish themselves and their Posterity, from their fellow Citizens, and form an Order of *hereditary Knights*, in direct Opposition to the solemnly declared Sense of their Country."[24]

Misgivings about the society's aristocratic inclinations also became a weapon wielded by those who opposed a standing army in the new country: kings, after all, need armies. Many of these opponents instead were supporters of militias, seen as armed symbols of state (not federal) sovereignty. There was even an endorsement of state sovereignty in the Treaty of Paris, ratified by the Congress of the Confederation in January 1784. His Britannic Majesty, the treaty said, acknowledged that United States consisted of thirteen "free Sovereign and independent States" and that he "treats with them as such."

Proponents of a republic now realized that the only way to get rid of the Articles of Confederation—which had given states nominal sovereignty and established only a weak federal government lacking taxation powers to fund a national army—was to convince Washington to endorse a federal republic. And, to achieve that drastic change, a constitution had to be written. But getting even that far would take some maneuvering.

Madison and Jefferson launched the quest for a federal constitution in 1785 when they asked commissioners from Virginia and Maryland to meet in Alexandria for a conference on regulating the Potomac. The two states' quarrel over use of the river epitomized all the contemporaneous interstate bickering about regulations, tariffs, taxes, and even currency. (By 1789, fourteen currencies were in circulation: one for each state, each denominated in pounds, and a continental currency, denominated in dollars.) The conflicts were further evidence of the impossibility of coordinating fourteen sovereign mini-governments within the body of a single nation. Rules for use of the Chesapeake Bay and the Pocomoke River, which flowed through Maryland and Delaware, were added to the agenda.

Virginia politicians, including Governor Patrick Henry—the fiery orator famed for coining the slogan "Give me liberty or give me death"—were disturbed by the idea of the conference. The governor and his supporters were ever on watch for any political move that threatened states' sovereignty. Henry managed, without leaving fingerprints, to make the Alexandria meeting collapse. But Washington saved the conference by inviting the participants to Mount Vernon.

There they produced the Compact of 1785, the first mutually binding agreement ever made between U.S. states. The commissioners of Virginia and Maryland agreed that their waterways would be "forever considered as a common Highway Free for Use and Navigation of any vessel belonging"[25] to the other. The commissioners also invited Pennsylvania to join an effort to improve the navigation of the Potomac River up to its headwaters, arguing that such a project would "have for their object the interest and convenience of [Pennsylvania's] Citizens and those of the other States in the Union."[26] Pennsylvania agreed to send delegates, and what Patrick Henry feared—states ignoring the doctrine of sovereignty—seemed to be happening.

Next, in September 1786, came the Annapolis Convention, a four-day meeting of twelve commissioners from New Jersey, New York, Pennsylvania, Delaware, and Virginia. Maryland, though the physical site of the meeting, sent no delegates. Two more states would have made a quorum—meaning, under the rules of the Articles of Confederation, the convention could become an official session, where the Constitution-writing goal of Madison and Jefferson would be exposed and debated. Unwilling to take chances with that possibility, the conclave ended abruptly after adopting its historic "Address," which called for a convention to meet in Philadelphia in May 1787. Hamilton, just elected to a one-year term in the New York Assembly,[27] wrote the call, which aimed to "render the constitution of the federal government adequate to the exigencies of the union."[28]

Although the Annapolis meeting appeared to be a failure, Madison saw it as a further demonstration of the need for a robust central government, and Washington endorsed that view. In a long letter to Madison written a few months later, Washington passionately called for a new and stronger federal government. "No Morn ever dawned more favourable than ours did, and no day was ever more clouded than the present! Wisdom, & good examples are necessary at this time to rescue the political machine from the impending storm. . . . the consequences of a lax, or inefficient government, are too obvious to be dwelt on. Thirteen Sovereignties pulling against each other and all tugging the federal head, will soon bring ruin on the whole."[29]

Reinforcing Washington's sense of imminent peril was the news he had received in a recent letter from Henry Knox, who ran the penniless War Department. "Our political machine, constituted of thirteen independent sovereignties, have been constantly operating against each other . . . ever since the peace," Knox wrote, pointing in particular to discontent among New England farmers, estimating that as many as fifteen thousand "desperate & unprincipled men" were ready to foment "a formidable rebellion against reason."[30]

David Ramsay, in his *History of the American Revolution,* noted that with "the return of peace," the "calamities of war were followed by another class of evils." People "were induced by seditious demagogues to make an open resistance to the operations of their own free government." Anti-tax sentiment bubbled beneath the surface of this turbulent era; Shays' Rebellion was its most dangerous eruption.

The rebellion convulsed western Massachusetts from August 1786 to February 1787, led in part by former Continental Army Captain Daniel Shays. Spurred by anger over seizures of property for delinquent debts, Shays mobilized a swiftly growing army of veterans, many of them bankrupted farmers. At first, Shays led protests at county court houses, thwarting debt collectors. Reacting to reports he was receiving, Washington wrote to Humphreys, saying, "commotions of this sort, like snow-balls, gather strength as they roll, if there is no opposition in the way to divide and crumble them."[31]

Lacking a strong federal government to call upon to quell Shays' rebel force, Massachusetts had to form its own army of militiamen, funded by merchants.[32] Shays' followers called themselves the Regulators, harkening back to disgruntled North Carolina farmers who rebelled against a royal governor in 1771. The original Regulators had protested a corrupt system of dishonest tax collectors and corrupt judges under British rule.[33]

During the rebellion, Madison kept working on his vision of a convention that would draw up the framework of a strengthened central government. He proposed that it be a *constitutional* convention, though that label was avoided in conversation and correspondence. Congress, then meeting in New York, approved the convention, providing that it would be held "for the sole and express purpose of revising the Articles of Confederation."[34] In December 1786, naturally expecting that Washington would lend his support to the creation of a federal republic, Madison asked him to attend the convention, to be held in Philadelphia in May 1787. Washington stunned Madison by initially turning down the invitation.

By a coincidence that added to general suspicions of a royalist conspiracy, the Society of the Cincinnati was planning to hold its triennial national meeting in the same city at the same time. Washington already had told the society he would not attend, but he felt he could not go to Philadelphia for the convention that Madison was organizing, either. "I should be too much embarrassed by the meetings of these two bodies in the same place, in the same moment," Washington wrote Madison. "I should feel myself in an awkward situation to be in Philadelphia on another public occasion during the sitting of this Society."[35]

The climax of Shays' rebellion came on January 25, 1787, when 2,000 farmers marched on the arsenal at Springfield, Massachusetts to seize its arms and ammunition. Some carried manure forks and clubs. Many shouldered muskets. Major General William Shepard, a state militia officer, took command of about 1,200 militiamen defending the armory. After Shepard warned the rebels they would be fired upon if they continued to advance, they ignored the warning and struggled forward through four feet of snow. Two warning artillery volleys "only hastened them onward," Shepard later said. He then ordered that the cannons be aimed at "waistband height" and fired, killing four marchers and wounding twenty. The survivors fled.[36] The rebellion was all but over, but its consequences lived on, giving added support to Hamilton's and Madison's quest for a federal Constitution.

Late in April 1787, Washington changed his mind about participating in the Convention. He had his principal aide, Tobias Lear, send an urgent letter to Knox, then in Philadelphia preparing to preside over the Cincinnati meeting, claiming that Washington would not be able to attend the society's meeting "in consequence of an account which he received by express that his Mother & only Sister lay dangerously ill, & that he was obliged to make all possible dispatch if he wishes to find them alive."[37] (That the statement might have been a fib is supported by the fact that his mother lived until 1789 and his sister, Betty Washington Lewis, until 1797.) In truth Washington was again feeling the tug of national duty, succumbing at last to the pleas not only of Madison but also of three prominent members of the Cincinnati who wanted him to attend the constitutional convention: Knox, whose hope for a Constitution trumped his enthusiasm for the society; Hamilton;

and a former aide-de-camp, Edmund Randolph.[38] Ailing relatives or no, Washington would attend the convention, which would last from May 25 to September 17, 1787.

As a result of events like Shays' Rebellion, David Ramsay observed, "the lovers of liberty and independence began to be less sanguine in their hopes from the American revolution, and to fear that they had built a visionary fabric of government." After the rebellion was put down, Ramsay said, Virginia urged "all the other States to meet in convention, for the purpose of digesting a form of government, equal to the exigencies of the union."[39] The Annapolis meeting, and alarm over Shays' rebellion, added to the pressure to revise the Articles of Confederation.

On its first day, once the convention had achieved a quorum, it unanimously chose Washington to be the president of the fifty-five delegates, who came from every state except Rhode Island, then noted more for its smuggling than for its civic virtue. Newspapers from Massachusetts to New York dubbed the notoriously corrupt state "Rogue Island," and the *Worchester Magazine* suggested that the state "be dropped out of the Union or apportioned to the different States which surround her."[40] Washington joined the chorus, singling out the state's "scandalous conduct, which seems to have marked all her public Councils of late."

For four months over the hot and humid summer of 1787, Washington sat at a desk on a raised platform and ran the convention largely through his commanding silence, maintaining order almost without speaking a word.[41] Despite Washington's presence, the question of the Cincinnati's patriotism was hovering over the convention: He was one of twenty-one convention delegates who were also members of the society,[42] causing some to wonder if the Cincinnatians might steer the gathering toward monarchism. Historian Mercy Otis Warren, for one, mocked the Cincinnatians as "panting for nobility and with the eagle dangling on their breast . . . ready to bow to the sceptre of a king."[43] Another observer who noted the presence of the Cincinnati bloc was Louis-Guillaume Otto, *comte de Mosloy*, acting French chargé d'affaires to the United States. He reported to the French Foreign Ministry that the Cincinnati were "interested in the establishment of a strong government" that would consolidate the states and "place at

their head ... Washington with all the prerogatives of a crowned head."
But Otto did not believe the Cincinnati were strong enough—or popular enough—to achieve their aims.[44]

Although the convention was supposed to have been called merely
to revise the Articles of Confederation, by mid-June, most delegates
began to realize that they had to build a new kind of national structure.
None of the delegates had been authorized by their state legislatures to
go beyond revising the Articles of Confederation. They decided essentially to discard the Articles of Confederation—and keep their lips sealed.

They decided there would be a strong central government. There
would be a Congress of two houses. There would be a complex, cen-
sus-based system for setting the number of seats allotted to each state
in the House of Representatives. And there would be the compromises
necessary to shape such a government. A key compromise was the convention's decision about whether to count enslaved people when deter-
mining the number of people in a state for the apportionment of taxes
based on population. Anti-slavery delegates wanted only free people
counted; proslavery delegates argued that enslaved people should be
counted as well.

In the end, however, the word *slaves* did not appear in the so-called
three-fifths clause of the Constitution, which said that tax apportionment would be determined by "adding to the whole Number of free
Persons, including those bound to Service for a Term of Years, and excluding Indians not taxed, three fifths of all other Persons."[45] The clause
would significantly bolster the power of slaveholding states, an imbal-
ance that would empower slavery states in the run-up to the Civil War.

The delegates had agreed to convene in secrecy to avoid public discussion of their undertaking. Explaining the secrecy rule to Jefferson,
Madison wrote, "It was thought expedient in order to secure unbiased
discussion within doors, and to prevent misconceptions & miscon-
structions without."[46] He later said, "No Constitution would ever have
been adopted by the convention if the debates had been public."[47]

The delegates proved surprisingly scrupulous about not revealing their debates or other daily activities. One morning, for example,
Washington was handed a document that someone had dropped on
the floor. Before adjourning for the day, he rose and said, "Gentlemen,

I am sorry to find that some member of this body has been so neglectful as to drop in the State House a copy of their proceedings, which was picked up and delivered to me this morning. I must entreat the gentleman to be more careful, lest our transactions get into the newspapers and disturb the public repose by premature speculation. I know not whose paper it is, but there it is"—he threw it down on the table— and, saying, "Let him who owns it take it," he bowed, took his hat, and, according to a delegate, "left the room with a dignity so severe every person seemed alarmed."[48]

The convention's secrecy rule was obeyed so well that a full accounting of its proceedings did not emerge until decades later. Madison kept notes on the proceedings but declared that they were not to be published until after his death, which came in 1836; they became public four years thereafter, as *Notes of Debates in the Federal Convention of 1787*.[49] Before then, most information about the convention had come from the notes of Robert Yates, an Anti-Federalist delegate from New York. His notes were published in 1821, twenty years after his death.[50]

A major topic of debate at the convention—as one might expect, given the suspicions swirling around its inclusion of Cincinnatians— was what powers should be granted to the president. Opponents of a strong executive raised the specter of a king; a president was just an elected monarch, said some Anti-Federalists. George Mason of Virginia advocated rotation in office for the presidency, saying, "As it now stands, he may continue in office for life; or, in other words, it will be an elective monarchy." [51]James Monroe agreed with Mason. Patrick Henry, denouncing the emerging Constitution, said that "among other deformities . . . it squints towards monarchy."[52]

But the ripples of concern were smoothed by a compromise, laid out in the Constitution's Article II, section 1, that allotted the president a limited term of four years and provided that he would be elected by electors chosen by the state legislatures, not by the direct vote of individual voters. Delegates feared that if citizens were to vote directly, they might choose a tyrant. That argument reflected the widespread distrust of ordinary citizens by the wealthy and the well-educated—the kind of men who served in state legislatures. As Hamilton put it in a Federalist Paper: "A small number of persons, selected by their fellow-citizens from the general mass, will be most likely to possess the information and discernment requisite to such complicated investigations."[53] The Electoral College became the answer to that problem: give the vote to the members of state legislatures. The number of representatives sent to Congress would be based on the states' populations, determined by a national census.

The delegates also fashioned impeachment clauses, giving the Senate "the sole Power to try all Impeachments," including the president, vice president "and all Civil Officers of the United States." Anyone convicted of "Treason, Bribery, or other high Crimes and Misdemeanors," would be removed from office.

In the hearts and minds of the delegates, the ultimate protection from crimes, from monarchy, or from tyranny was George Washington, who had already rebuffed opportunities to don the cloak of royalty. The overwhelming trust in his character meant he would almost certainly be elected the first president.

The final text of the Constitution began to take shape by the end of August 1787. The delegates appointed a five-man Committee of Style and Arrangement, consisting of Madison, Hamilton, William Samuel Johnson of Connecticut, whose legislative experience went back to the Stamp Act Congress of 1765; Rufus King of Massachusetts, who served on more convention committees than any other delegate; and Gouverneur Morris of Pennsylvania, who wrote much of the final version of the Constitution, including the iconic preamble, which begins, "We the People."[54]

Fifty-five delegates had arrived at the beginning of the convention, but only forty-two assembled on September 17, 1787, its last day. Thirty-nine of them signed the Constitution. The three men who refused were Elbridge Gerry of Massachusetts and two Virginians, Edmund Randolph and George Mason, who predicted that the Constitution would usher in a government that "would end either in monarchy or a tyrannical aristocracy."[55] Mason also persistently spoke of individual rights, especially the right to vote, and even though he was a slaveholder himself, he denounced the institution and called for ending the importation of slaves.[56] He wrote a withering denouncement of the Constitution, exposing what he believed to be its fallacies.

He particularly feared for the future of the presidency, writing, "The President of the United States has no Constitutional Council," making him "unsupported by proper information and advice, and will generally be directed by minions and favorites . . . or he will become a tool to the Senate—or a Council of State will grow out of the principal officers of the great departments."[57]

In fact, as a general running an army, Washington did seek and accept the advice of his staff. And, as president, he would quickly name members of his cabinet. Mason's prophecy signaled the opposition that the Constitution would face during the next phase of its creation: ratification by the sovereign states, as it could not go into effect until at least nine states decided to ratify it in conventions especially called for that purpose. (For the Articles of Confederation to become operative, all the state legislatures had to ratify it. And any changes in the Articles had to be accepted by all thirteen states. Allowing for ratification by only nine states was a drastic change.)[58]

In September 1787, Washington, as president of the convention, sent copies of the proposed Constitution to the state ratification conventions. Most states had bicameral legislatures whose members were typically wealthy landowners and descendants from old families. Madison and the other architects of the Constitutions hoped to curb political intrigue by stipulating that the states elect delegates to the ratification debates and not rely on state legislatures.

Immediately, as Ramsay wrote, "almost every passion which could agitate the human breast" exploded among members of state conventions as they debated whether to accept the Constitution and its unique, untried form of government. In a pamphlet aimed at his own South Carolinians, Ramsay urged them to ratify and to "consider the people of all the thirteen states, as a band of brethren . . . inhabiting one undivided country, and designed by heaven to be one people."[59]

Washington also sent copies of the Constitution to Jefferson, then serving as minister to France, and to his former comrade in arms Gilbert du Motier, Marquis de Lafayette. Anticipating the struggle for ratification, in his letter to Lafayette Washington called the Constitution "a child of fortune, to be fostered by some and buffeted by others," adding, "nor shall I say anything for or against it; if it be good I suppose it will work its way good; if bad, it will recoil on the Framers."[60]

Beginning on December 7, 1787, five states—Delaware, Pennsylvania, New Jersey, Georgia, and Connecticut—ratified the Constitution in quick succession. Boston's *Massachusetts Centinel* began publishing drawings that showed "Federal Pillars" rising to support a "Grand Republican Superstructure," adding a pillar as each state ratified. Then the rate of the rising pillars slowed. Some states (including Massachusetts itself) were opposing the Constitution because it failed to reserve unmentioned powers to the states and lacked constitutional protection of basic political rights, such as freedom of speech, religion, and the press.

After Federalists promised the states that amendments would be added to address their concerns, Massachusetts narrowly voted to ratify the Constitution in February 1788. (In the *Centinel* illustration, the relevant pillar seems to be nudged into place by a heavenly hand.)

Next came Maryland and South Carolina—and finally, on June 21, 1788, New Hampshire, the crucial ninth state.[61] On that date, with nine states on board, the Constitution itself became a reality. As it said of itself in Article VI, "This Constitution, and the laws of the United States which shall be made in pursuance thereof; and all treaties made, or which shall be made, under the authority of the United States, shall be the supreme law of the land."

The Constitution therefore could go into effect, but neither New York nor Virginia had yet acted. In New York, John Jay and Hamilton succeeded in getting their state to call a convention, which, by a vote of 30-27 voted for ratification on July 26, 1788. In Virginia, delegates Madison and John Marshall led the ratification effort, opposed by Mason and Henry. Addressing the Virginia convention, Henry denounced the Constitution, starting with its preamble: "That poor little thing—the expression, *We, the people*, instead of the *States*, of America. I need not take much pains to show that the principles of this system are extremely pernicious, impolitic, and dangerous. Is this a monarchy, like England—a compact between prince and people, with checks on the former to secure the liberty of the latter? . . . It is not a democracy, wherein the people retain all their rights securely."[62] On June 26, declining to accept Henry's dark warnings, the Virginia delegates voted 89-79 to ratify.[63]

As Ramsay recorded, "the ratification of it was celebrated in most of the capitals of the States with elegant processions, which far exceeded any thing of the kind ever before exhibited in America."[64] Rhode Island

and North Carolina held off. But with eleven states united by it, the Constitution came to life in 1789, the year the First Federal Congress assembled in New York City.

Yet much work remained to be done before the First Congress—and the first president—could begin, in 1789, to govern under the design now laid out for an entirely new sort of country.

Nor could Madison and his cohorts claim complete victory. New York was calling for a second convention at which constitutional amendments would be proposed, and, as Washington knew, bowing to that demand would "undo all that has been done." He feared that the Constitution would be "shipwrecked in sight of the Port."[65] The Constitution had been written and ratified. What could have happened next—a potentially lethal call for a second convention—did not come. Washington and Madison, among other veterans of the Constitution Convention, were relieved because they had feared that the reopening of the convention would give Anti-Federalists a new chance to attack the Constitution.

The ratified Constitution was a reality, a blueprint for the building of the engine that would be the First Federal Congress. But scattered through the ratifications were warnings that threatened the Constitution's claim to be the supreme law of the land. The states wanted more than a Constitution. Within their ratification statements they inserted demands for nearly two hundred amendments guaranteeing personal rights. Over time, these would be consolidated and evolve into a document added to the Constitution that came to be called the Bill of Rights. Madison chose to put the amendments crisis aside for a while so that the First Federal Congress could begin its work.

The task list for the new nation that fall and winter was thus a lengthy one: to create the Federal Congress, U.S. senators and representatives first had to be elected in all the states. And to install a president and a vice president, electors first had to be selected and the Electoral College created. (The word *college*, as used at that time, meant a group of people working on a common task.) A compromise between election of the President by a vote in Congress and election of the President by a popular vote of qualified citizens, the Electoral College would begin a long and contentious reign.

THE RELUCTANT PRESIDENT

*I*n late December 1788, in that luminous period after the Constitution had been ratified but before the First Congress took up its duties, George Washington told a Georgia politician, "The future is all a scene of darkness and uncertainty to me, on many accounts. It is known; that when I left the army, it was with a fixed determination, never to be engaged again in any public affairs. Events, which were not then foreseen, have since turned up."[1] Five years earlier, on December 23, 1783, Washington had resigned as commander-in-chief of the Continental Army before the assembled Congress of the Confederation in the State House at Annapolis, then the U.S. capital, and retired to Mount Vernon. Yet his acceptance of the presidency of the Constitutional Convention and the looming March 4 date for the opening of the new Congress were drawing Washington still further into public life.

By January 1789, Washington was grudgingly accepting the inevitability that he would become president; indeed, it seemed the American people would accept no other candidate, judging from the torrent of correspondence from ordinary and prominent citizens alike that had flooded into Mount Vernon, urging him to accept the office. But doubts nagged at him. He was a natural leader of men in war, but he had no way of knowing whether he had the skills and temperament to begin leading a nation. He was even considering what his first words as president should be, inviting David Humphreys, his literary former aide-de-camp, to draft the first inaugural address.

Humphreys earlier had urged Washington to write his memoirs, but the general had demurred, suggesting instead that Humphreys move to Mount Vernon and write an account of Washington as commander-in-chief of the Continental Army. Humphreys accepted, taking up residence at Mount Vernon in October 1787 and staying there until Washington went to New York for his April 1789 inaugural.[2] His worshipful book, *Life of General Washington*, lauded his subject as a near-perfect man, presenting various nuggets of hagiography for future biographers' consideration. For instance, Humphreys described Washington as "remarkably robust & athletic" and added, "I have several times heard him say he never met any man who could throw a stone to so great a distance as himself; and, that when standing in the valley beneath the natural bridge in Virginia, he has thrown one up to that stupendous arch," a 215-foot toss.[3]

But Humphreys's literary talents did not extend to speechwriting. By the dawn of 1789, his draft of the proposed inaugural address had grown to seventy-three pages, including a short space for a prayer.[4] Among its passages was, interestingly, a statement on slavery: "I rejoice in a belief that intellectual light will spring up in the dark corners of the earth; that freedom of enquiry will produce liberality of conduct; that mankind will reverse the absurd position that *the many* were made for *the few*; and that they will not continue slaves in one part of the globe, when they can become freemen in another."[5]

For editorial help and to condense the ponderous speech, Washington turned to James Madison, a political confidant. Madison, in Virginia's first federal election, had just run unsuccessfully for the Senate against Anti-Federalists backed by Patrick Henry. Madison had been nominated, against his will. He was defeated in a show of power by Henry, who picked for his Senate nominees Richard Henry Lee and William Grayson, a lawyer and wartime aide to General Washingon. Madison came in third in a bitter contest.

Madison nonetheless pressed on with a run for the House of Representatives, determined as he was to become a leader in the new Congress and implement the new Constitution. Madison's opponent was James Monroe. It was a historic contest not only because it put Madison into the First Federal Congress but because it was a race between two future presidents.

Washington, as he sought out help on the inaugural address, trusted Madison but not the postal system. "Is there any safe and tolerably expeditious mode by which letters from the Post Office in Fredericksburgh [Virginia] are conveyed to you?" he wrote to Madison in January 1789.

"I want to write a private & confidential letter to you, shortly, but am not inclined to trust to an uncertain conveyance, so as to hazard the loss or inspection of it."[6] Madison suggested that Washington send the letter through Fontaine Maury, the postmaster at Fredericksburg, about forty miles east of Montpelier, Madison's 2,650-acre estate. Neither Washington nor Madison described this "private & confidential" matter in any other letter of their cautious subsequent correspondence, but there is no doubt that they were referring to Humphreys's draft of the inaugural address.

Washington copied over Humphreys's entire speech himself— thereby proving to posterity that he had at least read the antislavery passage—and sent it on to Madison, identifying his ghostwriter merely as "a gentleman under this roof" but surely knowing that Madison would realize the author was Humphreys and that Washington wanted his aide's name kept confidential.

In the early nineteenth century, these seventy-three pages in Washington's hand were discovered by Jared Sparks, a scholar collecting Washington's writings for eventual publication. In a May 1827 letter to Madison, Sparks reacted much as Madison probably had when he first read the draft: "It is certainly an extraordinary production for a message to Congress, and it is happy, that Washington took counsel of his own understanding, and of his other friends, before he made use of this document.... I hardly need ask your advice, as to the expediency of publishing in his works any allusion to this draft of a message. I do not conceive that the public would derive benefit from them...."[7] Both Sparks and Madison were probably reacting to the tone and length of the Humphreys draft. Left unsaid was their relief that the antislavery passage had not become public.

Between 1834 and 1837, Sparks published twelve volumes of his *Writings of George Washington*, notoriously altering many of the originals by deleting words, correcting spelling, and supposedly improving grammar. He also discarded papers he considered trivial or unflattering and cut others into snippets that he gave to people seeking samples of the first president's prose. That was the fate of Humphreys's seventy-three pages.[8]

• • •

"Went up to the Election of an Elector (for this district) of President & Vice President. . . . Dined with a large company on venisen at Pages Tavn. and came home in the evening," George Washington recorded in his diary on January 7, 1789.[9] He had just voted in the first phase of the nation's first presidential election: the selection of electors from each state. The vote for electors was held throughout the states; the town courthouse in Alexandria, about fifteen miles upriver from Mount Vernon, was Washington's district polling place.

For many delegates to the Constitutional Convention in the summer of 1787, the most challenging issue had been the creation of a process for electing the president and vice president. Gouverneur Morris, a delegate from Pennsylvania, compared the convention's debates on the election system to the writing of *The Odyssey*: again and again, "every mode of electing the chief magistrate of a powerful nation hitherto adopted is liable to objection," he recounted in an 1802 letter.[10] Two competing ideas emerged from the scrum: election through a vote in Congress, and election by popular vote. Delegates decided they did not want either, especially not direct voting by citizens, and finally a committee produced a compromise—the complex system of electors—that both protected states' rights and bridged the two rejected ideas.[11] Yet how should those electors be chosen? The delegates pondered various options—even wondering, at one desperate point, whether a lottery should be used to pick electors—and decided to let states choose the method of selection.

Washington was among the 50 percent of Virginia white men whose ownership of land qualified them to vote; at that time, the state required that a voter own at least fifty acres of unimproved land—a requirement changed in 1785 from the earlier twenty-five acres of improved land to exercise the franchise.[12] By comparison, in some New England colonies and towns, only modest landholdings were required, such as an urban lot, and these rules made as many as three-quarters of white men there eligible to vote. Pennsylvania gave voting rights to all white taxpaying adult males; in 1787, an estimated 87.5 percent of that state's white men could vote. By 1792, after the admission of Vermont and Kentucky to the Union, seven of the fifteen states no longer used property qualifications for voting, at least in elections for their lower houses of assembly.[13]

Washington's mention of the Alexandria vote in his diary, offhand as it seemed, was a reference to the debut of an institution still vigorously debated during presidential election campaigns: The Electoral College. Each state was allotted a number of electors equal to the combined total of the state's Senate and House of Representatives delegations. A state, as noted, could decide on the manner of choosing its electors; Virginia decided to elect them by popular vote in elections that were held from Monday, December 15, 1788, to Saturday, January 10, 1789, in each legislative district.[14]

Washington could have voted for either of two candidates, both of them well known to him: physician David Stuart, a scion of the nearby Abingdon plantation and a representative in the Virginia House of Burgesses (as the state legislature was called), or Thomas Blackburn, a former colonel in the state militia who had been wounded during the battle of Germantown in 1777. Stuart had become a Washington relative in 1783 when he married Eleanor Calvert Custis, the widow of Martha Washington's late son John Parke Custis. Blackburn's daughter Julia Ann, meanwhile, was married to George Washington's nephew Bushrod Washington.[15]

It is not known for which man Washington cast his ballot, but Stuart won by a margin of 347 votes[16] and thus was among the Virginia electors who would gather in Richmond on February 4, 1789, to cast their votes for America's first president. Each elector could vote for two persons of his choice. To keep electors from voting for their own state's two favorite sons, however, only one of the two candidates could live in the elector's state. Nor could an elector cast both his votes for the same candidate. In the end, the person receiving the greatest number of votes would be elected president. Whoever came in second—among an extensive field including John Adams, Robert Harrison, John Jay, and John Rutledge—would become vice president.

Virginia was one of the ten states that were participating in the electoral process. North Carolina and Rhode Island were ineligible because their state legislators had so far failed to ratify the Constitution. In the New York legislature, the fight over ratification had included a Fourth of July burning of a copy of the proposed Constitution;[17] eventually the legislators did vote for ratification, but they remained so deadlocked on other issues that they could not produce a slate of electors. *Federalist* and *Anti-Federalist*—labels identifying legislators during New York's Constitution debate—caught on beyond the borders of the state and became the names of America's earliest political parties.[18]

At the end of January 1789, Washington wrote a long letter to the Marquis de Lafayette, his former comrade in arms and a young man he often treated like a son. The letter left no doubt that Washington was foreseeing his inauguration. Without directly saying that he was about to become president, he wrote that he would "assume the task with the most unfeigned reluctance." At the time of the letter, Lafayette was in France, about to plunge into the revolution looming there, and Washington expressed hope that the government simultaneously emerging from America's revolution "will not finally disappoint the expectations of her Friends." Washington also noted, more prosaically, that he had ordered himself a new suit of homespun cloth from a factory in Hartford, Connecticut, adding, "I hope it will not be a great while, before it will be unfashionable for a gentleman to appear in any other dress" besides that made in America. "Indeed we have already been too long subject to British prejudices. I use no porter or cheese in my family, but such as is made in America: both those articles may now be purchased of an excellent quality."[19]

On March 4, 1789—the day the Confederation Congress chose for the beginning of the Constitutional government—Washington wrote to Richard Conway, an Alexandria merchant and ship owner. Washington said he was attempting something he had "never expected to be reduced to the necessity of doing": borrowing money. Washington's landholdings were extensive, amounting to more than seventy thousand acres, including Mount Vernon's eight thousand.[20] Yet still he was cash-poor. As he told Conway, his land would "not command cash but at an under value. . . . Short Crops, & other causes not entirely within my Controul" had caused the lack of funds. Washington asked for £500, which he would use to pay off debts "in Alexandria &ca." * [21] And he added, in a not-so-casual aside, that he might need

---

*   It takes a double translation—one involving time, the other involving geography—to convert 1789 U.S. currencies to modern currency. In 1789 America had fourteen currencies, one for each state in pounds and a colonial currency in dollars. Washington's first loan, later increased to 625 Maryland

funds for a trip out of state, "if it shall not be permitted me to remain at home in retirement."[22] Although the election would not be certified by the House and the Senate until April 6, Washington clearly had few doubts that he was now president-elect and would soon travel to New York for his inauguration. In the end, he garnered sixty-nine of the electors' votes, and John Adams, winning thirty-four, became his vice president.

Looking back today at that epochal electoral victory, it seems incredible that people of Washington's time could see him, not in the new, mysterious role as president but rather as a potential monarch. Washington himself had marveled at the fact that even after he resigned his military commission and had been hailed a hero, "respectable characters speak of a monarchical form of Government without horror."[23] Those characters included Jefferson and Hamilton ("elective monarch"); Edmund Randolph, Washington's future attorney general ("foetus of monarchy"); Representative Thomas Tudor Tucker of South Carolina: ("people . . . Rage for Monarchy").[24]

If Humphreys' words had become part of the inaugural address, Washington might well have contributed to the scare, even as he sought to quell it, by floating the idea of a hereditary monarchy. Humphreys' text included this passage: "Divine Providence hath not seen fit, that my blood should be transmitted or my name perpetuated by the endearing, though sometimes seducing channel of immediate offspring. I have no child for whom I could wish to make a provision—no family to build in greatness upon my Country's ruins." In less flowery language, Washington was not a father with prospective heirs, and so a prospective dynasty would end with him.[25]

And shortly, as Washington was about to be inaugurated, John Adams would add himself to the roll of respectable characters: He would seek a royal title for the American republic's first elected president.

---

pounds, was the equivalent 625 x 2.6667 = 1666.70 dollars. That would buy in modern American currency about $40,000 worth of goods and services, See John J. McCusker, *A Historical Price Index* (Worcester, MA: American Antiquarian Society, 1992), 299-332.

4

OUT WITH THE OLD

The Congress of the Confederation, which had been meeting in New York since 1785, had a final task in the autumn of 1788: to put the Constitution "into operation in pursuance of the resolutions of the late Federal Convention."[1] On September 13, a committee of the dwindling members of the Confederation Congress had issued an ordinance establishing key dates on the future Congress's calendar: the first Wednesday in January 1789 for the appointment of electors; the first Wednesday in February for the electors to "assemble in their respective States, and vote for a President"; and the first Wednesday in March "for commencing Proceedings." The Congress of the Confederation, in its final official session on October 10, 1788, had decreed that the date for the opening of the First Federal Congress was to be March 4, 1789— and handed off to its successor the creation of the new government.

But where were those proceedings to commence? The logical site for the peripatetic Congress would seem to be to remain in New York City. However, members were so split on a location that instead of using the words "New York" in their ordinance, they employed the term "the present Seat of Congress."[2] The Congress of the Confederation had its last quorum on October 10, 1788, and its final meeting, at Fraunces Tavern in New York, on March 2, 1789. Besides the Congress's secretary, only one member was in attendance: Philip Pell, an Anti-Federalist of nearby Pelham, New York, his family's home since 1654.[3]

The process for selecting delegates to the First Federal Congress had been established via compromise at the Constitutional Convention in July 1787. Introduced by Connecticut's Roger Sherman and Oliver Ellsworth, the "Great Compromise" may have saved the argumentative convention from dissolution, calling as it did for proportional representation in the House and a sole representative per state in the Senate. After agreeing on two senators, the compromise passed.

Creators of the Constitution had to guess at states' populations to establish forty-three congressional districts. So representation varied widely and produced such differences as these: Representative James Jackson of Georgia had 16,250 constituents, George Thatcher of the Maine district of Massachusetts had 96,550. [4]

To provide members for the First Federal Congress, the eleven ratifying states ran elections so as to conclude them by the scheduled March 4, 1789 opening day for the First Federal Congress. North Carolina and Rhode Island still had not ratified. New York's senatorial candidates did not emerge from their election struggle until July 1789.

State legislatures chose the senators. States elected representatives at large or by districts. Of the elections' forty-three districts, only fifteen held serious contests. Federalists, running against Anti-Federalists, clearly won, electing twenty of the twenty-two senators and forty-nine of the fifty-nine representatives. [5]

New York politicians, in hopes that their city would become America's permanent capital, decided to transform their City Hall into Federal Hall and make it the home of the First Federal Congress. New York, after all, had been the home of the Congress of the Confederation for almost five years, after it spent stints in Philadelphia, Princeton, Trenton, and Annapolis.

In the winter of 1789, as the congressional delegates began streaming into the city in anticipation of their first session on March 4, local boosters eagerly anticipated a day when their city would become the permanent seat of government, (not *capital* because that is what states had.)

City Hall, at 26 Wall Street, had long been a historic site. In 1734, John Peter Zenger, printer of the *New-York Weekly Journal*, had been imprisoned in a jail cell on the second floor after his arrest on a charge of seditious libel; his newspaper had accused New York's royal governor, William Cosby, of tyranny. Also on the second floor was the courtroom where, in 1735, spectators cheered after a jury acquitted Zenger in the trial that began the American march toward constitutionally guaranteed freedom of the press. [6] Here, too, the Stamp Act Congress had met in 1765, when delegates from the colonies drafted the Declaration of

Rights and Grievances, which protested Parliament's imposing laws on the colonists without their consent.

Conversion of City Hall into Federal Hall had begun in September 1788, financed by a subscription of £3,200 from private benefactors. Work commenced under the supervision of five commissioners appointed by the city's Common Council and the architect, Major Peter Charles L'Enfant (who showed he was now an American by anglicizing his French first name, Pierre). During the Revolutionary War, like many French officers aiding the Americans, L'Enfant had served in the Continental Army. He had been wounded at the battle of Savannah, captured in the fall of Charleston, and later freed in a prisoner exchange.[7]

He was born in Paris in 1754 to Pierre L'Enfant, a painter in the royal court, and Marie Charlotte Leullier L'Enfant, the daughter of an official of the court. The elder L'Enfant had an important court position: overseeing the Gobelins Tapestry Works, which had supplied magnificent tapestries to the French court of the Sun King, Louis XIV, in the seventeenth century. At the age of seventeen, the younger L'Enfant began study under his father at the Royal Academy of Painting and Sculpture and became interested in drawing and architecture. He was twenty-two when he was recruited into the Continental Army by Silas Deane, an American secret agent in Paris. L'Enfant arrived in the United States in 1777, was commissioned as a captain of engineers in the Continental Army and assigned to the staff of Baron Frederick William Von Steuben, himself recruited in Paris by Ben Franklin.

After L'Enfant was discharged in 1784, he remained in America and worked as an architect of private homes and at least one park. He also planned the spectacular Grand Federal Procession in July 1788, which celebrated New York State's tardy ratification of the Constitution. The parade included five thousand marchers, a banquet for six thousand celebrants, and a twenty-seven-foot-long frigate christened the *Hamilton* after one of L'Enfant's influential New York friends.[8] Pulled by ten horses, the ship fired its thirty-two guns as it passed through the crowds.[9]

Two months after that extravaganza, in September 1788, L'Enfant volunteered to design "additions, alterations, and repairs" to the imminent home of the First Federal Congress. "Under pretext of a few necessary changes," French Ambassador Elénor-François-Élie, Comte de Moustier would later observe, "L'Enfant rebuilt almost all the old building bit by bit, so that it retained only its name and a few components of its old form.... Major L'Enfant was not guided or constrained by anyone." [10.]

L'Enfant's alterations were indeed extensive, including a rear addition that was ninety feet long and two and a half stories high. About two hundred workers toiled through the fall and winter on what was then New York's largest construction project. Many of the unskilled laborers were immigrants personally hired by L'Enfant, and some New Yorkers accused him of favoring "foreigners (even of the lowest class)" over locals.[11] Cost overruns forced Mayor James Duane to appeal, successfully, to the New York Legislature for a £13,000 tax on city residents, and another petition for funds led the legislature to allow the city to run lotteries to indemnify creditors up to another £13,000. Yet Duane and his supporters amiably accepted the rising costs of the project, given their hopes that their city would be the lasting seat of government.

L'Enfant's redesign not only expanded City Hall but also transformed it into a beautiful building that would make architectural history as an early exemplar of the Federal style. The central three-story vestibule had a marble floor and a skylight under a cupola. Off the vestibule stood a two-story, richly decorated octagonal room, sixty-five by fifty-five feet, which became the chamber of the House of Representatives. A spectators' gallery thrust fifteen feet into the House chamber, one story above the main floor. A smaller second gallery above was reserved for special guests. Members' desks formed two semicircles facing the Speaker. Members are believed to have carried on a tradition from the Continental and Confederation Congresses: representatives from New Hampshire through Delaware sat on one side of the House, and the rest of the representatives sat on the other.

On the second floor was the forty-by-thirty-foot, two-story Senate chamber and several smaller rooms for committees and the Senate secretary. Vice President John Adams would oversee the Senate from a chair "elevated several steps from the floor, and placed under a superb canopy of crimson damask. The chairs [are] arranged semicircularly, as in the room of the Representatives, with the window curtains, and hangings are also of crimson damask, and the floor is richly carpeted."[12] At the rear of the second floor were the two public galleries overhanging the House chamber, giving the Senate an architectural basis for calling itself the "upper chamber."[13]

L'Enfant, apparently anticipating the emergence of a patent law, included on the second floor a "machinery room" for the display of models of inventions, which inventors would be required to submit as part of their patent applications. Above a covered walk that ran along Wall Street was a second-floor balcony, the site that Congress would select for Washington's inauguration later that spring. Little is known about the third story except that it contained several small rooms, including a corner room that was given to the New-York Society Library and thus unofficially became the first library of Congress. [14] [15] One of its patrons would be George Washington.[16]

When the members of the First Federal Congress began arriving in New York, they walked the streets of a city that had not yet recovered from the great fires of 1776 and 1778 and its seven years of British occupation. The British had blamed the fire of 1776 on American arsonists, a claim that Washington always officially denied. Yet in a 1776 letter to his cousin Lund Washington, he seemed to give a wink and a nod to the idea that a nameless Patriot was responsible: "Providence— or some good honest Fellow, has done more for us than we were disposed to do for ourselves, as near One fourth of the City is supposed to be consumed."[17] Washington apparently thought that the fire would somehow hamper the operations of the British occupying force. The mystery of the great fire was never solved.

Many structures remained scorched even in 1789. Three ruined landmarks stood out as reminders: Trinity Church was still not restored; the derelict Lutheran church came to be called the Burnt Lutheran Church; the Middle Dutch Church was still under repair.

New York's city fathers believed that prosperity was on the way, given that the new Congress would meet here. Under British occupation, New York had not been allowed to expand, and thus the city covered only the tip of Manhattan Island by 1789. The city's northern boundary was at Byard Lane (today's Broome Street), roughly on the line of the present-day Williamsburg Bridge. On the west side of the island, the boundary was about at today's Reade Street. Greenwich Village and the Bowery were farmlands.[18] According to a city directory published on the Fourth of July 1789, New York had about 4,100 householders. Most buildings were made of brick, with tiled roofs, interspersed with the old, steeply peaked roofs of old wooden Dutch-style houses. Street lamps had been installed in 1762 but were badly maintained, and residents said the only dependable evening light came from the moon. The sanitation system consisted of buckets and the nearest river—the one called North or Hudson and the one called East. Wealthier New Yorkers ordered their servants to carry and empty the buckets.[19]

Some of these servants were enslaved, as abolition was a gradual process in New York. A state law passed in 1788 decreed that every "negro," "mulatto," or "mestee" (meaning an offspring of a white person and a "quadroon," or a person who was one-quarter black) who was then enslaved would remain so unless he or she was formally set free by a registered manumit certificate or by an owner's will. The law had been successfully lobbied for by the New York Society for the Manumission of Slaves and the Protection of Such of Them as Had Been or Wanted to Be Liberated. Its members included John Jay, Mayor James Duane, and several slaveholders, as well as Alexander Hamilton, who suggested that slave owners who wished to become members had to first free their enslaved servants. The society rejected his proposal. In 1789, coincidentally with the arrival of the First Federal Congress, Hamilton and the society founded the African Free School to divert free African American children from the "slippery paths of vice" and prepare them for abolition.[20]

Pressure to abolish slavery came not only from Americans but also from Britons, led by William Wilberforce, a lawyer and philanthropist. American newspapers covered the abolition movement in Britain, spreading to America details of the British efforts to end the slave trade. The *New York Daily Gazette* of Aug 17, 1789, for instance, devoted two full columns describing Wilberforce's crusade.[21]

In New York, as elsewhere in the early country, punishment for crime was often medieval. Under a 1788 law, death was the penalty for conviction of treason, murder, forgery, counterfeiting, rape, forcible detaining of women, robbing a church, housebreaking by day or night if the house was occupied, other forms of robbery, willful burning of a house or barn, and malicious maiming. During the year 1789, judges handed down ten death sentences in New York, all for burglary, robbery, or forgery. For minor offenses, there was the whipping post and stocks, which were on view next to the gallows. A miscreant brought before the public whipper could not be given more than thirty-nine lashes in one day. Reform legislation in 1789 lessened the punishment for vagrants and disorderly persons to six months of imprisonment, with hard labor and whipping imposed at the discretion of the court.[22]

Reigning over the city and its disorderly persons was New York society, with its aristocratic leanings, its taste for English fashions, and its preference for a style of entertaining that resembled that of England's royal court. New Yorkers of all classes wondered whether that courtly style would attract the newcomers of the Federal Congress.

By 1790 attending the House debates at Federal Hall had become the most popular social activity in New York." Yet fame did not last long for Federal Hall: the building was torn down in 1812 and its salvaged materials sold off for $425.[23]

Although its first home would be temporary, the First Federal Congress of 1789 was seminal: it was the first instrument of government to emerge from the newly ratified Constitution and become reality. Acts of this Congress would refine the complex presidential election system and establish the powers of the president, and from this Congress would emerge the law establishing the judicial branch of the government, with its Supreme Court and federal court system; the office of the attorney general; and the first executive departments of War, State, and Treasury.

No other nation in history so swiftly won independence from a powerful empire—and preserved that independence. Many critics in Europe and in America predicted swift or eventual failure. But America survived because the First Federal Congress survived, solving problems that challenged its existence and leaving to future Congresses a legacy of practical and effective governance.

The work of the First Congress became a guidebook for future Congresses. The First Congress, using patience and economic threats, succeeded in handling the initial refusals of North Carolina and Rhode Island to ratify the Constitution, bringing them back into the Union—

primarily by getting them to see that in union there was strength. Employing both persistence and tolerance of dissent, those first law-makers managed to create a strong federal government while accepting the foibles of states' rights. The First Congress invented a way to solve almost every problem of 1789 and many that would arise in the future. With a minimum of political guff the members figured out how to add amendments to the Constitution without damaging it and how to add states to the Union. Some problems that were not solved by the genius of compromise were simply ignored until a solution suddenly burst through.

But there was no solution for a haunting reality that could not be ignored. As a Massachusetts constituent put it to a member of the First Federal Congress: "southern & northern will often be the division of Congress—The thought is disagreeable; but the distinction is founded in nature, & will last as long as the Union." [24]

5

A NEW GOVERNMENT AWAKENS

At sunset on the evening of March 3, 1789, a thirteen-gun salute boomed from a New York waterfront fort to bid farewell to the Articles of Confederation. At dawn the next day, an eleven-gun salute hailed the states of the new Republic and the convening of its First Federal Congress. "The old government has gently fallen asleep—and the new one is waking into activity," wrote Representative George Thatcher, from the Maine District of Massachusetts, who had served in the "sleeping" Congress and would serve in the one that was awakening the next day.[1] Yet, of the fifty-nine representatives expected in New York for Congress's opening day, only thirteen had appeared by the morning of March 4: Thatcher plus twelve others. Of the twenty-two senators expected, only eight were present—travel problems delayed most of the absentees. The special elections of candidates for Congress had gone smoothly—except for New York State, which had not yet held elections to fill its congressional seats.

"I got to this place about seven o'clock this morning and did intend to have written a long letter," wrote Senator Robert Morris of Philadelphia of his first day on the job, "but the day has been consumed in firing of Guns, ringing of Bells, and receiving and paying visits, and in meeting at the new Federal Building (called the *Trap*)"—a comment bestowed on New York by members who preferred Philadelphia. "The Public's expectation," Morris continued, "seems to be so highly wound up that I think disappointment must inevitably follow after a while, notwithstanding that I believe there will be inclination and abilities in the two houses to do every thing that reasonable and sensible men can promise to themselves, but you know well how impossible it is for

Public measures to keep pace with the sanguine desires of the interested, the ignorant, and the inconsiderate parts of the Community."[2]

New Yorkers met the day flashing celebratory brass medallions stamped with a radiant sun and a scrawny version of the eagle on the Great Seal of the United States. Others bore medallions reading MEMORABLE ERA MARCH THE FOURTH 1789 or LONG LIVE THE PRESIDENT or just plain GW.[3] This was the day, after all, that the new American government was to start under President George Washington. Yet the president-elect himself was still in Mount Vernon, awaiting the formal notification that he had been elected and would be inaugurated.

Back in the hot summer of 1787, when the creators of the Constitution had convened in Philadelphia, no other issue produced more oratory than the debate over the nature of the "National Executive," the leader and personification of the strong new central government. Some convention delegates—including Benjamin Franklin, George Mason, and Edmund Randolph, who had served as an aide-de-camp to General Washington—questioned whether the National Executive had to consist of only one man. Randolph, for example, proposed an executive of three men as an antidote to fears of monarchy. Maryland, New York, and Delaware, too, opposed the concept of the one-man presidency, but a majority of the convention's delegates supported it. So the Constitution would declare a solo National Executive in its article II, section 1: "The executive Power shall be vested in a President of the United States of America." Many delegates envisioned that the presidency would land inevitably, and safely, in the hands of George Washington.

Compromise had been the mainstay of the Constitutional Convention, starting with the "Great Compromise," which laid out how congressional representatives were to be chosen. Yet in the First Federal Congress, *compromise* would be a word rarely heard. The day that had begun with celebratory cannon firing would end with the new Congress yearning for a quorum and the president-elect still at home in Virginia, wondering when he was going to be inaugurated.

Monitoring the situation in New York for Washington was Henry Knox, on whom Washington had depended since Knox joined the Continental Army and delivered to Washington the cannons that in

1776 had forced the British to evacuate Boston. On March 5, Knox wrote Washington to report a new number: eight senators and seventeen representatives. They had assembled and promptly adjourned. The delegates agreed to follow that routine every day until they achieved a quorum of twelve in the Senate and thirty in the House. In a more prosaic aside, Knox added that "superfine brown Hartford cloth"—the material of Washington's inaugural suit—would arrive in New York next week.[4]

Washington, continuing preparations for his trip to New York, wrote to the Alexandria shipowner Richard Conway again, asking him to raise the £500 loan by an extra £100. Conway increased the loan amount to £625 in "Maryland currency."[5] (See note on page 52.) Interest on the loan was at 6 percent a year; when Washington paid off the debt on December 15, 1790, the indebtedness would be nearly £650. In the same letter, Washington said he had "to discharge the last Act of *personal* duty" by visiting his mother, Mary Ball Washington, then around eighty-two and dying of what is believed to have been breast cancer.[6] She lived in Fredericksburg, about forty miles south of Mount Vernon, where the president-elect had bought a small house next door to his sister Betty Lewis. Washington would see his mother for the last time when he stopped at Fredericksburg on his way to New York, and the presidency.

There were empty seats in the Senate and House chambers on March 4, 1789, but on that day Congress truly launched the United States of America. Under the Constitution's article I, section 1, "All legislative Powers herein granted shall be vested in a Congress of the United States." The men gathering in New York were empowered to convert the new Constitution's abstract framework for "a Congress" into the reality of the hardworking First Federal Congress. The House, disregarding the fact that the Senate still lacked a quorum, achieved its own quorum (thirty members out of fifty-nine) and went to work on April 1, a day of snow-dappled rain.

As Speaker of the House, the members chose Frederick Augustus Conrad Muhlenberg, a native of Trappe, Pennsylvania, and a former Lutheran minister; *Columbian* magazine described him as having a "rubicund complexion and oval face, hair full powdered, tamboured satin vest of ample dimensions, dark blue coat with gilt buttons, and a sonorous voice, all corresponding in appearance and sound with his magnificent name."[7] The Pennsylvania delegation had nominated Muhlenberg with the understanding that he would be the northern leader who would balance Washington, the southern president. (Meanwhile, on the same day, Washington was still asserting his reluctance to assume the presidency at all, writing to Knox: "For myself, the delay may be compared to a reprieve; for in confidence I can assure *you*—with the *world* it would obtain *little credit*—that my movements to the chair of Government will be accompanied with feelings not unlike those of a culprit who is going to the place of his execution.")[8]

On the next day, April 2, the representatives appointed the eleven-man Select Committee on Rules, the first—and potentially the House's most powerful—select committee.[9] After only five days of give-and-take discussion, the committee produced the first set of parliamentary guidelines, outlining the functions of the Speaker and the steps of the legislative process. The committee also established the procedures for debate and for the Committee of the Whole. The latter device, which makes the entire House function as one big congressional committee, was borrowed from the British House of Commons and had been used by the Continental Congress. It would continue to be used in the Senate until 1986.

The rules of House and Senate were nearly the same in 1789, both allowing unlimited debate. As the House population grew, it would set limits on the time permitted for debate, but the Senate continued without such restrictions.[10] The first senators also set rules of protocol still practiced today, including "when two members rise at the same time, the President [meaning the vice president, who presides over the Senate] shall name the person to speak," and "When the yeas and nays shall be called for ... each member called upon shall ... declare openly, and without debate, his assent or dissent to the question."[11]

The Senate finally attained its twelve-man quorum on April 6.[12] Congress, trying to make up for lost time, swiftly carried out its first constitutional duties: counting the electors' votes for president and vice president and notifying the winners. Washington had received the maximum possible votes–sixty-nine—a feat that no president since has matched. John Adams had received thirty-four, making him vice-president.* Adams had hoped to receive enough votes to become a challenger to Washington, but he did not know that Alexander Hamilton, as "an essential point of caution," had confidentially convinced several politicians to see to it that Adams did not receive enough votes to make Washington look less than utterly victorious.[13] The president-to-be was also unaware of Hamilton's machinations.

The runners-up among the electoral votes, receiving a few each, were John Jay, whom Washington later would name as the first chief justice of the Supreme Court; Massachusetts Governor John Hancock; New York Governor George Clinton; John Rutledge of South Carolina, who would become the second chief justice; and Robert H. Harrison of Maryland, a wartime aide-de-camp to Washington. The president later would select Harrison for appointment to the Supreme Court, but he declined.

Newspapers immediately published the election results, but the official report did not come until April 6, when the House and Senate met in joint session to accept the vote counts in the electors' certificates that had been presented to Congress. To formally notify Adams that he had been elected vice president, Congress enlisted a man who happened to be in New York on business: Sylvanus Bourne, a young friend of Adams and a future consul general of the United States to the Netherlands. Bourne sailed to Rhode Island on a packet boat and, after traveling by stage coaches, reached Adams's home in Braintree, Massachusetts, fifty hours after leaving New York.

After receiving the news, Adams was sent on his way with a militia cavalry troop of horse, pealing bells, and an escort of more than forty carriages. At a stop in Hartford, the same manufacturer who already had provided brown broadcloth to Washington presented a bolt of the same to Adams, presumably for an inauguration suit like Washington's.[14] Adams's ceremonial procession continued on to New York, where, on April 20, he was met by numerous cavalry escorts and

---

*   Under the procedure set down in the original Constitution, the Constitution called for each elector to enter two votes, without any distinction indicating which vote was for president, and which for vice president. The person receiving the most votes became president, and the runner-up vice president. Thus, all 69 electors voted once for Washington, and then a second time for another candidate. This system proved unworkable and was altered by the Twelfth Amendment in 1804.

congressmen in carriages. He was officially presented to the Senate in a short session at Federal Hall on April 21. Thus, for a short while, the new nation had a vice president but no president.

Charles Thomson, longtime secretary of Congress, was chosen to go to Mount Vernon and officially inform the seemingly ambivalent Washington of his victory. Thomson was a man of humble origin who had achieved an office of great power and prestige. Born in Ireland to Scots-Irish parents in 1729, he was ten years old when he sailed for America with his widowed father and three brothers. The father became ill at sea and died within sight of land. The ship's captain, after confiscating most of the family's money and goods, put the boys ashore at Lewes, Delaware, and each brother set off to find a life on his own. Thomson was indentured to a blacksmith but soon ran away, hoping for something better. A benefactress, sensing his potential, arranged for him to attend the Philadelphia Academy, where he was introduced to the study of the Greek and Roman classics.[15] The French and Indian War of 1756–63 drew Thomson into politics as an opponent of the establishment's aggressive policy toward Native Americans. He also established himself as a successful merchant and a brilliant member of the Philadelphia intelligentsia. He became involved in Pennsylvanian Quaker politics, continuing to champion justice for Native Americans and, starting in 1774, "the Cause of Liberty." He was unanimously chosen as secretary of the First Continental Congress, a post he still held in 1789 as he headed to Mount Vernon on April 6.

Under the weak government of the Articles of Confederation, Thomson had performed duties that the First Federal Congress later would distribute among the Department of State, the secretary of the Senate, and the clerk of the House of Representatives. Under the new Constitution, Thomson had anticipated that he would hold all three merged jobs and rise to Cabinet rank, becoming the secretary for the Home Department, a post envisioned as being similar to that of the British home secretary. As Thomson set off for Mount Vernon, he expected that he soon would be promoted to the new position by Congress.

Around noon on Tuesday, April 14, eight days out of New York—and after conquering "tempestuous weather, bad roads, and many large rivers"[16]—Thomson arrived at Mount Vernon and was greeted at its doorway by Washington. Thomson took a document from his pocket and read it aloud:

> I have the honor to transmit to your Excellency the informa-
> tion of your unanimous election to the Office of President
> of the United States of America. Suffer me, Sir, to indulge
> the hope, that so auspicious a mark of public confidence will
> meet your approbation and be considered as a sure pledge of
> the affection and support you are to expect from a free and
> an enlightened people.[17]

Thomson finished reading and handed the letter to the president-elect. It had been written by John Langdon, a senator from New Hampshire who had just become the president pro tempore of the Senate. Langdon's words seem to indicate that he was unsure whether Washington had yet made up his mind to accept the presidency.

Washington's written answer both confirmed his acceptance and noted that he saw his election as a tribute, not a mandate:

> I have been long accustomed to pay so much respect to the
> opinion of my fellow citizens, that the knowledge of their
> unanimous suffrages having been given in my favour scarcely
> leaves me the alternative for an Option. Whatever may have
> been my private feelings and sentiments, I cannot, I believe,
> give a greater evidence of my sensibility for the honor they
> have done me than by accepting the appointment.

He also made a barbed remark about how long it had taken Congress to get organized:

> Upon considering how long time some of the gentlemen of
> both houses of Congress have been at New York, how anx-
> iously desirous they must be to proceed to business and how
> deeply the public mind appears to be impressed with the ne-
> cessity of doing it speedily, I cannot find myself at liberty to
> delay my Journey.[18]

Back in New York, Thomson's congressional foes, who included Vice President John Adams, had wiped out Thomson's long-held post as secretary of Congress. To these foes, the new Federal Congress did not need a man who symbolized the old Congress of the Confederation. As a final touch, they decided not to invite Thomson to the inauguration of the president. Afterward Thomson would no longer be a prominent participant in American history; although he had written more than thousand pages of a memoir about Congress, he destroyed that manuscript at some time after the Mount Vernon trip. Asked for his reason, he replied, "I should contradict all the histories of the great events of the Revolution. Let the world admire the supposed wisdom and valor of our great men. Perhaps they may adopt the qualities that have been ascribed to them, and thus good may be done. I shall not undeceive future generations."[19]

The men who wrote the Constitution wanted a strong federal government and a robust chief executive. From the beginning, back in Annapolis, Madison and his Federalist allies believed almost beyond any doubt, that the first chief executive would be George Washington. There could be no other man. They knew that he would establish the dimensions of the presidency, that he would mold presidential power in his own presidency, and that mold would be passed to the presidents who followed—a double gift to posterity.

If, at this fragile moment, anyone else had challenged him, the presidency and perhaps the Constitution itself could not have long endured.

6

"NOW A KING"

The most controversial phrase written at the Constitutional Convention is in the opening of Article II: "The executive Power shall be vested in a President of the United States." Anti-Federalists swooped down on the word *Power*, dismissing Federalists' assurances that presidential supremacy would be blocked by the checks-and-balances structure set up elsewhere in the Constitution. Anti-Federalists hated the Constitution. And no one was more passionate in his loathing than Patrick Henry, whose call for liberty had launched the Revolution. In his ringing speech before the Virginia Ratifying Convention on June 5, 1788, he warned that the so-called check was "a supposition" that the president "shall be honest." But the Constitution's "defective and imperfect construction" made it possible for "bad men" to have the "power to perpetrate the worst of mischiefs. . . . If your American chief be a man of ambition and abilities, how easy it is for him to render himself absolute!"[1]

A writer who called himself "an old Whig"—meaning anti-monarchy Patriot—in 1787 saw the president "as much a KING as the *King of Great Britain*, and a king too of the worst kind: an elective king." Looking beyond George Washington as president, the writer said that the chance of getting another Washington "is perhaps a chance of one hundred millions to one."[2]

The Federalists, who controlled the First Federal Congress, acknowledged the Anti-Federalists' warnings of monarchy by showing that the presidency was the creation of Congress. Members of Congress would be making all the decisions that would bring the president into the government. Members of Congress would supervise the counting of the presidential ballots, the formal notification of his election, and—in

71

one of the first tasks the new Congress took up—the planning of his inauguration. All the Constitution dictated about inaugural proceedings was that the president-elect had to take an oath upon inauguration ("Before he enter on the execution of his office, he shall take the following oath or affirmation: 'I do solemnly swear (or affirm) that I will faithfully execute the office of President of the United States, and will to the best of my ability, preserve, protect and defend the constitution of the United States'"). The vice president already had been sworn in so that the Senate could function, and the Speaker of the House had taken his oath for the same reason; no ceremony had been held for either position. But the presidential inauguration was so important that a historic observance was essential and would be the exemplar for all inaugurations in the future. So the new Congress set up a joint committee on the inauguration, merging the parallel discussions on the ceremony among members of the House and members of the Senate.

The only useful precedent for the inaugural ceremony upon which the committee could draw was the installation of state governors, which usually involved taking an oath. To add to the solemnity of the presidential occasion, the committee decided that a "divine service" would follow in a nearby church. The committee then recorded their decisions as a 13,500-word "Ceremonial" and published it as a broadside—a sizable sheet of paper printed on one side—that would be presented first to their colleagues and then to the public. Their key decision would be a hallmark of all the presidential inaugurations to come: The Oath of Office would be "administered to the President in the most public manner, and . . . the greatest number of the people of the United States, and without distinction, may be witnesses to the solemnity."[3]

For Washington, the inauguration was not a few minutes with his right hand on a Bible, but a long procession that finally ended on the second-floor balcony of Federal Hall. On the morning of April 16, two days after he had received and replied to John Langdon's official notice of his election, Washington "bade adieu to Mount Vernon, to private life, and to domestic felicity; and, with a mind oppressed with more anxious and painful sensation than I have words to explain, I set out for New York," accompanied by Charles Thomson and David Humphreys.[4] Traveling separately in his entourage were Tobias Lear, who had been

Washington's principal aide and confidant since 1786, and Billy Lee, an enslaved manservant who had been with Washington in peace and war.

Martha Washington, concerned about his age and health, said good-bye, wondering, as she later wrote in a letter to a nephew, "when or whether he will ever come home again god only knows."[5] Washington, too, had pragmatic reasons to worry during his departure: he had left behind detailed plans for the running of his five unprofitable Mount Vernon farms, and he was not confident that they would make money while he was gone.

Crowds saw off Washington at Mount Vernon and later at Alexandria, where he continued to reveal his reluctance to become president: "I ought not to conceal, yet I cannot describe, the painful emotions which I felt in being called upon to determine whether I would accept or refuse the Presidency of the United States." He said that the unanimous electoral vote induced "an ardent desire on my own part to be instrumental in conciliating the good will of my country-men towards each other."[6] During a stop at Alexandria's Wise's Tavern, locals slowed down his journey with a celebration that included thirteen toasts. Washington and his party then boarded a ferry and crossed the Potomac to Georgetown (then part of Maryland), where another crowd hailed him. And so it went, in town after town, for all eight days of the slow procession northward.

On April 20, as he neared Philadelphia, Washington stepped out of his carriage and mounted a white horse. At a bridge leading to the city, he was welcomed by a structure that evoked a Roman arch of triumph, supported by thirteen pillars and festooned with laurel. As his horse trotted under it, a contraption designed by artist Charles Willson Peale dropped a crown of laurel upon his head. Not much farther down the route, Billy Lee, suffering from an old knee injury, found himself un-able to continue onward. Washington asked a friend in Philadelphia to care for him until he recovered.[7] (He would arrive in New York "safe & well," but not until June.[8])

Lee perhaps knew George Washington as well as anyone could; pur-chased in 1768, he had become Washington's valet, or enslaved manser-vant. He had ridden by Washington's side during all eight years of the American Revolution, helping him dress, serving him meals, and delivering personal correspondence. He had also accompanied Washington to Philadelphia for the Constitutional Convention.[9]

As Washington journeyed northward, a newspaper exulted with a quotation from Revelations that would reverberate in many who glimpsed royalty in George Washington: *"And I looked, and behold, a white horse! And its rider had a bow, and a crown was given to him, and he came out conquering, and to conquer."*[10] This mention of "a crown" is noteworthy: many Americans still believed that only a king could rule a country. That conviction had haunted Washington since the final days of the Revolutionary War, when troops mutinied, and disgruntled officers talked of a military coup d'état. Little had changed in the six subsequent years; even before he left Mount Vernon, James McHenry, a former aide had told him, "You are now a king under a different name."[11]

In Trenton, New Jersey, on April 21, the bridge across Assunpink Creek was festooned with garlands of greenery and an arch emblazoned with the 1776 date of the town's liberation, along with the words "The Defender of the Mothers Will Also Defend the Daughters." On the bridge, waiting to greet him, a chorus of young girls and matrons sang:

> *Welcome, mighty Chief once more!*
> *Welcome to this grateful shore;*
> *Now no mercenary foe*
> *Aims again the fatal blow;*
> *Aims at thee, the fatal blow.*
> *"Virgins fair & Matrons grave,*
> *These thy conquering arm did save."*[12]

When Washington reached Elizabethtown, New Jersey, on April 23, he was met by a committee of senators and representatives who escorted him to the waterfront, where a barge—named *Hamilton* after the man who had paid for it—awaited him. Manning its oars were thirteen harbor pilots in white uniforms. The *Hamilton* bore Washington up the New Jersey shoreline and into New York Harbor, where a women's chorus on another barge serenaded him while flutes paced the strokes of the oarsmen. Porpoises surfaced and swam near Washington's barge, "as if," wrote a dazzled Representative Elias Boudinot, "they had risen up to know what was the Cause of all this Joy."[13] A celebratory flotilla of barges and ships filled the waters of New York Harbor. A Spanish sloop-of-war fired a thirteen-gun salute and ran up the flags of two dozen nations. A chorus sang "God Save the King," but with new lyrics:

> *Thrice welcome to this shore,*
> *Our Leader now no more,*
> *But Ruler thou;*
> *Oh, truly good and great!*
> *Long live to glad our State,*
> *Where countless Honours wait*
> *To deck thy brow.*[14]

At Murray's Wharf, near the foot of Wall Street, Washington disembarked onto a red carpet while yet another thirteen guns boomed. Various dignitaries welcomed him to New York and formed a procession that passed thousands of cheering people. "He frequently bowed to the multitude and took off his hat to the ladies at the windows, who waved their handkerchiefs, threw flowers before him, and shed tears of joy and congratulation," a witness remembered. "The whole city was one scene of triumphal rejoicing."[15]

Indeed, Washington was much beloved by the city fathers of New York, as illustrated by an event that had occurred earlier in April, probably on Palm Sunday weekend. A nasty anonymous cartoon portraying the president-elect had been peddled on city streets; it showed Washington holding Billy Lee in his arms and riding a jackass led by David Humphreys.[16] "The Entry," as the cartoon was titled, also had a couplet: "*The glorious time has come to pass / When David shall conduct an Ass.*" In a testimonial to New York's adoration of Washington, copies of the cartoon were treated like pornography and rapidly suppressed. None is known to exist today, and we know about it only because of a reference to it in a letter from one participant in the Newburgh Conspiracy to another: John Armstrong Jr. wrote to his former superior, Horatio Gates, that "all the world here and elsewhere are busy in collecting flowrs & sweets of every kind to amuse and delight" Washington. "Yet in the midst of this admiration there are Sceptics who doubt its propriety and wits who amuse themselves with its extravagance. The first will grumble, and the last will laugh, and the Presidt should be prepard to meet the attacks of both with firmness and good Nature." The cartoon, he wrote, was "full of very disloyal & profane allusions."[17]

As Washington proceeded into the city, "the windows, stoops, and streets were crowded, the latter so closely you might have walked upon people's heads for a great distance," Don Diego de Gardoqui, Spain's ambassador to America, reported in a dispatch to the Spanish minister of foreign affairs. "Every house is illuminated except those of the Quakers."[18] Washington, ignoring the carriage assigned to him, waved at Gardoqui, who hopped out of his own carriage to join the French ambassador, the welcoming officials, and the troop of horse accompanying Washington. The walk ended at what Gardoqui called "the humble house which had been provided as his residence," a three-story structure at No. 1 Cherry Street.

Washington's own narration of his arrival in New York was more equivocal; in his diary entry of April 23, 1789, he wrote, "The display of boats which attended and joined us[19] on this occasion, some with vocal and some with instrumental music on board; the decorations of the ships, the roar of cannon, and the loud acclamations of the people which rent the skies, as I passed along the wharves, filled my mind with sensations as painful (considering the reverse of this scene, which may be the case after all my labors to do good) as they are pleasing."

Washington's new home was owned by Samuel Osgood, originally of Massachusetts. He had served in the Revolutionary War as a colonel and assistant quartermaster, and after Washington became president, he would appoint Osgood the first United States postmaster general. The house at No. 1 Cherry Street had been built in 1770 for Walter Franklin, a wealthy Quaker merchant who rented out the residence to presidents of the Congress of the Confederation. Osgood acquired the mansion after marrying Franklin's widow, Maria Bowne Franklin—a joining of wealth and social authority that was common among the well-to-do in North and South. Although the house was somewhat out of the way, the First Federal Congress requested it for Washington's residence. The president would remain here for ten months, at a cost to the Congress of $845, before relocating to larger quarters at 39-41 Broadway.

Osgood expanded the drawing room for presidential entertaining and gave responsibility for additional improvements to his wife, who in turn enlisted the help of her socialite friend Catherine Alexander Duer, whose aristocratic airs had earned her the title "Lady Kitty." She was the daughter of William Alexander, a Continental Army major general known as Lord Stirling (a Scot title that he claimed), and Sarah Livingston, a socialite from an old, immensely wealthy Hudson Valley family. Lady Kitty's kin included the man who would shortly administer the presidential oath of office to Washington: Robert Livingston, chancellor of New York—the state's highest judicial official.

The flirtatious Lady Kitty, who was once wooed by Alexander Hamilton, married British-born William Duer instead. When Hamilton became secretary of the Treasury, he made Duer his first assistant secretary. An inside trader involved in events leading to the financial panic of 1792, Duer later would inspire Jefferson's fury over market manipulators and give Jefferson an opportunity to obliquely criticize Hamilton: "the credit and fate of the nation seem to hang on the desperate throws and plunges of gambling scoundrels."[20] Duer would die in debtors' prison in 1799.

In the words of a woman who saw the transformed house before Washington moved in, there was "the best of furniture in every room—and the greatest quantity of plate and china that I ever saw before, the whole of the first and second story is papered and the floors covered with the richest kind of Turkey and Wilton Carpets . . . they spared no pains nor expense in it."[21] The house may have been superbly furnished, but quarters were so cramped that three presidential secretaries—Humphreys, Robert Lewis, and Thomas Nelson—had to share a room. Humphreys would sometimes awaken and, in moments of inspiration, stride across the floor, reciting his verses and waking up his roommates. In 1790, much larger quarters, the four-story Macomb House on Broadway, became available, presumably to the relief of Lewis and Nelson.

Washington had sent Tobias Lear ahead to New York to act as his personal aide in such matters as hiring servants. In 1786, Lear had, as Washington put it, successfully applied to "come into my family in the blended characters of preceptor to the Children, and as a Clerk or private Secretary to me." Born in Portsmouth, New Hampshire, Lear graduated from Harvard and was recommended to Washington by General Benjamin Lincoln. Lear had moved into Mount Vernon, sat at the family table, and had his linens and stockings mended and washed along with the laundry of family members.

Arrving in New York, Lear engaged fourteen people: a coachman, a porter, a cook, maids, footmen, laundresses, and a man he called a *valet de chamber,* a label that traced back to the English royal household, where French was the language of the court. Lear also arranged for seven enslaved servants to be brought from Mount Vernon. The staff would be supervised by Samuel Fraunces, whose nickname, "Black Sam," has inspired modern speculation that he may have been a free African American.

Fraunces also owned the tavern (run by his wife) in a four-story building at 54 Pearl Street where the last, one-delegate meeting of the Congress of the Confederation had been held in December 1788. (See page 55.) The same building would eventually become the first location of the departments of Foreign Affairs, Treasury, and War.

Fraunces Tavern was already a storied place for Washington. At noon on December 4, 1783, after Royal Navy ships had carried off the last British occupation troops and thousands of Loyalists, Washington had invited his officers to the tavern's second floor. There he lifted a glass and said, "With a heart full of love and gratitude, I now take leave of you. I most devoutly wish that your latter days may be prosperous and happy as your former ones have been glorious and honorable." Tears streaming down his cheeks, he embraced or shook the hand of each officer and then left the tavern to begin his journey home. On December 23, before the assembled Congress of the Confederation in the State House at Annapolis—then the U.S. capitol—he handed in a copy of his congressional appointment, dated June 15, 1775, and resigned as commander-in-chief.[22]

The joint congressional committee on the inauguration declared that the precise site of the inauguration would be on the balcony known as the Outer Gallery, which opened off the Senate Chamber in Federal Hall. The Ceremonial also laid out the movements of the players with the precision of a theatrical script: "When the President shall proceed to the gallery to take the Oath, he be attended by the Vice-President, and be followed by the Chancellor of the State, and pass through the middle door, that the Senators pass through the door on the right, and the Representatives, preceded by the Speaker, pass through the door on the left." Inaugural "assistants" were appointed and prominent seats designated for them; their ranks included Colonel William Stephens Smith, John Adams's son-in-law, appointed by the New York chapter of the Society of the Cincinnati to present the society's congratulations to the president. L'Enfant, without explanation, declined his appointment as an assistant.

April 30, Inauguration Day, was nearing when an unexpected question arose in the Senate: What should George Washington be called after he became president? The answer was entrusted to a three-man Senate committee, and two days later the House created a similar committee so that the two could confer. The senators wanted to call Washington "His Highness the President of the United States, and Protector of Their Liberties." *Their*, referring to the states, showed that the senators had not fully realized that they belonged to the First *Federal* Congress and that the president presided over a federal nation. The representatives chose to stick with the Constitution, which uses the phrase *"President of the United States" six* times and does not offer alternative title suggestions. Representative Madison eloquently gave his own reason for rejecting titles: "I am not afraid of titles because I fear the danger of any power they could confer, but I am against them because they are not very reconcilable with the nature of our government, or the genius of the people."[23]

Other titles were circulated as well. Elénor-François-Élie, Comte de Moustier, the French ambassador, wrote that he heard "Elected Majesty," "Most Serene Highness," and "Most Illustrious Highness" proposed.[24] John Adams, the vice president, promoted various titles for the president, prompting Senator Ralph Izard of South Carolina to assign Adams one of his own: "His Rotundity," which stuck for a long time.[25]

Another witness to the parade of honorifics was Senator William Maclay of Pennsylvania, an irascible observer and a caustic commentator in his diary. His legacy to posterity is his diary, which contained whatever he saw in the secret debates behind the closed doors of the Senate chamber. The decision to keep those doors shut was deliberate policy. The first employee hired by the Senate was a doorkeeper, who was ordered to bar the entry of sightseers and members of the House of Representatives. (Noticing how their House colleagues got much more publicity than the secretive Senate, the Senate decided to swing its doors open – but not until December 9, 1795.[26])

Maclay took extensive notes during Senate debates and later made them into entries for his journal. These recollections—spanning March 1789 to March 1791—are the only sustained record of those historic days in the first Senate. His journal is full of brash words, sharp observations (in one debate, he said he could see a senator's "Nostrils Widen, and his nose flatten like the head of a Viper"),[27] and a loathing for Vice President John Adams, beginning when he suggested that Washington should have a title—such as "His Majesty the President"[28]—raised for Maclay and others the fear that the desire for a monarchy stalked the Republic.

The diary, so invaluable for understanding the first Senate, was not discovered until sometime after his death in 1804. His heirs showed some of the three volumes to a few people, but the diary remained unpublished until the late nineteenth century.[29] Maclay often veered off from reporting Senate matters to make remarks that bequeathed to posterity a rare view of the Senate's human side.

Maclay became the leading congressional critic of what he called "pompous Titles" and said he had "uniformly opposed as far as I was able every thing of this Kind. and I believe have sacrificed every chance of being popular, and every grain of influence in the Senate, by so doing. but be it so. I have the testimony of my own conscience that I am right."[30]

Maclay kept close watch on Senator Richard Henry Lee of the powerful Virginia family. Lee, a leading Anti-Federalist, had called the Constitution the products of oligarchs. "Either monarchy or an aristocracy will be generated," he had predicted.[31] In the Senate, Lee rekindled a friendship with Adams that dated to the Continental Congress, and he shared with Adams an appreciation of titles, noting that ancient Greeks and Romans bestowed titles while governing republics.[32]

Lee and Adams, a strong South-North axis, had pushed Charles Thomson out of his job and off the inaugural invitation list. Thomson was "ill used," Maclay wrote. "This is Wrong."[33] Maclay discovered that Lee was not only serious about convening a committee on titles but also moved that the Senate "pass a Vote for the transmitting it down" to the House. "This was truly ridiculous," Maclay continued in his typically jagged, punctuation-challenged style. "But mind, this base business, had been went into solely" on the motion of Vice President Adams. "This was bare faced indeed—but now Lee wanted to bring it on motion plain enough."[34] Allying himself with Senator Charles Carroll of Maryland, Maclay attempted to "throw out the part about Titles altogether," but they "lost the question. . . . however I could plainly see that we had gained Ground with the House. . . . And from this Omen, I think [Adams] may go and dream about Titles for none will he get."[35] Debate over the title would continue even after the inauguration: a persistent but unconfirmed story went around that Washington would never talk to Speaker of the House Frederick Muhlenberg after the speaker had audibly laughed when hearing that Washington himself preferred "His Mightiness the President of the United States."[36] Another version of this anecdote was set at a presidential dinner, where both Muhlenberg and Representative Henry Wynkoop, a huge man, was among the guests. Washington said he favored "His Mightiness" and asked Muhlenberg his opinion. The speaker replied, "If all the incumbents were to have the commanding size or yourself or of my friend Wynkoop here, the title might be appropriate, but if applied here to some lesser men it would provoke ridicule." Some diners were said to have laughed, but Washington was not amused.[37]

Vice President Adams, in his role as president of the Senate, argued that Washington's title should be "His Highness" or, "if you will, His Most Benign Highness is the correct title that will comport with his constitutional prerogatives and support his state in the minds of our own people or foreigners."[38] Another possibility, imported from the fading Polish idea of a regal democracy, was "Elective Majesty."[39] Finally Adams surrendered, accepting the House's choice of "the president," without any modifying royal adjectives.

At nine o'clock on the morning of Thursday, April 30, bells rang as people gathered in New York churches to pray for the new government and its president on his Inauguration Day. Senator Maclay recorded in his diary that Vice President Adams, in the Senate chamber on the second floor of Federal Hall, appeared agitated. "Gentlemen, I wish for the direction of the Senate," Maclay quoted him as saying. "The President will, I suppose, address the Congress [after the swearing-in]. How shall I behave? How shall we receive it? Shall it be standing or sitting?" Adams, joined by Senator Lee, wondered about using as a precedent the words typically used in Parliament's respectful response to the delivery of a speech from the king. "Mr. Lee began with the House of Commons (as is usual with him) then the House of Lords then the King & then back again," Maclay wrote, sniffing a whiff of monarchy. "God forgive me, for it was involuntary, but the profane Muscles of my face, were in Tune for laughter, in spite of my indisposition."[40] The dialogue went on until the clerk of the House knocked at the closed Senate door. The House members, he said, were waiting to set off to Washington's residence. The chosen senators sped away to join their waiting colleagues and their carriages, leaving Adams behind with his questions and Maclay with his observations.

The line of carriages carrying members of Congress and other dignitaries pulled up to Washington's residence — one hour and ten minutes behind schedule.[41] He stepped out wearing white silk stockings, shoes with silver buckles, and a dark-brown suit made of the cloth he had ordered from the Hartford factory, each of its gilt-metal buttons bearing an eagle with outspread wings. Strapped about his waist was a dress sword in its scabbard.

The president-elect "made his way towards the hall of Congress with the pomp suitable to the first magistrate of a great republic," Elénor-François-Élie, Comte de Moustier, wrote later. Led by some five hundred New York militia troops, the procession began its passage through streets lined with some ten thousand spectators. Near Federal Hall, the soldiers formed an honor guard in double lines. Washington left the carriage, walked past the troops, and entered the hall. He climbed the stairs to the Senate chamber, where members of both houses awaited him, the representatives to the left side of a raised seat that had the look of a throne, the senators to the right. Washington sat down, and, after a long pause, Adams solemnly asked Washington if he was ready. "I am ready to proceed," he responded.[42]

In his conversion of City Hall, L'Enfant had designed a balcony that projected over the street from the second-floor Senate chamber. It was the perfect platform for the first inauguration, as it placed Washington in full view of the public but also on congressional terrain and surrounded by elected officials. It was here that Chancellor Robert R. Livingston—New York State's chief judicial officer—would administer the presidential oath.

The Constitution's description of the president's duties and powers includes the words of the presidential oath (which appear inside the only quotation marks used in the Constitution). It does not specify that a Bible must be used during the oath or that a presidential address be delivered thereafter, but the congressional arrangers of the ceremony had specified both. In Washington's pocket, accordingly, was his labored-over speech, which he and Madison had honed down to a lean eight pages. At the last minute, Chancellor Livingston realized he did not have a Bible to hand. He sent off an aide to borrow a Bible from the nearby St. John's Lodge of Free Masons. The Bible, printed in London in 1765, was placed on a crimson cushion on a table draped in velvet. It had been randomly opened to Genesis 49–50, which begins, "Then Jacob called for his sons and said: 'Gather around so I can tell you what will happen to you in days to come.'"[43] A witness wrote:

> The words of the oath were audibly, distinctly repeated by Washington after the Chancellor, in a solemn and impressive manner, and after he had reverently kissed the book [the Bible], the Chancellor advanced to the balcony of the portico—and in a loud voice proclaimed to the assembled multitude "Long live George Washington—President of the United States."

"Till then," wrote another witness, "a silence had been preserved by this immense assemblage in unison with the solemnity of the occasion; but now there burst forth, as if from one voice, such thundering peals, as seemed to shake the foundations of the city; and long and loud were they repeated, as if their echoes never were to cease."[44] Another spectator said Washington looked down at the crowd, placed his hand on his heart, and bowed several times. One newspaper account said he kissed the Bible after he spoke the oath. No contemporary report has him mention "God" at the end of the oath.

But author Washington Irving, who said he witnessed the inauguration at the age of six, recalled that he had heard Washington end the oath with "So help me God." Irving said he was at the corner of New Street and Wall Street, about two hundred feet away from Washington.[45] In 1789, many Americans believed that they lived in a nation blessed by God—a belief still heard in modern times.

The new president returned to the Senate chamber to deliver his inaugural address to the joint Senate and House. Maclay was there to record the scene: "This great Man was agitated and embarrassed more than ever he was by the levelled Cannon or pointed Musket, and he trembled, and several times could scarce make out to read, tho it must be supposed he had often read it before. he put the part of the fingers of his left hand, into the side of what I think the Taylors call the fall, of his Breetches. changing the paper into his left hand, after some time, he then did the same with some of the fingers of his right hand . . . . he made a flourish with his right hand, which had left rather an ungainly impression. I sincerely, for my part, wished all set ceremony in the hands of the dancing Masters. and that this first of Men, had read off, his address, in the plainest Manner without ever taking his Eyes off From, the paper. for I felt hurt, that he was not first in every thing.[46]

"Among the vicissitudes incident to life," Washington began, "no event could have filled me with greater anxieties than that of which the notification was transmitted by your order. . . . I was summoned by my Country, whose voice I can never hear but with veneration and love." He spent some time questioning his own qualifications, saying that the "magnitude and difficulty of the trust to which the voice of my Country called me" should awaken "a distrustful scrutiny into his qualifications" and, since he was "unpractised in the duties of civil administration," he "ought to be peculiarly conscious of his own deficiencies."

The word *God* did not appear in his address, but *Heaven* did. So did "that Almighty Being who rules over the Universe" and "the Great Author of every public and private good," as well as "the invisible hand, which conducts the Affairs of . . . the People of the United States." And he declared his core belief: "Every step" Americans took toward creation of their nation "seems to have been distinguished by some token of providential agency."[47]

The president noted that the Constitution said that it was "the duty of the President 'to recommend to your consideration, such measures as he shall judge necessary and expedient.'" He avoided any specific recommendations, ending instead by expressing hope for "the temperate consultations, and the wise measures on which the success of this Government must depend." As he had promised when he became commander-in-chief of the Continental Army in 1775, he said he would "renounce every pecuniary compensation" as president. (But, because the Constitution said the president was to be given compensation, Congress voted to pay the president $25,000 a year and the vice president $5,000.)[48]

The speech was well received. Representative Fisher Ames of Massachusetts later said he had "sat entranced" in the chamber, listening to what, he confessed, seemed to him "an allegory in which virtue was personified."[49]

Maclay recorded in his diary that Adams had "called it his most gracious Speech," but then added an observation on his own behalf: "I cannot approve of this. a Committee was appointd on it." Deciphered, Maclay meant that he could not approve of Adams's phrasing because it echoed the way that Parliament paid tribute to the king, not the way that Congress should speak to a president or vice versa. As for the inauguration committee, Maclay did not approve of its members producing the kind of response that sounded like Parliament politely responding to the king. Maclay mirrored the feelings of people who feared that royal threads were already appearing in the executive tapestry.

The inauguration was followed by what Maclay called "a grand Procession" to St. Paul's Chapel, which was serving the Trinity congregation while its burned-down home church was being rebuilt. Senator Lee, a member of the joint committee that arranged the inauguration, had scheduled the St. Paul's service, apparently on his own. His solo performance upset both Maclay and representatives on the joint committee, not because it had mixed church and state but because, as Maclay put it, it caused "dissension" between Senate and House.[50]

In the chapel, Washington sat in a canopied presidential pew. The Right Reverend Samuel Provoost, Episcopal bishop of New York and chaplain of the Senate, read prayers from the *"Proposed"* Book of Common Prayer, a trial version of the *American Book of Common*

Prayer, which would be published later in 1789. The book served as a reminder to America's former Anglicans that they were now members of the Protestant Episcopal Church and that they were to pray for the president of the United States, not King George III.

After the church service, Washington was escorted to a carriage that took him to his residence, where he dined alone. When night came, the New York sky burst with fireworks, including one fiery portrait that a witness called "the best likeness I have yet seen of him, so much like him that one could hardly distinguish it from life—excepting for the situation, over a beer-house, a place he never frequents." [51]

When the Senate convened the day after the inauguration, a motion was introduced officially bestowing the phrase "most gracious speech" upon Washington's inaugural address. Maclay boldly challenged the wording of Vice President Adams' speech, claiming that the "Words prefixed to the President's Speech are the same that are usually placed before the Speech of his Britannic Majesty" and moved that they be "struck out."

Adams rose in his chair and, according to Maclay "expressed the greatest Surprise, that any thing should be objected to on account of its being taken from the practices of the British government, 'under which we had lived so long and so happily formerly.' "—an odd and tone-deaf description of the monarchy that had been firmly and eloquently replaced the day before by a republic and its first president.

7

ETIQUETTE ADVICE FOR THE PRESIDENT

After staging his first social events as president, Washington seemed to be having second thoughts about whether he had behaved correctly. Writing in an imperial third-person style, he addressed a formal note to Vice President Adams: "The President of the United States wishes to avail himself of your sentiments on the following points." The first of his nine questions set forth his concern: "Whether a line of conduct, equally distant from an association with all kinds of company on the one hand and from a total seclusion from Society on the other, ought to be adopted by him?" One of his nine specific questions used an odd phrase: He wanted to know if he should receive "visits of Compliment" more often than once a week.[1]

Adams promptly replied, essentially reassuring Washington, point by point, that he was right to be concerned about the presidential image. "The system of the President," Adams wrote, "will gradually develop itself in practice, without any formal communication to the legislature, or publication from the press." As for how many days to devote to meeting people, experience will eventually "elucidate this point." Adams also counseled Washington against handing off petitions to "a minister of state." Rather, he should learn about the petitioners' requests and at times "admit the party to a personal interview." Such interviews should be screened by "a chamberlain, or gentleman in waiting."[2] Those monarchical-sounding positions were never filled.

The presidency, Adams wrote, "has no equal in the world. . . . If the state and pomp essential to this great department are not, in a good degree, preserved, it will be in vain for America to hope for consideration with foreign powers."[3]

Washington had also turned to Madison, Hamilton, and other trusted advisers. Hamilton gave the advice of a seasoned politician: "The notions of equality are yet in my opinion too general and too strong to admit of such a distance being placed between the President and other branches of the government as might even be consistent with a due proportion."[4] Hamilton also suggested that Washington favor senators over representatives as dinner companions. Senators, he wrote, "are coupled with the President in certain executive functions; treaties and appointments. This makes them in a degree his constitutional counsellors and gives them a peculiar claim to the right of access." And no matter who is invited to dinner, this should be the rule: "The President never to remain long at table."[5]

David Stuart, the Virginia physician and elector who had become a Washington family connection by marriage, wrote to Washington and told of a report that Adams always appeared publicly "with a coach and six horses," contributing to the rumors of the administration's monarchial tendency.[6] Washington denied the six-horse report, but did blame Adams for starting royal rumors with his campaign for a noble presidential title.[7]

Old Virginia, for the upper class, was essentially English and aristocratic. At Mount Vernon, Farmer Washington—as he liked to think of himself—added his own simple but refined personal style to derived English customs. He set a fine and bountiful table and was generous with his port and Madeira. At a typical dinner with eight diners, "the table was arranged with a leg of boiled pork at the head, a goose at the foot, and the following dishes arranged around the table: roast beef, round cold boiled beef, mutton chops, hominy, cabbage, potatoes, pickles, fried tripe, and onions. Beverages offered during dinner included wine, porter, and beer. The tablecloth was wiped off before the second course, which included mince pies, tarts, and cheese. The cloth was then removed altogether and port and madeira, as well as two kinds of nuts, apples, and raisins were set out. The eight diners were attended by three servants."[8]

In New York, President Washington had to project an image that was urbane, commanding, and detached. He could not serve a farmer's dinner; instead, he had to think about levees as a setting for his appearances.

The levee, its name drawn from the French *lever* ("to rise") and meaning a daily audience with a sovereign, was a tradition steeped in the practices of European nobility. While its function was partially pragmatic (it allowed Washington to speak informally with a variety of visitors), it was also richly ceremonial, with visitors announced, led in, and allotted their time with the president according to a strict schedule and decorum. With its monarchical roots and its odor of court politics, the levee proved controversial once planted in American soil.

As Jefferson told it, Washington "resisted for three weeks" and then turned to Humphreys to arrange presidential levees. At one of the first levees, those "who were to pay their court" were assembled in an ante-chamber of the presidential residence. After Washington and Humphreys passed through the ante-chamber, "the door of the inner room was thrown open and Humphreys entered first, calling out with a loud voice, 'The President of the United States!' The President was so much disconcerted by it that he did not recover in the whole time of the levee; and when the company was gone, he said to Humphreys, 'Well, you have taken me in once, but, by God, you shall never take me in a second time.'"[9] Washington, the Virginian aristocratic, was embarrassed by the new demands of his new role. He seemed to be cautiously adapting to the European tradition of the nobility gathering for a reception that inevitably included a political undercurrent.

David Stuart warned that the levees had become targets of Anti-Federalists in Virginia. "I suspect the old Patriot [Patrick Henry] has heard some extraordinary representations of the Etiquette established at your Levees," Stuart wrote. He quoted a House member as saying to Governor Beverley Randolph and others at a dinner, that there was "more pomp" around Washington "than at [the Court of] St. James's, where he had been, and that your bows were more distant & stiff."[10]

The president defended his levees by picturing himself as a president besieged. He said he needed a way to break out of the clutches of his numerous admirers. Looking back at his earliest presidential days, Washington later told an old friend, "By the time I had done breakfast, thence 'till dinner, & afterwards 'till bed time. . . . I had no leizure to

read, or answer the dispatches which were pouring in from all quarters
. . . the Table was considered as a public one, and every person who
could get introduced to the President, conceived that he had a right to
be envited to it."[11]

Washington's levees were an inevitable target for Senator William
Maclay's pen as he recorded events in his journal. Maclay was coming
back from the post office on the morning of Monday, May 4, when he
met Arthur St. Clair, governor of the Northwest Territory. Striking up a
conversation, St. Clair asked Maclay what he thought of the president's
"new arrangements." When Maclay looked puzzled, St. Clair replied,
"The President is neither to entertain nor receive invitations. He is to
have levee days on Tuesdays and Fridays, when only he is to be seen."

This news inspired a burst of verbiage in Maclay's diary: The president "stood on as difficult Ground, as he ever had done in his life.
That to suffer himself to be run down, on the one hand, by a Croud of
Visitants so as to engross his time, would never do, as it would render
the doing of Business impracticable. but on the other hand for him to
be seen only in public on Stated times like an Eastern Lama would be
equally offensive."

As a practical matter, Maclay said if the president could be seen only
in levees, "nothing confidential could pass between him and any individual." And if he did spend time with someone during a levee, "and he
could not escape the Charge of favouritism. all Court would be paid to
the supposed favourite."[12]

The announcement of Washington's two-levee schedule, shortly after his inauguration, was hailed by a friendly newspaper, the *Gazette of
the United States,* because he showed that he was "determined to pursue that system of regularity and economy in his household which has
always marked his public and private life." The *Gazette* also noted that
he had instructed his steward, Samuel Fraunces, "to guard against any
waste or extravagance that might be committed by the servants."[13]

Washington's staff made certain that flattering stories of the president's frugality were circulated. Fraunces, for one, told of a breakfast
that he once served to Washington: he offered the president shad, a
costly and luxurious dish. "It is very early in the season for shad," the
president remarked. "How much did you pay for it?"

"Two dollars."

"Two dollars! I can never encourage this extravagance at my table. Take it away—I will not touch it."

Fraunces took it away and served it to himself.[14] This kind of story was in keeping with how most Americans viewed their hero—firm, prudent, never extravagant. But levees, modeled on those of a royal court?

Baron Frederick William von Steuben was in New York successfully lobbying the First Congress for the annuity promised by the Continental Congress in gratitude for his work in transforming the starving men at Valley Forge into a disciplined army. Steuben, who remembered monarchial notions arising during the Revolutionary War, was not surprised that "our politicians are now bussi [busy] in settling the Etiquette of the New Court." Asked for his suggestions, "As an old Courtier," he recommended "abolishing all nut cracking after the desert."[15]

Steuben was prophetic about the levees, which had the look of a royal court, especially to those who feared a drift toward monarchy. To Maclay, "it seems as if a Court party was forming" around Washington, and "the Creatures that surround him, would place a crown on his head."[16] Maclay was dutiful about attending levees, believing it helped keep Washington aware of Pennsylvania, even if Maclay merely "went to the Levee made my bows, walked a[b]out, turned about, and came out."[17]

Washington tried to keep his balance—petitioners on one side, powerful on the other. At the core of the levee system was the fact that some were invited while others were not. Initially, among those without invitations were the Lees of Virginia, who were not accustomed to being outsiders. Arthur Lee, who helped to negotiate the treaty of alliance with France, was shocked. In a letter to his brother, Francis Lightfoot Lee, a signer of the Declaration of Independence, Arthur indignantly wrote, "The President has two Levees a week no public dinners, nor does he accept of any invitation."[18]

An old comrade, a member of the Society of the Cincinnati, in a letter to a fellow member, seemed to view Washington as a recluse: "I attend the Presidents Levee (which is on Tuesdays & Fridays between two & three OClock) generally every ten days or two Weeks, & I have the Honor to say that the Old Gentleman looks kindly yet on a

Regimental Coat—He lives very retired, neither entertains Company, nor dines out, frequently walks the Streets with no other person but Colo. Humphrys & sometimes rides."[19] Humphreys was Washington's chief screener, deciding who was entitled to be in Washington's presence and who should be politely turned away. But the new President had more than one political operative.

Tobias Lear, having journeyed from Mount Vernon to get the presidential residence on Cherry Street ready for Washington, made himself the first presidential advance man. He soon began signing himself "Secretary to the President," gradually expanding his role to include managing Washington's expense reports to Congress and giving the President advice on what today would be called public relations; he encouraged the levees for giving "a dignity to the President."[20]

On the morning of May 27, President Washington and several officials arrived at Elizabethtown Point, New Jersey, to escort Martha Washington to the white presidential barge that had borne the president-elect to New York the month before. As the barge neared New York, a thirteen-cannon salute welcomed her to the city. A cheering crowd and Governor Clinton guided her to her new home at 1 Cherry Street.[21]

She had brought with her from Mount Vernon two grandchildren and seven enslaved house servants. The president's household staff might be described as lean, compared to the fleets of servants and footmen found in a European court: it consisted of five white servants who wore liveries, six black servants (including Billy Lee, who arrived later after recuperating from his Philadelphia injuries), two black maids, and a housekeeper, assisted by three other women (presumably white), a valet, and the steward Fraunces. For his personal staff, Washington had a secretary, an assistant, and three aides. Based on newspaper want ads of the day, the Washingtons also sought out a waiter, a cook, and a coachman (although these employees do not appear in the household expenses account from May 24 to August 24.)[22]

Martha Washington also had brought American-made fashion; at the Baltimore stop on her journey to New York, a journalist noted that "like her illustrious husband, she was clothed in the manufacture of our country, in which her native goodness and patriotism appeared to the greatest advantage."[23]

"I have not had one half hour to my self since the day of my arrival," she wrote to her niece, Fanny Bassett, in Mount Vernon. "My first care was to get the children to a good school." She loved watching Nelly, "a little wild creature," who "spends her time at the windows looking at carriages, &c passing by." But Martha Washington's time was immediately far more devoted to the social obligations of the president's wife than to the joys of being a grandmother. Her title was now Lady Washington or Our Lady Presidentess.[24]

On the evening of Friday, May 29, two days after her arrival, Mrs. Washington held her first levee. The president continued his levees on Tuesday afternoons. For his wife, the schedule was eight to ten every Friday evening, and he always dropped in. "I found it quite a crowded Room," Abigail Adams wrote in a letter to her sister:

> The form of Reception is this, the servants announce—& col Humphries or mr Lear—receives every Lady at the door, & Hands her up to mrs washington to whom she makes a most Respectfull curtzey and then is seated without noticeing any of the rest of the company. the Pressident then comes up and speaks to the Lady, which he does with a grace dignity & ease, that leaves Royal George far behind him. the company are entertaind with Ice creems & Lemonade, and retire at their pleasure performing the same ceremony when they quit the Room.[25]

The drawing room's ceiling was low, and the candlelit chandelier lower. At one of Mrs. Washington's levees, as a "belle of New York" walked under the chandelier, a long ostrich feather in her headdress caught fire. As an account of the event says, "Major Jackson, aide-de-camp to the President, with great presence of mind and equal gallantry, flew to the rescue of the lady, and, by clapping the burning plumes between his hands, extinguished the flames."[26]

Mrs. Washington had sent from Mount Vernon, via ship out of Alexandria, "many articles of taste and luxury, including a few pictures, vases, and other ornaments, which had been presented to the General by his European friends," according to a critique of the presidential residence. "The family plate was melted soon after it was brought to the city, and reproduced in more elegant and harmonious forms. . . . Each piece displays the arms of the Washington family. The state coach was the finest carriage in the city. It was usually drawn by four horses, but when it conveyed the President to Federal Hall, always by six."[27]

Late in the summer, the Washingtons limited their entertaining because Washington was in formal mourning for his mother, who had died at the age of eighty-one on August 25 at her home in Fredericksburg, Virginia. In her will, she left five enslaved people, including "my negro woman, little Bet, and her future increase," to various relatives. "I give my son, General George Washington, all my land in Accokeek Run, in the County of Stafford, and also my negro boy George, to him and his heirs forever. Also, my best bed, bedstead, and Virginia cloth curtains (the same that stand in my best bedroom), my quilted blue-and-white quilt, and my best dressing glass."[28] Washington ordered his household staff to don black cockades and ribbons. He wore a black badge for five months, and many in New York wore black symbols of bereavement.[29]

Washington continued to host Thursday dinners. Maclay, in his stream-of-recollection diary style, once sketched a Washington dinner he attended one night in August 1789. Other diners were Vice President Adams and Mrs. Adams; Governor Clinton and his wife; President Pro Tem of the Senate John Langdon of New Hampshire and "a Lady perhaps his Wife"; John Jay (who was named Chief Justice of the United States Supreme Court in September 1789) and his wife; Senator Richard Bassett of Delaware; and "and a Mr. Smith" (who may have been William Stephens Smith, son-in-law of John and Abigail Adams.)[30] Tobias Lear, Langdon's cousin, was also at the table, but as more a staff person than a guest. Another man with that status was twenty-year-old Robert Lewis, a copyist in what the president called his "official family," a military term for a high-ranking officer's staff. Lewis had accompanied Mrs. Washington from Mount Vernon to New York and often escorted her on trips about the city. He was the son of Fielding Lewis, a wealthy Virginian planter and international merchant, and George Washington's sister, Betty.

The president and Mrs. Washington, Maclay wrote, "sat opposite each other in the Middle of the Table. the Two Secretaries one at each end ... the middle of the Table was garnished in the usual tasty way. with small Images flowers (artificial) &ca. It was a great dinner & the best of the kind ever I was at. the room however was disagreeably warm." The meal began with soup that Maclay did not describe. Then came "Fish roasted & boiled meats," including "Gammon" (bacon), "Fowls &ca. The dessert was, first Apple pies puddings &ca. then iced creams Jellies &ca. then Water Melons Musk Melons apples peaches nuts."

"It was the most solemn dinner ever I sat at," Maclay continued. "not an health drank scarce a Word said. untill the Cloath was taken away. then the President filling a Glass of Wine with great formality drank the health of every individual by name round the Table. every body imitated him changed glasses and such a buz of health sir and health Madam, & thank You sir and thank You Madam. never had I heard before indeed I had like to have been thrown out in the Hurry but I got a little Wine in my Glass, & passed the Ceremony. the Ladies sat a good While and the Bottles passed about. but there was a dead Silence almost. Mrs. Washington at last withdrew with the Ladies.

"I expected the Men would now begin. but the same Stillness remained the President told of a new England clergyman who had lost an hat and Wig in passing a River called the Brunks [Bronx]. he smiled And every body else laughed. he now and then said a Sentence or two on some common Subject. and What he said was not amiss. Mr. Jay tried to make a laugh by mentioning the Consatina of the Duchess of Devonshire leaving no *Stone* unturned, to carry Fox's Election."[31]

The man named Smith "mentioned, how Homer described Æneas leaving his Wife and carrying his father out of flaming Troy, he had heard somebody, (I suppose) witty on the Occasion—but if he had ever read it he would have said *Virgil.* The President. kept a fork in his hand when the Cloath was taken away I thought for the purpose of picking nuts. he ate no nuts but played with the Fork striking on the Edge of the Table with it. We did not sit long after the Ladies retired the President rose and, went up Stairs to drink Coffee. the Company followed. I took my hat and came home."[32]

Washington's love of the theater was well known. During the Revolutionary War, General Washington encouraged his men to put on plays. He even approved of "Washington's Strolling Players" performing in the cold and hunger of Valley Forge. Washington's favorite play was *Cato* by the British playwright Joseph Addison. First performed in 1713, *Cato* pitted the tyranny of Julius Caesar against men of republican virtue. Washington often ordered the play produced during the war. As President, he was frequently seen in the President's Box at the New-York Theater.

On November 24, for example—along with Mrs. Washington, Mrs. Adams, Hamilton and his wife, and others—the president filled the presidential box at the New-York Theater. On stage was *Darby's Return,* a comic sketch by William Dunlap, the first American professional playwright. The son of a Loyalist father, Dunlap built his theatrical career as a patriotic writer. His first play, *The Father; or American Shandyism,* debuted at the New-York Theater, which he later ran as manager and director.[33]

In one scene of *Darby's Return,* Darby, an Irish lad, happens to be in New York on Inauguration Day. The eyes of the audience turned toward Washington, Dunlap remembered, "to watch the emotions produced"—especially when "the looks and changes of countenance of the great man became intense."

Darby says, "I saw some mighty pretty shows. . . . " The president smiles. Darby continues:

> A man who fought to free the land from woe,
> *Like me,* had left his farm, a soldiering to go. . . .
> But having gained his point, he had, *like me,*
> Returned to his own potatoe-ground to see.
> But then he could not rest. With one accord,
> He is called to be a kind of—not a lord—
> I don't know what. He's not a *great man,* sure,
> For poor men love him just as he were poor.

The president looks grim. Another player, Kathleen, asks, "How looked he, Darby? Was he short or tall?"

The president's "countenance showed embarrassment, from the expectation of one of those eulogiums which he had been obliged to hear on many public occasions, and which must doubtless have been a severe trial to his feelings."[34]

Darby answers that he had not seen Washington—and the Washington in the box "indulged in that which was for him extremely rare—a hearty laugh."[35]

Like the audience who watched George Washington watch Darby, most of the chosen attended Martha Washington's Friday-night levees so that they could see her husband. Her levees were always simply dignified meetings between a reluctant public figure and the people she, as a handmaiden to her husband, had invited. "I lead a very dull life here and know nothing that passes in the town," she wrote five months after her arrival. "I never goe to any publick place—indeed I think I am more like a state prisoner than anything else, there is certain bounds set for me which I must not depart from—and as I cannot doe as I like I am obstinate and stay at home a great deal."[36]

Toward the end of 1789, she wrote to her old friend Mercy Otis Warren, the Massachusetts writer and historian: "I little thought, when the war was finished, that any circumstances could possibly happen which would call the General"—her usual name for him—"into public life again. I had anticipated that from that moment we should be suffered to grow old together in solitude and tranquility. That was the first and dearest wish of my heart. I will not, however, contemplate with too much regret, disappointments that were inevitable. . . . I cannot blame him for having acted according to his ideas of duty in obeying the voice of his country."

On Thursday, December 31, the first year of the Republic ended. Next day, Mrs. Washington had her regular levee, but, according to a recollection, "on no previous occasion had one been graced with so much respectability and elegance. The air was almost as gentle as it should be in May, and the full moon shone so brightly that the streets to a late hour were filled with a delicious twilight." [37] When "the hall struck nine," Mrs. Washington, "with a complacent smile observed: 'The General always retires at nine, and I usually precede him.' At this hint the ladies instantly rose, adjusted their dresses, made their salutations, and retired."[38]

"ALL IS BARE CREATION"

*B*etween April and September 1789, the First Congress completed a dizzying list of tasks, creating the departments of State, Treasury, and War; devising a federal judiciary system consisting of "the Supreme and other Courts"; building a financial structure for the raising and collecting of taxes and tariffs; approving a plan for funding the foreign and domestic war debts; establishing a national bank; asserting the right to transform swaths of North America into additional states of the Union, and passing the numerous laws needed by the new Republic to regulate such matters as the naturalization of immigrants, the patenting of inventions, the conducting of a national census, and the building of lighthouses. They also proposed twelve constitutional amendments, ten of which became the Bill of Rights. And the members, after arguing about other sites, granted President Washington the authority to move the nation's permanent capital to somewhere along the Potomac River in Virginia.

The Judiciary Act was a colossal example of lawmaking. The 7,600-word act began with a description of one creation—the Supreme Court of the United States—and ended with a description of another conception: the Attorney General. Most crucial was the establishing of judicial supremacy. "No future session of Congress will ever have so arduous and weighty a charge on their hands," said the *Georgia Gazette* on July 30, 1789 quoting the *Gazette of the United States* for June 24, 1789. "No examples to imitate, and no striking historical facts on which to ground their decisions—All is bare creation."[1]

Later, Congress passed the Punishment of Crimes Act, which produced the first list of federal crimes, including treason, piracy, murder, and robbery in federal jurisdictions on land or on the high seas. The act—written at a time when physicians usually obtained corpses for dissection and study from grave robbers—authorized judges to order that bodies of convicted federal murderers "shall be delivered to a Surgeon for dissection" by "Such Surgeon as the court shall direct for the purpose."[2]

"We are in a wilderness without a single footstep to guide us," Representative James Madison told Thomas Jefferson soon after the First Federal Congress convened. "Our successors," he continued, "will have an easier task, and by degrees the way will become smooth short and certain."[3] In fact, success did come—in the First Congress itself. Ninety-five men[4] ventured into that congressional wilderness and built a government, defying naysayers who had warned that in a world of kings and queens no self-governing republic could possibility rule a population so large and extend its power over a territory already large and growing larger. But much as Washington hoped for a First Federal Congress with a nonpartisan approach to the creating of a nation, the creators were divided. Ever since the campaign to scrap the Articles of Confederation, the past had been arguing with the future, politicians of the North and the South had been eying each other warily, and the idea of a strong federal government versus a government of empowered states had been the heart of all debates.

The labels *Federalists* and *Anti-Federalists* appeared frequently during the Constitutional Convention, though differences were not as clear as the labels implied. Many of the Anti-Federalists actually favored the Constitution but wanted amendments. The Federalists essentially wanted the Constitution as it was when they sent it off to the states for ratification. Elbridge Gerry, a longtime politician from Massachusetts, said that since the argument was over ratification, the labels should be "rats and antirats."[5] The labels stuck, adding unsubtle name-calling to the debate.

Fifty-five senators and sixteen representatives were members of the Society of the Cincinnati, who supported legislation favoring veterans.[6] They began the tradition of a veterans' bloc in every Federal Congress that dealt with the aftermaths of wars.

Not all members were revolutionaries. Senator William Samuel Johnson of Connecticut, a judge of the state's supreme court, chose to work for peace. In 1779 Johnson declined to endorse independence and was arrested on charges of communicating with the enemy. He defended himself successfully and was released.[7] He was elected to the Continental Congress, chaired the Committee of Style, and campaigned for ratification by the Connecticut legislature.

The men of this first Congress, hailed by the *Georgia Gazette* as creators, were not idealists striving for a perfect Union. They represented their homelands—their states—and had to balance the old idea of states' rights with the new idea of a federal government. Nor were they newcomers to politics. Forty-two had been members of the Continental Congress or the Congress of the Confederation. Eighteen had been delegates to the Constitutional Convention. More than forty had served in ratifying conventions of their states. Nine had been governors. Eighty-four had served in their home legislatures. One, Jesse Franklin of North Carolina, was captured by Loyalists during a battle and hanged by his own bridle. It broke, and he escaped.[8]

Southern members, most of them owners of plantations worked by enslaved laborers, held disproportionate power because of the Constitution's "three-fifths clause."[9] The southern advantage would wane as the population of Northern states grew more rapidly than that of the Southern states.

Most of the members were husbands and fathers. Five were widowers, and four of them would woo and marry New York women. Virginian Representative John Page complained that New York's "rich Widows are ugly & old & the rich maids too young," but he found a soulmate, who, like him, was a poet. They would have eight children.[10]

In the romance most gossiped about, chubby-faced Representative Isaac Coles of Virginia married Catherine Thompson, a high-born English woman whose brother was in the Queen's Guard and whose sister was the wife of Representative Elbridge Gerry of Massachusetts. A member of the Gerry household noted that Coles "was reported to be immensely rich in land and negroes, and, though older than her father, and not so good looking, being lame from repeated attacks of gout."[11] When the question of abolishing slavery came up for debate one day, Coles voted for it and his brother-in-law voted against it. In a campaign in 1797, Coles' opponent won after vilifying Coles for not marrying "a Virginia girl."[12]

"The House," said Fisher Ames, a Federal member from Massachusetts, "is composed of sober, solid, old-charter folks. . . . There are few shining geniuses; there are many who have experience, the virtues of the heart, and the habits of business." After two months in the House, he complained about "the yawning listlessness of many here"[13] while still believing that the "House is composed of very good men, not shining, but honest and reasonably well-informed."[14] About half of those very good men of the House would dutifully attend but would not speak a word in debates.[15] Among gentlemen, there was an understanding, going back to Continental Congress days, that men of a certain station were obliged to serve as a civil responsibility and did not necessarily have to become politicians.

A rare critique of a politician by a politician came from future president John Quincy Adams, who enjoyed sitting in the public gallery and rating members. "The greatest speakers in the house, as to quantity," he wrote "are Gerry, Jackson of Georgia, and Burke of S. Carolina; and as to quality, Ames, Maddison, and Vining." But none of them resembled a Demosthenes or a Cicero.[16]

Most members reached New York after long, rigorous journeys. New Englanders usually chose stagecoaches that originated in Hartford or New Haven, Connecticut. Others sailed from Providence, hoping for calm seas. The fare was six and a half dollars, covering food and a berth in a single large cabin accommodating up to a dozen or more passengers.

Brissot de Warville, a French journalist who traveled in America during the Constitutional Convention, wrote, "American stagecoaches are truly political vehicles," offering members of Congress a chance to sit "side by side with the shoemaker who elected him and fraternizes with him; they talk together on familiar terms." He was also enthusiastic about American taverns, saying they were safer than French inns. At least two members of the First Congress, robbed en route to New York, would disagree.[17]

"A stage," wrote an anonymous passenger, "is a heavy, unwieldy vehicle, generally drawn by four jaded horses, urged along by a vulgar, insolent driver. There are some exceptions, some drivers being respectable, and some stages are mere lumber wagons."[18] A voyage by sea from

Providence might have been faster than a stagecoach trip, but the sea route added the uncertainty of westerly winds and the risk of seasickness. The ship was usually a packet boat built to carry cargo and mail to coastal ports. Captains based their schedules on the needs of cargo owners, not members of Congress. And voyages to New York had to pass through Hell's Gate, the whirlpool where the East River flowed into Long Island Sound.

Delegates from the Carolinas usually headed for New York by land-and-sea routes, braving the Outer Banks, a graveyard of ships, to reach Philadelphia. From there, they were hauled through a New Jersey road maze, making frequent stagecoach changes and five ferry crossings, including passage across the wide Hudson River. Adding the Philadelphia–New York leg to their trip meant added travel expenses. This amounted to about what their New England colleagues were spending for transportation from their states: four dollars for two days of travel plus a little more for room and board.

The stagecoach fare for New England travelers was three to four pence per mile, with roughly eight shillings per day for a tavern's room and board. A coach traveled about sixty miles a day, and members spent about three dollars per day on travel. They were reimbursed thirty cents a mile for travel from and to their homes. Congress voted its members a salary of six dollars for each day they attended plus travel expenses. Senators insisted that, since there were fewer of them, they deserved higher pay. A compromise provided them a dollar-per-day raise, beginning in 1795. If the absence of a senator or representative during a session was due to sickness, he received full pay.[19]

The sea voyage from the South was the riskiest way to reach New York. Representative Aedanus Burke of South Carolina spent more than a week getting there after his ship foundered off Delaware's Cape Henlopen. Gales threatened the ship carrying Representative James Jackson on a return trip to Savannah. Violent storms also plagued the passages of Representatives George Mathews of Georgia and Thomas Tudor Tucker of South Carolina. Southerners' tales of storm-tossed travel aided their campaign to move the permanent seat of government to Virginia.

Most people of the era, well aware of the travails of even short-distance travel, tolerated the tardiness of representatives and senators that caused the long delay after March 4. And, given the primitive state of medicine and hygiene, they also accepted unspecified illnesses from several latecomers and specific excuses from others, such as an ulcerated tooth or gout. And, by March 4, several members had not even been elected. Late elections or late counting of election returns held up New Jersey's representatives and the entire delegation from New York. One Massachusetts district required a fifth runoff election before Theodore Sedgwick could claim his House seat; and in New Hampshire, erratic Benjamin West's last-minute refusal to serve necessitated a second election, won by Representative Abiel Foster, whose arrival in mid-July finally completed the forming of the first Federal Legislature.[20]

The First Congress acted under the spell of the new Constitution, using it as a strict guide to every detail in the forming of the new government. The Constitution began with the words "We the People," not "We the States," and most of the time the men sent to New York by their states understood the difference. Once in New York, most members left their states behind and worked to build the new nation.

Constituents, who had lived through the failure of the Articles of Confederation, could only hope that the new government would be an improvement. They were rewarded by the work of the First Federal Congress. Historian Charlene Bickford, assessing the accomplishments of the First Federal Congress, said, "Our Constitution and the governmental structure that it created have weathered crises, adapted to change, and stood the test of time, and the United States Congress is at the heart of that enduring structure. The Founders saw the legislature as the first branch of government, and its duties and powers are much more clearly and extensively defined in the Constitution than those of the other two branches. . . .

"We often see Congress as an institution where parties and issues are too divisive; the legislative process is unbelievably complex; the rules are quite arcane; and frequent gridlock seems to make progress impossible. . . . Congress often seems more than a little dysfunctional."[21] But it has endured.

9

THE CONSTITUTION AS BLUEPRINT

Vice President Adams was lampooned as "Old Daddy Vice" in one of the nasty bits of doggerel by his colleagues during his quixotic quest for a royal presidential title. His conduct cost him respect, both personally and for his office. Stubbornly, he warned that failure to produce an adequate title would bring on "the Contempt, the Scorn and the Derision of all Europe."[1] In fact, Europe accepted the new republic into the family of nations, and it was Adams who inherited the contempt. More importantly, the failure to find a royal title showed Congress that there was little support for a monarchy. That idea had been a mere distraction that faded away as the real work began and a republic started to take shape.

Working like carpenters guided by a blueprint called the Constitution, members of the First Congress steadily built a structure of government. The two master builders were James Madison, a Virginian politician whose Virginia Plan—which outlined a central government of three checked and balanced branches—and Alexander Hamilton, who had his own plan to finance the government. Hamilton, with Madison and John Jay, anonymously wrote the eighty-five "Federalist Papers," published in 1787 and 1788, which urged ratification of the Constitution.

Madison was thirty-eight, Hamilton about five years younger. Both were short and slim, Madison usually plain-dressed, Hamilton dashing with an elegant touch.

Madison, whose words had made their way into his envisioned Constitution, had been in Virginia politics since he was twenty-five years old. He had made many friends and few foes. Hamilton was well connected in New York politics through his marriage to Elizabeth

105

Schuyler. She was from a fabulously wealthy Hudson River Valley family that gave Hamilton entrée to New York's ruling class. When the New York Legislature finally had an election, Hamilton's father-in-law, Philip Schuyler, would be a senator and an ally of Hamilton.

Madison and Hamilton made an odd pair, but they shared the vision of a strong national government, and both of them spoke sternly and clearly about their vision. Their power stemmed from their political skills, their roles as Washington's closest advisers, and, thanks to a Federalist majority, their ability to turn ideas into laws. Madison dominated the first session as the self-designated leader of Congress.

The Senate, having achieved a quorum on Monday, April 6, had promptly accepted the credentials of the twelve senators present. Both senators from the states of New Hampshire, Connecticut, New Jersey, and Pennsylvania, were there. Massachusetts, Delaware, Virginia and Georgia each had one senator present.[2] Missing on quorum day were senators from New York, whose strife-torn legislature had not yet managed to stage an election for its senators and representatives. Nor were Maryland or South Carolina represented. There were no senators or representatives from North Carolina or Rhode Island because those states had still not ratified the Constitution.

The senators also adopted a set of procedural rules that resembled those of the Continental Congress and the Congress of the Confederation. And the Senate appointed Ireland-born James Mathers, who had been wounded in the Revolutionary War, as "doorkeeper"— to guard the Senate's closed sessions from the eyes of the public and the press. Mathers and his one aide also maintained the Senate's two horses and bought the Senate firewood. Mathers later was given a title that still exists: sergeant at arms. He served at both posts until his death in 1811.[3]

The senators chose John Langdon, a wealthy New Hampshire merchant and politician, as the president pro tem to preside over the Senate in the absence of the vice president. Langdon was a veteran of the Revolutionary War, the Continental Congress, and the Constitutional Convention, for which he had to furnish his own expenses and those of a second delegate because his state refused to pay.[4]

Creation of a working republic took time. Not until June 1 was the first act of Congress—the Act to Regulate the Time and Manner of Administering Certain Oaths—signed into law by President

Washington. The law, seemingly bland, was the last act in a debate that had been going on since the Constitutional Convention. The Constitution, stated in Article VI, clause 3 that "The Senators and Representatives before mentioned, and the Members of the several State Legislatures, and all executive and judicial Officers, both of the United States and of the several States, shall be bound by Oath or Affirmation, to support this Constitution." Opponents believed that if state officials had to take the oath, it would establish the supremacy of the federal government.

On June 3, Langdon administered the oath to Vice President Adams, and then Adams did the same to Langdon and seventeen other senators. Oath-taking went on sporadically into late July in between debates and other Senate business.[5]

The Senate had to stage a lottery to carry out the instructions of Article I, Section 3, which told how the six-year terms of the first set of Federal Congress senators had to be dispensed "so that one third may be chosen every second Year." The Senate, moving at its own slow pace, had only gotten around to that required task on May 14, when twenty senators were present. A special committee divided them into three "classes," with no class containing two members from the same state.

On the next day, three senators, each representing a class, as proscribed by the Constitution, climbed the steep stairs to the Senate chamber in Federal Hall. One of them was Tristram Dalton of Massachusetts, who had served in the Continental Congress. With his Harvard classmate, Vice President Adams, and a dozen senators looking on, Dalton pulled a slip of paper out of a small wooden box. Holding up the paper for all to see, he shouted, "Number One!" He and six other senators became members of "Class One," meaning their terms of office would expire in two years. (William Maclay was in the Senate's "Class One," and was not re-elected, and so his caustic and garrulous diary historically covers only those two years.)

The ritual was repeated twice more that morning. Senator Paine Wingate of New Hampshire drew number two, putting his group of senators in "Class Two" with a term of four years. By default, the remaining senators were in the third class. But the ceremony of drawing papers went on as John Langdon, also of New Hampshire, drew the third paper and six senators went into "Class Three," granting them full six-year terms.[6]

•••

Because the new nation had no source of funding, Madison and Hamilton had to find a way to raise money quickly and fairly. The House clearly had the constitutional obligation to finance the government under Article I, section 7, clause 1: "All Bills for raising Revenue shall originate in the House of Representatives; but the Senate may propose or concur with amendments as on other Bills." And Article I, section 9, clause 7: "No Money shall be drawn from the Treasury, but in Consequence of Appropriations made by Law."

So on April 8—before Washington had even set off from Mount Vernon for his triumphant journey to New York—Madison rose in the House to introduce a resolution calling for a tax in the form of a tariff on imported alcoholic beverages and other commodities. Three days later came the first lobbying reaction: a petition from Baltimore "Tradesmen, Manufacturers and others" asking for tariffs on imported goods, alerting members of Congress to "the present melancholy State of his country; the Number of her Poor increasing for want of employment; foreign debts accumulating; houses and lands depreciating in value; trade and manufactures languishing and expiring."[7] The 750 signers of the petition asked for tariffs that would discourage the importation of foreign versions of items that were made in and around Baltimore, such as candlesticks, stationery, and chocolate, along with everything needed to build and outfit a ship.

One of the vigorously disputed tariff items was molasses, imported from the West Indies to make rum in America. (Molasses is the sticky, dark byproduct produced when sugar is made by boiling down crushed sugar cane.) Under Madison's guidance in the House, aided by Hamilton's private conversations with representatives, the legislators searched for the most effective—and politically least hurtful—tariff on molasses.

Hovering unseen and unacknowledged over the debate was the notorious old international enterprise called the Triangle Trade: Africans were bought with New England rum and then sold as enslaved workers to the plantations in British Caribbean "Sugar Islands" for sugar or molasses, which was shipped back to New England distillers to make into rum.

That longtime trade system seemed to be in the mind of George Thatcher, an antislavery Federalist from the Maine district of Massachusetts, who said during the debate, "Suppose a member from Massachusetts was to propose an impost on negroes; what would you hear from the southern gentlemen, if 50 dollars was the sum to be laid? And yet this is not more than the proportion laid upon molasses." By mentioning "negroes" and implying "slavery," Thatcher was raising a subject that few members, from the North or from the South, wished to bring to the floor.

Madison responded to Thatcher by not speaking directly of the slave trade: "I shall make no observation, Mr. Speaker, upon the language of the gentleman from Massachusetts because I do not conceive it expresses either the deliberate temper of his own mind, or the good sense of his constituents." He went on to say, "In Virginia, the habits of the people are so strong in favor of rum, both foreign and domestic, that it requires the greatest exertion to change them; they consume vast quantities of this article."[8]

Madison proposed that dozens of goods would begin carrying duties—taxes in the form of tariffs. His list began with "distilled spirits of Jamaica proof, imported from any kingdom or country whatsoever, per gallon, ten cents." Then came the rest of the goods on his list. A sample:

> On all other distilled spirits, per gallon, eight cents.
> On molasses, per gallon, two and a half cents.
> On Madeira wine, per gallon, eighteen cents.
> On all other wines, per gallon, ten cents.
> On every gallon of beer, ale or porter in casks, five cents.
> On brown sugars, per pound, one cent.
> On cocoa, per pound, one cent.
> On all candles of tallow, per pound, two cents.
> On all candles of wax or spermaceti, per pound, six cents.
> On cheese, per pound, four cents.
> On soap, per pound, two cents.
> On boots, per pair, fifty cents.[9]

Quick to follow Madison's tariff proposal were petitions to Congress from people who wanted high tariffs on imported goods that competed with such growing American products as pottery and glass. "These protections and commercial regulations will surely lead us a wild dance," Representative Abraham Baldwin of Georgia complained in a letter. Southerners were mostly against tariffs used to protect American manufactures.[10] When the tariff reached the Senate, the tariff on molasses became the essence of the debate. Some senators favored three cents while others wanted a four-cent tariff.

When the debate ended in a tie, Vice President Adams voted in favor of three cents. The duty on molasses was finally set at three cents per gallon and on rum ten cents per gallon. Merchants who re-exported molasses in the form of rum got a five-cents-per-gallon "drawback"— an import duty refund. A five-cent-per-barrel drawback was also given to salt merchants who imported fish for pickling. Jamaican rum cost about forty-five cents per gallon, making a duty of ten cents effectively a 22 percent tax. Molasses cost about sixteen to twenty cents per gallon, so its duty was essentially a tax on consumers ranging from 12 to 16 percent.

The ship *Sally*, owned by Representative Jeremiah Wadsworth of Connecticut, was the first ship to pay the new impost duties in the Connecticut port of New London. She was carrying molasses. Wadsworth, a former ship's captain who became one of the richest men in America, had argued for a lowering of impost duties, especially for molasses. He had begun his accumulation of ships and wealth as commissary general for purchases for the Continental Army, raking off a 3 percent commission on each transaction. After the war, he began the Hartford Manufacturing Company, the first machine-powered woolen factory. To promote his product, he made sure that Washington, Adams, and all the Connecticut members of the First Congress wore suits made of Hartford broadcloth to Washington's inauguration.[11]

The tariff on every imported chaise, carriage, or other wheeled vehicle, and for parts, was fifteen percent of the value. Buyers of shoe buckles and mirrors paid the price plus an extra 10 percent. The tariff on buttons and hats and ready-made clothing was seven and a half percent.[12]

The swift enactment of the tariff act led to passage of three related laws—and the founding of the new nation's federal bureaucracy. The Collection Act, a long and complicated piece of legislation, designated ports from Portland to Savannah as custom-collection ports. The Coasting Act set up the registration and regulation of all American ships plying coastal waters. The Tonnage Act placed a duty, based on size, on any ship entering an American port: six cents per ton on American-owned ships and ships of nations having commercial treaties with America and fifty cents per ton on all other ships.[13]

All the laws treated the ports of Rhode Island and North Carolina as foreign territories but offered them an incentive to join the Union: their ships would be treated as American until January. Elénor-François-Élie, Comte Moustier, the French ambassador, noted in a report to the French foreign minister that

> the tonnage act is . . . a result of the private interest of a certain class of Citizens, those who engage in navigation. The Southern States, who have almost no vessels, find themselves almost entirely at the mercy of Northern navigators . . . Rhode Island and North Carolina which have not yet adopted the new Constitution are considered foreigners and charged the duty of 50 cents per ton, but Congress, in hopes of drawing them into the confederation, has given them a reprieve that will expire next January. At that time their vessels will be treated as foreign.[14]

Each of the designated ports was to be manned by a set of civilians with specific titles. The "naval officer" and his assistants inspected cargoes; the "collector" calculated what was owed and gathered the tariff charges; the "surveyor" checked on ships' registration and handled customs paperwork. Suddenly, President Washington had to appoint more than one hundred revenue officials, not only beginning the Federal bureaucracy but also forcing him to establish requirements for federal jobs.[15] The paperwork of federal regulations also began, including the registrations of ships and the printing of revenue forms.

Topping off the nautical laws was the Lighthouse Act, which would be funded by the tonnage payments. Proposed lighthouse legislation inspired surprising geographic responses. America's northern shoreline was rockier and more treacherous than its southern shore. So northern lawmakers wanted not only lighthouses but also beacons, buoys, and public piers added to the proposed bill. Southern legislators, with less need for lighthouses, were against federal takeover of what was a state function. The southern coast only had two lighthouses: one at Tybee Island, Georgia, and the other in Charleston harbor. While the South opposed federal control, the North endorsed it; Philadelphia merchants even wrote their own version of a bill favoring their port. Finally, the bill evolved into a law that contained the navigational enhancements that those merchants and the North wanted.[16] In its second session, Congress passed and Washington signed a bill that authorized the building of ten cutters "of from thirty-six to forty feet keel," each armed with swivel guns, for guarding the coast against smugglers. This was the beginning of the U.S. Coast Guard, then known as the Revenue Marine. The first cutter, the two-masted *Massachusetts*, was launched in 1791. Her master took a double oath to support the Constitution and to detect and prevent frauds. Coast Guard officers still take that oath—one of the many 1789 bits of the past that live on.[17]

The Constitution called for a Supreme Court and a federal judiciary but left the details to Congress. Madison and the other leading Federalists knew that the emerging nation needed a judicial system as much as it needed a revenue system. On the day after achieving a quorum, the Senate acted, putting on the docket bill number one: the Act to Establish the Judicial Courts of the United States.

The Senate appointed a Bill Number One committee, composed of Maclay and a senator from each of the nine other states (The New York legislature was still at war over how to elect two senators.) Connecticut's Oliver Ellsworth received the most votes for chairman and conducted the debate. Maclay led the charge against this audacious trampling of states' rights. "I opposed this bill from the beginning," he wrote. "It certainly is a Vile law System . . . with a design to draw by degrees all law business into the federal Courts."[18]

Maclay was right. A legal system with its Supreme Court was at the heart of the federal plan. As Madison wrote many years later, "A supremacy of the Constitution & laws of the Union, without a supremacy in the exposition & execution of them, would be as much a mockery as a scabbard put into the hand of a Soldier without a sword in it."[19]

What emerged from the debates, mostly held in the Senate, was the foundation for an enduring American judicial system. The Supreme Court, consisting of five associate justices and a chief justice appointed by the president, ruled on constitutional questions and had jurisdiction over actions between states or between a state and the federal government. Each state had a District Court whose judge was a local person appointed by the president. District Courts ruled over some criminal cases, along with admiralty and maritime issues, and civil cases with federal aspects. Three Circuit Courts (Eastern, Middle, and Southern), each conducted by the local U.S. district court judge and two traveling justices of the Supreme Court, "riding circuit" twice a year in each judicial circuit. Thus, the act made the Supreme Court Justices circuit judges, who took to the road and sat on cases. The Circuit Courts primarily heard cases involving interstate conflicts.

The act also created the post of attorney general, chosen by the president and envisioned as a legal adviser to the president. Also appointed by the president were district attorneys, who served as federal prosecutors, and federal marshals, whose appointments marked the beginning of the U.S. Marshals Service.[20]

Two days after Washington signed the Judiciary Act, he nominated for chief justice John Jay, who had served as a minister to Spain and to France. Jay continued to give Washington political advice, a practice then not considered untoward. But Jay declined to give Hamilton a requested endorsement of his plan for federal assumption of state war debts, and thus established the independence of the Supreme Court.[21]

Washington established the precedent of geographical diversity in his selection of the Associate Justices from Virginia, Massachusetts, Pennsylvania, South Carolina, and North Carolina—even though the latter state was not in the Union.

The Supreme Court did not move swiftly. Its first session was scheduled for February 1, 1790, in the Royal Exchange Building in New

York, but because three justices were held up by travel problems, the historic event took place on the next day. For months, the Supreme Court justices worked out the details of running of their new institution and granting commissions to lawyers for appearing before it. The court handed down its first opinion on August 3, 1791. The ruling, on a procedural matter pertaining to the mechanics of the circuit court, stemmed from a farm-mortgage case that went back to 1763. As a result of the court's decision, the farmer's family eventually lost the farm.[22]

More than laws were being made in Federal Hall in those nation-building days. Public access to the House gallery had begun the American pastime of watching Congress at work. Among the watchers on the First Congress's first day was James Kent, a twenty-six-year-old lawyer who would become a renowned authority on American law and a justice on the New York Supreme Court. As he recalled that day in the gallery, "all ranks and degrees of men seemed to be actuated by one common impulse, to fill the galleries as soon as the doors of the House of Representatives were opened for the first time. . . . I was looking upon an organ of popular will, just beginning to breathe the breath of Life, and which might in some future age, much more truly than the Roman Senate, be regarded as 'the refuge of nations.'"[23]

The public gallery became a destination for constituents as well as tourists. Women began attending almost as soon as the gallery opened, getting views of an elected government that did not allow them to vote. New York and New Jersey congressmen could expect that they would be watched by men who would be deciding whether to vote for the legislature they watched. Members of the audience often ate in the galleries, and the noise of teeth cracking nuts and feet walking on nutshells so annoyed one visitor that he sent a letter to a newspaper pleading that nut crackers do it at home.[24]

The representatives being watched by the nut crackers and other members of the public faced another unprecedented problem. The number of representatives was supposed to be proportional to the number of people in their respective states. And that meant finding out, as accurately as possible, just how many people there were—and where they were.

COUNTING WE THE PEOPLE

"We the People" still delivers in three words the idea that Americans are united. The three words begin our Constitution and give us the image of a unity that we know has yet to be achieved—an image that, as the Founders well knew, did not exist. In 1789, about twenty-five percent of Americans were African American, and ninety percent of them were slaves whose population was doubling every twenty years.[1] Yet, on May 18, 1789, when members of the House of Representatives routinely appointed a committee to prepare a bill authorizing the first U. S. census, Congress gave as its purpose "the actual enumeration of the inhabitants of the United States." In reality, that would not be true. Many Americans in the territory west of the Ohio River would not be counted because they were not yet living in states. And thousands of Americans would be only partially counted—the three-fifths Americans whose imaginary existence fulfilled a need: to be "in conformity to the Constitution, and for the purposes therein mentioned."[2] The Constitution ordered the so-called enumeration—America's first national census—to determine how many representatives each state should have, based on the Constitution's formula of one representative per 30,000 residents.

But suppose a state found a way to cheat to get more representatives than it deserves? A few words in the Constitution made cheating unlikely: "Representatives and direct Taxes shall be apportioned . . . according to their respective Numbers." So a high population number obtained by cheating would not only produce more representatives. A high number would also bring more taxes. And the states could not cheat because they would not be doing the counting. The enumeration bill made the census a task of the federal government. The writers of the Constitution reached back in history to determine who would be counted. In 1783, members of the Confederation Congress attempted to amend the Articles of Confederation so that the burden of war and other common expenses should be borne by the states. The idea that slaves should not be counted as equals with freemen for taxation purposes was first raised by Virginian Benjamin Harrison during the amendment debate on the Articles of Confederation. Harrison was a plantation owner, a delegate to the First and Second Continental Congresses, and a signer of the Declaration of Independence.[3] The sharing would be based on a triennial census of "the whole number of white and other free citizens and inhabitants of every age, sex, and condition, including those bound to servitude for a term of years, and three-fifths of all other persons not comprehended in the foregoing description, except Indians not paying taxes, in each State."[4]

All the states except New Hampshire and Rhode Island approved the recommendation. But because the Articles of Confederation required unanimous agreement, the proposal was defeated. When the Constitutional Convention met in 1787, Madison brought up the Harrison three-fifths idea and it became Article I, section 2, of the Constitution: "Representatives and direct Taxes shall be apportioned among the several States which may be included within this Union, according to their respective Numbers, which shall be determined by adding to the whole Number of free Persons, including those bound to Service for a Term of Years, and excluding Indians not taxed, three fifths of all other Persons."[5] Known as the Three-Fifths Clause, in this passage the term "other Persons" referred to *slaves*.

The enumeration bill stemmed from the Judiciary Act, which generated a polite but sharply-worded debate when it reached the House in August 1789. Representative Samuel Livermore of New Hampshire led the attack, focusing his ire on the act's creation of federal district courts: "We have supported the union for 13 or 14 years without such courts," he said, "from which I infer that they are not necessary, or we should have discovered the inconvenience of being without them."[6]

Livermore and other congressional foes of the act missed a loophole in the Judiciary Act. It did not say who was to appoint the district attorneys, the attorney general—and the members of the newly created

U.S. Marshals Service.[7] Although attached to the court system, the marshals would carry out orders issued by judges, Congress, or the president.

President Washington decided to give himself the power to appoint marshals and drew up a list of names. Congress, meanwhile, increased the judicial districts to sixteen, and so Washington named three more marshals. Fourteen were Revolutionary War veterans, and most had been involved in politics in the districts where they served. They ranged in age from twenty-five to fifty-seven. On September 26, 1789, Washington signed the commissions of the first thirteen marshals, thus establishing the U.S. Marshals Service as America's oldest law-enforcement organization.[8]

In responding to the Constitution's call for a census, the First Federal Congress was, as usual, proceeding without precedent. No other country had ever produced a regularly held census.[9] Congress decided to order the U.S. Marshals Service[10] to run the census. Marshals would continue to take on that task until 1880, when trained census-takers would replace them.[11]

By the early nineteenth century, the marshals were the lawmen dispatched westward with the people heading for what were officially known as America's unorganized territories[12]—and unofficially as the Wild West. By the mid 1800s, marshals, wearing badges and six-guns, were the representatives of federal law. They became the inspiration for countless books and movies about the taming of the West and the integrity and courage of marshals—more than two hundred of whom have died on duty.[13]

The marshal service emerged from the Judiciary Act. But the marshals escaped the attacks that focused on the act, probably because critics saw the need for some kind of federal law enforcement. *Marshal*, a British word tracing to medieval times, replaced *federal sheriff* as a possible title and ultimately prevailed, probably to lessen confusion over *sheriff*, a recognizable word for state or county law enforcers

Each of the sixteen federal district courts had a marshal to "carry out all lawful orders issued by judges, Congress, or the President." The marshals and their deputies served subpoenas, summonses, writs, warrants, and other court orders. They also made arrests and handled prisoners.[14]

The federal courts became the focus of representatives' opposition to the Judiciary Act. Representative Fisher Ames of Massachusetts, in a letter to a lawyer friend, said, "The idea of submitting to a foreign and hostile jurisdiction—as some of the state courts will be, and, in time, perhaps, all of them—the important office of enforcing and interpreting the Laws seems, *a priori,* awkward and improper."[15] Representatives Aedanus Burke of South Carolina, referring to the entire Judiciary Act, said he had "turned himself about to find some way to extricate himself from this measure, but which ever way he turned, the Constitution still stared him in the face, and he confessed he saw no way to avoid the evil."[16]

The Constitution was also staring in the faces of supporters of state sovereignty, who fumed over the fact that the census-takers would be using federal court districts, rather than the states, to define the canvassing areas. Some of the court districts did not have boundaries consistent with state boundaries. This was a federal action, and so state borders were overshadowed by the boundaries of the judicial districts. The plan called for each district marshal to canvass his district, with the aid of deputies if needed. So technically the federal districts—not the states—would be the providers of census results.

The canvassing areas encompassed the original thirteen States (including North Carolina, which ratified the Constitution on November 21, 1789, and Rhode Island, which did so on May 29, 1790) plus the districts of Kentucky; the state of Vermont; the Southwest Territory, which contained future Tennessee; and Maine, which was a political district of Massachusetts and would not become a state until 1820. The Northwest territory's population was not counted in 1790. For the census, the Maine District was described as "that part of the state of Massachusetts which lies easterly of the state of New-Hampshire." The Kentucky District consisted of part of Virginia.[17] The state of Kentucky did not come into the Union until 1792. The marshals were told to start the count on the first Monday in August 1790 and end it within nine months. They did not have forms to write on, and there was no uniform system for recording information. For New England and one or two of the other states, for instance, the population was broken out by counties and towns, while New Jersey appeared partly by counties and towns and partly by counties only.[18] Unfortunately, while the overall totals survived, the 1790 detailed counts for Delaware, Georgia, Kentucky, New Jersey, Tennessee, and Virginia were destroyed when British troops burned the Capitol during the War of 1812.[19]

The periods for canvassing were later extended, the longest being eighteen months for South Carolina. District marshals could appoint as many deputies as they need; the total was estimated to be 650.[20] Thomas Jefferson had general supervision of the census, as that was then a duty of the Secretary of State. The marshals were told not only to count people but also to place them in six categories: (1) heads of families; (2) free white males of sixteen years and upward for potential militia use; (3) free white males younger than sixteen; (4) free white females, including heads of families; (5) all other free persons; and (6) slaves, each of whom was counted as three-fifths of a white person.[21]

The 1790 census reported a population of 3,929,328 people. The official results include districts labeled "Kentucky" and "Vermont," and "the Southwest Territory." A table of results for the first census appears on the following page.*

Both George Washington and Thomas Jefferson were skeptical about the final count, expecting a number that exceeded the roughly 3.9 million inhabitants reported in the census. They were probably right.[22]

Aside from the general undercount Washington and Jefferson suspected, the 16 "slaves" in Vermont were never there. A 1908 report on the 1790 Census states that "an examination of the original manuscript returns shows that there never were any slaves in Vermont. The original error occurred in preparing the results for publication, when 16 persons, returned as 'Free colored' were classified as 'Slave.'" That same 1908 report noted an addition error for Delaware that resulted in an undercount of two. And the 1908 report duly reproduces the original 1791 report in providing a line for reporting the population of the Northern Territory, but failing to enter any numbers showing anyone actually residing there. And of course people were living, dying, and

---

*   Following a common convention in the early days of the Republic, the original Census listed the States from North to South—New Hampshire to Georgia. This was already becoming unwieldy by 1790, with Kentucky, Vermont and Maine throwing things off. The 1908 report from which the table below is drawn followed the north-to-south style as closely as practical. It has been reorganized in alphabetical order, as per modern-day convention.

District	Free white males (16 years and up), incl: heads of families	Free white males under 16 years	Free white females, incl. heads of families	All other free persons	Slaves	Total
Connecticut	60,523	54,403	117,448	2,808	2,764	237,946
Delaware	11,783	12,143	22,384	3,899	8,887	59,096
Georgia	13,103	14,044	25,739	398	29,264	82,548
Kentucky	15,154	17,057	28,922	114	12,430	73,677
Maine	24,384	24,748	46,870	538	None	96,540
Maryland	55,915	51,339	101,395	8,043	103,036	319,728
Massachusetts	95,453	87,289	190,582	5,363	None	378,787
New Hampshire	36,086	34,851	70,160	630	158	141,885
New Jersey	45,251	41,416	83,287	2,762	11,423	184,139
New York	83,700	78,122	152,320	4,654	21,324	340,120
North Carolina	69,988	77,506	140,710	4,975	100,572	393,751
Pennsylvania	110,788	106,948	206,363	6,537	3,737	434,373
Rhode Island	16,019	15,799	32,652	3,407	948	68,825
South Carolina	35,576	37,722	66,880	1,801	107,094	249,073
Vermont	22,435	22,328	40,505	255	16	85,539
Virginia	110,936	116,135	215,046	12,866	292,627	747,610
Total number of inhabitants of the United States exclusive of S. Western and N. Territory						
	807,094	791,850	1,541,263	59,150	694,280	3,893,637

	Free white males of 21 years and upward.	Free males under 21 years of age.	Free white females.	All other persons.	Slaves	Total
S.W. territory	6,271	10,277	15,365	361	3,417	35,691
N. territory	---	---	---	---	---	
TOTALS						3,929,328

Results of the 1790 Census

moving about without much worrying about the accuracy of the census. The numbers were as good as they could be, but they were not perfect.

A modern-day analysis by the U.S. Census Bureau came up with a very slightly lower headcount for 1790: 3,929,214. The Northeast population was put at 1,968,040, the South at 1,961,174.[23]

By 1790 Virginia was far and away the most populous state overall, and had the largest number of slaves: 292,627. Virginia had 42 percent of all slaves in the United States. South Carolina, North Carolina, and Maryland each had more than 100,000 slaves.[24] The 1790 census dispensed with the Constitution's cautious locution, "other Persons." Enslaved black men, women and children were listed in columns labeled "slaves."

What the Census report called the Northern Territory was generally called the Northwest Territory. Although no hard count was made there in 1790, a 1792 estimate put the white population of the Northwest Territory at 7,820.[25] Those very few persons were spread out over what would eventually become part or all of six states: Ohio, Indiana, Illinois, Michigan, Wisconsin and Minnesota.

Indians also went uncounted in the official census. Secretary of War Knox in 1789 estimated the total Indian population in the territory of the United States to be 76,000, with one-fourth of them believed to be warriors—or "gun men," the term then in use.[26] However, one modern source estimates the Native American population of the United States in 1800 to be 600,000.[27]

While there is great dispute over the exact numbers at any one time, it is beyond all dispute that the Native American population was in drastic decline. By some estimates, about 1.4 million Indians had lived in North America at the end of the seventeenth century—some 250,000 of them east of the Mississippi River. By the end of the eighteenth century, relatively few Indians could be found in New England. Elsewhere, historian Gordon S. Wood wrote, "the colonists had continually tried to draw lines between themselves and the Indians, offering them bribes to surrender more and more of their lands as they relentlessly pushed them westward. Many of these native peoples believed that they could move no further and were increasingly determined to protect their dwindling hunting grounds."[28]

• • •

For whites, a new, growing society was emerging. A modern British demographer calculated that the 1780 to 1790 decade was the fastest period of population growth in American history.[29] The Naturalization
Act, passed in March 1790, was welcoming and made citizenship easily
obtainable: Any free white alien who lived in the United States for two
years could become a citizen by applying to do so in a court of a given
state after living in that state for at least a year and taking an oath to
support the Constitution. Citizenship was extended to any children
under the age of twenty-one. The act contained only 276 words.[30]

The population boom came not only from immigration but also
"from people marrying earlier and having an extra child," according
to Wood. "If you lower the marriage age by two years, the population jumps. The reason people were marrying earlier is that their out-
look was good. They thought they were going to be okay. There was a
fast-growing population in a time of great exuberance, excitement, and
prospects. I think the pursuit of happiness that Jefferson talked about
was being fulfilled for lots of Americans in the 1780s."[31]

Scattered among the general American population was another kind
of "Others"—Loyalists, disparagingly known as Tories, and despised
by fellow citizens. They were against the Revolution after the battles of
Lexington and Concord in 1775, against independence in 1776, and
thousands of them took up arms to fight for the king when the war began. Tens of thousands of Loyalists left America with the British troops
who evacuated Boston at the beginning of the war and New York at the
end. Most of them fled to Canada. Today four to six million Canadians
claim a Loyalist ancestor, including descendants of runaway slaves who,
having been freed by the British, sailed to Canada.[32]

Throughout the Revolutionary War, Loyalists and Patriots fought
each other, in battle and in private acts of revenge or hatred. Although
there were occasional executions based on state treason laws, violence
against Loyalists was rare. But Patriots fought guerrilla warfare, particularly in the southern states. Here is an eyewitness account of a Patriot
recruitment foray in North Carolina: "An officer or committeeman en-
ters a plantation with his posse. the Alternative is proposed, Agree to

join us, and your persons and properties are safe. . . . But if you refuse, we are directly to shoot your pigs, burn your houses, seize your Negroes and perhaps tar and feather your self."[33] When the Confederation Congress ratified the treaty ending the war in January 1784, the official status of Loyalists, according to the treaty, was that Congress would "earnestly recommend" to state legislatures that they recognize the rightful owners of all confiscated lands and "provide for the restitution of all estates, rights, and properties, which have been confiscated." In fact, the fate of Loyalists was not determined by Congress but by the legislatures of the states. There was no way that any state was going to obey the treaty's recommendations.

Most self-exiled Loyalists did not return to America, and most of them lost their properties to people who chose the war's winning side. Philadelphia patriots and other local groups from New York and Boston to Charleston, South Carolina passed resolutions demanding that Loyalists be barred from returning.

Many would never come back. They had fled, had chosen to reset-tle elsewhere and begin new lives. Most of those who chose Canada were awarded large tracts of land and sometimes the materials and tools for building houses.[34] The self-exiles to England, often treated as fleeing "Americans," had trouble finding hospitable niches in British society.[35] Many others sailed to new lives in the sugar islands of the British Caribbean. They took their slaves with them, put them to work on plantations, and enjoyed an island life little changed from life in Georgia or South Carolina.[36]

Most Loyalists who remained in the United States kept quiet, hun-kered down, and paid little for not actively supporting the war. In Connecticut, inconspicuous Loyalists living near the New York bor-der had traded with British occupiers and managed to escape post-war punishment.[37] Typical of the states' treatment of Loyalists was a Connecticut law that divided Loyalists into three classes and punished them proportionally to their deeds: (1) those who supplied the British with provisions or military stores, gave intelligence or other aid; (2) those who wrote or spoke in ways that "defame the resolves of Congress"; and (3) those "reported to the local authorities as 'inimical.'" Loyalists accused of violating various laws could be found in nearly every jail in every state.[38]

Washington did his part to show good will toward Loyalists by allowing one, the artist John Ramage, to paint the first portraits of Washington as president. The sitting, which produced two portraits, took place on October 3, 1789. Ireland-born Ramage joined Irish-British forces formed to fight the rebels, but spent most of the war in British-occupied New York as a member of a growing artist community.[39]

One nonviolent Loyalist was Constant Tiffany, a cantankerous fourth-generation American confined to his Hartland, Connecticut, farm by neighbors. He decided to fight by wielding his pen, setting down his version of a "Shocking and unhappy Struggle Between prince and people." He accused non-Loyalists of taking over pulpits: "Twas Rare To hear a Sermon, but what was a mixture of both The art of war Civil pollicy end Gilded over wIth a Thin Coat of Devinity. In short, if Ther was any authority, it was Cheifly Lodged among Those That were once Esteemed The Giddy, Rude and profligate."[40]

The liturgy of the Church of England included prayers for the good health of King George III. Members of that denomination, also known as Anglicans, were frequent targets of Tory hunters. At least one Anglican clergyman was shot at—and he armed himself by keeping two pistols handy while preaching.[41] During the war, some Anglican ministers who had remained in the colonies started planning an American church. The Protestant Episcopal Church of the United States emerged from a 1789 convention, which also revised the *Book of Common Prayer*, mostly to clarify liturgical issues—and, almost incidentally, to drop the prayer for the king and replace with a prayer "For the President of the United States and all in Civil Authority."[42]

Early in the war, when Americans had to choose between the revolution or the king, revolutionaries demanded treason laws with capital punishment. In 1777, John Van Cortlandt, a New York politician, said, "The Tories . . . are plotting from New Hampshire to Carolina. . . . a Thousand of them must in 2 or 3 Months be hanged and then all will be Peace."[43] From a Massachusetts politician came a call for Congress to pass laws for "exterminating traitors." Some death-penalty laws were passed. Predictions about punishing Loyalists were vengeful and bloody. Most casualties were victims of battles, guerrilla raids, or murders inspired by vengeance.

When the British ended their nine-month occupation of Philadelphia in September 1777, the Supreme Council of Pennsylvania published a list of people charged with aiding the occupiers. [44] Ordered to surrender, most of them fled to England or joined Loyalist military units. The Pennsylvania government arrested 638 people on suspicion of treason, seized the property of more than 100 of them, and hanged two men, both Quakers. [45]

Alexander Hamilton, as a New Yorker, defended in court many New York Loyalists whose property had been taken. He wrote that "The world has its eye upon America. The noble struggle we have made in the cause of liberty, has occasioned a kind of revolution in human sentiment. The influence of our example has penetrated the gloomy regions of despotism." [46] Elsewhere he recorded that "Instead of wholesome regulations for the improvement of our polity and commerce," he wrote, "we are labouring to contrive methods to mortify and punish tories and to explain away treaties." [47]

What could never be adequately explained away was the internal contradiction between a new republic that presented itself as the bastion of liberty—and yet profited from the enslavement of hundreds of thousands of fellow humans.

11

AMERICA'S "OTHER PERSONS"

The year 1789, the birth year of America, was also a milestone on the long, long trail that led to the abolition of slavery. An earlier point on that trail was the Revolutionary War, a marker of change in attitudes toward slavery. Initially, General Washington barred slaves from the Continental Army. Then, on November 7, 1775, when Lord Dunmore, the royal governor of Virginia, declared "all indented servants, negroes, or others" were free and "able and willing to bear arms" in the British Army,[1] Washington changed his mind, allowing the enlistment of slaves. In Rhode Island, state legislators promised to free all black, Indian, and mulatto slaves who enlisted in a new nonwhite regiment.[2] In Virginia, Dunmore formed the Ethiopian Regiment—300 men clad in uniforms bearing the words *Liberty to Slaves*.[3]

Thousands of slaves left the United States during the war —some as freed Americans accompanying British troops sailing to Canada, others as slaves fleeing from their masters—or with their masters. When the British evacuated Savannah on July 11, 1782, some 2,000 white Georgians and about 4,000 slaves headed for British-controlled East Florida (only to learn that the peace treaty of 1783 returned Florida to Spain). About 400 whites with some 5,000 slaves chose Jamaica.[4] In the 1782 evacuation of Charleston, South Carolina, more than 9,000 slaves and their masters left for Halifax, New York, East Florida, Jamaica, and St. Lucia.[5] Ex-slaves settled in Canada as freed people; in the Caribbean, most continued their lives in enslavement.

The war had no direct effect on the Founders who owned slaves— Washington, Jefferson, Madison, George Mason and Patrick Henry. Even Ben Franklin had owned people. He kept slaves as a young man and accepted advertisements for runaway slaves in his *Pennsylvania*

Gazette.[6] In 1751, when he wrote about slavery for the first time, he focused on the expenses inherent in keeping a slave, rather than on any moral consideration. For example, he cited the "expense of a driver to keep him at work, and his pilfering from time to time (almost every slave being by nature a thief)."[7]

Other Founders did write about their moral qualms over possessing slaves. James Madison said, "American citizens are instrumental in carrying on a traffic in enslaved Africans, equally in violation of the laws of humanity and in defiance of those of their own country."[8] Privately, Madison wondered about establishing a settlement of freed blacks in Africa, possibly encouraging "manumission in the Southern parts of the U. S. and . . . an end to the slavery in which not less than 600,000 unhappy negroes are now involved."[9]

George Mason called slavery a "slow Poison, which is daily contaminating the Minds & Morals of our People. Every Gentlemen [*sic*] here is born a petty Tyrant."[10]

In a letter, Washington wrote, "I can only say that there is not a man living who wishes more sincerely than I do, to see a plan adopted for the abolition of [slavery] but there is only one proper and effectual mode by which it can be accomplished, and that is by Legislative authority."[11] Washington was the only slaveholding Founder to put provisions for manumission in his will.[12]

Of all the slave-owning Founders, only Ben Franklin became an active abolitionist. In 1787 he began to serve as president of the Pennsylvania Society for Promoting the Abolition of Slavery. The organization's roots went back to 1775 (as the Society for the Relief of Free Negroes Unlawfully Held in Bondage.) Franklin formally submitted the society's petition, which asked for Congress to abolish slavery and "every species of traffic in slaves" in February 1790. The submission of the petition was his last public act. He died on April 17, 1790, at the age of eighty-four, two months after Congress had tabled the petition. Members of the House of Representatives wore black crepe armbands of mourning for a month, but, because Vice President Adams had long been feuding with Franklin, mostly over clashing views of the French Revolution, he did not ask the Senate to mourn, symbolically or otherwise. Neither President Washington nor any other members of the executive branch mourned, perhaps because, he said, he wished to avoid the look of royal mourning practices in Europe. No members of Congress were among the 20,000 people who attended his funeral in Philadelphia.[13]

As the First Federal Congress settled into routines, the members showed great respect for petitions submitted by their constituents. But when, at about the same time as Franklin's petitions, two Quaker anti-slavery petitions appeared without warning in the second session, some Representatives from the South panicked. The House was debating Hamilton's highly controversial proposal that the federal government assume state war debts. The sudden arrival of the Quakers' petitions unexpectedly changed the topic. To the Southern delegates, that meant switching from a significant issue worthy of Congress to an annoying intrusion by abolitionists who knew their petitions were futile—and dangerous to the slave states. The petitions also forced Congress to face an unwelcome issue.

The two petitions were based on resolutions that had passed at Quaker annual meetings in Philadelphia and New York. The petitions triggered a hot-tempered House debate that lasted for six days near the beginning of the second session. Southern Representatives reverted to an old canard: Quakers were noncitizens who were causing trouble as outsiders who had clung to treasonous pacifism during the Revolutionary War. In fact, many Quakers, including Major General Nathanael Greene, were expelled from Quakers meetings for violating the religion's anti-violence edicts by going to war.[14]

Representative Aedanus Burke of South Carolina was a leading congressional defender of the slave trade. In debate he accused the Quakers of blowing the "trumpet of sedition." To morally justify slaveholding, Burke turned to the Bible with a bit of oratory: "The master has a property over his servant the same as over his slave. Whether religion sanctifies slavery [I] will not pretend to say. If these good people would search out Bible in Genesis, slavery was from the original."[15] "What do they expect?" asked one representative, referring to the Quakers.[16] "Do [they] expect general emancipation of slaves [to] the United States? Do they mean to purchase these slaves? How came these Quakers to take upon themselves—Are they the only men who have religion and morality?"[17]

Connecticut Representative Jonathan Trumbull, Jr., complained that "the whole of the past Week has been wasted with the Quakers & the Negroes," adding, "The So. Carolina & Georgia Members have taken up the Matter with as much warmth & zeal as though the very existence of their States depended on the decision on the Comtee." (He was apparently referring to the Committee of the Whole.)[18]

Southern Representatives irrationally feared that the petitions would lead to a vote on abolition—and they vowed to secede from the Union if that ever happened.[19] The Senate took no action on the petitions. The House referred them to a select committee, which in turn reported to the Committee of the Whole. That powerful body killed them by ordering the petitions "to lie on the table" and then made sure they were dead by ruling that Congress had no authority to interfere with the slave trade until 1808.[20]

Many Southern and Northern members of the First Congress naively believed that slavery, one of the most contentious issues in the debates of the Constitutional Convention, had been defused by the so-called slave clauses in the Constitution. As discussed already, the key pro-slavery clause allowed Southern states to treat slaves as three-fifths of "other Persons." Another clause anticipated a fugitive-slave law. Topping all other pro-slavery laws was the Constitution's guarantee that no law prohibiting importation of slaves would go into effect before January 1, 1808. The clause did not require an end to the trade. However, in the event, Congress ultimately did ban the trade effective January 1, 1808.

On March 15, as the impact of the well-publicized Quaker petitions were fading away, David Stuart wrote a warning to his old friend, President Washington: "A spirit of jealousy which may become dangerous to the Union, towards the Eastern States, seems to be growing fast among us." Stuart went on to say that "the Northern phalanx is so firmly united, as to bear down all opposition, while Virginia is unsupported, even by those whose interests are similar with her's." As to the Quakers, the petitions "will certainly tend to promote this spirit—It gives particular umbrage, that the Quakers should be so busy in this business—That they will raise up a storm against themselves, appears to me very certain."[21] In response, Washington, surprisingly raised the issue of secession: "What would Virginia (and such other States as might be inclined to join her) gain by a seperation?"[22]

Congressman William Loughton Smith condemned the Quakers as "intemperate & bigoted" men "who seemed to take pleasure in accusing us of infamous & inhuman proceedings & who were pursuing with eager steps the ruin & destruction of our happiness & property." He perceived "an attempt made to deprive us of our property so soon after we had established a government for the express purpose of protecting it, & in the face of a solemn compact."[23]

"Our State is weak in the Union—it certainly is," Smith said in a letter to Edward Rutledge, a future governor of South Carolina. "We have no state to support our peculiar rights, particu[larl]y. that of holding Slavery, but Georgia: She will be generally represented by men of moderate abilities—indeed I fear the smallness of the pay will not entice our best men to make the necessary sacrifices & come to Congress."

Smith predicted that the presidency would evolve into a hereditary New England institution. "What chance then," he asked Rutledge, "will a Southern man have of being appointed to office?"[24] The South, he said, needed to curb the influence of "These high-flyers [who] want to depreciate the Senate and & substitute a privy council, behind the Curtain.[25] "The Gentlemen from S. Carolina & Georgia are intemperate beyond all example and even all decorum," Madison wrote in a letter to Benjamin Rush, a crusader for abolition. "They are not content with palliating slavery as a deep-rooted abuse, but plead for the lawfulness of the african trade itself."[26]

Rush turned to science to strengthen his abhorrence of slavery. He developed and published a bizarre medical theory to explain Africans' skin color was due to a form of leprosy.[27] As for the slaves' supposedly placid acceptance of servitude, Rush further believed that enslaved people were intellectually wounded by the mental burden of their fate.[28]

The *Maryland Journal*, reporting on the House's handling of the anti-slavery petitions, cited the historic North-South divide that intensified the debate. Representatives Thomas Scott of Pennsylvania, Elbridge Gerry of Massachusetts, Elias Boudinot of New Jersey, and John Vining of Delaware "advocated the cause" of the Quakers "and vindicated their characters, with great ability, eloquence and liberality" while South Carolina Representatives William Loughton Smith and Aedanus Burke, along with James Jackson of Georgia, treated the Quakers "with a degree of acrimony and invective, which ill become American Legislators."[29]

Claims about the North-South divide on slavery, highlighted in the Quaker petitions debate, overlooked the fact that America's leading slave traders were Northerners—distinguished citizens of Rhode Island. During the 18th century, Rhode Island slave traders launched about one thousand voyages to the coast of Africa to acquire slaves.[30]

Rhode Island's ties to the slave trade were overlooked during the petitions debate in Congress because the state was not yet in the Union. Rhode Islanders had boycotted the Constitution Convention, contending that the convention had not had congressional authority to replace the Articles of Confederation. The state's powerful advocates of paper money also opposed a strong central government, which presumably would introduce a federal monetary system. Ironically, Rhode Islander abolitionists also were against ratifying the Constitution because of compromises that allowed the continuance of the slave trade.[31]

Newspapers called Rhode Island "the perverse sister," "an evil genius," and the "Quintessence of Villainy." The name that stuck was "Rogue Island," featured in a poem that began:

> Hail, realm of rogues, renown'd for fraud and guile,
> All hail, ye knav'ries of yon little isle;
> There prowls the rascal cloth'd with legal power,
> To snare the orphan, and the poor devour.[32]

In May 1787, the Rhode Island house of representatives had voted to send delegates to the Constitutional Convention, but the Rhode Island senate voted against. A month later, the senate voted in favor— but the house voted against.[33] Between September 1787 and January 1790, Rogue Island's legislature rejected eleven attempts to ratify the Constitution.[34]

The new nation, conceived in liberty, had a deeply rooted cynical and hypocritical attitude toward the slave trade, which attracted leading Northern citizens seeking sound investments. Rhode Island's dominance of the slave trade, for instance, came in the 1750s, when Henry Laurens, who would later succeed John Hancock as president of the Continental Congress, ran the largest slave trading operation in North America. He enslaved more than 8,000 Africans during that decade alone.[35]

When rum began outranking French brandy as an important trade item, Rhode Islanders' high-proof rum surpassed all its competitors. Captains of Rhode Island slave ships became known as the Rum Men. Their Rhode Island product began appearing on the African coast in 1725. During the next ten years, twenty-five ships sailed from Newport, Rhode Island, to Africa. The rum was traded for Africans fated to work on the sugar plantations of the Caribbean. On those islands the slavers bought molasses, which they brought back to Rhode Island for the distilling of more rum.[36]

A slave bought in Africa for £4 to £6 could be sold at Jamaica for £50 to £55.[37] That incredible ten-to-one profit margin was irresistible to investors. In 1764, Rhode Island Governor Stephen Hopkins, first chancellor of the College of Rhode Island and later a signer of the Declaration of Independence, was a slave owner. Nevertheless, he was able to write, "Liberty is the greatest blessing that men enjoy, and slavery is the heaviest curse that human nature is capable of." The quotation is from the opening of his 1764 *Rights of the Colonies Examined*, one of the earliest American documents challenging British colonialism.[38]

Coincidentally, Nicholas Brown and Company—a partnership of brothers Nicholas, John, Joseph, and Moses Brown—had sent a slave ship, the *Sally*, to West Africa around the time that Stephen Hopkins published his stirring words on liberty. The *Sally*'s captain was Stephen Hopkins' brother Esek. He later served as commander-in-chief of the Continental Navy during the Revolutionary War. In late 1764 the Brown brothers forwarded a copy of Stephen Hopkins's pamphlet to Esek Hopkins "for your amusement." At the time, the *Sally* was off the Windward Coast of Africa (modern Liberia and Ivory Coast).[39] The Brown brothers had ordered Hopkins to trade his cargo—including spermaceti candles, tobacco, onions, and 17,274 gallons of rum—for slaves. He was then to sell those slaves in the West Indies. The brothers also asked him to bring "four likely young slaves," boys of fifteen years or younger, back to Providence to work for the family.[40]

Hopkins acquired 196 Africans, twenty of whom had died by the time the *Sally* sailed for the West Indies. They included several children and a woman who "hanged her Self between Decks," according, not to the ship's log, but to the account book that kept track of profit and loss. On the eighth day at sea, "Slaves Rose on us was obliged fire on them and Destroyed Eight and Several more wounded badly a Thye and ones Ribs broke." Some captives later "drowned themselves Some Starved and others Sickened & Dyed." In all, sixty-eight Africans died at sea and twenty died after the ship reached the West Indies, bringing the total death toll to 108. En route to Providence, the 109th person died; he was one of the four "likely young slaves."[41]

The survivors, auctioned in Antigua, were so sickly that they sold for about one-tenth of the prevailing price for a "prime" slave. Hawkins apologized for "the Bad Voyage," but the Brown brothers told him, "your Self Continuing in Helth is so grate Satisfaction to us, that we Remain Cheerful under the Heavey Loss of our Int[erest]s."[42] Three of the brothers—Nicholas, Joseph, and Moses—abandoned the slave trade. Moses became a Quaker and an advocate for antislavery legislation.[43]

The year 1789, which launched America, also marked the beginning of the end of the slave trade in Britain. And in that same year a link was forged between abolitionists in Britain and in America, where many seemed to see a profound connection between ending slavery and founding a nation. On May 12, 1789, William Wilberforce, leader of the abolitionist movement in Parliament, rose in the House of Commons and for three hours described the horrors of slavery, particularly voyages of the slave ships. He ended the speech by saying, "having heard all of this you may choose to look the other way but you can never again say that you did not know."[44] But, despite widespread support for an end to slavery, Britain did not abolish the slave trade until 1807.[45]

Around this time an investigation of slave ships by Thomas Clarkson, another British abolitionist, led to the publication of the shipbuilders' plan for the *Brookes,* a British slave ship. The widely reproduced image was horrifying —454 men, women, and children crammed into the hold. It transformed the public perception of the slave trade. What had been an abstract concept became an indelible mental image of human beings in unspeakable conditions. That image of the Brookes was published for the first time in America by Mathew Carey in the May 1789 edition of the magazine *American Museum* and in a print run of 2,500 copies as a broadside.

The *Brookes* image was not enough to wipe out the slave trade. Nor were such murderous voyages such as that of the *Sally*. But they gave new strength to the abolitionists' crusade. And in a time when Americans fought for liberty and then worked to build a nation, slavery began to fade away in the North. But each state used its sovereignty to decide how to abolish slavery. Rhode Island, for example, in 1784 enacted a Gradual Abolition Act, which specified that every person born in the state after March 1 of that year would be free. But the law did not change the status of those born before then. And free-born children had to serve their mothers' owners for twenty-one years before assuming their freedom.[46]

Delaware outlawed the importation of slaves in its 1776 constitution and in 1789 forbade slave ships to enter its ports, but in fact did little to abolish its homegrown slavery.[47] In 1777, Vermont, which did not enter the Union until 1791, amended its constitution to ban the enslavement of males age twenty-one and older and females eighteen and older; child slaves had to wait for freedom until their twenty-first birthday. Some wealthy Vermont landowners continued to own slaves into the early nineteenth century.[48]

Pennsylvania passed a law of gradual abolition in 1780, freeing slaves when they reached the age of twenty-eight.[49] Massachusetts never formally abolished slavery, but in 1781 its State Supreme Court ruled that slavery was incompatible with the phrase "All men are born free and equal" in its state constitution.[50] Connecticut passed the Gradual Abolition Act of 1784, which emancipated slaves born into slavery after they reached the age of twenty-five.[51] New Jersey, whose slave population was 14,000 in 1790, did not begin its slow abolition until 1804.[52] In 1799, New York passed the Gradual Emancipation Act, freeing slave children born after July 4, 1799, but indenturing them until they were young adults. A subsequent law freed slaves born before 1799 when they entered the year 1827. By the 1830 census, there were only seventy-five slaves in New York, and the 1840 census listed no slaves in New York City.[53]

Absolute abolition of slavery would not come until December 6, 1865, when the Thirteenth Amendment was ratified. The amendment, declaring that "neither slavery nor involuntary servitude ... shall exist within the United States," finally put the word *slavery* into the Constitution.

But that day was far off. Much closer at hand was an effort to write some equally vital amendments—yet another process for which there was no precedent at all.

A TUB FULL OF RIGHTS

The First Federal Congress was only a few weeks old, when on June 8, 1789, James Madison wrote down some notes for a speech about amendments to the Constitution:

> Reasons urging amendts.
> 1. to prove fed[eralis]ts. friends to liberty
> 2. remove remaining inquietudes
> 3. bring in N[orth]. C[arolina]. & R[hode]. Island.
> 4. to improve the Constitution
> Reasons for moderating the plan
> 1. No stop if door opend to theoretic amendts.
> 2. as likely to make worse as better till trial
> 3. insure passage by 2/3 of Congs. & 3/4 of Sts.
> Objectns. of 3 kinds vs. the Const[itutio]n.
> 1. vs. the theory of its structure
> 2. vs. substance of its powers—elections & direct taxes
> 3. vs. omission of guards in favr. of rights & libertys.[1]

On a printed page, those handwritten notes look remarkably like a modern PowerPoint presentation. And, as in many such presentations, their meaning is lost without some background. 1 and 2, for instance, went to the heart of Madison's belief that he needed to "improve the Constitution" through amendments. He knew that during the Constitutional Convention the word *amendment* had two meanings:

1. to prove fed[eralis]ts. friends to liberty: Because of their focus on the creation of a strong central government, Federalists like Madison were accused of ignoring the need for definite protection of personal liberty.

2. remove remaining inquietudes: This seems to be Madison sensing a restlessness that still inspired some members of Congress to distrust the structure of the government—even though they were now part of that structure. Madison knew that he had to keep a tight control over the amendments debate. Otherwise, *No stop if door opend to theoretic amendts.*[2] Madison's notes show how deliberative and focused he was about introducing prospective amendments to the Constitution. But many members, seeing no point in shifting away from the urgent task of lawmaking, questioned Madison's motives, comparing his move to Jonathan Swift's *Tale of a Tub:* "Seamen have a custom, when they meet a whale, to fling him out an empty tub by way of amusement, to divert him from laying violent hands upon the ship."[3]

Nevertheless, Madison, inspired by the Virginia Declaration of Rights, drew up amendments—he also called them "articles"—that would give Americans constitutionally guaranteed rights: freedom of speech, press, assembly, and religion, along with the right to bear arms and to receive fair justice. He believed that his amendments could be injected into the Constitution rather than being attached to it.

Many Federalists saw no need for any amendments at all because they admired the Constitution just as it was. An anonymous observer, writing in Philadelphia's *Pennsylvania Gazette,* said that "if we must have amendments, I pray for merely amusing amendments, a little frothy garnish."[4] Anti-Federalists, however, were not amused. They wanted the First Congress to devote its time to issues that had to do with governance, not personal rights. During the convention that created the Constitution, Anti-Federalists Elbridge Gerry of Massachusetts and George Mason of Virginia had proposed that the Constitution contain explicit rights of individuals. As Mason put it, "It would give great quiet to the people." The delegation from Virginia—and all the other states that attended the convention—agreed with Madison by voting against the proposal.[5] Few legislators then had the vision to see the potential Bill of Rights as the heart of the Constitution, the words that would foster, down the years, an all-American assertion: "I know my rights!"

The basis for the *Tale of a Tub* ridicule was the suspicion that Madison was hoping to use amendments to distract the House members from possible attempts to introduce "alterations" in the Constitution itself.

To open up the Constitution for the purpose of inserting alterations meant revisiting old debates and perhaps forcing a second round of state-by-state ratifications. Or, worse, tinkering with the Constitution might inspire a second Constitutional Convention, where anything might happen in the growing battle between Federalists and Anti-Federalists.

The need for a bill of rights had become a blazing political issue by the time Madison failed to become one of Virginia's senators in the First Congress and then ran for the House and won. Originally, Madison saw no need for a bill of rights, but in his campaign he became a supporter, even suggesting that the addition of rights might bring Rhode Island and North Carolina into the nation.[6] As an architect of the Constitution, Madison foresaw the need of a built-in process for proposing amendments. The process is built into Article V:

> The Congress, whenever two thirds of both houses shall deem it necessary, shall propose amendments to this Constitution, or, on the application of the legislatures of two thirds of the several states, shall call a convention for proposing amendments, which, in either case, shall be valid to all intents and purposes, as part of this Constitution, when ratified by the legislatures of three fourths of the several states.

A state could ratify *and* submit proposed amendments. Using that device, ratification conventions in three states had narrowly approved the Constitution and included amendments in the official ratification notices sent to Congress. Anti-Federalists in Massachusetts and Pennsylvania proposed amendments that the ratification conventions rejected, but the Anti-Federalists, as a signal of dissent, published them. Virginia proposed a twenty-article bill of rights and twenty alterations. New York wanted twenty-two alterations and a rights packet containing twenty-three proposals and "Explanations."

Most of the requested amendments were aimed at narrowing the powers of the new federal government.[7] Prominent among the proffered amendments was the idea of a Bill of Rights, once defined by Thomas Jefferson as "what the people are entitled to against every government on earth, general or particular, and what no just government should refuse."[8]

Noah Webster, already well known as a chronicler of the American language, added his voice to Federalists who opposed what they saw as the pointless bother of creating a Bill of Rights. Anonymously attacking Madison, Webster wrote, "It seems to be agreed on all hands that paper declarations of rights are trifling things and no real security to liberty. In general they are a subject of ridicule. . . . Mr. Madison's talents should be employed to bring forth amendments, which, at best can have little effect upon the merits of the constitution. And may sow the seeds of discord from New-Hampshire to Georgia."[9]

Soon after the Constitutional Convention ended, individuals and organizations began calling for amendments or changes in the Constitution. A long complaint from the Pennsylvania minority members especially railed against convention secrecy: "The proposed plan had not many hours issued from the womb of suspicious secrecy, until such as were prepared for the purpose, were carrying about petitions for people to sign, signifying their approbation of the system, and requesting the legislature to call a convention . . . and *tar and feathers* were liberally promised to all those who would not immediately join in supporting the proposed government."[10]

Madison accepted a delay in the timetable so that the tariff act could be debated. Then, on June 8—the day he wrote his notes—he "moved the house to go into a committee of the whole in order to take into consideration" the amendments he had selected: the embryonic Bill of Rights. He launched his motion with a 5,100-word speech in which he said that "this house is bound by every motive of prudence, not to let the first session pass over without proposing to the state legislatures some things to be incorporated into the constitution, as will render it as acceptable to the whole people of the United States, as it has been found acceptable to a majority of them." He also admitted that he had changed his mind about "what may be called a bill of rights," primarily because "the people of many states, have thought it necessary to raise barriers against power in all forms."[11]

Of the nearly two hundred amendments and alterations submitted by the states, many were duplications. So, when Madison decided to produce his set of potential changes, he had about one hundred to choose from.[12] His selections had to be acceptable to two-thirds of the House and Senate, and then they had to be approved by three-quarters of the states. He assembled a set of seventeen potential changes and, after a series of delays, presented them to the Committee of the Whole House for debate and vote on July 21. Later, by a vote of thirty-four to fifteen, the issue would be transferred to a select committee consisting of one member from each state. Madison was Virginia's member.

Madison's first proposal was his own creation and was designed to precede the Constitution's great "We the People" preamble. His words were to be "prefixed to the constitution" and declare that "all power is originally rested in, and consequently derived from, the people." The preamble also said, "Government is instituted and ought to be exercised for the benefit of the people; which consists in the enjoyment of life and liberty, with the right of acquiring and using property, and generally of pursuing and obtaining happiness and safety." Madison's words were voted down, as was a proposed amendment promising a federal guarantee of rights against violation by the states. Another amendment would prohibit a sitting Congress from raising its members' salary. That one passed.

Most of the rest of Madison's proposals had to do with personal rights. One of the proposals most debated (and hotly debated still) was designated number six in the committee report of July 28: "*A well regulated militia, composed of the body of the people, being the best security of a free State, the right of the people to keep and bear arms shall not be infringed, but no person religiously scrupulous shall be compelled to bear arms.*" Representative Gerry moved that "*trained to arms*" be inserted, but no one seconded the motion. And Madison had not selected a suggested amendment from New Hampshire: "Congress shall never disarm any Citizen unless such as are or have been in Actual Rebellion."[13]

Jackson moved, at the suggestion of Representative William Smith of South Carolina, to change this phrase to "No one, religiously scrupulous of bearing arms, shall be compelled to render military service in person, upon paying an equivalent." This was rejected, twenty-four to twenty-two.

Then Representative Aedanus Burke of South Carolina moved that the following words be inserted into the bearing-arms amendment: "A standing army of regular troops in time of peace, is dangerous to public liberty, and such shall not be raised or kept up in time of peace but from necessity, and for the security of the people, nor then without the consent of two-thirds of the members present of both houses, and in all cases the military shall be subordinate to the civil authority."

The "standing army" insert was discarded by what the House report called "a majority of thirteen" without indicating the actual number of pro and con votes.[14] Questions about the need for a standing army would frequently reverberate in the First Congress, but in their assay of Madison's proposals, the representatives did not linger over issues. They went through his articles one by one, changing a word here, a phrase there, or suggesting a string of words that would make a major difference in the article.

Motions and soaring oratory poured forth from both Federalists and Anti-Federalists for weeks. One seemingly minor suggestion from Representative Roger Sherman of Connecticut was accepted: place the amendments at the end of the Constitution as supplements. That became the precedent for all the amendments that would follow—and it would have the effect of enshrining the Bill of Rights as a document separate from the Constitution.

"We cannot incorporate these amendments in the body of the Constitution," Sherman said. "It would be mixing brass, iron, and clay." Later in the debate that he had inspired, he said, "The amendments reported are a declaration of rights, the people are secure in them whether we declare them or not."[15] The debate dragged on, occasionally flaring into language that could have inspired challenges for duels. But, as one observer noted, "The maxim here [is] that no member of the legislature is responsible outside for what he said in the course of the debates."[16]

A phrase in one of the articles—"*Congress shall make no law respecting an establishment of religion*"—touched off a short, fervent debate. Representative Daniel Carroll of Maryland, a signer of the Declaration of Independence and a prominent Catholic, welcomed recognition of "Rights of conscience." But Representative Benjamin Huntington of Connecticut, a Congregationalist, feared that the article actually endangered religion because it might touch on local laws that enforced tithing. Madison suggested that "national" be inserted before "religion." Gerry rose quickly and challenged the word "national" because it suggested a "consolidated" nation, thus lessening and weakening state power. Madison promptly withdrew the word, insisting that he had not meant to imply "a national government."[17]

Much of the debates had to do with extremely minor matters, such as Burke's motion to change the word "vicinage" to "district or county" in a phrase regarding the right of the accused to a trial where the crime was committed. Burke wanted language that was "conformable to the practice of the state of South Carolina." (The phrase ultimately became "*district wherein the crime shall have been committed.*")

Another word-change motion came from Burke's fellow South Carolinian, Thomas Tudor Tucker, a foe of Madison's twelfth amendment: "*The powers not delegated to the United States by the Constitution, nor prohibited by it to the States, are reserved to the States respectively.*" Tucker wanted "expressly" inserted so that the phrase would read, "*The powers not expressly delegated by this constitution . . .*" Madison objected and, according to the *Gazette of the United States* report, said it was "impossible to confine a government to the exercise of express powers," and so "there must necessarily be admitted powers by implication, unless the constitution descended to recount every minutiae."[18]

Knowing that he had little chance of making any significant changes, Tucker nevertheless moved for the acceptance of a cherished Anti-Federalist amendment: "The congress shall never impose direct taxes, but where the moneys arising from the duties, imposts, and excise, are insufficient." To Anti-Federalists, a direct tax—one on income or profits, rather than on goods or services—was an abomination. Representative Samuel Livermore of New Hampshire, a Federalist who sided with the Anti-Federalists, called the tax proposal the most important of all the amendments to be debated in the House. As for the rest of them, he said, his constituents "would not value them more than a pinch of snuff."[19]

After long debate, the tax amendment was voted down, as were four more fruitless Anti-Federalist attempts to change Madison's seventeen-article package. Finally, on August 24, the House passed a joint resolution containing seventeen "articles" rather than "amendments" and sent them to the Senate in the form of three broadsides: large sheets of paper printed on one side. The broadsides, which survive in the National Archives, bear brown-ink blots, cross-outs, inserts, and scrawled strings of words that show the changes made by the senators as they rephrased and whittled down the House's seventeen articles.[20]

Senator Maclay was uncharacteristically taciturn in his diary about debates over the articles, which he rightly called amendments. Because of illness, he had missed most of debates. He wrote only that the amendments had been "treated contemptuously" by Senator Ralph Izard of South Carolina (as usual, referred to as "Z" by Maclay), Senator John Langdon of New Hampshire, Dalton, and Senator Robert Morris of Pennsylvania. They wanted to postpone consideration of the amendments until the second session, which would begin in January 1790. The motion was voted down.[21]

Under the rules established by the First Congress, the House and Senate then formed a Conference Committee to produce the final document, which would be presented to President Washington for signature or veto. The House appointed Madison, Sherman, and John Vining of Delaware; the Senate's members were Carroll, Oliver Ellsworth of Connecticut, and William Paterson of New Jersey. The House agreed to reduce its seventeen articles to the twelve that contained the senators' rearrangements, rewrites, and editing.

The House and Senate treated the amendments as they would a regular piece of legislation and submitted their joint bill to President Washington. He signed it, and on October 2 sent it off to the governors of the states as "amendments proposed to be added to the Constitution of the United States." As a courtesy, he also sent copies to Rhode Island and North Carolina, which could not ratify the amendments because they had not yet accepted the Constitution.

New Jersey and Delaware were the first states to ratify the amendments; by January 1790, Maryland, South Carolina, and New Hampshire had done the same. In November 1789, North Carolina ratified both the Constitution and the amendments, and Rhode Island followed in May 1790. They fulfilled Madison's prophecy that the amendments would lure them back into the Union. By March 1791, with Vermont in the Union, the two-thirds ratification requirement changed from nine out of thirteen to ten out of fourteen. On December 15, 1791, Virginia became the tenth state to ratify, making the Bill of Rights the law of the land.

Two of the twelve amendments submitted to the states failed to get sufficient ratifications. One, which involved a system for establishing the number of representatives, was never seen again. The other, which concerned pay for representatives and senators, lived on to become the Twenty-seventh Amendment in 1992.*

---

* In 1982, Gregory D. Watson, a sophomore at the University of Texas-Austin, while searching for a topic for a paper, discovered that Madison's Second Article ("No law varying the compensation for the services of the Senators and Representatives shall take effect, until an election of Representatives shall have intervened") had been ratified by Maryland, North Carolina, South Carolina, Delaware, Vermont, and Virginia between 1789 and 1791. Kentucky, entering the Union in 1792, ratified the article, probably to show acceptance of the Bill of Rights. Ohio (1803) and Wyoming (1890) ratified the Madison article to protest Congressional salary increases. Watson's professor gave him a C. But Watson pressed on, finding that the Supreme Court had ruled in 1939 there was no deadline for ratification of the amendment.

Urged on by then-Senator William Cohen, Maine ratified it in 1983, and Colorado in 1984. Watson began a writing campaign to state legislatures, urging ratification. In 1992, the U.S. archivist, who administers the ratification process certified that the required thirty-eight states had ratified the amendment, and it joined all the preceding twenty-six. At first people thought that Michigan's May 7, 1992 ratification was the thirty-eighth. But, years later, the fact that Kentucky had in fact ratified it in 1792, a detail that essentially had been forgotten, was rediscovered. That meant that the amendment had passed muster on May 5, 1992 when Alabama ratified. Missouri had acted mere hours earlier on the same day. Due to this muddle, various sources list different states in reporting which one put this amendment over the top.

Sources: *Archivist certification of the Twenty-seventh Amendment, May 18, 1992,* https://catalog.archives.gov/id/1512313. Accessed August 31, 2017.

See also National Constitution Center, "Congressional Compensation," https://constitutioncenter.org/interactive-constitution/amendments/amendment-xxvii. Accessed November 3, 2017.

See also http://tennesseestar.com/2018/08/02/exclusive-the-202-year-ratification-saga-of-the-27th-amendment/ accessed June 15, 2019.

"HE SHALL HAVE POWER"

Under constitutional instructions, the First Federal Congress built itself, along with the judiciary system and the presidency. Compared to Congress and the creation of the courts, the presidency might seem much simpler: it was embodied in one man whose powers were well described. But that first Congress was always there, hovering over that first president.

Look what happened when Washington issued the first presidential proclamation on the decidedly noncontroversial issue of Thanksgiving. In September 1789, Representative Elias Boudinot of New Jersey introduced a resolution calling on the House to ask the President to recommend to the people of the United States a day of public thanksgiving and prayer, acknowledging God's help in the creation of the Constitution.

Aedanus Burke and Thomas Tudor Tucker, both representatives from South Carolina, both hammered the idea. Burke "did not like this mimicking of European customs" while Tucker thought the House "had no business to interfere in a matter which did not concern them."[1] He went on to wonder how people could give thanks for a Constitution "until they have experienced that it promotes their safety and happiness." Anyway, he continued, "it is a religious matter, and, as such, is proscribed to us. If a day of thanksgiving must take place, let it be done by the authority of the several States."[2] Once again, the quest for states' rights fueled criticism of a strong central government.

Washington ignored the opposition, sending each governor a proclamation making Thursday, November 26, a day "devoted by the People of these States to the service of that great and glorious Being, who is the beneficent Author of all the good that was, that is, or that will be."

Most newspapers printed the proclamation and many churches used Thanksgiving Day an occasion for seeking donations to aid the poor. One donor was Washington, who contributed "twenty five dollars to be applied towards relieving the poor of the Presbyterian Churches."[3]

The First Congress assured that its accomplishments would be known to contemporaries and posterity by publishing a book. One copy of it became particularly of interest to the new president.

After the first session ended, on September 29, the First Congress ordered the printing of six hundred copies of a 105-page book containing the texts of all the acts passed during the first session.[4] One of those books was unlike any of the others. It had an elegant binding, and on its cover, embossed in golden letters, was *President of the United States.* When he received the book, George Washington pasted his armorial bookplate to the front inside cover and penned his sweeping signature on the title page.

The book begins with a notice from the clerk of the House and the secretary of the Senate that the acts in the book were "prefixed" by "a correct Copy of the Constitution of the United States." The surprising word *correct* stemmed from the existence of two versions of the Constitution, one penned on parchment, the other printed. The differences were insignificant, but one had to be made official. Congress, as *Acts of Congress* shows, chose the printed version. This was the same copy of the Constitution sent to the states for the ratifications.[5] *

Some time after receiving his *Acts of Congress,* Washington opened his book to the correct Constitution, picked up a pencil, and wrote in the margin, something he rarely did. He read Article I, Section 7: *"Every bill which shall have passed the House of Representatives and the Senate, shall, before it become a law, be presented to the President of the United States. ... "* In the margin he drew a long, neat bracket alongside the words of Section 7 and wrote "President."

Section 7 continued on the next page: *"the votes of both Houses shall be determined by yeas and nays, and the names of the persons voting for and against the bill shall be entered on the journal of each House respectively. If any bill shall not be returned by the President within ten days (Sundays excepted) after it shall have been presented to him, the same shall be a law,* in like manner as if he had signed it, unless the Congress

---

*   See Appendix 1: The "Correct" Constitution of the United States.

by their adjournment prevent its return, in which case it shall not be a law." Again, in the margin, he placed a bracket and "President."

Section 7 ended on the next page and received a bracket and "President": *"Every order, resolution or vote to which the concurrence of the Senate and House of Representatives may be necessary . . . shall be presented to the President of the United States; and before the same shall take effect, shall be approved by him, or being disapproved by him, shall be re-passed by two-thirds of the Senate and House of Representatives."*

Article II, Section 1, of course, caught his eye: *"The executive Power shall be vested in a President of the United States of America. He shall hold his office during the term of four years, and, together with the Vice-President, chosen for the same term, be elected, as follows . . . "* Again he wrote "President" and added a bracket.

Alongside the long paragraph that began, *"The President shall be commander in chief of the army and navy of the United States, and of the militia of the several states . . . ,"* he wrote "President" and added a bracket. Then he added a word: *"Powers."*

Finally, at Article II, Section 3, he added a long bracket and added *"Required."* That paragraph said: *"He shall from time to time give to the Congress information of the State of the Union, and recommend to their consideration such measures as he shall judge necessary and expedient; he may on extraordinary occasions, convene both houses, or either of them, and in case of disagreement between them, with respect to the time of adjournment, he may adjourn them to such time as he shall think proper; he shall receive ambassadors and other public ministers; he shall take care that the laws be faithfully executed, and shall commission all the officers of the United States."*

His interpretation of what the Constitution expected of *the president* was in those seven marginal words. With a few presidential pencil strokes, he left to history his testimony: He saw a basic difference between the *power* the president is given and the presidential duties that are *"required."*

Deeper in *Acts of Congress, Washington* would find twenty-two pages dedicated to *"An act to regulate the COLLECTION of the DUTIES imposed by Law."* The act listed, state by state (except Rhode Island and North Carolina) the ports that must be used by ships bearing imported goods. For each of the dozens of ports, the act called for at least three federal appointees to inspect cargoes, calculate what was owed, and collect the tariff. Suddenly, for Washington, dispensing federal jobs was a *required presidential action.*

"The first thing done under our new Government," Senator Maclay wrote, "was the creation of a Vast number of Offices and Officers."[6] Applications had been pouring into Washington's office ever since Congress passed the tariff act. In fact, the Congress of the Confederation had begun the federal bureaucracy, which stumbled through handling the logistics and debts of the Revolutionary War. One of those government workers was twenty-two-year-old Joseph Nourse, sometimes called the "first federal worker," who had begun his government career in March 1776 as secretary to Continental Army General Charles Lee. In June 1777, Nourse became assistant clerk of the Board of War, the Congressional committee that handled finances for the military. He remained in the fiscal side of government and in 1781 became register of the Treasury under the Confederation Congress and eventually serving under Robert Morris, superintendent of finance.

On September 11, 1789, Tobias Lear handed to Vice President Adams for perusal of the Senate a list of nominees for positions in the newly created Treasury Department, beginning with Alexander Hamilton for secretary. On the list was Joseph Nourse to continue as register of the Treasury under the new Federal Constitution. Next day, the Senate approved all the appointees. Nourse would remain in federal service as a Treasury executive through the administrations of George Washington, John Adams, Thomas Jefferson, James Madison, James Monroe, and John Q. Adams. Finally, in 1828, President Andrew Jackson, in a political move that included claims of malfeasance, fired Nourse, ending a fifty-two-year federal career that made him a symbol of bureaucratic durability.[7]

Nourse was one of nearly one thousand individuals that Washington nominated and sent to the Senate. Most of the men were nominated to fill the jobs that stemmed from the Tariff Act. Washington depended upon Hamilton, Madison, and other political advisers for some of the nominations, but he favored his former comrades in arms whatever their politics. One of the applications was from Peter L'Enfant, designer of Federal Hall. He reminded Washington of his military service as an army engineer and asked for a chance to design "the Capital of this vast Empire." His plan would be "drawn on such a scale as to leave room for that aggrandizement & embellishment which the increase of the wealth of the nation will permit it to pursue." He also volunteered to design fortifications for American ports and suggested that he be named "Engineer to the United States."[8]

L'Enfant's request to design a grand city came just as the House was in the midst of a debate about where to locate the seat of government, also known as the permanent residence of Congress. L'Enfant would have to be patient. So would members of Congress and all the other Americans who were wondering where the federal government was going to be next.

By the time Washington made his marginal notes about *Power* and what was *Required,* he had learned lessons that were not written in the Constitution. And he knew, as he told Madison, that he dealt with "the first of every thing," establishing precedents that "may be fixed on true principles."[9] In his relationship with the Senate, at least twice he did not establish precedents. They were imposed upon him by the Senate.

Both the House and the Senate had worked out protocols for dealing with each other and with the president. For instance, the doorkeeper of the Senate was instructed to admit the clerk of the House, rather than House members. As for the president, when he had to deliver a document to the Senate, he gave it to twenty-seven-year-old Tobias Lear, the first presidential chief of staff. Lear signed himself "S.P.U.S.," for "Secretary to the President of the United States." He controlled access to the president, and often drafted Washington's speeches.[10] Lear based his influence on the invention of a phrase that subsequent chiefs of staff would use to declare their place in the power structure: "The president has directed me to . . . ."

As Washington accumulated nominations, he listed the names in a series of documents he sent, through Lear, to the gentlemen of the Senate. The president was carrying out a Constitutional mandate: "He shall have Power" to nominate not only ambassadors and high-level officials but also "inferior Officers," such as tariff collectors and Treasury clerks—but only "with the Advice and Consent of the Senate." The handing of the lists to Lear for delivery became routine. The Senate approved the presidential nominations, batch by batch, day after day. Then, on August 3, Washington handed Lear a seven-page routine list of nominees, each with his assigned port and position. Soon after Lear presented the list, the senators went over the names and a clerk noted the Senate vote by writing *Aye* next to each name.

When the list was returned to Washington, *Aye* appeared next to every name except one: Benjamin Fishbourn, nominated for the naval officer of Savannah, Georgia, a post he already held as an appointee of the governor. No reason was given for the rejection of Fishbourn, a member of the Society of the Cincinnati who had served as an aide-de-camp to General Anthony Wayne. Fishbourn had been warmly endorsed by Wayne.[11]

The rejection of Fishbourn stunned Washington.

What happened next probably would have remained undocumented by the secretive Senate. Maclay certainly would have commented, but he was absent because of illness on the day of the rejection. History had to wait until 1933, when a book culled from "the records and accounts of Tobias Lear" revealed what Tobias's son, Benjamin Lincoln Lear, knew about the incident. Benjamin's recollection came in the form of an 1818 letter to the *National Intelligencer:* after learning of the rejection, "The President immediately repaired to the Senate Chambers & entered, to the astonishment of every one." The Lear account continues,

> The Vice-President left his chair & offered it to the President, who accepted it & then told the Senate that he had come to ask their reasons for rejecting his nomination of Collector &c. After many minutes of embarrassing silence, Genl. [James] Gunn rose and said, that as he had been the person who had first objected to the nomination, & had probably been the cause of its rejection, it was perhaps his office to speak on this occasion. That his personal respect for the personal character of Genl. Washington was such that he would inform him of his grounds for recommending this rejection, (and he did so,) but that he would have it distinctly understood to be the sense of the Senate, that no explanation of their motives or proceedings was ever due or would ever be

given to any President of the United States. Upon which the President withdrew.[12]

Senator Gunn of Georgia despised Fishbourn and almost certainly disparaged him in the later private conversation with Washington. The feud between Gunn and Fishbourn began during the war, when they were fellow officers. In 1785, Gunn had challenged Major General Nathanael Greene to a duel, and somehow that had led to an "affair of honor" between Fishbourn and Gunn. The Fishbourn-Gunn duel was stopped by the "Interference of the seconds" and mediated. When Gunn saw a chance to deny Fishbourn a job, he did so. Greene's wife, Catharine, once called Gunn "the Most ignorant and infamous fellow in the whole army," an assessment, she indicated, that was shared by many.[13]

Without revealing what Gunn had told him, Washington reacted by sending Tobias Lear back to the Senate with a letter that lavishly praised Fishbourn, as a wartime officer, a member of the Georgia legislature, and a man already working faithfully as a state employee. Washington also icily suggested that "where the propriety of Nominations appear questionable to you, it would not be expedient to communicate that circumstance to me, and thereby avail yourselves of the information which led me to make them, and which I would with pleasure lay before you."[14]

To replace Fishbourn, Washington nominated Lachlan McIntosh, a controversial Georgian veteran of the Revolutionary War and a member of the Society of the Cincinnati. As a brigadier general during the war, he had clashed with his military and political rival Button Gwinnett, a signer of the Declaration of Independence. Much of the state had been a Loyalist sanctuary under British control. Gwinnett, the state executive officer for Georgia, arrested the brother of General Lachlan McIntosh for treason, an act that inspired a pistol duel on May 16, 1777. Both the general and Gwinnett were wounded; Gwinnett died a few days afterward. McIntosh reentered Georgia politics after the war and became a Gunn ally.[15]

Two members of the First Federal Congress had fought a duel before their Federal service. In 1782, State House Representative Ralph Izard of South Carolina, known as "planter-boss of the lowcountry," used his power to prevent the election of Thomas Tudor Tucker to the state body. This led to a duel, which ended with Tucker shot in the left leg. Both men continued to engage in the state's rough-and-tumble politics and both were elected to elected to the historic Congress, Izard as a senator and Tucker as a Representative.[16]

Three weeks after he had stormed into the Senate chamber, Washington calmly returned, saying he was seeking "advice and consent" about a Native American treaty he wished to sign. Again he chose to sit in John Adams's canopied chair, and Adams retreated to the desk of the secretary of the Senate. This time Senator Maclay was present. Later, in his erratically punctuated prose, he recorded a long description of the scene: "The President . . . rose and told us bluntly that he had called on Us for our advice and consent to some propositions respecting the Treatie with the Southern Indians." Washington had brought along Secretary of War Henry Knox, who handed a paper to Adams, followed by an Native American agent's report he had just received. Adams read the report aloud. "Carriages were driving past and such a Noise" was coming through the open windows, Maclay continued, "I could tell it was something about indians, but was not master of one Sentence about it."[17]

The paper that Washington had brought ended with seven points about the treaty. He wanted the senators to advise and consent by responding aye or no, point by point. After the president read the first point, Maclay's Pennsylvania colleague, Senator Robert Morris, rose and said that "the Noise of carriages had been so great that he really could not say that he had heard." Washington read the words again "and put the Question do you advise and consent &ca. There was a dead pause. Mr. Morris wispered to me, we will see who will venture to break silence first. . . . I rose reluctantly indeed, and . . . it appeared to me, that if I did not, no other one would. and we should have these advices and consents ravish'd."

After saying Native American treaties were "new to the Senate" and "it is our duty to inform ourselves as well as possible," Maclay asked for time so that the senators could read the documents and then records, "I cast an Eye at the President of the United States [and] I saw he wore an aspect of Stern displeasure." But the president and Knox continued to read documents, the words droning on. Several senators vaguely commented on the treaty or suggested that the treaty and accompanying papers be handed over to a committee. Maclay rose again and, "in a low tone of Voice," proposed a postponement until Monday.

When Maclay sat down, "the President started up in a Violent fret. *This defeats every purpose of my coming here,* were the first words that he said. . . . We waited for him to withdraw, he did so with a discontented Air. . . . I cannot now be mistaken the President wishes to tread on the Necks of the Senate."

Two days later, Washington returned—"placid and Serene and manifested a Spirit of Accomodation"—to witness the Senate's approval of the treaty. "Yet a shamefaceness, or I know not what flowing from the presence of the President kept every body silent." The president, however, did not remain silent, According to another source: "He said he would be damned if he ever went there again."[18]

A short while after the president left, the doorkeeper asked Maclay to step out of the chamber and speak to Washington's aide David Humphreys. "It was to invite me to dinner with the President," Maclay wrote. He dutifully accepted. But "all the dinners he can nor give or ever could, will make no difference in my Conduct."[19]

Washington had produced another precedent by accepting the reality that would be accepted by every president who followed him: "as the President has a right to nominate without assigning his reasons, so has the Senate a right to dissent without giving theirs."[20] Ever since his third—and last—visit to the Senate, presidents, with their Cabinet members and advisers, have negotiated treaties and then submitted them to the Senate for ratification.

Early in his presidency, Washington wrote, "In our progress towards political happiness my station is new; and . . . I walk on untrodden ground. There is scarcely any part of my conduct wch. may not hereafter be drawn into precedent."[21] Ahead on that ground many Americans still saw the vision of a king. A South Carolinian congressman, for instance, wrote, "Verily I believe that a very great Proportion are ripe for a King & would salute the President as such with all the Folly of Enthusiasm."[22]

Many hours of the first session were devoted to examining and interpreting Article II of the Constitution: *"The executive Power shall be vested in a President of the United States.*" Debate over definition of *executive power* and *President* often took members of Congress down the road to *monarchy*. Congress contributed to the fears of monarchy by borrowing rules and procedure from the British Parliament. For example, when an "affair of honor" threatened to evolve into a duel between Representative Aedanus Burke of South Carolina and Alexander Hamilton, the First Congress turned to an intervention used in Parliament: an unofficial committee of senators and representatives negotiated an honorable solution and prevented a duel.[23]

Washington himself added to the image of monarchy with his grand six-horse carriage, his liveried servants, and his glamorous levees, which often had the look of a royal court. And, when Federalists argued that the president had the right not only to appoint officials but also to remove them from office, Anti-Federalists cried monarchy. The power to dismiss officials, said Representative James Jackson of Georgia, "may hold good in Europe where monarchs claim their powers *jure divino* [by divine right], but it never can be admitted in America."[24]

"That every Part of the Conduct and feelings of the Americans tends to that Species of Republick called a limited Monarchy I agree," wrote John Adams to Benjamin Rush, physician, philosopher, and a signer of the Declaration of Independence. "They were born and brought up in it. Their Habits are fixed in it: but their Heads are most miserably bewildered about it."[25]

Washington had heard the monarchy chatter, and he knew he had to end it because it was hurtful to the new nation. He decided that if Americans could see him—and if he could see and talk to them—perhaps they would see that a president was not a king. Once Congress was between sessions, and he was free to travel, he would eventually journey to all the states—but he would begin with the ones he knew the least: the states of the North. But any such journeying would have to wait until Congress was out of session.

That would not happen until the autumn of 1789. In the meantime, summer would see America come close to losing her newly installed leader—and see her greatest ally descend into chaos.

14

STRICKEN WASHINGTON, FEARFUL NATION

In mid-June 1789, a few weeks after the flags and the cannons and the bells had celebrated the inauguration of George Washington, word began to spread that he was deathly ill, the victim of a "slow fever" that struck during an influenza epidemic sweeping across the city. White men then had a life expectancy of thirty-six and a half years.[1] They knew they were stalked by early death—and that a long fever often was a sign of the coming of the end.

At the time, death at birth or in early infancy claimed four children in ten. Smallpox, cholera, and tropical fevers periodically ravaged the adult population. Death did not care for rank or social station, either. Ben Franklin suffered through many diseases; long plagued by boils that covered much of his body, he attempted to eradicate them with mercury pills, which not only failed but also caused him to lose three teeth. Of Abigail Adams's six children, one was stillborn, and the second lived only thirteen months. George Washington himself, though he had no children, lost his beloved stepdaughter "Patsy" (Martha Parke Custis) to epilepsy at age seventeen. His stepson "Jacky" (John Parke Custis) had survived childhood only to fall victim to "camp fever" (typhus) at age twenty-six, soon after he joined his stepfather at Yorktown.[2]

Washington's personal life expectancy was not long. His grandfather had died at thirty-seven, his father at forty-nine, most likely from one of many untreatable infectious diseases.[3] But luckily for Washington, he suffered from a treatable ailment and was the patient of Samuel Bard, the family doctor for many prominent New Yorkers, including the Hamiltons and their children.[4] And Bard had been trained in Edinburgh, the era's mark of a physician's excellence.[5]

Bard examined the source of Washington's intense pain—a carbuncle on his left thigh—and deduced that the fever was a reaction
to "anthrax," which then meant the cause of a carbuncle "that arises in
several Parts surrounded with fiery, sharp, and painful Pimples."[6] Bard,
fearing that lethal gangrene would soon set in, decided to remove the
carbuncle immediately. To aid in the operation, he called in another
distinguished New York physician: his retired seventy-three-year-old
father, Doctor John Bard.

While the younger Bard was alone with the president, Washington
asked for a frank opinion of his chances. "Do not flatter me with vain
hopes," Washington demanded, "I am not afraid to die, and therefore
can bear the worst." Bard replied that he was hopeful but had apprehensions. "Whether tonight or twenty years hence makes no difference," Washington responded. "I know that I am in the hands of a good
Providence."[7]

On June 17, in a room of the presidential residence on Cherry Street,
Washington lay, fully conscious, as the elder Bard took up a knife to
begin. But, according to a Washington family account, the physician,
"being somewhat doubtful of his nerves, gave the knife to his son, bid-
ding him 'cut away—deeper, deeper still; don't be afraid you see how
well he bears it.'"[8] The younger Bard cut out the carbuncle, leaving a
deep wound. The fever soon faded away and the wound slowly healed.
Streets around Washington's residence were strung with ropes to prevent coaches from nosily passing by and disturbing the recovering president. Straw was strewn on the sidewalk to muffle footsteps.

Madison had assured Attorney General Edmund Jennings Randolph
on June 24 that the operation was a success "and the alarm is now over."
Ever the politician, Madison coolly added, "His death at the present
moment would have brought on another crisis in our affairs."[9]

In May 1790, a severe form of pneumonia felled Washington, and
again there were cries of crisis, warnings that the Republic was
doomed. Secretary of State Thomas Jefferson told a friend, "We have
been very near losing the President."[10] Abigail Adams, realizing that
Washington's life was entwined with the life and destiny of America,
wrote that "the union of the States, and consequently the permanency

of the Government, depend upon his life. . . . His death would, I fear, have had most disastrous consequences." [11]

Fear of his death arose from the widespread belief that only Washington could guide the new Republic. And rooted deep in the people was the realization that, for everyone, death was ever nigh.

Abigail Adams reported that Washington had been treated with James's Fever Powder, an English nostrum touted as a cure not only for fever but also for gout, scurvy, and distemper in cattle.[12] The powder was prescribed for King George III's cataracts, rheumatism, and dementia. In 1791, an esteemed British physician discovered that the powder's secret formula was a mix of calcium phosphate, the main mineral of bone, and antimony, which is toxic and potentially fatal.[13] Washington's illness, which began with a bad cold, was diagnosed as influenza worsening into pneumonia. James Madison, who had just recovered from influenza himself, described Washington's illness as "peripneumony united probably with the Influenza."[14]

An influenza epidemic was sweeping through much of the country when Washington was struck. New York was particularly hard hit. Senator Richard Henry Lee of Virginia described the city as "a perfect Hospital—few are well & many very sick—among the latter is unfortuneately placed our most worthy P. of the U.S."[15] Maclay wrote to Dr. Benjamin Rush as an authority on epidemics. In a characteristically wandering commentary on both Congress and Washington, the Senator said, "Our Proceedings are slow beyond all bearing. . . . The Spring is very backward at this place. And let me add very Unhealthy. The influenza is almost Universal, and has been in some instances Mortal. The President of the U.S. is so affected by it as to have nearly lost his hearing. The effect this place has had on him is visible to every one. such a change has taken place on him in the last year, as seems plainly to say the Measure of his life, will not fill his first Presidency."[16]

In early April of 1790, concern over Washington's illness was the major topic in Congress. Representative Richard Bland Lee of Virginia told David Stuart, a longtime Washington friend, that "the President has been unwell for a few days past." Soon afterward, according to Pennsylvania Representative George Clymer, Washington's condition had worsened. "I do not know the exact state of GW's health for a day or two last," Clymer wrote, "but it is observed here with a great deal of anxiety that his general health seems to be declining. For some time past he has been subject to a slow fever." Representative Theodore Sedgwick of Massachusetts reported on May 16, "About five oclock in the afternoon yesterday, the physicians disclosed that they had no hopes of his recovery. But about six he began to sweat most profusely, which continued untill this morning and we are now told that he is entirely out of danger, if he should not relapse." [17]

Another House member, Representative John Page of Virginia, wrote, "The Whole city nay whole Countries around us, have been & still are suffering under the Influenza, or Catahral [catarrhal] Fever," including the President, whose "Life was yesterday despaired of." Page called on him and "had the Pleasure to find that his Disorder had taken the happy turn."[18]

"The Influenza is an amazingly irksome Disorder—I have been plagued off and on for a month" and have "almost habitual Sore Eyes," wrote Maryland Representative Michael Jenifer Stone in mid-May. "The President is mending so Slowly that it is three Days now since the Doctors pronounced him out of Danger and he is not yet (unless within a few Hours) out of Bed."[19]

Just as he had done after his bout with pneumonia in 1789, Washington decided that a tour would cure him of his ills. His journey was "contrary to the advise of his Friends," Abigail Adams wrote. But off he went, and for a while his personal prescription of vigorous exercise seemed to work. Robert Morris reported to his wife that he had attended a levee and saw Washington, "who . . . has regained his looks, his appetite & his Health."[20]

In this era, thousands of Americans depended upon a British physician's book for their day-to-day medicine. *Buchan's Domestic Medicine or The Family Physician* advertised itself as "showing people what is in their own power, both with respect to the prevention and cure of diseases."[21] The first edition of William Buchan's book was published in 1769; eighty thousand copies, in nineteen British and American editions, were printed before his death in 1805.[22]

"I think the administration of medicine always doubtful," Buchan wrote, "and often dangerous, and would much rather teach men how to avoid the necessity of using them, than how they should be used." He was particularly critical of the "high living" of the wealthy. "We seldom find a barren woman among the labouring poor," he wrote, "while nothing is more common amongst the rich and affluent. The inhabitants of every country are prolific in proportion to their poverty, and it would be an easy matter to adduce many instances of women who, by being reduced to live entirely upon a milk and vegetable diet, have conceived and brought forth children, though they never had any before."[23]

Buchan's distrust of medicine did not discourage the widespread use of natural cure-alls or the public's faith in medicine peddlers. The bark of the cinchona tree (also known as Peruvian bark or Jesuit's bark) had been a cure available in North America since the 1720s. The basis for quinine, it was used for recurring fevers and other symptoms similar to malaria.[24]

Belief extended to all classes. Representative Roger Sherman, signer of the Declaration of Independence and the Constitution, excitedly wrote his wife to say, "I have got a new medicine for the toothake & other disorders. . . . I have also the name of a person on long Island who cures cancers."[25] Senator William Maclay's cure for rheumatism included "a tea Spoonful full of the Flour of Brimston taken every Morning before Breakfast."[26] Purges of bitter, foul-smelling asafetida, the dried latex exuded from the tap root of the tall flowering plant of that name, were popular in the eighteenth century. The substance can still be found on the modern medicine market today, in the form of a hard, resinous gum, which, among other benefits, is touted as a cure for flatulence.[27]

Bleeding was a cure-all for nearly any ailment. A Rhode Island man who "Had a violent pain in the side," typically went to a doctor who "took about 20 ½ ounces" of blood.[28] Besides Washington, other believers included Abigail Adams and Ben Franklin. Benjamin Rush, the most famous physician of the time, treated almost any illness by removing prodigious amounts of blood from the patient.[29] By Rush's calculations, most people had twelve quarts of blood flowing through their bodies—an estimate twice the actual average amount. His fame spanned decades, as did his faith in bleeding. "To him," wrote a modern medical historian, "more than any other man in America, was due the great vogue of vomits, purging, and especially of bleeding, salivation and blistering, which blackened the record of medicine and afflicted the sick almost to the time of the Civil War."[30]

He frequently he took five quarts from his patients in two days. British journalist William Cobbett wrote that Rush's bleeding was "one of those great discoveries which have contributed to the depopulation of the earth." [31] That was one of the accusations that inspired Rush to sue Cobbett for libel—successfully. Rush's victory in court extended the use of bleeding. For supporters of bleeding, such as George Washington, the blood would keep flowing out of them until their final days.

Even as President Washington was recovering from the first of his illnesses, a foreign crisis was brewing. Across the Atlantic, America's ally, France, inspired by America's successful Revolution, was suddenly convulsed by its own rebellion against monarchy. And there, the blood would flow in horrifying abundance.

15

WASHINGTON GETS A BASTILLE KEY

On July 14, 1789, the French Revolution exploded. A huge wild mob stormed a symbol of tyranny, the Bastille, releasing prisoners and killing the prison's commanding officer and then parading through Paris with his head on a pike. The Marquis de Lafayette took command of a national guard mustered to keep order and, as a symbol of freedom, was given the major key to the Bastille. In France, July 14, a day of blood and terror, would become known as National Day, Bastille Day—or, to Americans, the French Fourth of July.

Thomas Paine, who was visiting Paris and planning to return to the United States, agreed to present the key to Washington, along with a drawing of the demolished Bastille. Lafayette arranged for a ceremony in a former royal garden near the Tuileries Palace. Paine—who was becoming entangled in the French Revolution—accepted the key for delivery to Washington. Paine spoke briefly, asserting, with a touch of bravado, "The principles of America opened the Bastille."[1]

In London, Paine changed his plans and handed off "those trophies of liberty" to an American he had met. He was John Rutledge Jr., son of Associate Supreme Court Justice Rutledge, who would succeed John Jay as the court's second chief justice. The key and the drawing finally arrived at Washington's New York presidential residence, Macomb House, in August 1790.[2]

In a letter that had arrived earlier, Lafayette said, "Give me leave, My dear General, to present you With a picture of the Bastille just as it looked a few days after I Had ordered its demolition, with the Main Key of that fortress of despotism—it is a tribute Which I owe as A Son to My Adoptive father, as an aid de Camp to My General, as a Missionary of liberty to its patriarch."

The president first put the key on view at a Macomb House levee in his New York and showed it off again in Philadelphia, when the seat of government moved there in the fall of 1790. After Washington retired from the presidency in 1797, the key was enshrined at Mount Vernon in a windowed case in the first-floor passage. In 1858, John A. Washington III, the last of the family to reside at Mount Vernon, sold the property to the Mount Vernon Ladies' Association. Among the objects he donated was the Bastille Key, which still is hanging in the first-floor passage.[3]

A few weeks after he began his presidency, Washington knew that a revolution was brewing in France and Lafayette was in the midst of it.[4] "I am in great pain for the M. de la Fayette," Thomas Jefferson, America's ambassador to France, wrote Washington. "His principles you know are clearly with the people, but having been elected for the noblesse of Auvergne, they have laid him under express instructions" that "would ruin him with the *tiers etat* [Third Estate], whose radical advocates believed that France no longer had need for the other two estates stemming from the monarchy: the clergy and the aristocracy."

"I have not hesitated to press on him to burn his instructions & follow his conscience as the only sure clue which will eternally guide a man clear of all doubts & inconsistencies," Jefferson continued. "If he cannot effect a conciliatory plan, he will surely take his stand manfully at once with the tiers etat."[5]

To many Americans—especially former Continental Army officers who knew him in combat—Lafayette symbolized the link between America and France created by France's military aid during the Revolutionary War. As a major general, he had been the highest-ranking foreign volunteer in the Continental Army. He was wounded in the battle of Brandywine and served at such sites of valor as Valley Forge and Yorktown. Now, as revolution rumbled in his birthplace, he headed a relatively moderate party of liberals as vice president of the French National Assembly and commander of the National Guard.

Washington and Lafayette often treated themselves as aloof father and worshipful son. But Washington seemed even more aloof than usual on October 14, 1789, in his first letter to Lafayette since becoming president. He wrote "more with a view of assuring you that you are still remembered by me with affection—than with an intent to convey any political intelligence." Washington said that the French Revolution "is of such magnitude and of so momentous a nature that we hardly yet dare to form a conjecture about it. We however trust, and fervently pray that its consequences may prove happy to a nation . . . and that its influence may be felt with pleasure by future generations."[6]

By the time Washington had written his wishful letter, Paris streets were bristling with poles upon which were heads of nobles and others murdered as enemies of the people. At the time, news from France took six weeks or more to reach New York. So, as the French revolutionaries turned against Lafayette, Washington and members of Congress were hailing the revolution, which, they believed, would end in peaceful treaty negotiations, like America's.

Hamilton and Jefferson, already clashing over their views of America's Federalist destiny, also had opposing views of the French Revolution. Hamilton urged a hands-off policy, maintaining that Britain would stop trade with America if the Washington administration favored France. Jefferson wanted America to support French citizens and honor the U.S. treaty of alliance with France. In August 1789 he even allowed revolutionaries to meet and plot in his Paris residence.[7] [8]

In 1792, Washington appointed Gouverneur Morris U.S. Minister Plenipotentiary to France—an ambassadorial choice narrowly confirmed by the Senate. In a remarkably candid message that contained inserted observations from then-Secretary of State Jefferson, Washington told Morris why the Senate's advice and consent was so slight: "Whilst your abilities, knowledge in the affairs of this country and disposition to serve it were adduced and asserted on one hand, the levity and imprudence of your conversation, and in many instances of your conduct were as severely arraigned on the other . . . your mode of expression was imperious, contemptuous and disgusting to those who might happen to differ from you in opinion: and among a people who studied civility and politeness more than any other nation it must be displeasing.—

That in France you were considered as a favorer of Aristocracy, and unfriendly to it's revolution."[9]

In response, Morris wrote, "I make the Promise that my Sense of Integrity may enforce what my Sense of Propriety dictates."[10] Morris was a brilliant, unpredictable character. He had, for instance, done the final edit on the Preamble to the Constitution. The first draft read, in full: "We the People of the States of New–Hampshire, Massachusetts, Rhode-Island and Providence Plantations, Connecticut, New-York, New-Jersey, Pennsylvania, Delaware, Maryland, Virginia, North-Carolina, South-Carolina, and Georgia, do ordain, declare and establish the following Constitution for the Government of Ourselves and our Posterity."

Aside from it being leaden prose, there were other problems. It was not at all certain all the states would ratify the Constitution. Would the names of contrarian states need to be scratched out? Besides that, the Constitution provided for adding new states. Would those states want their names inserted? Morris removed all those headaches by deleting the list of state names and replacing that text with the immortal and lyric phrases that set down the purposes and intents of the document.[11]

A droll wit, he often made light of having one leg. He had lost his left leg in a carriage accident in Philadelphia. Fifteen years later in France, he was riding with a woman in an ornate carriage that attracted angry, anti-aristocratic revolutionaries who started shaking the carriage. Morris ended the threat by removing his peg leg, shoving it through the window, and waving it, shouting, "Vive la Révolution!" The revolutionaries cheered and the carriage sped away. [12]

Soon after promising Washington that he would be discreet as a diplomat, Morris became involved in a failed plan to help the royal family escape from Paris. Morris also found himself dealing with the imprisonment of a man who had been a hero of two revolutions, Thomas Paine.

Paine's *Common Sense*, which had helped to launch the American Revolution, had been translated into French, exporting to France an attack on monarchy and a desire for democracy. After the British condemned the French Revolution, Paine wrote *Rights of Man* in refutation and joined revolutionaries who were writing the French Constitution.

In the short celebratory phase of the revolution, Paine, Washington, Hamilton, and Madison were given honorary French citizenship. In Boston, a celebration of the French Revolution was the largest public event ever held in North America.[13]

But the abolition of the monarchy came in 1792, soon after the first executions by means of the newly invented guillotine. King Louis XVI and Marie Antoinette were put to death by guillotine in 1793. Paine, who had opposed the execution of the king, was arrested by the revolutionary government in December 1793 and awaited his own execution.

Morris, seeing Paine as a menace to America's delicate diplomacy, told French authorities that Paine—an England-born American with honorary French citizenship—could not officially pass as an American.[14] While Paine suffered through a fever in a dank prison, Morris gave him no support. In a haughty letter to Secretary Jefferson, Morris wrote, "Lest I should forget it, I must mention that Thomas Paine is in prison, where he amuses himself with publishing a pamphlet against Jesus Christ. I do not recollect whether I mentioned to you that he would have been executed along with the rest of the Brissotins if the advance party had not viewed him with contempt. I incline to think that if he is quiet in prison he may have the good luck to be forgotten."[15]

In November 1794, James Monroe, Morris's successor as ambassador, responded to Washington's urging to do something for "poor Paine." Morris seems to have been right when he predicted that Paine would be officially forgotten. Monroe was able to get him released. Paine remained in France until 1802, when, responding to an invitation from Thomas Jefferson, he returned to America. He was greeted with surprising loathing, inspired in part by certain of his writings, such as this paragraph:[16]

> I do not believe in the creed professed by the Jewish church, by the Roman church, by the Greek church, by the Turkish church, by the Protestant church, nor by any church that I know of. My own mind is my own church. All national institutions of churches, whether Jewish, Christian or Turkish, appear to me no other than human inventions, set up to terrify and enslave mankind, and monopolize power and profit.[17]

Lafayette had been going through his own ordeal. In August 1792, after the overthrow of the doomed Louis XVI, the Legislative Assembly impeached Lafayette. He was in the French Army, serving on the northern French border in a war against soldiers of a Prussia and Austria coalition. He fled, heading for a Dutch port in the hope of boarding a ship for America. But he was taken prisoner, despite his claim that his honorary status made him an American citizen. After being confined to several prisons, he was finally held in the Austrian fortress of Olmütz. His wife, Adrienne, and two daughters were eventually given permission to join him. Adrienne's mother, grandmother, and sister had been guillotined in 1794. Adrienne had been spared only because of American diplomatic warnings to France that the execution of Madame de Lafayette would turn Americans against France.

When Napoleon Bonaparte conquered Austria in 1797, a clause was added to the treaty calling for the release of Lafayette. An American diplomat in Hamburg was Lafayette's host on the night of his release on September 19, 1797. After spending two years in exile in Holland, he returned to France in 1799. [18]

The crisis begun by the French Revolution in 1789 would embroil American domestic and foreign politics for a decade. Again and again, confusing news that the revolution had ended came from Americans who had desperately boarded ships and fled the carnage. It was over in October 1789, when King Louis XVI appeared in Paris and was unharmed. Or it was over in July 1791, when the National Assembly moved against a mob demanding the end of monarchy. Or it was over in 1795, when a constitution appeared. But, as historian Peter McPhee writes, "In the end, it was Napoleon Bonaparte's seizure of power in December 1799 which was the most successful of such attempts to impose stability." [19]

In the autumn of 1789, however, no one could know how long the agonies of France would go on. In the meantime, President Washington was eager to get out and see his own people, and be seen by them. In so doing, he sought both to demonstrate and to reinforce a degree of domestic stability—and progress.

SEEING AMERICA'S FARMS AND FACTORIES

Talking to Hamilton one day in early October 1789, Washington said he wanted to tour what he called "the Eastern states" to learn "the temper and disposition of the Inhabitants towards the new government."[1] Hamilton urged him to make the trip, thinking it made for good politics. But, for the future of America, the most important reward for the trip was what would come when he would later tour southern states and see the contrast between the plantation South and the rapidly industrializing North—an amazing sight for the man of Mount Vernon. In one diary entry, he cites an unnamed Connecticut town as if it were a symbol of modern times: *"In this place there is but one Church, or in other words but one steeple—but there are Grist & saw Mills and a handsome Cascade over the Tumbling dam—the source of mill power."*[2]

By the end of the first session of Congress, Tobias Lear, the smart and ambitious secretary to the president of the United States, controlled access to Washington. Lear often drafted Washington's speeches, and kept him apprised of the mood of Congress.[3] Lear realized that people in New England were particularly suspicious about the loss of their states' sovereignty.

Washington accepted Lear's suggestion that the president's northern tour be a goodwill visit to New England, and Lear went to work drawing up an itinerary: north into Connecticut and Massachusetts, with a major stop in Boston, and a quick trip up the coast to Lear's hometown, Portsmouth, New Hampshire. Washington avoided Rhode Island, which was not part of the Union because it had not yet ratified the Constitution.[4]

Lear—and Washington—were well aware of the monarchy chatter in Congress. The President did not want his travel to resemble a royal progress with a long train, proceeding from fiefdom to fiefdom. He would travel in an open carriage with servants in livery, followed by a baggage wagon and his white horse. He usually chose to enter a welcoming town or city riding the horse.

John Jay, newly appointed chief justice of the Supreme Court, highly approved of the proposed trip. Jay, a New Yorker, added that a similar visit would be expected by the southern states. Washington accepted the advice, even though he was, above all else, a man of the South and believed he knew the Southland far better than the northern states. He lived most of his life in that world of plantations and rural gentility, mirrored in Mount Vernon. Yes, he would still need to show himself to the South. But the North beckoned. He wanted a firsthand view of life in the North, where manufacturing was said to be taking hold.

On the rainy morning of October 15, 1789, Washington and his entourage set out on the Post Road toward the Connecticut state line. He rode in a white and gold coach pulled by four bay horses.[5] The postilions and coachmen were in red-and-white livery. Behind the coach was a baggage wagon driven by one of six male slaves—invariably referred to as servants, not slaves. One of them rode the white charger that Washington would mount, usually at the edge of a town, when he left the carriage to enter a town on horseback.[6] Also accompanying him were Lear and two other experienced members of his staff: David Humphreys, and William Jackson, who had been secretary to the Constitutional Convention and became a presidential aide in 1789.[7]

As Washington's entourage reached Wethersfield, Connecticut, the Governor's Troop of Horse Guards rode up to escort him. The riders wore bearskin dragoon hats, white coats "brilliant with lace and braid of gold, red belt above tight pants, and boots with yellow tops."[8] At the head of the column was Colonel Jeremiah Wadsworth, the owner of the factory that produced the cloth for the inauguration suits worn by Washington, Adams, and all the members of Connecticut's congressional delegation. As the largest shareholder of the continent's first bank, the Bank of North America, he was one of America's richest men and the state's leading entrepreneur.

Orphaned as a child, he went to sea at eighteen and became a seagoing merchant who decided where to sell and how to price his cargoes. During the Revolutionary War he was first the commissary general to the Continental Army and then commissary to the French soldiers and sailors serving in America. He had an interest in a factory producing glasswork and another turning out linen. He was a partner in a distillery served by a fleet of ships carrying molasses from the West Indies. Wadsworth plunged into politics in 1788, becoming a member of the Continental Congress and the Constitutional Convention while still minding his businesses. By the time he rode up to welcome Washington, his most important holding was the Hartford Woolen Company, the first American mill to use power machinery to weave broadcloth.[9]

Washington learned enough about Wadsworth's company to wonder whether Virginia could begin a woolen industry. "By a little Legislative encouragement," he wrote to Governor Beverley Randolph after he ended his trip, "the Farmers of Connecticut have, in two years past, added one hundred thousand [sheep] to their former stock." In Virginia, he went on, "If a greater quantity of Wool could be produced, and if the hands (which are often in a manner idle) could be employed in the manufacturing it; a spirit of industry might be promoted." [10]

Washington would also meet Governor Samuel Huntington, who spurred the development of "useful Manufactures" in Connecticut. This included the first industrial company to be incorporated in the United States, a silk manufacturing firm. Farmers grew mulberry trees as feeding sources for silk worms that produced cocoons of fine, strong, glossy fiber that farmers' wives and children reeled and spun. In 1789, one town, Mansfield, produced approximately two hundred pounds of raw silk valued at $5 a pound.[11]

As Washington's northern journey began, so did his travel diary. Its pages were richer in detail and keen observations than what is found in his usual bland, quotidian entries. He notes the number of bushels of wheat per acre, and sometimes seems surprised by what he sees and learns. In Connecticut, for instance, he sees "*a great equality in the People of this State—Few or no oppulent Men and no poor.*"[12]

Throughout the trip Washington would follow a rigid rule: To avoid an appearance of favoritism, he would not stay in private homes.

He preferred inns, taverns, or boarding houses. And he followed a strict travel schedule: retire at or near 9 p.m., rise at 4 a.m., and get moving before having breakfast a few miles down the road. He thus could assume that he and his retinue would be able to achieve some distance before being met by troops of horse or crowd of greeters, who not only slowed him down but also kicked up clouds of dust.

Although he did meet cheering crowds at every stop, the adulation was far less important than what he was seeing and learning about a changing America. Only once did a visit become an incident. As he neared Boston, Massachusetts Governor John Hancock invited him stay at his mansion on Beacon Hill. Washington declined. He was staying in Boston at the Widow Ingersolls's *very decent & good house*," and expected Hancock to come there to greet him.

Hancock, through his secretary, begged off because he was indisposed, supposedly by an attack of gout. It was really an attack of anti-federalism, demonstrating the sovereignty of a state governor over a national president. Next day, apparently rethinking his snub, Hancock appeared at Washington's lodgings, wrapped in red bandages and borne in the arms of servants.[13] After Washington left Boston, an epidemic of respiratory infections struck the city. People called it "the Washington Influenza."[14]

Washington's most elaborate welcome came as he approached Newburyport, Massachusetts. Two companies of cavalry escorted him to the edge of town, where everyone halted to hear a chorus sing:

> *He comes! He comes! The hero comes.*
> *Sound, sound your Trumpets, beat, beat your Drums:*
> *From Port to Port let Cannons roar.*

Real drums rat-tat-tatted after the chorus sang, "Drums," and real cannons roared after the chorus sang the word *"Cannons."* Then came a parade whose marchers included "Tradesmen and Manufacturers, Captains of Vessels, Sailors, Schoolmasters, and about four hundred Scholars, all with Quills in their hands."[15] Washington's next stop was the Massachusetts town of Beverly—*which "makes a handsome appearance."* And there he saw the future. Washington was taken into a plain three-story brick building housing the Beverly Cotton Manufactory, which had begun operating in 1788 and claimed to be the first cotton mill in America.

However, Samuel Slater, a skilled British textile worker, had a rival claim. He had memorized the designs of cotton-mill machines he had been operating in England. In 1789, at the age of twenty-one, he left the Derbyshire town of Belper, boarded a ship in London, and sailed for New York.

Parliament, wanting to preserve the exclusive British hold on such machinery, passed legislation prohibiting textile workers from immigrating to America. Slater posed as a farmer and did not carry any documents mentioning textile machinery. Soon after landing he went to Rhode Island, where he provided investors with the secret of the machinery he had operated in his native land. His disclosures led to the founding of Rhode Island's textile industry and his title as "Father of American Manufactures."[16]

But there was a cotton mill operating in Beverly before Slater had even sailed to America. In 1786, the Massachusetts legislature granted the two Barr brothers, Scottish weavers and machinists, a £200 subsidy for the development of new weaving methods. They ran a foundry for making firearms and probably manufactured the Beverly machinery. [17] The Massachusetts Legislature supported the factory in its early years, first with a grant of land and then by authorizing the raising of funds through a state lottery.

Washington, obviously fascinated by what he saw at the Beverly factory visit, produced one of his longest diary entries. "*In this Manufactury*," he wrote, "*they have the New Invented Carding and Spinning Machines*[18]—*one of the first supplies the work; and four of the latter; one of which spins 84 threads at a time. . . . There is also another Machine for doubling and twisting the threads for particular cloths. This also does many at a time. . . . A number of Looms (15 or 16) were at work with Spring shuttles which do more than dble. work. In short the whole seemed perfect, and the Cotton stuffs wch. they turn out excellent of their kind.*"[19]

Many, if not most, of the workers were women, pioneers of a labor force no longer all-male. The investors were also pioneers, who "hazarded, some their whole fortunes, and others very large sums" to build the Manufactory and install costly machines. They kept losing money and resorted to barter, trading exported codfish for imported raw cotton, using Yankee ingenuity to support two local industries.[20] Not long after Washington's visit, stores in Beverly and Salem were advertising "corduroys from the Manufactory Warranted equal for service to any imported, and at as low prices."[21]

Water power would run Slater's first mill, built in Pawtucket, Rhode Island, in 1793. The Beverly Manufactory had a different source of power. In a basement pit, boys as young as seven drove two horses that turned a capstan, transferring horsepower to the machinery overhead. Elderly women picked the seeds out of the cotton and, to clean it, men laid it on a net and whipped it with sticks, separating strands of cotton fibers from their seeds. At the next stage of carding and spinning, machines operated by trained workers took over.[22]

Washington's interest in the manufactory was inspired by more than curiosity. He, like Hamilton, was an enthusiast for American self-sufficiency through industry. Rather than import finished goods, they wanted Americans to make the goods themselves.

Beverly incorporators included George Cabot, who would be elected to the U.S. Senate in 1791; two Cabot brothers, their sister, and a brother-in-law. The Cabot brothers owned several ships, which they envisioned as bringing cotton into Beverly from foreign sources because American cotton, dirty and short-fibered, was not suitable for their plant's mechanized system.[23]

The textile industry quickly spread as new cotton-mill developers in Connecticut and Rhode Island lured Beverly workers away. George Cabot, a friend of Hamilton and an acquaintance of Washington, showed himself to be an early practitioner of lobbying. The out-of-state mills were getting "the benefit of the knowledge & information we have purchased," he wrote to Representative Benjamin Goodhue, a Salem merchant and politician, to whom Cabot sent a petition seeking tariff changes that would aid his company. Goodhue, by his marriage to Martha Prescott, was the brother-in-law of both Representative Roger Sherman of Connecticut, and Henry Gibbs, another Salem merchant and staunch Federalist.[24]

Cabot won a land grant from the state, and from the First Congress, in response to his petition, a raise of the duty on imported cotton goods from 5 to 7.5 percent of value.[25] As a senator, he would support Hamilton's policies and would later be named a director of the Bank of the United States, which Congress would charter in 1791.

Cabot's lobbying resembled the practices of Jeremiah Wadsworth. Washington was seeing not only a functioning cotton mill but also a functioning interplay between industry and politics. In a letter to Hamilton in 1791, Cabot expressed the essence of the enterprising Yankees: "[We] must at last depend on the People of the country alone for a solid & permanent establishment . . . so that of the 40 Persons now employed in our workshop 39 are natives of the vicinity."[26]

Delegates to the First Congress had spoken more words about where the Federal Government should ultimately reside than how to raise and collect taxes.[27] The Constitution did not proclaim where the Seat of the Government of the United States should be, but merely that it not exceed ten miles square and that it was to be formed "by Cession of particular States."

No fewer than twenty-three sites had been proposed during the long and fervent debates over the location of the "seat of government."[28] In one of the many debates over the permanent seat of Congress, for example, the House ignored the Potomac River desires of President Washington and voted for the East-bank of the Susquehanna River. "We had better build *thirteen* federal towns," said a newspaper, "and let Congress go in rotation, as we all have the same right and claim."[29]

The long location fight ended on July 16, 1790, when Washington signed The Residence Act that called for a permanent seat, or residence, for the Federal Government, to be established on the Potomac River. (When referring to the home city of the Federal government, many still preferred the term "seat of government," reserving "capital" for the cities that hosted *state* governments.) The Act did not specify an exact location for the new seat of government, but merely that it be located somewhere on the Potomac River between the Eastern Branch (today's Anacostia River) and Connogochgue Creek. President Washington was authorized to select three commissioners who would in turn select the precise location.

Under the terms of the Act, Philadelphia became the temporary seat of the Government of the United States for ten years. Washington moved to The President's House at 6th & Market in Philadelphia in November 1790.[30]

Washington's persistent demand for a Potomac site helped to transform him from a hallowed and benign leader to the reluctant chief of a political party who wanted to have his way. Shortly before his departure on his southern tour in the spring of 1791, Washington became a party to a blatant political deal that every member of Congress since 1789 would recognize: *I do something for you, and you do something for me.* Near the end of the third session of Congress, Washington signed a bill establishing the controversial National Bank proposed by Hamilton—and opposed by Jefferson and Madison. Hamilton argued that such a bank would smooth the payment of taxes and payment of the states' Revolutionary War debts by the federal government.[31] In exchange, supporters of the bank quickly reciprocated, passing a supplemental bill that added Alexandria, Virginia—near Mount Vernon—to the federal district.[32] After a week of desultory debate, the National Bank bill was passed on February 8, 1791, by a vote of 39 to 20, and President Washington signed it into law on February 25. Thirty-three members who voted for the bank represented New York, New Jersey, and Pennsylvania; fifteen of the negative voters were from Virginia, the Carolinas, and Georgia. It was another example of how the First Congress began what would become the lasting struggle between North and South.

When the third session of Congress, held in Philadelphia, ended on March 3, 1791, Washington waited impatiently to begin a tour of southern states. He had laid out the itinerary himself: an 1,800-mile, three-and-a-half-month journey across the South, from Annapolis to Savannah and then back by a mostly different route to Philadelphia.[33] He wanted to start the journey right away, before "the warm and sickly months" of summer afflicted the South. But heavy rains and floods had muddied the roads around Philadelphia, and he had to postpone his departure from Philadelphia until March 21 at about 11:00 am, but only getting as far as the nearby town of Chester, as the roads were "exceedingly deep, heavy & cut." He was in Annapolis by March 25.[34]

Much had changed aside from the location of the Federal seat of government since his tour of the northern states in the fall of 1789. When he toured the north, he had been the new president of the new nation, getting more acquainted with northern people and northern places. Now, in 1791, he was the experienced president of a growing nation at a crucial time. The frontier beyond the Ohio River was wild and getting wilder. Spain was emerging as a shadowy adversary controlling the Mississippi. British soldiers were still manning northern borderland forts, contrary to the peace treaty. And France was being torn apart by revolution.

This time his journey included an uncharacteristically slick scheme that involved the Constitution's instructions about the size and location of "the Seat of Government": ("not exceeding ten Miles square"). On March 28, 1791, he stopped at the busy Potomac port of George Town, Maryland, [35] where his mission shifted from presidential traveler to presidential lobbyist pressing for his preferred location of the nation's capital. (For further discussion of the agreement as to the permanent seat in relation to the assumption of the debt, see page 198.)

Maryland and Virginia donated land for the formation of the federal government's ten-miles-square. But Washington wanted more. In George Town, "Finding the interests of the Landholders . . . much at varience," Washington wrote in his diary, "I requested them to meet me . . . at my lodgings" and "convinced them to surrender for public purposes, one half of the land they severally possessed" to the federal district. [36]

To lay out the boundaries of the district, the president appointed a well-qualified surveyor, Andrew Ellicott, who had as an assistant Benjamin Banneker, a free Ethiopian American who was a self-taught mathematician and astronomer; he later became publisher of a highly successful almanac.[37] Washington also hired Peter (Pierre) L'Enfant, the designer of Federal Hall, to make "drawings of the particular grounds most likely to be offered for the site of the federal town and buildings." L'Enfant had a reputation of being argumentative and uncooperative. Later, when he was asked for an engraving of his plan in a campaign to sell lots for the federal city, he refused. Washington fired him.

In the years to come, after the locations of the government buildings were laid out, more than 10,000 lots were available for sale at $249 each. The funds from lot sales would go toward the construction of government buildings. Virginia donated $120,000 and Maryland $72,000 toward the same goal.[38] Washington named three commissioners who would supervise the launching of the District: Daniel Carroll of Maryland, from a prominent Catholic family; Thomas Johnson, a Maryland judge; and physician David Stuart of Virginia, a longtime friend who had been one of the electors who had voted for Washington.

Business done, on March 30, Washington departed George Town, stopped in Alexandria for dinner, and then traveled on to his beloved Mount Vernon where he remained until departing for his southern tour proper on April 7, 1791.[39]

Washington duplicated his northern routine: up near dawn, get started, have breakfast, and begin another day of dinners, balls, cannon salutes, receptions, mayors, and governors, and poets with their odes. The going was not always smooth. He traveled down what his coachman called "the devil's own roads"[40] and twice suffered near-disasters while crossing rivers. But Washington, as ever, soldiered on.

Washington's diary of his southern trip lacks the thrill of discovery found on his northern pages. Traveling in the South, he was under the region's spell. He finds "The manners of the people . . . orderly and Civil . . . happy, contented and satisfied" with the federal government.[41] In the North, he talked to farmers about their crops. In the South, he also talked about crops—and slaves. One day, at Petersburg, near Richmond, he visited Davies Randolph, "a man who is fully entitled to the reputation which he enjoys of being the best farmer in the whole country." Washington reported that Randolph owned "Eight negroes (of whom two are little better than children)." In a succinct description of slavery economics, Randolph "declares that each of his negroes last year produced to him, after all expences paid, a net sum of three hundred dollars."[42]

And in the South, the style of homage enthralled Washington, as did the adoration shown by many upper-class Southern ladies who flocked to the dances and dinners and parties in his honor. At one stop, a newspaper reported, "he was introduced to upwards of fifty ladies who had assembled (at a Tea party) on the occasion."[43] At a ball in Charleston, according to another newspaper account, "nearly 250 ladies, elegantly dressed," presented themselves."[44] And "sixty ladies who upon his entering the room arose and made an elegant appearance."[45]

Newspaper reports and diary entries repeatedly mention ladies. For example: "60 & 70 well dressed ladies . . . about fifty ladies . . . about twenty ladies who had been assembled for the occasion. . . . Dined with the Members of the Cincinnati, and Was visited . . . by a great number of the most respectable ladies of Charleston, and in the evening went to a very elegant dancing Assembly at the Exchange—At which were 25 elegantly dressed and handsome ladies." [46] In Columbia, South Carolina, "he was conducted to the room of the representatives in the statehouse, where were assembled sixty-seven ladies, who upon his entering the room, arose and made an elegant appearance. . . . Went to a Ball in the evening, at which there were 62 ladies . . . receiving a number of visits from the most respectable ladies of the place (as was the case yesterday.) In the evening went to a Concert at the Exchange at wch. there were at least 400 ladies, the number & appearance of wch exceeded any thing of the kind I had ever seen."[47]

Before setting out, Washington had given Adams, Jefferson, Hamilton, and Knox copies of his itinerary—the old soldier called it his "line-of-march"—in case a crisis should summon him back to Philadelphia. From March 21 until mid-May. his route took him close to the King's Highway, the longtime mail road that ran along the coast from Charleston and Savannah to Boston. But from the time that Washington left Savannah on May 15 until he reached Fredericksburg, Virginia on June 10, he was out of the lines of any regular mail service. On May 15, Jefferson assured him, "We are still without any occurrence foreign or domestic worth mentioning to you." [48]

But a more personal sort of domestic crisis was brewing. On April 5, Tobias Lear wrote to President Washington from Philadelphia: Attorney General Edmund Randolph "called upon Mrs. Washington today, and informed her that three of his Negroes had given him notice that they should tomorrow take advantage of a law of this State, and claim their freedom—and that he had mentioned it to her from an idea that those who were of age in this family might follow the example. After a residence of six months should put it in their power. I have therefore communicated it to you that you might, if you thought best, give directions in the matter respecting the blacks in this family."[49]

Randolph was discreetly warning Mrs. Washington about a 1780 Pennsylvania law whose passage had reflected the northern states' slow and steady embrace of state-level abolition. Designed for the gradual abolition of slavery in Pennsylvania, the law automatically freed any slaves who had been brought into the state and kept there for an uninterrupted residence of six months.

In a second letter, forwarded "by a private conveyance," Lear wrote that he had talked with Randolph about the Washington household slaves at the presidential residence in Philadelphia without letting Washington know that Randolph had already "heard from you on the subject." Because Washington would be on the road when the six-month residence would expire, Lear, "with the concurrence of Mrs Washington," decided to solve the problem by exploiting a loophole: if, before the expiration of six months, a slave left the state, even for a single day, a *new* six-month residence would begin when he or she returned.[50]

Lear said he would tell Hercules, Washington's esteemed chef, that "he will be wanted at home in June when you return" to Mount Vernon after the tour—duping Hercules into breaking the six-month term. "If Hercules should decline the offer which will be made him of going home," Lear added, "it will be a pretty strong proof of his intention to take the advantage of the law at the expiration of six months." Mrs. Washington would do her part "with an excursion as far as Trenton," in a carriage, taking with her Oney Judge, Martha's personal maid, and another slave, thus breaking their six-month residence in Pennsylvania with a few hours in New Jersey.[51] Lear's scheme worked; all the Washington slaves missed the chance to take advantage of the law.

In 1796, during Washington's second term, Oney would flee. Washington advertised for her capture, offering a $10 reward and describing her as "a light mulatto girl, much freckled, with very black eyes and bushy black hair."[52] She eluded capture and settled in New Hampshire, where she married Jack Staines, a free black man.[53]

Hercules ran away in 1797, after he had been demoted to laborer at Mount Vernon. He was never caught.

No more is heard about the plotting to deny Washington's slaves a chance for freedom. The incident came at a time when Washington—like many other Americans—was pondering the future of slavery. "The unfortunate condition of the persons, whose labor in part I employed," Washington said, "has been the only unavoidable subject of regret. . . . to lay a foundation to prepare the rising generation for a destiny from that in which they were born; afforded some satisfaction to my mind & could not I hoped be displeasing to the justice of the Creator." [54]

There were other Americans, enslaved overseas, under quite different circumstances. Washington could at least work to free them, and to protect American merchants plying the oceans of the world. But at the start of his presidency, he lacked one of the basic tools needed in such cases—the ability to defend American interests on the high seas.

MANY PIRATES—AND NO NAVY

*F*or the American colonies, one benefit to being governed by a British king had been the protection of American ships by the Royal Navy. Unlike other seafaring nations, colonial America did not have its own navy to guard its many ships—the great fishing fleet of the Grand Banks off Newfoundland, the whalers hunting in the North and South Atlantic, and the merchantmen that carried American exports to such ports as the "sugar islands" of the British Caribbean.

The hull designs of American merchant ships were typically boxy, to create a big cargo space. Ships that expected to escape from pirates had a trimmer design that chose speed over cargo space.[1] The colonies could build big cargo ships without worry about pirates and privateers. But in 1776, when the colonies declared independence, their seagoing world changed.

Not only did American ships lose the Royal Navy shield but Britain also closed off the prime American trade destination: the sugar islands. Thousands of slaves on the islands' sugar and coffee plantations lived on beef, flour, pork, and salted fish imported from the American colonies. Banned from Britain's Caribbean, many American merchants suffered sudden losses and were condemned to debtors' prison. "Our West Indies business is ten times worse than it was before the war and God only knows that was bad enough then. Trade and commerce is almost at a stand," a U.S. merchant reported.[2]

"Without a Respectable Navy—Alas America!" wrote Captain John Paul Jones of the Continental Navy early in the American Revolutionary War.[3] Jones was seeking a navy by writing directly to Robert Morris of the Continental Congress, a financier of the war, a member of the standing marine committee of Congress, and the future

U. S. Superintendent of Finance. Morris, like many merchants, saw the need for a navy, but the United States had no money for shipbuilding—or, for that matter, for the feeding and equipping of a respectable army.

When France entered the war, some American warships were able to sail out of French ports and harass the British "Lords of the Ocean," the title that Ben Franklin bestowed on the Royal Navy. America's most important navy was the privateer fleet, which did far more damage to British shipping than the official Continental Navy.

Privateers were, simply put, privately-owned warships. Privateers were usually employed by weaker maritime powers. Generally converted merchant ships, they were armed with whatever cannon and other gear they could scrounge up—but also with what were effectively hunting licenses, called letters-of-marque, issued by a government. These licenses made what would otherwise be piratical, legal: the seizure and possession of merchant ships—and cargoes—of enemy nations.[4] The individual states and Congress issued some two thousand commissions for privateers.

A congressionally appointed commission approved the building of thirteen light frigates for what was envisioned as the seagoing partner of the Continental Army. But, unlike the army, the navy did little fighting. Many of the commissioned frigates spent years in shipyards waiting for rigging, armament, and crews. Seven of the frigates that made it to sea were captured; four were deliberately destroyed to keep them from being seized by the British.[5]

Almost forgotten in the victorious siege and battle of Yorktown was the fact that France's most crucial aid came by sea, most of all when François Joseph Paul, comte de Grasse, commanding officer of the French fleet, kept British warships from entering Chesapeake Bay. The French warships thus thwarted the British plan to resupply or withdraw their besieged soldiers. That action should have shown the vital need for a strong U. S. Navy.

America's most sustained early maritime encounter was far beyond U.S. shores and began after the war, during the woeful governance of the Articles of Confederation. On July 25, 1785, off Cape St. Vincent, Portugal, Algerian pirates seized the schooner *Maria* of Boston. Five days later, about 170 miles off Lisbon, Algerian pirates in another ship had taken the *Dauphin* of Philadelphia. The pirates sailed both ships, with their cargoes and crews, to Algiers. There, crews and captains were declared infidels and condemned to spend the rest of their lives as slaves—unless they were ransomed.

The horrors of Algiers were well known to Americans. The master of the *Dauphin*, Richard O'Bryen, would be enslaved for about ten years. O'Bryen continually prodded the conscience of America through correspondence with Washington and Jefferson.[6] Here are excerpts, dated February 19, 1790, from O'Bryen's journal. Her crew was enslaved by the Dey of Algiers. (*Dey* was the title given to the rulers of the Algeria, Tripoli, and Tunis, which were semi-autonomous provinces under the Ottoman Empire.) O'Bryen called they De "the King of Cruelties":

"Picture to yourself your Brother Citizens or Unfortunate Countrymen in the Algerian State Prisons or Damned Castile, and starved 2/3rd's and Naked. . . . The Chains of their Legs, and under the Lash . . . Beat in such a Manner as to Shock Humanity. . . . No Prospects of ever being Redeemed or Restored to their Native Land & Never to See their Wives & Families. . . . Viewing and Considering of their approaching Exit, where 6 of their Dear Country-man is buried with thousands of other Christian Slaves of all nations . . . Once a Citizen of the United States of America, but at present the Most Miserable Slave in Algiers."[7]

O'Bryen would later become American consul-general to Algiers and live through a bubonic plague that would kill about two hundred Christian slaves, including several crewmen of the *Dauphin*.[8]

The following is from a sailor who was a prisoner in Algiers for several years: "The roll is called every night in the prison before the gates are locked.—If any one neglects his call, he is immediately put in irons, hands and feet, then chained to a pillar, where he must remain until the next morning. Then the irons are taken from his feet, and he is driven before a task-master. He commonly orders 150 or 200 Bastinadoes [caning the soles of the feet]. . . . The person is laid upon his face, with his hands in irons behind him, and his legs lashed together with a rope.—One taskmaster holds down his head and another his legs, while two others inflict the punishment upon his breech, with sticks some what larger than an ox-goad. After he had received one half his punishment in this manner, they lash his ancles to a pole, and two Turks lift the pole up, and hold it in such a manner as brings the soles of his feet upward, and the remainder of his punishment, he receives upon the soles of his feet."[9]

In 1786, an agent working for the Americans secretly offered the pirates a ransom of $550 per man for twenty-one American captives. The Algerians demanded $2,833 per captive, for a total of $59,496. At that time, there were 2,200 enslaved captives from various nations in Algiers. By 1789 the number had been reduced to 655 "by Death or Ransom." Six of the dead were Americans who had died in cruel captivity, and a seventh had been ransomed in a private deal made by his friends.[10]

By December 1790, the United States of America had been operating under the Constitution for about eighteen months. Thomas Jefferson was secretary of state. He presented to President Washington a 4,400-word report on what was known about "our suffering Citizens" in Algeria and what could be done to free them.[11]

Another Jefferson agent, his diplomatic aide William Short, persistently—and vainly—tried to strike a bargain with the Muslim pirates. "My last letters will have informed you of the present situation of the business relative to the American Captives at Algiers," Short wrote Jefferson. "You will have seen that nothing has been done, or possible to be done, for their redemption; still I will leave nothing untried, and will write you regularly as you desire respecting it[12].... the people will cost for their redemption at least twelve hundred hard dollars pr. head: the number is twenty-one. Your Excellency sees how feeble we are."[13]

Much of the report to Washington had to do with the fluctuating and complicated ransom demands. In his report to Washington, Jefferson included the potential ransoms for two captains ($8,000), two mates ($6,000), and eleven mariners ($1,300 each), plus a fee and "Sundry Gratifications [tips] to Officers of the Dey's Household, and Regency." At one point, Jefferson was told by another agent that the men could be ransomed for $1,200 apiece, although Spain had paid $1,600.[14] In frustration, Jefferson turned from the numbers to "another Expedient": force.

"Captures made on the Enemy, may, perhaps, put us into Possession of some of their Mariners, and Exchange be substituted for Ransom," he suggested. "It is not indeed, a fixed Usage with them to exchange Prisoners. It is rather their Custom to refuse it. However, such Exchanges are sometimes effected, by allowing them more or less of Advantage. They have sometimes accepted of two Moors for a Christian, at others, they have refused five or six for one."[15]

Jefferson's prisoner trade idea would have been a logical step toward war by a nation that had a navy. All the United States possessed were the authorized wartime frigates. And a month before the capture of the *Maria* and the *Dauphin*, Congress had voted to sell the last of the frigates. That meant America's only defense at sea were the Treasury Department's revenue cutters.

But America's trade with foreign ports was growing, and so were attacks on U.S. merchant ships. Pressure increased on Congress, and many members, along with Washington, believed that to attain the status of a major power, America needed a Navy.

The Constitution gave Congress power to raise money to "provide and maintain a navy," implying a permanent navy. [16] As for an army, the Constitution granted the power "to raise and support Armies," but added "no Appropriation of Money to that Use shall be for a longer Term than two Years." There was no such restriction on naval appropriations.

There was no army in large part because lawmakers, reflecting their constituents' beliefs, refrained from creating a standing army. Madison was a leader of the anti-army majority, warning: "A standing military force, with an overgrown Executive will not long be safe companions to liberty. . . . [17]

As Thomas Jefferson had once observed, "A naval force can never endanger our liberties, nor occasion bloodshed; a land force would do both."[18] Or, as James Madison put it, a navy could "never be turned by a perfidious government against our liberties."[19] In short, many legislators looked benignly upon the navy while seeing a threat when considering a standing army.

Slowly, the idea of creating a navy developed in Congress. Washington endorsed the building of a navy in his annual address to

Congress on December 3, 1793: "If we desire to avoid insult, we must be able to repel it; if we desire to secure peace, one of the most powerful instruments of our rising prosperity, it must be known, that we are at all times ready for War."[20] A short time later, Congress learned that Portugal and Algiers had negotiated a truce that allowed Barbary pirates to prowl the Atlantic, threatening American ships in their trade with Europe.

On December 16, Washington forwarded to Congress documents on the unsatisfactory negotiations with the Algerians. On January 2, 1794, the House resolved "that a naval force adequate to the protection of the commerce of the United States, against the Algerine corsairs, ought to be provided," and appointed a committee that was to determine what kind of naval force was necessary. Eighteen days later, committee chairman Thomas Fitzsimons of Pennsylvania reported a resolution to authorize the building and procurement of six frigates; five were given names: *Constitution, United States, President, Constellation,* and *Congress;* the name *Chesapeake* came later.

Washington began the perpetual practice of spreading defense dollars by authorizing the building of the frigates at six sites: Portsmouth, New Hampshire; Boston, New York, Philadelphia, Baltimore, and the Gosport Shipyard in Norfolk, Virginia, on land seized from a Loyalist. To hold costs down, government workers, rather than contractors' employees, would build the ships. The government leased the shipyard from Virginia and in 1794 started to build the 36-gun USS *Chesapeake.*[21]

In 1796 the threat of pirates suddenly eased when negotiations between Algiers and the United States produced a treaty that awarded nearly $1,000,000 in ransom for American prisoners—and the building of a 32-gun frigate for the Dey's fleet. Congress reacted by authorizing the completion of only three of the six frigates. But they were not allowed to be fitted out and manned. America had the beginning of a fleet that could float but not fight.[22] But on April 30, 1798, President John Adams signed a bill establishing the Department of the Navy,[23] and Congress followed through by authorizing funds to finish building and fitting out *Congress, Chesapeake,* and *President.*

Then came a test of the reborn U.S. Navy—war at sea.

Reacting to war between Britain and France, President Washington on April 22, 1793, proclaimed neutrality. France, by then roiled for years by her own revolution, responded by sending the French ambassador to the United States, Charles-Edmond Genêt, to America to appeal for American aid and counter Washington's policy of neutrality. The ambassador called himself Citizen Genêt to emphasize his revolutionary sentiments. He carried with him letters of marque that gave him the theoretical ability to recruit a fleet of American privateers. He also attempted to stir up trouble between Americans who were for and against the French Revolution. At the same time, Britain and the United States negotiated an agreement intended to resolve residual differences after the Revolution, but the so-called Jay Treaty created its own hornets-nest of trouble—and infuriated the French, who reacted by harassing American vessels at sea, and setting off a naval conflict that did not quite rise to the status of full-blown war. [24]

Genêt managed to revive support for France among the American public. But he outraged newly-elected President John Adams, who plunged into what was called the Quasi War. Undeclared and unfettered, the war, fought entirely at sea, went on for two years. American and British warships, although were fighting the same French Navy foe, did not coordinate their operations[25].

Washington, finally enjoying retirement at Mount Vernon, was drafted by Adams to serve as commander-in-chief in anticipation of the war spreading to major a land-and-sea military campaign. But the war remained at sea, and the U.S. Navy, fighting mostly in the Caribbean, made prizes of about eighty-five French ships.

An odd legacy of the Quasi War is the Logan Act, passed in 1799 and still in effect. The law criminalized unauthorized diplomatic negotiations. It was named for a pacifist Quaker, George Logan, who went to France to negotiate, as a private citizen, with French diplomats, including Foreign Minister Talleyrand. Logan returned to the United States "announcing Talleyrand's peaceful intentions" and competing with official American negotiations, according to the U.S. State Department version of the incident.[26] The Senate did not ratify the final version of the treaty until December 18, 1801.

As was true of the French Revolution itself, the man who truly ended the war was Napoleon Bonaparte, who seized control of France in 1800 and officially declared the undeclared hostilities concluded. The darkest fear of America's Founding Fathers had always been that their Revolution would, in the end, produce a monarchy, an absolute ruler. That the French Revolution ended with Napoleon, and that the Quasi War was ended by a word from Napoleon, showed how real the danger could be.

That an American constitutional republic still in its infancy was slow and late in creating a navy was, perhaps, understandable. But it was remarkable how much else the brand-new government was able to accomplish in the remainder of the First Federal Congress.

THE SECOND SESSION: HOPE AND ANGST

The First Federal Congress had made 1789 the true birth year of the United States. The three branches of government had been established, as had a revenue system, and the Bill of Rights became a reality. By any measure, these were major accomplishments. Then 1789 gave way to 1790, and Congress began its second session on January 8.

The second session of Congress began in style. Washington "set out . . . in my Coach—preceded by Colonel Humphreys and Majr. Jackson in Uniform (on my two White Horses.)"[1] Six horses pulled Washington's coach. Its body and wheels were cream-colored with gilt moldings. It had Venetian blinds and, for cold weather, leather curtains. On the coach's four panels were allegorical decorations portraying the seasons, in reproductions of the famed Italian artist Giuseppe Ceracchi, who fancied cupids and festoons of flowers. Emblazoned on the door was the Washington coat of arms, which included the hereditary family motto, *exitus acta probat*—the outcome justifies the deed.[2]

Following the coach on horseback were aides Tobias Lear and Thomas Nelson, Jr. Next came the carriages of the chief justice, the secretary of the treasury, and the secretary of war. As he did for his inauguration, Washington wore a suit of Connecticut-made cloth, this one described by an authority of fashion as "of that beautiful changeable hue called crow color, which is remarked in shades not quite black."[3] At Federal Hall he entered the Senate chamber, the site for joint addresses to Congress, and sat on a raised seat that looked to some like a throne.

With Speaker Muhlenberg and the members of the House to his left and Vice President Adams and the Senate to his right, he stood and delivered the first Annual Message to a Joint Session of Congress, fulfilling the instructions of the Constitution, which states that the

President, "shall from time to time give to the Congress Information of the State of the Union, and recommend to their Consideration such Measures as he shall judge necessary and expedient."

Washington began by hailing the North Carolina Legislature for voting, 194 to 77, to ratify the Constitution and thus enter the Union.[4] He also praised the First Congress for its labors and urged them to take on further tasks, such as dealing with the new government's finances, establishing "Uniformity in the Currency, Weights and Measures of the United States," creating laws for the naturalization of citizens, and paying "a due attention to the Post-Office and Post Roads." He further observed that "providing for the common defense will merit particular regard." This was so because "[t]o be prepared for war is one of the most effectual means of preserving peace."[5]

He had given what would someday be called the State of the Union Address.[6]

Once the pomp and ceremonies were complete, the House and Senate faced three spiky issues that they had left unresolved: the handling of state and national debts, the location of the United States Capital, and the creation of a federal army.

As a retired general, Washington had a natural desire for a national army. But he did not call his envisioned force an army. He preferred "Peace Establishment." Several members of Congress preferred to call the permanent force "a standing army." The persistent label resurrected for many the image of Redcoats camping on Boston Commons in 1768.

Washington had first chosen to unveil his idea of a Peace Establishment in June 1783, when, shortly after snuffing out a possible military coup d'état, he said farewell to the Continental Army with "my last official communication." He also sent the long goodbye—4,115 words—to all state governors in the form of a circular letter, which was widely printed in newspapers, touching off countless conversations among friends and foes of a standing army.[7] Deep in the document he listed "The adoption of a proper Peace Establishment" as one of four necessities "essential to the well being, I may even venture to say, to the existence of the United States as an Independent Power." The other three were rhetorical: "An indissoluble Union of the States under one Federal Head"; "a Sacred regard to Public Justice"; and "pacific and friendly Disposition, among the People of the United States, which will induce them to forget their local prejudices and policies".[8]

"This," he said in the 1783 circular letter, "is the moment to establish or ruin [America's] national Character for ever." The success of the republic would demonstrate to all living under monarchies that government by the people was possible. Conversely, if the Union crumbled, the notion of self-government would be rendered a failure. In this way, Washington solemnly observed, Americans held in their hands the "destiny of unborn Millions."[9]

Washington was not an admirer of militias. Early in the Revolutionary War, as commander in chief of the Continental Army, he had railed against the militias, saying their soldiers were "men just dragged from the tender scenes of domestic life." When fighting trained troops like the British redcoats, he said, militiamen "are timid and ready to fly from their own shadows."[10]

But militias were the heart of his Peace Establishment plan for an army of 2,651 men who would garrison a citadel at West Point, maintain borders, defend against Indian uprisings, prevent "the encroachment of our Neighbours of Canada and the Florida's" and "guard us at least from surprises." He also envisioned federally maintained arsenals, military academies, and a navy, as soon as the nation was able "to raise funds more than adequate to the discharge of the Debts incurred by the Revolution."

The Peace Establishment would include a "well organized Militia" drawn from all the states on the premise that "every Citizen who enjoys the protection of a free Government, owes not only a proportion of his property, but even of his personal services to the defence of it, and consequently that the Citizens of America (with a few legal and official exceptions) from 18 to 50 Years of Age should be borne on the Militia Rolls, provided with uniform Arms, and so far accustomed to the use of them, that the Total strength of the Country might be called forth at a Short Notice on any very interesting Emergency."[11] The impotent Confederation Congress took no action on Washington's plan or the proposals presented by Hamilton and the other committee members.

Nothing meaningful would happen about a standing army until the emergence of the First Federal Congress, although it was constitutionally empowered to "raise and support armies" and "provide and maintain a navy." But, busy with the task of creating a government in the first session, Congress basically ignored the need to create an army or a way to pay for it. So the two entwined issues of defense and taxes were passed to the second session—as was a third and epic issue: the location of the national capital.

Reporting to the Minister of Foreign Affairs soon after the second session began, Louis Guillaume Otto, the astute French ambassador, wrote, "The first session of Congress has had for its aim only the general organization of the government. The second will be more important and more delicate: it will decide about the purse and the sword. All information relating to finances and to the country's defense has been carefully prepared and will guide the two Houses. . . . A third object, much less interesting, may give a more perceptible shock to the new confederation. It is the eternal discussion about the residence."[12]

Otto was right. In the second session there was a sword, but it was legislatively sheathed. Congress would not pass a national militia act until 1792. As for the purse, it contained the "Report of the Secretary of the Treasury on the Public Credit," Alexander Hamilton's magnum opus—a 36,000-word plan for a sound federal fiscal policy. The plan addressed an issue that threatened the existence of a united nation: paying the Revolutionary War debts.

Hamilton began with a primer showing the need for public credit: "States, like individuals, who observe their engagements, are respected and trusted: while the reverse is the fate of those, who pursue an opposite conduct." America's future success, he said, would be based on attracting European investment capital. And that depended on settlement of a mammoth debt that stemmed from wartime borrowing: $54 million owed by the nation—mostly to the French monarchy and Dutch investors[13]—and a total of $25 million owed by the states. Article VI of the Constitution said, "All debts contracted and engagements entered into, before the adoption of this constitution, shall be as valid against the United States under this constitution, as under the confederation." Hamilton was thus following the Constitution when he proposed that the newly created government assume the national debt. America would do this, he said, by borrowing new money at the low interest rates that are awarded to fiscally responsible nations.

As he explained his plan, America's debt payments would almost entirely be made on the interest on the debt, not the principal. New government securities would be exchanged for old notes with an interest yield of about 4 percent. He would get the payment money "from the present duties on imports and tonnage, with the additions, which, without any possible disadvantage either to trade, or agriculture, may be made on wines, spirits, including those distilled within the United States, teas and coffee."[14] In what sounded like a sermon, Hamilton pointed out that all of the taxed articles are

> in reality—luxuries—the greatest part of them foreign luxuries; some of them, in the excess in which they are used, pernicious luxuries. And there is, perhaps, none of them, which is not consumed in so great abundance, as may, justly, denominate it, a source of national extravagance and impoverishment. The consumption of ardent spirits [strong alcoholic liquors made by distillation, such as brandy, whiskey, or gin] particularly, no doubt very much on account of their cheapness, is carried to an extreme, which is truly to be regretted, as well in regard to the health and the morals, as to the economy of the community.
>
> Should the increase of duties tend to a decrease of the consumption of those articles, the effect would be, in every respect desireable. The saving which it would occasion, would leave individuals more at their ease, and promote a more favourable balance of trade. As far as this decrease might be applicable to distilled spirits, it would encourage the substitution of cyder and malt liquors, benefit agriculture, and open a new and productive source of revenue. . . . Experience has shewn, that luxuries of every kind, lay the strongest hold on the attachments of mankind.[15]

The most controversial part of Hamilton's plan was federal "assumption" of the state debts. And that inspired a fiery congressional debate, fueled by the millions of dollars in public bonds that states had originally sold to their soldiers and investors. But by 1787 most of the debt certificates were no longer in the hands of original holders, those Americans who had actually loaned money or given services to the United States. This was because some Americans, particularly in the commercial North, saw speculation in state and federal debt certificates as a means of making more money much faster than in the relatively respectable field of land speculation.[16]

Debate on the report began on February 8. Many members accepted the plan, but Madison deplored the addition of the states' debts to the federal debt. And he questioned the fairness of the windfall that assumption would bring to speculators who had bought bonds from original holders at pennies on the dollar.[17]

The plan was still being debated on April 12 when Madison made a 5,000-word speech explaining his objections. The *Daily Gazette* boiled down the speech to this: "A public debt is, in fact, a debt from one part of the citizens to the other part; it resolves itself into private debts, the government being the collector for the parties. In this point of view the debts of Virginia are far greater than those of Massachusetts, and the inequality would be increased by the proposed assumption."[18] Massachusetts, Connecticut, and South Carolina owed almost half of the total state debts.[19]

Senator Maclay walked down the stairs to the House gallery to watch the House defeat, 31 to 29, a resolution endorsing assumption. Maclay recognized Representatives George Clymer and Thomas Fitzsimons of Pennsylvania; Representatives Theodore Sedgwick, Elbridge Gerry, and Fisher Ames of Massachusetts; Egbert Benson of New York; Elias Boudinot of New Jersey; and Jeremiah Wadsworth of Connecticut, all among those who voted yes. Maclay recorded in his diary:

> Sedgwick from Boston pronounced a funeral Oration over it, he was called to Order, some Confusion ensued he took his hat & went out. When he returned his Visage to me bore the visible marks of Weeping. Fitzsimons reddened like Scarlet his Eyes were bringm full, Clymer's color always pale now verged to cadavereous a deadly Whiteness. his lips quavered, and his neither Jaw shook with convulsive Motions. His head neck & Breast consented to Gesticulations resembling those of a Turkey or Fowl Goose, nearly strangled in the Act

of deglutition. Benson bungled like a Shoemaker who hads lost his End.[20] Ames's Aspect was truly hippocratic, a total change of face & feature. he sat torpid as if his faculties had been benumbed. Gerry exhibited the advantages of a cadaverous appearance. at all times palid, and far from pleasing. . . . Wadsworth hid his Grief Under the rim of a round hat. Boudinot's wrinkles rose into ridges. and the Angels of his mouth were dpressed, and their apperture assumed a curve resembling an horse Shoe—[21]

Congress was deadlocked, although its members went through the routine of meeting and adjourning "from day to day without doing anything, the parties being too much out of temper to do business together," Jefferson remembered.[22] Some members feared that the issue would split the new nation in two. Representative Richard Bland Lee, of the great Virginia dynasty, raised the specter of secession in a letter to his brother, Charles, a former member of the Virginia General Assembly. "I confess that I feel myself often chagrined by the taunts against the ancient Dominion," he wrote, "but disunion at this time would be the worst of calamities. The Southern States are too weak at present to stand by themselves. . . . And when we shall attain our natural degree of population I flatter myself that we shall have the power to do ourselves justice, with dissolving the bond which binds us together."[23] Another brother, Henry "Light-Horse Harry" Lee III, would be the father of Robert E. Lee, a general who would fight a war to dissolve the bond.

Assumption of foreign debts was accepted by Congress, as was Hamilton's raise in tariffs on alcoholic "luxuries," which produced an average increase about only 2.5 percent over the 1789 rates.[24] The state-assumption dispute, however, was not a dollar-and-cents issue. It went to the heart of the clash between state sovereignty and the power of the federal government.

On June 2, the House enacted the funding bill—minus the assumption. Hamilton knew he had to make a deal to save his plan.[25] So did several other political operatives. As Maclay told it in his diary, Robert Morris, Pennsylvania's other senator, had learned of a secret meeting where an assumption-residence deal had been discussed.[26] The participants, he said, were Tench Coxe, a thirty-five-year-old Philadelphian merchant who had been made assistant secretary of the Treasury by Jefferson, and William Jackson, a stalwart aide to Washington. Both Coxe and Jackson had to be acting as surrogates of their superiors.

According to Maclay's punctuation-challenged report, Cox and Jackson were "to negotiate a bargain. the permanent Residence in Pennsylvania, for her Votes for the Assumption." After learning of that meeting, Morris wrote a note to Hamilton that said, "I would be walking early in the Morning on the Battery [a public walk at the tip of Manhattan Island], and if Col. Hamilton had anything to propose to him, he might meet him there as if by accident."

When Morris approached the rendezvous, he found Hamilton waiting and ready for a deal: "One Vote in the Senate and five Votes in the House of Representatives" in exchange to place "the permanent Residence of Congress" at Germantown, near Philadelphia, or the Falls of Delaware, near Trenton. Morris said he had to consult the Pennsylvanian delegation, but he "proposed that the Temporary Residence of Congress in Philada. should be the Price. They parted upon this."[27]

On June 18, Maclay reported that Hamilton had met with Morris and Pennsylvania Representative Fitzsimons and told them that "the New-England Men will bargain to fix the permanent Seat at the Potowmac or in Baltimore."[28] The only way out of the deadlock was a compromise between supporters of assumption and supporters of putting the U.S. capital on the Potomac. Maclay had seen the dawn of the deal. Now came the next move, which introduced a new player, Thomas Jefferson.

In the early nineteenth century, Jefferson assembled numerous documents, letters, and snippets of notes, describing them as his "most secret communications, while in the office of state." He called his effort *Anas*, implying that it was a collection.[29] But one item in *Anas* stands out, not as an act of statesmanship but as a story told about a decisive moment in history: the secret meeting that fostered the Compromise of 1790. The story begins on a June day in 1790 outside Washington's mansion at 39–41 Broadway, his residence and the office of the

President. (He had moved out of the Samuel Osgood House four months before.)[30] Jefferson began:

> Going to the President's one day, I met Hamilton as I approached the door. His look was sombre, haggard, and dejected beyond description. Even his dress uncouth and neglected. He asked to speak with me. We stood in the street near the door.
>
> He opened the subject of the assumption of the state debts, the necessity of it in the general fiscal arrangement and its indispensible necessity towards a preservation of the Union: and particularly of the New England states, who had made great expenditures during the war, on expeditions which tho' of their own undertaking were for the common cause: that they considered the assumption of these by the Union so just, and its denial so palpably injurious, that they would make it a sine qua non of a continuance of the Union. That as to his own part, if he had not credit enough to carry such a measure as that, he could be of no use, and was determined to resign.
>
> He observed at the same time, that tho' our particular business laid in separate departments, yet the administration and its success was a common concern, and that we should make common cause in supporting one another. He added his wish that I would interest my friends from the South, who were those most opposed to it....
>
> It was a real fact that the Eastern and Southern members (S. Carolina, however, was with the former) had got into the most extreme ill humor with one another. This broke out on every question with the most alarming heat, the bitterest animosities seemed to be engendered, and tho' they met every day, little or nothing could be done from mutual distrust and antipathy. On considering the situation of things I thought the first step towards some conciliation of views would be to bring Mr. Madison and Colo. Hamilton to a friendly discussion of the subject.

I immediately wrote to each to come and dine with me the next day mentioning that we should be alone, that the object was to find some temperament for the present fever, and that I was persuaded that men of sound heads and honest views needed nothing more than explanation and mutual understanding to enable them to unite in some measures which might enable us to get along.[31]

They came. I opened the subject to them, acknowledged that my situation had not permitted me to understand it sufficiently, but encouraged them to consider the thing together. They did so. It ended in Mr. Madison's acquiescence in a proposition that the question should be again brought before the House by way of amendment from the Senate, that tho' he would not vote for it, nor entirely withdraw his opposition, yet he should not be strenuous, but leave it to its fate.

It was observed, I forget by which of them, that as the pill would be a bitter one to the Southern states, something should be done to soothe them; that the removal of the seat of government to the Potomac was a just measure, and would probably be a popular one with them, and would be a proper one to follow the assumption.

It was agreed to speak to Mr. [Alexander] White and Mr. [Richard Bland] Lee, whose districts lay on the Potomac and to refer to them to consider how far the interests of their particular districts might be a sufficient inducement to them to yield to the assumption.

This was done. Lee came into it without hesitation. Mr. White had some qualms, but finally agreed. The measure came down by way of amendment from the Senate and was finally carried by the change of White's and Lee's votes. But the removal to Potomac could not be carried unless Pennsylvania could be engaged in it. This Hamilton took on himself, and chiefly, as I understood, through the agency of Robert Morris, obtained the vote of that state, on agreeing to an intermediate residence at Philadelphia.

This is the real history of the assumption, about which many erroneous conjectures have been published. It was

unjust, in itself oppressive to the states, and was acquiesced
in merely from a fear of disunion, while our government
was still in its most infant state. It enabled Hamilton so to
strengthen himself by corrupt services to many that he could
afterwards carry his bank scheme and every measure he proposed in defiance of all opposition; in fact it was a principal
ground whereon was reared up that Speculating phalanx, in
and out of Congress which has since been able to give laws
and to change the political complexion of the government
of the U.S.

Many historians question the accuracy of the *Anas* story. But there is
no doubt that Jefferson, Hamilton, and Madison were the architects of
what became both the Hamilton plan complete with state assumptions
and An Act for Establishing the Temporary and Permanent Seat of the
Government of the United States. The act declared that the temporary seat for ten years would be Philadelphia. Then the permanent site
would be a federal district on the Potomac ten miles square. (See page
177 for discussion of George Washington negotiating the precise location, size, and terms of transfer for the new seat of government.)

On July 1, the Senate passed the bill, 14 to 12. Ten of the winning
votes came from all the Senators of the five states from Pennsylvania
south to North Carolina. Added to them were singleton Senators
from South Carolina, Georgia, New Jersey, and New Hampshire.[32]
After three days of intense debate and numerous failed amendments,
on July 9 the House voted 32 to 29 for the bill. Most of the affirma-
tive votes came from southerners.[33] Washington delayed signing the
bill until he conferred with Jefferson, who, backed by Madison, assured
Washington that the bill was constitutional.[34] The compromise was
fulfilled by the same coalition, which added the assumption to the already acceptable Funding Act. It was signed into law on July 6 as the
second session neared adjournment.

In something of an anticlimax after years of debate and delay, North
Carolina, without drama, ratified the Constitution in November 1789.
However, the other hold-out provided ample additional drama by
continuing to live up to its wry nickname.

Between September 1787 and January 1790, Rogue Island had repeatedly failed to ratify the Constitution. In March 1790, when Rhode Island legislators at last realized the economic impact of their contrariness, state legislature Federalists lobbied for a ratification convention bill, which passed, 32 to 11, in the state House—and then tied in the state Senate. The governor broke the tie with a vote to hold the convention.

Congress ran out of patience, and, in May 1790, the Senate passed the Act to Restrict Trade with Rhode Island, essentially aimed at making the state a foreign country if it did not agree to ratification. Faced with economic disaster, Rhode Island held the convention in Newport, where delegates voted 34 to 32 to ratify the Constitution. Four delegates were absent; had they attended, they would have voted to reject ratification. Thus, by the narrowest of margins, the state officially entered the Union on May 29, 1790.[35]

On Thursday, August 12, 1790, Congress adjourned until the first Monday of December, when the government was to begin its ten years in Philadelphia.

After years of gnarled negotiations with New York and New Hampshire, along with some intriguing with Canada, on February 9, 1791, President Washington presented Vermont's petition for statehood to Congress.[36] The First Congress approved it and then marked the end of its third and final session on March 3, 1791. On March 4, 1791, the act that made Vermont the fourteenth state of the United States came into effect.[37] The admission of Vermont established the precedent and process followed down the centuries as more and more states were admitted—starting with Kentucky in 1792.

Kentucky statehood established another precedent—keeping a very close balance between the number of northern and southern states.[38] In later decades, this would evolve into the deliberate policy of keeping the number of slave states equal to the number of free states.[39]

But Kentucky's admission was no smooth or simple process. It was instead part of a tangled web of intrigues, plots and conspiracies as the new United States struggled to bring some sort of order to the vast territories it had so recently gained.

ON THE FRONTIER, SPIES AND PLOTS

*I*n the treaty ending the Revolutionary War, Britain ceded land that doubled the size of the new nation, stretching it from the coast of Maine to the Mississippi River and north to the Great Lakes. The usually slow-moving Confederation Congress reacted quickly, by a 22-to-2 vote, passing the Ordinance of 1784, which proclaimed that the land "shall forever remain" part of the United States. The subsequent Ordinance of 1787 asserted Congress's right to admit new states from the Territory, guaranteed that the created states would be equal to the original thirteen states, and outlawed slavery in the Territory.[1] Eventually, Ohio, Indiana, Illinois, Michigan, and Wisconsin, as well as northeastern Minnesota would emerge from what became the Northwest Territory.

Brigadier General Rufus Putnam chose the legal way to acquire land. While he and other discontented officers were encamped at Newburgh, New York, awaiting the disbanding of the Continental Army, he campaigned for the Territory land bounties that Congress had promised veterans. In 1786 he founded the Ohio Company of Associates and contracted for a 1,800,000-acre tract of land at the confluence of the Ohio and Muskingum Rivers.

Two years later, Putnam left his home in Rutland, Massachusetts, and on April 7, 1788, leading forty-seven New Englanders, reached the site, in present-day Ohio, of what would be the first United States settlement in the Northwest Territory. He named it Marietta in honor of Queen Marie Antoinette of France. (At that time, many officers, particularly members of the Society of the Cincinnati, were passionately thankful for France's aid in the Revolutionary War.)[2] On a high bluff, the settlers built a stockade for defense against Indian attack. They named the fortification Campus Martius, after the military camp in Rome where legions trained.[3]

Congress also created the Southwest Territory out of land that North Carolina had once claimed but then ceded to the United States. However there was an illicit state in the territory: Franklin. The state was created, without congressional approval, in August 1784 by a convention of over-mountain settlers. The State of Franklin maintained an ambiguous existence for five years in what is now Upper East Tennessee.[4] In 1796, the Franklin land became part of the new state of Tennessee.

Congress appointed Arthur St. Clair, another former general—and Cincinnati member—governor of the Northwest Territory. In 1789 St. Clair induced some Indians to sign a treaty requiring them to give up land in Ohio to white settlers.[5] What looked like a smooth takeover of Indian land was more image than reality. The Territory, in the words of a Connecticut observer, was a realm of strife and intrigue, with "the Briton on the North, the Spaniard on the South, and the Savage on the West." [6]

Connecticut, along with Virginia, Massachusetts, and New York, still claimed parts of the Northwest Territory for themselves. Connecticut's claim extended to northeastern Ohio and included a large region known as the Firelands or the Sufferers' Land—a tract dedicated to the relocation of families whose homes had been torched in British and Loyalist raids upon Connecticut communities. Because of legal and political delays that extended into the War of 1812, many Connecticut people who acquired Firelands property were too old to migrate.[7]

"Can we retain the western country with the government of the United States? And if we can, what use will it be to them?" Representative Fisher Ames of Massachusetts asked Putnam.[8]

Ames was not alone in his wondering. One of the most outspoken opponents of unregulated migration into the Territory was Representative George Clymer of Pennsylvania, who wanted migration to be a gradually "extending circle" of civilization rather than a heedless flight of pioneers from the old states. He believed that the typical migrant, lured westward by visions of a wonderland, "can never propose to himself any thing beyond runing a few hogs loose and scratching his ground for as much Indian corn and wheat as will feed his ragged family."[9]

Clymer's interest in the Territory was rare in the First Federal Congress. Representative Alexander White of Virginia complained to Washington "that a disposition prevailed among the Eastern & northern States ... to pay little attention to the Western Country."[10] But land speculators were certainly taking an interest. And Clymer's vision of a migrant's ragged family often became real.

In 1790, several of Marietta's people died of smallpox. Inoculations saved many, and then came another scourge—the loss of most of the corn crop to a fungal disease. "By the middle of May," a historical account says, "the scarcity was felt generally. There were but few cows in the country to afford milk; no oxen or cattle to spare for meat, and very few hogs. The woods, which were full of game in 1788, were now nearly as bare of it was in an old settled country—the Indians having killed, or driven away, nearly all the deer within twenty miles of Marietta. In this great scarcity it was wonderful how little there was of selfishness, and how generally kindness and good feeling abounded."[11] All this while, Indians were ambushing river boats bringing more settlers to steadfast Marietta.

Kentuckians zigzagged toward their future, starting even before the Confederation Congress gave way to the First Federal Congress. For several years after the end of the war, there was reason to fear that the Kentucky District of Virginia was on a tortuous road that might not lead to statehood—but instead to Spanish or British control.

The British controlled Upper Canada and Quebec. From 1763 to 1801, the Spanish laid claim to the Louisiana Territory, a vast expanse of land including all the land west of the Mississippi River. Directly across, on the eastern shore, was the border of the Kentucky District, and thus of the United States. It was by no means clear which power would have long-term control over what territory.

"Now a dreadful & dangerous conspiracy is discovered to be carrying on between the People of Kentuke and the Spaniards," Senator William Maclay reported acidly in April 1790. Maclay questioned whether there was anything to the wild stories, but in fact plots had long been afoot.[12] The beginnings of the conspiracies could be traced back many years.

The enclave of the Kentucky District was beyond the Appalachians, a two- or three-week journey from Richmond, too far away for a quick response to Indian raids and too untamed to be considered truly part of stolid Virginia. Politicians in Virginia mostly ignored the Kentuckians. This stoked Kentuckians' anger over Virginia's failure to protect them.

At the same time, trade was far easier via the river routes of the Mississippi and the Ohio leading west and south, as opposed to the difficult land route east through the Cumberland Gap. Geography led Kentuckians to turn their backs on the coastal states to the east, and instead face west. They began looking at drastically different possible futures: separation from Virginia to become a new state of the Union; separating to become an independent colony; becoming a Spanish colony; or, alternately, plotting with a British secret agent sent to maneuver the territory into some degree of alliance with Britian.

The British agent in question was John Connolly, a native of Lancaster, Pennsylvania, and a well-known frontier trader and land speculator. Improbably enough, in 1770, in Pittsburgh, he met a more refined land speculator—George Washington himself—who was on a land-shopping journey along the Ohio and Kanawha Rivers. Connolly talked with him about organizing a government for an envisioned settlement near the Pittsburgh area.[13] Soon after, Connolly acquired some thousands of acres of land in what would become Louisville, Kentucky.

During the Revolutionary War, Connolly chose the Loyalist side. In late 1775 he developed and got approval for plans to attack Fort Pitt (at Pittsburgh), to secure Detroit and to incite "the Ohio Indians to act in concert with me against his Majesty's enemies." His servant, William Crowley, tended toward the Patriot side. Crowley "was acquainted with Washington" and alerted him. Washington in turn alerted the Maryland Committee of Public Safety to watch for Connolly, who was captured near Hagerstown while carrying letters detailing his plans.

Connolly was held as a prisoner in one form or another for five years, during which time he was suspected of various deceptions and attempts at escape. He was paroled and exchanged in late 1780. Returning to duty, he was assigned command of Loyalist forces in Virginia and North Carolina. He was again captured near Yorktown in the fall of 1781 and brought before General Washington, who was not best pleased to see him. As Connolly put it, "I can only say the friendly sentiment he once publicly professed, for me no longer existed." Connolly was again a prisoner, then a parolee, and then a prisoner again on the ground of violating his parole. In March 1782 he was permitted to go to British-occupied New York and then sail for England.[14]

Like many Loyalists, Connolly believed that Americans would soon return to British rule or form a new monarchy with Washington as king. And, like many Loyalists, Connolly's land and property was confiscated. He spent much of his time in England applying for compensation for his losses.

At some point he traveled to Quebec, and, in the winter of 1787-88, from there to Detroit, then still under *de facto* British control. While Connolly was in Detroit, he received a report that Kentuckians wanted to split off from the federal government, declare their independence and get the protection of the British government. He traveled on to Louisville.

Northwest Territory Governor St. Claire wrote about Connolly to John Jay, reporting that "The Reason he assigned, at Detroit for his Journey to Louisville was, that he might obtain Certificates of the value of his Property in that Country which had been confiscated in order to support the Claim he had made upon the british Government for Compensation: My Information is, that he is sent to tamper with the People of Kentuckey and induce them to throw themselves into the Arms of Great Britain, and to assure them of protection and Support in that Measure—if that cannot be brought about, to stimulate them to Hostilities against the Spaniards, and at [any] rate to detach them from the united States." [15]

Thomas Marshall, father of Chief Justice John Marshall, was an advocate of transforming a piece of Virginia territory into Kentucky. Trying to recruit Marshall and his associates into his pro-British plans, Connolly spoke of Canadian troops moving south to wrest control of the Mississippi River from the Spanish, perhaps as far south as New Orleans.[16]

Harry Innes, a Virginia judge who was attorney general for the District of Kentucky, warned Washington about Connolly—and about Canada's yearning for Kentucky, hoping to "connect her with

Upper Canada." In 1789, perhaps as a reward, Washington appointed Innes district judge for Kentucky.

But Connolly was not the only one scheming on behalf of a foreign power. In 1784 when former Brigadier General James Wilkinson of the Continental Army, his wife, and their two sons moved from Philadelphia to the wilderness of the Kentucky District of Virginia.[17] At age twenty-seven Wilkinson could already look back on a distinguished military record: combat officer, aide-de-camp to Nathanael Greene, to Benedict Arnold, and to Horatio Gates; brevet brigadier general, secretary to the board of war. As a civilian, he continued to call himself General.[18] Wilkinson immediately plunged into the incendiary politics of the Kentucky District.

Thomas Marshall reported to George Washington as well, writing that in the spring of 1787 Wilkinson went to New Orleans with a cargo of tobacco, knowing that he would be stopped and interrogated by Spanish officials who controlled navigation of the Mississippi River. The Spanish governor asked Wilkinson to "give his sentiments freely in writing respecting the political interest of Spain and the Americans of the United States inhabiting the western waters."[19] He submitted an essay about fifteen or twenty pages long. Marshall managed to read a version of it.

Wilkinson had written that Kentucky could become a Spanish colony and, as a reward for making that happen, he wanted Kentucky to have free trade rights on the Mississippi River. Wilkinson seems to have spoken openly about these ideas, perhaps even at one of the Kentucky statehood conventions, but he was far from open about his motivations. In August 1787 Wilkinson had met in New Orleans with Spanish Governor Esteban Rodríguez Miró, offered to help make Kentucky a Spanish colony, and signed a document "transferring my allegiance from the United States to his Catholic Majesty," King Charles III.[20] He became Agent 13 in the Spanish Secret Service.

In the same letter to Washington, Thomas Marshall reported on Connolly's efforts to develop Kentucky support for a combined British/Kentuckian move against on Spanish Louisiana and New Orleans. Marshall plainly did not trust Connolly, but observed that "had I not before been acquainted with his character as a man of intrigue and artful address I should in all probability have given him my confidence." At the close of his letter he wrote that "[we] shall I fear never be safe from the machinations of our Enemies as well internal as external until we have a seperate state and are admitted into the union as a federal member."[21]

The two conspiracies collided with each other. Incredibly, in November 1788, Connolly lobbied Wilkinson—already a Spanish agent—and tried to get *his* support for the *British* invasion. Wilkinson reported that he listened to all Connolly had to say—then warned him that Kentuckians were very anti-British. He arranged for a hunter to assault Connolly, and then warned Connolly his life was in danger. Connolly asked for and received an escort out of the country. Wilkinson thus did his part to forestall the British. He continued to scheme with and on behalf of the Spanish.

Meantime, the Kentucky District's journey to statehood was still nothing like plain sailing. Kentuckians who wanted American statehood had to petition the Virginia General Assembly in Richmond, which passed a cumbersome enabling act that would allow Kentucky to sever its ties if its advocates were to hold two conventions: one where delegates would vote on independence, leading to a second where delegates would write a constitution. Next, Congress would decide when to admit that piece of Territory into the Union.

The first statehood convention took place in 1784, but accomplished little beyond agreement to hold a second convention the next year, followed soon after by a third. The Congress of the Confederation laid down new conditions that required several further meetings—but then in late 1787 the process ground to a halt as all parties awaited the outcome of the effort to ratify the new Federal Constitution. At the seventh convention, in 1788, James Wilkinson, secretly in the pay of the Spanish, called for a vote for independence from Virginia, which failed. Instead, petitions were sent to Washington and Richmond, but then the Congress of the Confederation set new conditions, leading to two more conventions. The ninth meeting voted 24 to 18 in favor of statehood, and received approval from Richmond and the new Federal Congress.

After *nine* contentious conventions over a span of eight years, on February 4, 1791 the First Federal Congress finally passed Kentucky's act of admission.[22] A tenth and final convention met to write the state constitution in April 1792. [23] But because of a legislative technicality, Kentucky's official entry was to be June 1, 1792, so that Kentucky became the fifteenth state—behind independent Vermont, which had been admitted on March 4, 1791, after flirting with the idea of becoming part of Canada.[24]

After failing to link Kentucky to Spain, Wilkinson left the new state, rejoined the American Army, and continued to be Spanish secret Service Agent 13. He soon regained his rank as brigadier general and assumed command of the Army in 1797. George Washington, the first of four Presidents who were served by Wilkinson during his treacherous career, said of him as a military officer, "General Wilkinson has displayed great zeal & ability for the public weal since he came into Service—His conduct carries strong marks of attention, activity, & Spirit, & I wish him to know the favorable light in which it is viewed."[25] His treachery was often suspected during his life, but not proven until long after his death.[26]

Washington long viewed the Northwest Territory as the path westward for "a rising Empire."[27] In his pre-presidential years he had believed that "Settlement of the Western Country and making a Peace with the Indians are so analogous that there can be no definition of the one without involving considerations of the other. . . . attempting to drive them by force of arms out of their Country . . . is like driving the Wild Beasts of the Forest which will return us soon as the pursuit is at an end and fall perhaps on those that are left there. . . . "[28]

As President, Washington wanted to achieve peace with the Indians by treating tribal chieftains as leaders of quasi nations. He demonstrated his faith on August 13, 1790, when he and Jefferson, as Secretary of State, publicly ratified what was known as the Treaty of New York, between the United States and the Creek Nation. Twenty-three headmen, chiefs, and warriors staged the public ratification of the first Indian treaty negotiated and ratified under the Constitution.

The treaty established the boundary between the United States and the Creek Nation, whose Kings, Chiefs, and Warriors "do acknowledge themselves, and the said parts of the Creek Nation, would be under the protection of the United States of America, and of no other sovereign whosoever"—a clause aimed at Spain, which did not recognize

American land claims in the Territory or borderlands. The treaty gave the Creek Nation control over tribal lands in Georgia and Alabama and guaranteed federal protection from white settlers, who were prohibited from hunting or even entering Creek lands. The Indian signatories also agreed to free American prisoners and hand over runaway slaves, who had sought freedom in Indian lands.[29]

The treaty made Alexander McGillivray "the Agent of the United States in the said nation with the rank of Brigadier General and the pay of one thousand two hundred dollars per annum, on his taking the usual oaths required by law." Anticipating the treaty, McGillivray had sent a letter to James White, superintendent of Indian affairs in North Carolina, South Carolina, and Georgia. "In the meantime," McGillivray wrote, "the chiefs should advise all the young Warriors to attend Closely to hunting, during the winter, instead of risquing their lives for a scalp." He considered them "an oppressed people" and "had agreed to give them assistance to enable them to obtain a good peace: but they were not to Consider me as engaged to support them in an unjust and an unnecessary war."[30]

McGillivray was the son of a Scot trader and a Creek woman whose father was French. Because the Creeks had a matrilineal society, he was treated as a Creek and full member of her clan. As the son of a successful father, he was well educated. In adulthood he acquired a plantation, became a slave owner, and had several wives. A colonel in the British Army during the Revolutionary War, he never became a trustworthy ally of the United States. But, as a smart, English-speaking Indian leader, he helped maintain communication between his people and the Washington administration.[31]

Both sides failed to carry out many provisions of the treaty. But there was great value inherent in that document with the Americans' signatures and the Indians' *X*s. For the treaty confirmed that federal power could trump states' rights, set the nation's Indian policy, and direct westward expansion through the creation of new states.

The scene of the unprecedented ratification ceremony was Federal Hall, and among the spectators in the packed gallery was Judith Sargent Murray, one of America's first female crusaders for educational and social equality of the sexes.

At the ratification ceremony, she sat in "a brilliant circle of Ladies, richly habited, and displaying some of the most beautiful faces." They included Mrs. Washington, who brought her grandson, George Washington Parke Custis, and granddaughter Eleanor Parke Custis.

"Suddenly rude, and tumultuous sounds are heard—frightfully terrific they vibrate tremendously upon the ear. Now the most dreadful shrieks wear the semblance of horrid yells, and now they characterize ceaseless riot, and unlicensed mirth—'What sounds are these?'—Every eye seems to ask—It is the song of praise as sung by the Kings, Chiefs, and Warriors, of the Creek Nation. . . . They are in a complete uniform of blue, faced with red, and McGillivray takes the lead, and all are fancifully painted, and decorated with earrings, and Nose jewels."

Washington arrived, listened to the secretary read the treaty, and then "supplicated the great Spirit, the Master of breath, to forbid an infringement of a Contract, formed under such happy auspices" and McGillivray "returned a short speech." Some Indians took the President by an elbow, entwined their arms with his, and sang a song of peace.[32][33]

The treaty ceremony was the federal government's last official function in New York City's Federal Hall.

The move of Congress to Philadelphia for the third session went smoothly. Many of the members were familiar with the city where they had served on Continental and Confederation Congresses. The lawmakers' new home was Congress Hall, formerly the County Court House, a two-story brick building in the Georgian style. The interior lacked grandeur. It bore no sign indicating the new title with its ten-year lease. Pennsylvanian Representative Thomas Fitzsimons had unsuccessfully recommended that the Philadelphians hire L'Enfant as the conversion architect. Again, the Senate was where the Senators thought they should be: on the second floor, above the House on the first.

The House gallery could hold about three hundred people. The *General Advertiser* published the complaint of a visitor who reported that the view was obstructed by Quakers who refused to remove their hats and by spectators in the first three rows who stood on their chairs. House members sat in black leather-upholstered armchairs arranged in a semicircle. Senators sat at individual desks in red-leather armchairs, kept warm by four fireplaces.[34]

When the session opened on December 6, 1790, the most important issue awaiting the lawmakers was Hamilton's proposal for a National Bank, which he portrayed as a vital ingredient of his economic plan. He cited the Constitution's *"necessary and proper" clause,* part of Article I, as the authority for the bank, setting off a debate over whether the Constitution permitted Congress to make laws that were not among the *enumerated powers.*

After a week of desultory debate, the bill was passed on February 8, 1791, by a vote of 39 to 20. Thirty-three members who voted for the bank represented New York, New Jersey, and Pennsylvania; fifteen of the negative voters were from Virginia, the Carolinas, and Georgia. It was another example of how the First Congress began what would become the lasting clash between North and South.

As for what else was accomplished in that session, Senator Maclay provided a summary in his diary: "Nothing of Consequence to the Continent, was transacted this day . . . unless it was the Report, of the Committee on the Algerine business."[35]

The Algerine business would not be fulfilled until the United States had a Navy and unleashed its frigates against the pirate regimes of the Barbary Coast. It would be fifteen years before the U.S. Marines reached the shores of Tripoli in the first of the two Barbary Coast wars. As for the fate of the tribes of the Frontiers, 1791 was the year President Washington lost any chance for peace between Indians and whites.

Eventually, Washington could not ignore pleas for protection from the Ohio Valley frontier. Settlers were streaming into the valley despite Indian attacks. On January 8, 1790, in his first State of the Union address to Congress, Washington felt he had to respond to pleas for protection from the Ohio Valley frontier, where one land syndicate alone, organized by former New Jersey politician John Cleves Symmes, who had moved to Ohio and was hoping to buy, owned about 330,000 Territory acres.[36]

Washington asked for an effective army, declaring, "To be prepared for war is one of the most effectual means of preserving peace."[37] To underline the need to protect the frontier, he passed along an exhaustive proposal by Secretary of War Knox to enlarge the Army. Maclay's comment: "give Knox his Army, and he will soon have a War on hand."[38] Maclay was right.

Brigadier General Josiah Harmar commanded the small force guarding the Ohio frontier against native uprisings and Canadian squatters. He operated from Fort Harmar at the site of today's Marietta, Ohio, but later shifted to the settlement he named Cincinnati, obviously in honor of the Society. Harmar and St. Clair developed a strategy to send a powerful punitive force in a two-prong attack against Indian villages along the Wabash and Maumee Rivers.

In the fall of 1790 about 1,500 men—regular army soldiers, Philadelphia and Kentucky militiamen, levies, and hired levy replacements—gathered at Cincinnati. On October 7, 1790, they set out with their six hundred packhorses, shadowed by Indian scouts.[39] On October 17, part of Harmar's force reached five abandoned Miami villages, which they destroyed, burning wigwams, log houses, and hoards of food.

On October 21, mission completed, Harmar headed back to Fort Washington, In short and bloody battles, warriors armed with British muskets and led by Little Turtle of the Miami Nation got their revenge. By the time Harmar and his men reached Fort Washington, the regulars had lost seventy-five men killed out of the three hundred and twenty in the original force; militia losses were also high. Most reports list one hundred and eighty-three men killed or missing.[40]

Washington and Knox reacted to that battle, which would be called Harmar's Defeat[41] by preparing for another expedition. This one would be a 3,000-man invasion force. Its objective would be to build a "strong post and garrison" at Miami village and a string of support units from there to Fort Washington. Knox predicted that the invasion and fortifications would "curb and overawe not only the Wabash Indians, but ... all others who might be wavering. . . ."[42]

On September 17, 1791, Arthur St. Clair, acting as a major general and the governor of the Northwest Territory, led about 1,400 men, including regulars, Kentucky volunteers, and six-month volunteers, out of Fort Washington. Building forts along the way, they had gone only about ninety miles when Little Turtle and his warriors struck, killing six hundred and thirty-seven, wounding two hundred and sixty-three, and driving off the survivors. The battle, which left nearly half the U.S. Army dead or wounded, became known St. Clair's Defeat.[43]

Americans' abhorrence of a standing army quickly faded. Congress, responding to the massacre, authorized a force organized into what would be called the Legion of the United States. Instead of consisting of separate infantry, cavalry, and artillery units, all three would be integrated into four Sub-Legions of 1,280 men each. The Legion's mission was to be guardian of the Territory, under the command of Major General Anthony Wayne.[44] "I hope," Wayne told Knox, "that by this time every Idea of peace is done away."[45]

For good and ill, the process of rapid and continuous expansion westward that had its start in those early days became part of the American heritage, part of the American identity. The process of creating that identity, of defining a new people, had many other aspects. How people spoke, how they wrote, and what the words conveyed held a mirror up to all that was happening in the new and growing nation.

TOWARD AN AMERICAN LANGUAGE

One day in the fall of 1782, lexicographer Noah Webster, after a Hudson ferry crossing en route to a new teaching job in Goshen, New York, passed through the Continental Army encampment near Newburgh. He listened to the soldiers' talk and was surprised by what he heard—not because there was so much grumbling and discontent but because the soldiers spoke so many languages. Several of the soldiers spoke French to one another. Others spoke German, or Dutch, or Swedish, or one of the Gaelic dialects of Scotland and Ireland. He even had trouble understanding some of the soldiers' regional versions of English.[1]

The soldiers' chatter became an inspiration to the lexicographer: America needed the unifying bond of an American language, he decided, and American students needed a book to replace the old ones, with their outdated pledges of allegiance to the king. In 1783, Webster published volume 1 of *A Grammatical Institute of the English Language* (also known as *The American Spelling Book* but best known as the *Blue-Backed Speller* for the color of its binding).[2] The book sold a million copies a year, producing income for Webster for the rest of his life. It is still in print.[3]

In Webster's *Dissertations on the English Language*, published in 1789, he wrote, "As an independent nation, our honor requires us to have a system of our own, in language, as well as government. Great Britain, whose children we are, and whose language we speak, should no longer be *our* standard."[4] He saw as part of his work a declaration of independence, both culturally and linguistically. "Let us then seize the present moment," he wrote, "and establish a *national language* as well as a national government."[5]

Establishing a national language, however, can be frustrating. What
the Webster *Dissertations* said in 1789 is still true today: the persistence
of "local peculiarities in pronunciation," particularly "among the country people in New England." The "great error in their manner of speaking proceeds immediately from not opening the mouth sufficiently,"
Webster wrote. "Hence words are drawled out in a careless lazy manner,
or the sound finds a passage thro the nose. Nothing can be so disagreeable as that drawling, whining cant that distinguishes a certain class of
people; and too much pains cannot be taken to reform the practice."[6]

After the creation of the First Federal Congress in 1789, America quickly became a new nation with new ideas that were presented, discussed,
and debated in scores of newspapers and magazines. Pennsylvania allowed Philadelphia to open theaters. New York playgoers saw a play
that made American theatrical history. Book readers were turning the
pages of the first American novel.

Except for some baffling spelling, odd punctuation, and a strange
s that looks like an *f*, we modern Americans usually have little trouble reading printed documents written from much of our past. (Not
so for handwritten cursive documents!) As we read them, we might
see unfamiliar spellings: *gaol* instead of *jail*, *honour* instead of *honor*,
publick instead of *public*, *travelled* instead of *traveled*, and *centre* instead
of *center*. Back in the late eighteenth century, however, more and more
Americans, whether feeding a printing press or dipping a quill pen
into an inkwell, were writing *jail*, *honor*, *public*, *traveled*, and *center*.
They were disciples of the new *American* language.

The notion of getting rid of "superfluous or silent letters" came from
Webster, who, with the dour persistence of a zealot, devoted his life to
a quest for a simpler, more sensible alphabet. Most people did not accept some of his bizarre new spellings, such as *ake* instead of *ache*, *soop*
instead of *soup*, *tung* instead of *tongue*, and *wimmen* instead of *women*.[7]

But at the same time, Americans were discarding old words and
adopting or coining new words. "A living language," Webster wrote,
"must keep pace with improvements in knowledge, and with the multi-
plication of ideas."[8] Those ideas made their way into the consciousness
of American who were reading new magazines, newspapers, and books.
Another Webster crusade sought copyright protection for authors.

Webster, traveling continually, became a champion for copyright by individual states in lieu of a federal copyright law. But copyright became a Federal responsibility on May 31, 1790, when the president signed what was called the *Act for the Encouragement of Learning*.[9] That first such law protected books, maps, and charts for fourteen years with a renewal of another fourteen years.

The nation's first literary magazine, *The American Museum, or Repository of Ancient and Modern Fugitive Pieces*, did not have a long life: it extended only from volume 1 in January 1787 to volume 12, the final issue, in July 1792.[10] But it had lasting influence on what Americans expected from their magazines: contemporary American literature and poetry, articles on politics, economics, and excerpts from newspapers.[11]

The *American Museum*'s founder and publisher, Dublin-born Mathew Carey, got started with a contribution equivalent to $400 from Marquis de Lafayette, who happened to be in New York when Carey was in the city looking for subscribers and supporters.[12] One of Carey's subscribers was President Washington, who replied to a plea for funds not with a contribution of money but with what today would be called a blurb—a free advertisement: "discontinuance of the Publication for want of proper support would, in my judgment, be an impeachment on the Understanding of this Country."[13]

Among the thirty-eight articles in *Museum*'s final issue were "Reflexions on the State of the Union," "Letters to a Young Lady" (on several topics, including affection, Voltaire, and observations on bees), and "Rules for Changing a Limited Republican Government into an Absolute Hereditary One" This last was a brilliant 2,900-word satirical piece by poet Philip Freneau, and among his rules was this one: "Nothing being more likely to prepare the vulgar mind for aristocratical ranks and hereditary powers than titles, endeavor in the offset of the government to confer these on its most dignified officers."

Freneau is also the author of one of the five poems in the issue, "Ode on the fourteenth of July," the day of the storming of the Bastille.

By coincidence—or perhaps because of a new America-inspired creativity—1789 was the year that six new magazines started up. *Children's Magazine* failed after only four issues, presumably because neither parents nor schoolmasters could understand why children needed a magazine of their own. *Courier de Boston*, devoted to promoting friendly relations between America and France, lasted only six months before it became a casualty of the French Revolution. *Arminian Magazine*, supported mostly by the Methodist Episcopal Church, ceased publication after a year of spreading the theology of John Wesley. *Christian's, Scholar's, and Farmer's Magazine* had an encyclopedic tone, offering entries on history, belles-lettres, and classical knowledge. *Gentleman and Ladies Town and Country Magazine* filled its pages with sentiment and sensibility for two years and then ceased publication.[14]

The most successful of the 1789 publications was the *Massachusetts Magazine*, which had an eight-year lifespan devoted to history, genealogy, and biography. The magazine's invitation to women writers attracted, among others, Judith Sargent Murray, a poet, playwright, and advocate of women's equality. Her dazzling contribution, "On the Equality of the Sexes," began as a poem—"That minds are not alike full well I know / This truth each day's experience will show"—and evolved into a long essay that asked whether "the minds of females are so notoriously deficient, or unequal? . . . Will it be said that the judgment of a male of two years old is more sage than that of a female's of the same age? I believe the reverse is generally observed. As their years increase, the sister must be wholly domesticated, while the brother is led by the hand through all the flowery paths of science. . . . Yes, ye lordly, ye haughty sex, our souls are by nature *equal* to yours."[15]

In New York, Noah Webster, gaining fame as the sentinel of the American language, launched *American Magazine*. It appeared on January 1, 1788, unfurling its motto: "Science the guide, and truth the eternal goal." Determined to teach Americans how to read and write the American language, Webster wrote fourteen essays on education. He was so critical of American newpapers' coverage of scandals and casual attitude toward facts that he proposed putting constraints on the press.[16]

Webster's magazine, much of it written in his pedagogical style, did not catch on. In December 1788, he passed *American Magazine* to a would-be publisher, but it was never published again.

The new copyright law did not specifically mention the type of art it covered, but the Constitution embraces "the progress of science and useful arts." The Puritans and their intellectual descendants would not call theaters useful, but by the mid-eighteenth century, most people no longer considered theaters as dens of iniquity, and some would even argue that theater was art. The old Puritanical bans on theater in major cities were falling away. There were theatrical sessions not only in New York but also Annapolis, Williamsburg, and Charleston.[17]

The last holdout was Philadelphia. In 1789, when the First Congress was beginning the acrimonious debate about the location of the nation's capital, Philadelphia was competing against New York—and its theaters. So the Pennsylvania Legislature, defying Quaker opposition, passed a bill allowing theatrical performances in Philadelphia.[18]

Royall Tyler's *The Contrast* was the first play by an American to be put on stage by a professional company. The play debuted in at the John Street Theatre in New York in April 1787. It was still running when the First Federal Congress arrived in New York. We know that because at least one member, Representative Jeremiah Wadsworth of Connecticut, on June 3, 1789, sent a note to a friend, asking him "to find for him a good theater box for the performance of *The Contract*," misspelling its name in a slip of the quill.[19]

The playwright Royall Tyler was a Boston lawyer who had served in the Revolutionary War and one day decided to go to New York and write a play. Using English Restoration comedies as a model, he conceived a sardonic view of the new nation. The play "points out the excesses of the wealthy, the folly of grandstanding righteousness, and the dangers of speculation without substance," wrote a modern critic about the play when *The Contrast* had a revival in 2009 at New York's Metropolitan Playhouse.[20]

Critiques of the emerging new society also came from the newspapers that were sprouting throughout the republic. By 1789, at least ninety-two papers were being published, ranging from the *Cumberland Gazette* in Portland, Maine,[21] to the *Gazette of the State of Georgia* in Savannah.[22] Several of them assigned reporters to cover Congress. Anticipating today's Associated Press, some shared their articles with papers that did not have congressional reporters.

Two entrepreneurs—Thomas Lloyd and John Fenno—arrived in New York with the idea of covering congressional debates. Lloyd planned to publish the debates exclusively and sell subscriptions. Fenno started a newspaper, *Gazette of the United States*, that reported accurately while supporting Hamilton and the Federal cause.[23] Its motto was "He that is not for us, is against us." Hamilton anonymously contributed essays and letters to the *Gazette*.[24]

Newspaper readers in 1789 were not only learning about what was going on in Federal Hall. Their newspapers delivered a variety of useful everyday information. The *New-York Journal and Weekly Register* for October 22, 1789 devotes most of a page-one column to the prices for dozens of items, some of which are still on store shelves: superfine flour, nails, cocoa, tobacco, soap, butter, and sugar. Below the list is a notice from the New York Supreme Court naming two farmers as "absconding and absent debtors." There is also a notice of the auctioning off of a Loyalist's confiscated lands in New Jersey. An advertisement from an agent in London informs American "Merchants and Planters" that he can ship their goods to ports in Italy, Spain, France, Greece, and Ireland—a short list that nonetheless reveals the widening span of America's international trade.[25]

The *Wilmington Centinel* of Wilmington, North Carolina, for February 19, 1789 published on the front page two slave stories, one a routine advertisement about three runaway slaves possibly heading to a port to board a ship to Nova Scotia or the Bahamas. The other slave story could have been written by an abolitionist: "A captain of a Guinea [Africa] ship is now in jail in London.... on account of having cruelly treated and maimed a number of English sailors under his command." A London abolition group provided evidence in another case involving the same captain: "A young negro woman, with her infant at her breast, was kidnapped away from her husband and parents, and offered, by the dealers in human flesh, to the commander for sale, but he could not have anything to do with the brat. Ho[w] ever, as they could not be separated, he purchased them both. At the same time deliberately he dashed out the brains of the infant on the deck of the ship, and threw it overboard in the mother's presence.—As she was a young woman of uncommon beauty, in less than an hour she was dragged by the captain to his bed, and compelled to endure the embraces of her child's murderer."[26]

The *Salem* (Massachusetts) *Mercury* contains a cure for a disease affecting the feet of sheep. News from Georgia comes in an excerpt of a letter: "I have had a small attack with the Creeks and Cherokees, within 300 yards of the house I lived at. My overseer is dangerously wounded, and myself plundered of my horses. We killed one Indian."

The *Herald of Freedom and the Federal Advertiser* of Boston for January 30, 1789 has an advertisement from Thomas H. Perkins, who is sending a ship to China and invites passengers—"Any Persons wishing to adventure."[27] (Perkins was a wealthy Boston merchant. Other ships he owned picked up Turkish opium at $2 a pound and sold it in China at $16 a pound.[28])

The *Daily Advertiser* of New York for February 4, 1789 devotes extensive space to the nation's leading public intellectual, Dr. Benjamin Rush, who is concerned about the medical effects of the Revolution. "Many persons of infirm and delicate habits," he writes, "were restored to perfect health" by the U.S. victory, and "hysterical women" were calmed. The New York Society for the Encouragement of American Manufactures is raising funds to find jobs for the poor. A very short story tells of the romance between Maria and Eugenio; the latter "tremble[s] with strong emotions" when his beloved speaks. They part, and soon consumption "terminated her existence." As for Eugenio, "a pistol procured him the same burial and the same grave."[29]

There is also an ad with the headline "First American Novel." It was William Hill Brown's *The Power of Sympathy* or *the Triumph of Nature*, dedicated to the Young Ladies of America and "intended to represent the specious causes and to inspire the fatal consequences of SEDUCTION; to inspire the female mind with a principle of self-complacency, and to promote the economy of human life."

Published in 1789, *The Power of Sympathy*[30] began the penchant of American novelists for basing their plots on real events—"ripped from the headlines," as we say today. Brown, who published this novel anonymously, paralleled in fiction the real characters of a real scandal.

There are other claimants as the first American novel, depending on what counts as being American—and, for that matter, what counts as being a novel, still a fairly new literary form in those days. At the very least, *The Power of Sympathy* can call itself the first novel written in America, by an author born in America, published first in America, set in America, and about something that happened in America, and all of those facts mattered. As noted by the New England Historical Society, "the novel achieved lasting popularity in America—because it had an American author, an American publisher, an American setting and an American subject."[31]

The real people were Perez Morton, his beautiful wife, poet Sarah Wentworth Morton; and Sarah's sister, Fanny Apthorp. Perez Morton was a Harvard graduate, a Patriot leader in Massachusetts, an aide to Governor John Hancock, a friend of John Adams, and an influential Boston lawyer. Sarah Apthorp, born in Boston in 1759, was the daughter of James Apthorp, and thus part of a prosperous Boston merchant family. Her mother was Sarah Wentworth Apthorp, whose family was also in the rich-merchant class. Young Sarah and Morton were married in 1781 and had five children before the scandal became public and stunned Boston.[32]

Peter and Sarah lived in the Apthorp family mansion and made their landmark home a salon for the Boston literati. In 1786, Sarah's younger sister Fanny moved into the mansion. Sometime later, she was seduced by Perez Morton. If fiction matched reality, he desired to have her as his mistress. She bore him a child in 1787 or 1788 and killed herself by swallowing an overdose of laudanum. (In the book, the seducer also kills himself. Next to his body lies an English-language copy of Goethe's *The Sorrows of Young Werther*: the scene is meant to mirror the suicides of young European men who killed themselves in imitation of lovelorn Werther. The deaths were the first recorded cases of "copycat suicides.")

Under the law of the time, Morton was guilty of both adultery and incest.[33] A jury implicated Morton in the suicide, but he was not punished for it. His friends, John Adams and former Governor James Bowdoin, defended him. He and the scandal were so well known that they did not use his name. In an open letter, they wrote that, after their inquiry, they decided that their unnamed friend had been the victim of "a late unhappy event" and was worthy of "friendship and affection."[34]

Brown probably chose to publish the book anonymously because he was both a neighbor and friend of the Mortons and did not want to reveal his treachery. But the plot so resembled what really happened that Sarah Morton was believed to have been the author. Her writings were well known in her circle, but it seemed odd that she, the victim of her husband's infidelity, would make a novel of it. Literary historians worked with meager clues before a definitive article settled the mystery in 1933: The author was William Hill Brown. [35]

Brown also wrote the romantic tale "Harriot, or the Domestic Reconciliation" which was published in the first issue of *Massachusetts Magazine*. He also wrote a play, poetry, and essays. *Ira and Isabella*, a short novel, repeated *Sympathy*'s themes of seduction and incest. It was published posthumously in 1807.[36] He died of "seasonal fevers" in Murfreesboro, North Carolina, in August 1793, at the age of twenty-eight.[37]

Sarah Wentworth Morton remained married to Perez Morton and began sending poems, often lengthy, to the new *Massachusetts Magazine*, which began publishing in 1789. Among her poems was "*The African Chief*," an antislavery work that must have infuriated her father, whose wealth mostly came from the slave trade.[38] She wrote under the name Constantia or Philenia.

Massachusetts Magazine's list of potential contents reflect the wide interests of Americans of those days: "illustrated articles and observations on agriculture, poetry, music, biography, history, physics, geography, morality, criticism, philosophy, mathematics, agriculture, architecture, chemistry, novels, tales, romances, translations, news, marriages, deaths, and meteorological observations."[39]

The American Geography, or, A View of the Present Situation, was also a bestseller of 1789.[40] It was the most widely read description of the nation since the ratification of the Constitution.[41] The author, Connecticut-born Jedidiah Morse, a clergyman, began his other career as a geographer while at Yale studying theology and planning to become a pastor. On the side, he worked as a schoolmaster.

Morse became particularly riled about European textbooks that gave his students inaccurate geographic information about America. So, he wrote *Geography Made Easy*, whose first edition was published in 1784. That work, the first geography by an American, launched his fame as a geographer. He kept gathering information, and a new book evolved: *The American Geography*,[42] with its "astronomical geography" and "geographical definitions." [43] But the book was far more than pages of geographic fact. Morse sometimes provided vivid descriptions about the state's inhabitants.

"The Virginians who are rich are in general sensible, polite and hospitable, and of an independent spirit," says a traveler quoted by Morse in his profile of Virginia. "The poor are ignorant and abject—and all are of an inquisitive turn, and in many other respects, very much resemble the people in the eastern states. They differ from them, however, in their morals: the former being much addicted to gaming, drinking, swearing, horse-racing, cock-fighting, and most kinds of dissipation. There is a much greater disparity between the rich and the poor, in Virginia, than in any of the northern states."

"'The young men,'" another traveler observes, "generally speaking, are gamblers, cock-fighters, and horse-jockies. To hear them converse, you would imagine that the grand point of all science was properly to fix a gaff [a spear for taking fish or turtles], and touch, with dexterity, the tail of a cock while in combat. He who won the last match, the last game, or the last horse-race, assumes the airs of a hero or German Potentate."[44]

No state gets a better depiction than Morse's home state of Connecticut, which "resembles a well cultivated garden, which, with that degree of industry that is necessary to happiness, produces the necessaries and conveniences of life in great plenty." Well-educated clergymen—presumably including Morse—"have hitherto preserved a kind of aristocratical balance in the very democratical government of the State."[45]

Morse also occasionally compares states and their people: "migrants from Pennsylvania always travel to the southward. The soil and climate of the western parts of Virginia, North and South-Carolina, and Georgia, afford a more easy-support to lazy farmers than the stubborn but durable soil of Pennsylvania. Here our ground requires deep and repeated plowing to render it fruitful; there scratching the ground once or twice affords tolerable crops." [46] Moses, an ardent abolitionist, attacked slavery as the "bane of industry. It renders labour, among the whites, not only unfashionable but disreputable. Industry is the offspring of necessity. . . . Slavery preludes this necessity; and indolence . . . is the unhappy consequence." [47]

Besides the thirteen states, Morse covers states-in-waiting (Indiana, Kentucky, Vermont) and the "Western Territory." He is especially a booster of Kentucky: "The progress in improvements and cultivation which have been made in this country, almost exceeds belief. Eleven years ago Kentucky lay in forest, almost uninhabited, but by wild beasts. Now, not withstanding the united opposition of all the western Indians, she exhibits an extensive settlement, divided into seven large and populous counties, in which are a number of flourishing little towns—containing more inhabitants than are in Georgia, Delaware or Rhode Island states—and nearly or quite as many as in New Hampshire."[48]

The American Geography contained excellent maps and detailed descriptions of Europe, Asia, and Africa, giving the book a potential appeal beyond the nation's borders. The book was sold in Britain by an unscrupulous publisher who took advantage of Morse's failed attempt to get it copyrighted in that country. But an unexpected result of the overseas edition was that it promoted immigration to America. One of the many letters from Britain told of a man who tells his children, "Study the book, as North America is the place you will probably go to."[49]

American diaries and journals contain nuggets of history. And, since it is the nature of a nugget to be rare and hidden, the searcher usually must sift through chunks and lumps before the ah-hah! moment. Journals also yield such moments. Describing a collection of 359 American diaries and journals, a historian wrote, "Some are full and informative; others spotty and thin, occasionally little more than daily recitals of the weather conditions." [50] The same could be said of the entries made by the prime American diary keeper of his time: George Washington. During his Mount Vernon respites between calls to duty, his entries were mundane and often agricultural. New Year's Day of 1789—"Clear Morning and wind tho' not much of it"—he wrote: "Went out after breakfast . . . to measure an old field which is intended to be added to Muddy hole Plantation."

Washington and the other Founders knew that posterity would be far more interested in their letters for researching the biographies and history books that were to come. Beyond the Founders, some diary keepers reveal their secrets and give us eyewitness reports of incidents we would not otherwise know about. Without Senator William

Maclay's diary, for instance, we would miss much that went on behind the Senate's closed doors in the First Congress.

Most books about war are written from the point of view of the generals or leaders, or from the lofty, dispassionate perch of the academic historian. But readers in the new democracy—and Americans ever since—were also eager for accounts as told from the perspective of the ordinary soldier. One of the first examples of such was Private Joseph Plumb Martin's account of his service in the Revolutionary War. It was a something beyond the ordinary diary. He was fifteen years old when he enlisted in the Continental Army, and he stayed in until the war ended. His book—*A Narrative of a Revolutionary Soldier*—takes the reader to war, sometimes going beyond battle to recall moments of misery, especially at Valley Forge: "The army was now not only starved but naked; the greatest part were not only shirtless and barefoot, but destitute of all their clothing, especially blankets."[51]

To read another soldier's narrative, more than a thousand subscribers from New England to Tennessee paid for the initial printing of *The Life and Travels of John Robert Shaw: A Narrative of the Life and Travels of the Well-Digger, now resident of Lexington, Kentucky, Written by Himself*. Shaw had arrived in Rhode Island as a British redcoat. As he told it, fate eventually made him a prisoner of war and he fought on the American side. Shaw was an exuberant spirit whose rowdy drinking bouts and related predicaments alternated with periods of wholehearted efforts at reform. His autobiography, written while he recuperated from injuries from one of several explosions (an occupational hazard for the frontier well-digger), recalls the rough and boozy life on the postwar frontier—and his faith in discovery of virtue and labor.

Shaw was the new American of the Territories. Such were the people who were moving beyond the original thirteen states, but retaining the spirit that said you could defy a king and create a nation. "Through all the career of my folly, vice and intemperance, I made it a point never to lose sight of industry," he wrote. Industry and virtue were his creed: "to aim at perfection" and "to have courage enough to withstand ridicule, the weapon of the wicked, in their subtil attacks upon virtue."[52]

He was one of the discoverers of what the new land held, what people could make of the American land and what the land could make of them.[53]

It was George Washington, too often described as a haughty aristocrat, who, as much as anyone, made possible an America where new Americans like John Robert Shaw, however raw and crude, could thrive. Washington was more than the indispensable man. He had, in the eyes of many, become something more than just a human being. He was turned into a symbol, a personification, of the American ideal.

The new America, and the new Americans, would soon be forced to learn that the man, if not the ideal, was mortal, after all.

EPILOGUE

IN RISING GLORY

On September 19, 1796, Philadelphia's *American Daily Advertiser* published a statement from President George Washington, addressed to "Friends and Fellow Citizens." He chose to publish rather than speak these words, which would become known as his Farewell Address. Nearing the end of his second term, he said he had chosen not to seek a third. In his sobering assessment of what he still called "an experiment," he warned against forces that pitted North against South, and party against party.[1]

His farewell had an air of finality, a sign of something more than the end of George Washington as President.

During his second term, he signed a bill that levied the first national internal revenue tax to raise money for the national debt and to assert the power of the national government. The tax had been proposed by Secretary of the Treasury Hamilton "upon spirits distilled within the United States and for appropriating the same." Jefferson opposed the law, which hit western Pennsylvania much harder than Washington or Hamilton had expected. They did not know—or care to know—that the Pennsylvania farmers did not harvest their corn, rye, and grain as food but as drink. They distilled their grain crops into whiskey. Wealthy, big-land farmers made enough money to afford the tax, which was a burden for farmers tilling smaller fields.

After trying to tamp down the farmers' protests, Washington reprimanded them for resisting federal law. Then, in July 1794, nearly 400 protesters set fire to the home of the regional tax collection supervisor near Pittsburgh. Urged on by Hamilton, Washington donned his general's uniform, mobilized a militia force of 12,950 men and led them toward western Pennsylvania, warning locals "not to abet, aid, or com-

fort the Insurgents . . . as they will answer the contrary at their peril."
About 150 insurgents were tried for treason; two were found guilty
and would later be pardoned by Washington.[2]

Although Washington's handling of the Whiskey Rebellion
demonstrated the awesome power of the federal government, his
use of military force was haunted by the brutal fact that his large
armed force was big enough to stage a coup d'état—the nightmare
of Newburgh.

A bit more than two years later, Washington performed the one
most powerful action he could take to drive that nightmare back into
the darkness. Simply by refusing to stand for a third term and step-
ping down from office, Washington established one more precedent,
perhaps the most important one of all. The world was not much used
to witnessing the orderly, law-bound, voluntary, peaceful transfer of
power. Willingly relinquishing office was not a thing that monarchs
did. By doing it, Washington demonstrated one more time that the
first President was no King, and nor would be the second, or third,
President, or any President at all. Twenty-first century Americans can
look back on more than two hundred years of such peaceful transfers
of power, and accept them as the normal course of events. It was eighteenth-century Americans who brought such a thing new into the world.

In 1797, after completing his second term, Washington finally could
retire to his beloved Mount Vernon. At last he would become what
he had so long yearned to be: "a private citizen on the banks of the
Potomac, & under the shadow of my own Vine & my own Fig-tree." [3]

But beyond Mount Vernon, as the end of the century neared, many
Americans feared for the future of their struggling democracy. The
United States was in an undeclared naval war with France. Men who
had fought alongside Washington were being accused of hatching monarchial plots to take over the country. Washington's Federalist supporters, concerned about Adams' unpopularity, had tried in vain to get
Washington to run for a third term and save "your injured country."

Washington's successor, President John Adams, stung by attacks on
his administration, signed into law the notorious Alien and Sedition
Acts, aimed at suppressing political opposition from Thomas Jefferson

and his Republicans. Newspaper editors were arrested for "false, scandalous and malicious writing" and had their newspapers shut down. [4]

George Washington was not supposed to die. He was supposed to live on and on. His existence, even in retirement, seemed, in some mystical way, to guarantee the continued existence of the nation he had led, first in war, then in peace. He was the first American hero, the spirit of American character, the American symbol of leadership and self-sacrifice.

After rising soon after sunrise on Thursday, December 12, 1799, Washington took note of the temperature: thirty-three degrees. "At about ten o'clock it began to snow, soon after to hail, and then to a settled cold rain," he recorded in his diary. But at ten o'clock he had mounted his horse, and, lashed by drenching winds, made his usual ride around his Mount Vernon farms.

Five hours later, he returned home, soaked. Tobias Lear saw that Washington's "neck appeared to be wet and the snow was hanging upon his hair." When Lear asked him if he wanted to change before dinner, Washington said his great coat had kept him dry. Lear handed him some letters for him to mark for franking. (Washington was granted the very rare privilege of franked, or free, postage.[5]) Washington did so, but told Lear not to send a slave to the Post Office in Alexandria, about eight miles away, because "the weather was too bad."[6]

One of the letters was to Alexander Hamilton, who had asked Washington's advice about the establishment of a military academy. Although Washington saw the academy as "an Object of primary importance to this Country," he said he "must now decline making any observations on the details of your plan." Washington apparently wanted to maintain neutrality between Hamilton and his nemesis, President Adams. Hamilton had engineered Adams' appointment of Washington as commander in chief of what Hamilton and his supporters called The New Army. [7]

On July 4, 1798, President Adams had commissioned Washington "Lieutenant General and Commander in Chief of all the Armies."[8] On July 7, Congress rescinded all treaties with France, and Adams had ordered the U.S. Navy to seek and destroy French warships and privateers that were attacking American merchantmen. So, as Washington rode his wintry land on December 12, 1799, he was also aware that a day might come when he would again be riding into battle.

Next day, snow three inches deep covered the fields. But when the snow let up, Washington went out, this time to walk the ground at the front of Mount Vernon. He had planned some new landscaping, and he needed to mark the trees that he wanted removed for a walkway.

"As usual with him, he carried his own compass, noted his observations, and marked out the ground," noted George Washington Custis, Martha Washington's nineteen-year-old grandson.

Washington, saying he had a chill, went inside about one o'clock. That afternoon, after his daily collection of newspapers were brought in, he sat in the parlor with Martha and Lear. After she left, the two men talked politics. Washington had a glass of his favorite Madeira and asked Lear to order more from a merchant in Philadelphia. When Washington started complaining about James Madison and James Monroe's behavior in the Virginia Assembly, Lear remarked that Washington sounded hoarse and told him he should take something for his cold.

Washington shook his head, saying, "You know I never take anything for a cold. Let it go as it came."

He excused himself for "a slight indisposition" and went into the library. Mount Vernon was operating at a loss. He wrote a letter to his farm manager, James Anderson, and enclosed an exhaustive plan that called for the renting out of his enterprises—a Potomac River fishery, a whiskey distillery, a grist mill—and the sale of one of the five Mount Vernon farms. The date for launching his plan was to be January 1, 1800.

Martha Washington went to bed. About eleven o'clock, she was still awake. She had not heard the sound of the library door's closing, the long-familiar signal the George Washington's day had ended. When he finally came to bed, she chided him for staying up late while he was not feeling well.

About two o'clock on Saturday morning, Washington, shaking and sweating, awakened Martha. Gasping for breath, he said he had ague, a fever that racked the body. He refused her offer to call a servant, waiting until a house slave, Caroline, arrived at dawn to make a fire in the bedroom. Martha sent her to get Lear, who found Washington "breathing with difficulty" and "hardly able to utter a word intelligibly."

Lear sent for one doctor, Martha for another, knowing he was closer. Washington, a great believer in bleeding as a cure for assorted ills, called in his young, recently hired clerk, Albin Rawlins, and ordered him to open a vein. Rawlins hesitated. "Don't be afraid," Washington said in a hoarse whisper. Rawlins plunged a double-edged lancet into Washington's arm. "The orifice is not large enough," Washington croaked. But the blood began to flow freely into a porcelain bowl.

For hours, first one, then another doctor treated Washington. They later described what they did, leaving to posterity a report that would be familiar to the survivors of eighteenth-century medicine but horrifying to anyone who read it in a doctor's waiting room today.

The doctors continued the bleeding, draining more than five pints of blood from Washington's body. They also forced him to swallow a purgative now known to contain poisons.

Washington interrupted his doctors' treatments to call Lear to his bedside. "I find I am going," Washington said.

About half-past four, Washington called Martha to his bedside and asked her to go to his desk, find two wills, and bring both to him. He looked them over, handed one to her, and ordered her to burn it. She placed it in the fireplace, left the room to put the other will away, then returned to the bed and took Washington's hand.

In July 1799, Washington had drawn up a new will—without the aid of a lawyer, as noted in the document itself. His will was a 7,669-word testament to his character and a look at his world of family, land, and slaves.

He identified himself not as a Virginian but as "a citizen of the United States." And, for the first recorded time, called the Federal District, which he had founded, "the City of Washington." [9]

His estate included vast tracts of land in Virginia, Kentucky, Maryland, New York, Pennsylvania, and Ohio. Besides some 50,000 acres of farm and forest and his other properties, he owned a large work force of slaves. Their fate involved his most complex bequest.

At the time of his death, there were a total of 317 enslaved people at Mount Vernon, many of them "dowry slaves" who had belonged to

Martha's first husband, and in whom Martha had a life interest. By law, neither George nor Martha could free these dower slaves.[10]

The slaves he owned were to be freed after Martha died. "To emancipate them during her life," he wrote, "would, tho' earnestly wished by me, be attended with such insuperable difficulties ... as to excite the most painful sensations, if not disagreeable consequences.... " He named and personally freed one slave—"my Mulatto man, William (calling himself William Lee)," who had served his master for more than thirty years.

Washington's scrupulous listing of his assets included a listing of his personal belongings and a meticulous inventory of objects in his Mount Vernon mansion, providing future curators and researchers with invaluable knowledge.

Leaving one of his swords to each of nephews, he imbued the bequest with his thought of peace at a time of possible war: "These swords are accompanied with an injunction not to unsheath them for the purpose of shedding blood, except it be for self defence, or in defence of their Country & its rights.... " [11]

About ten o'clock, Washington gestured for Lear to come nearer. Twice Washington tried to speak. Then Lear heard faint words: "I am going."

Washington found enough strength to continue: "Have me decently buried, and do not let my body be put into the Vault in less than two days after I am dead." Lear nodded silently.

"Do you understand me?" Washington insisted.

"Yes, sir," Lear replied, aware of the nightmare that had inspired Washington's instructions. Lear knew that Washington, like many people of the time, was afraid of being buried alive.

"'Tis well," Washington said.

Martha Washington sat at the foot of their bed. James Craik, one of the doctors and a longtime friend, sat by the fire. Servants—accounts never refer to them as slaves—stood by the door.

Washington put his right hand to his left wrist to take his pulse. Lear asked Craik to come to the bedside. Washington's right hand fell. Lear grasped the hand and touched it to his breast. Craik closed Washington's eyes.

Martha gave her farewell and left the room. Lear, taking charge, had the body removed to a downstairs room. Lear saw to it that entombment was delayed, according to Washington's wishes.

As Washington's corpse lay in the cold room, another doctor arrived and suggested ways to resuscitate him, including cutting his throat and warming the corpse. Resuscitation of people from apparent drowning was known at the time, as was piercing the neck and getting air into the lungs. The other doctors politely rejected his suggestions.

Washington had said in his will that it was his "express desire that my Corpse may be Interred in a private manner, without parade, or funeral Oration." But, because Washington was a Mason, Martha allowed a local lodge to arrange a funeral procession from the mansion to the family's red-brick tomb on Wednesday, December 18.

Militiamen carried the lead-lined coffin. Six veterans of the Revolution, five of them Masons, carried the black velvet pall shading the coffin. Dozens of mourners slowly followed.

A local clergyman read the Episcopal Order of Burial. Then another clergyman and Dr. Dick, a high-ranking Mason, led the traditional Masonic funeral rites. After this, the shroud was briefly withdrawn to allow a final viewing before Washington's body was placed in the family tomb.

The funeral lasted three and a half hours and was punctuated by cannon fire—from guns hauled up by Virginian militiamen and from a U. S. Navy ship off the Potomac shore of Mount Vernon.

Five slaves, including Frank Lee, the family's mulatto butler and brother of William Lee, Washington's aged valet, took part in the ceremonies. After the interment, guests lingered for food and drink. Leftovers were later distributed to some of the slaves.

Martha Washington, in her private act of remembrance, burned the letters exchanged between her and her husband, depriving history of insights into their marital life. She closed the second-floor bedroom that she and George had shared and moved to a reclusive life in a room on the third floor.

Martha went into deep mourning: black lace shawl, black gloves, and black shoes. She had outlived four children, two husbands, and seven siblings. Now she made her will and prepared for her own death.

Her grandchildren, George Washington Custis and Nelly Custis Lewis, and Nelly's husband, along with their two young daughters, remained at Mount Vernon. Her other grandchildren, Elizabeth Parke Custis Law and Martha Parke Custis Peter visited often, bringing their children and easing her grief.

Abigail Adams visited Mount Vernon in December 1800. Later, writing about Martha Washington's slaves, she said: "In the state in which they were left by the General, to be free at her death, she did not feel as tho her Life was safe in their Hands, many of whom would be told that it was [in] their interest to get rid of her—She therefore was advised to set them all free at the close of the year." Martha freed her husband's slaves on January 1, 1801.[12] After her death in 1802, her own slaves were inherited by her four grandchildren. She bequeathed Elish, the one slave she owned outright, to her grandson George Washington Parke Custis.[13]

Washington's death inspired a national unity not seen since the Revolution. From Castine, Maine, to Savannah, Georgia, in the churches of more than three hundred communities, congregations gathered at symbolic funerals and heard tributes to Washington. Added to those sermons were eulogies in hundreds of town halls, Masonic lodges, and schoolhouses. Politicians, Masons, and clergymen organized the "mock funerals" held across the nation.[14] In one of them, in Boston, Masons carried a golden urn containing a lock of Washington's hair, contributed by Martha Washington.[15]

Countless individuals and organizations eulogized Washington with long, effusive orations. Many portrayed Washington as a leader who embodied the Enlightenment and its concept of a republic. Hundreds of orations were printed, extending the lives of the words and spreading to all parts of the county eloquent reminders of the Washington era, when hope and unity blessed the Republic.

Congress had declared a period of mourning from the day of Washington's death to February 22, his birthday. Some groups, such as the Masons, extended the mourning period beyond February. Men, including every man in the small American army, wore black arm bands. Women followed the example of First Lady Abigail Adams, donning the black dresses and gloves of formal mourning. Abigail said she would remain in mourning until spring. Shops throughout the county ran out of black cloth.

The official public, symbolic funeral came on December 26. At dawn, sixteen cannons boomed in Philadelphia, signaling the start of the capital city's farewell to George Washington. Every half-hour that morning, the cannons were fired as troops assembled.

Shortly after noon, the procession began, paced by a somber march and the sound of muffled drums. Hundreds of federal troops and militiamen escorted a riderless horse, caparisoned in black. Soldiers carried an empty coffin, followed by Senators and Representatives, along with members of the Society of the Cincinnati and the Masons. The procession ended at the German Lutheran Church, where President Adams and Abigail Adams watched the coffin placed on a bier in the middle aisle. About 4,000 people packed the church. Many wore pewter medals commemorating Washington's death or silver and gold memorial rings.

Alexander Hamilton, who had succeeded Washington as commander in chief of the American army, had also succeeded him as head of the Society of the Cincinnati. Washington, in his years as the Society's first president, was troubled because it was evolving into an aristocratic organization and was dangerously linking the army and politics. Thomas Jefferson warned Washington that the Society could produce "an hereditary aristocracy which will change the form of our governments from the best to the worst in the world."

Hamilton, no longer restrained by Washington, took over the arrangements for military commemorations of Washington. The army dominated the service in Philadelphia. Henry "Light-Horse Harry" Lee, combat veteran of the Revolution and a member of Congress, delivered the most famous line of the hundreds of eulogies: "First in war, first in peace, and first in the hearts of his countrymen. . . . " In that same eulogy, Lee imagined Washington in the afterlife giving a warning to an America torn by political strife: "Control party spirit, the bane of free government."

Hamilton displayed his martial power beyond Philadelphia by deploying Army troops at funerals throughout the country. The Detroit rites, for example, were conducted by Colonel John F. Hamtramck, Society member and commander of the Western Army. The Detroit service was particularly significant, for the city represented a patriotic victory. Despite the treaty ending the Revolutionary War, the British had occupied Detroit until 1796, and it was Hamtramck who led the march into Detroit to assert that the city was under American control.

The military funerals in Detroit and elsewhere not only honored the Father of the Country but also advertised the power of the post-Revolution army. And Hamilton helped the Society of the Cincinnati by giving its members prominent roles in the ceremonies, thus spiritually connecting them to Washington.

In October 1799, Mason Locke Weems, an Anglican cleric turned traveling salesman, told his publisher that he had "on the Anvil and pretty well hammr'd out a piece that will sell. . . . "

Weems' working title for his project was *The True Patriot or Beauties of Washington,* which contained anecdotes "Curious & Marvellous." It was published as *A History of the Life and Death, Virtues and Exploits of General George Washington.*

Less than a month after Washington died, Weems wrote the publisher again, saying "Millions are gaping to read something about him. I am very nearly prim^d and cock^d for 'em." In 1800 Parson Weems, as he called himself, published his first edition of Washington's life, which, in the words of a 19th-century historian, was a brew of "pernicious drivel." Weems' most famous fabrication, the I-cannot-tell-a-lie cherry tree tale, was first published in the 1806 edition. A permanent bestseller, the biography was read by Abraham Lincoln as a boy and is still in print.

Weems' description of Washington's death ended with a celestial scene: "Swift on angel's wings the brightening saint ascended while voices more than human were warbling through the happy regions and hymning the great procession towards the gates of heaven."

That baroque ascension was the beginning of a remarkable process that made Washington into a god. When an enterprising engraver published a bestselling work called *The Apotheosis of Washington,* people understood that its symbolism and piety had deified their departed Father. "Every American," wrote a European visitor, "considers it his sacred duty to have a likeness of Washington in his home, just as we have images of God's saints."[16]

APOTHEOSIS OF WASHINGTON

As portrayed in the engraving, Washington, still in his burial shroud, sits on a cloud far above Mount Vernon. An angel bestows immortality upon him in the form of a laurel wreath. He is welcomed to heaven by two Revolutionary War heroes killed in battle.

Another engraving, copied from a painting by Irish-American artist John James Barralet, depicts Wingéd Immortality and Father Time lifting Washington from his tomb as he begins his celestial ascent.

Decades later, after the death of Abraham Lincoln, a popular engraving portrayed him as being welcomed to heaven by George Washington.

The idea of apotheosis continued and was enshrined in the capital city that Washington founded on the Potomac and in the Capitol whose cornerstone he laid in 1793. The Architect of the Capitol commissioned Constantino Brumidi to create what would become a spectacular example of allegorical painting in the central place of honor. He was to fashion an immense panorama of heavenly majesty. Brumidi, who had painted in the Vatican and Roman palaces before emigrating to the United States, was a master at creating the illusion of three-dimensional forms. He completed the work in 1865.

Stand in the U.S. Capitol's Rotunda and look up at the dome. There, 180 feet above, is George Washington. Grim in his general's uniform, he holds a blood-flecked sword. Flanking him are Liberty and a trumpeting Fame. A rainbow arches at his feet, and thirteen states-as-maidens complete the circle around him. In the swirling celestial clouds below him is Freedom, her sword raised and her red cape billowing as she tramples Tyranny and Kingly Power.

The painter, Constantino Brumidi, called his masterpiece *The Apotheosis of George Washington*.

APPENDICES

APPENDIX 1:

THE "CORRECT" CONSTITUTION OF THE UNITED STATES

The parchment transcription of the Constitution was inscribed by Jacob Shallus, a clerk in the Pennsylvania General Assembly, on four large sheets. He began engrossing immediately after the adjournment of the Constitutional Convention in Philadelphia on Saturday, September 15, 1787.

When Shallus was ready to hand his work to a printer, he went back over the document in search of mistakes. Many of them were omissions, which he corrected with insertions. At the bottom of the fourth sheet, he listed his corrections by insertions and reported an "Erazure"—a scraping away of the ink with a sharp knife—to make a change produced during the convention's Monday session: Delegates changed the maximum allowable number of representatives from one per 40,000 persons to one per 30,000.[1]

The following rendition of the U.S. Constitution is copied from the "correct" version as published in Acts Passed at a Congress of the United States of America, published in New York in 1789 by Francis Childs and John Swaine, Printers to the United States.

•••

We the People of the United States, in Order to form a more perfect Union, establish Justice, insure domestic Tranquility, provide for the common defence, promote the general Welfare, and secure the Blessings of Liberty to ourselves and our Posterity, do ordain and establish this Constitution for the United States of America.

ARTICLE I.

Sect. 1. All legislative Powers herein granted shall be vested in a Congress of the United States, which shall consist of a Senate and House of Representatives.

Sect. 2. The House of Representatives shall be composed of Members chosen every second Year by the people of the several states, and the electors in each state shall have the qualifications requisite for electors of the most numerous branch of the state legislature.

No person shall be a Representative who shall not have attained to the age of twenty- five years, and been seven years a citizen of the United States, and who shall not, when elected, be an inhabitant of that state in which he shall be chosen.

Representatives and direct taxes shall be apportioned among the several states which may be included within this Union, according to their respective numbers, which shall be determined by adding to the whole number of free persons, including those bound to service for a term of years, and excluding Indians not taxed, three-fifths of all other persons. The actual enumeration shall be made within three years after the first meeting of the Congress of the United States, and within every subsequent term of ten years, in such manner as they shall by law direct. The number of Representatives shall not exceed one for every thirty-thousand, but each state shall have at least one Representative; and until such enumeration shall be made, the state of New-Hampshire shall be entitled to chuse three, Massachusetts eight, Rhode-Island and Providence Plantations one, Connecticut five, New-York six, New-Jersey four, Pennsylvania eight, Delaware one, Maryland six, Virginia ten, North-Carolina five, South-Carolina five, and Georgia three. The actual enumeration shall be made within three years after the first meeting of the Congress of the United States, and within every subsequent term of ten years, in such Manner as they shall by law direct. The number of Representatives shall not exceed one for every thirty-thousand, but each state shall have at least one Representative ; and until such enumeration shall be made, the state of New-Hampshire shall be entitled to chuse three, Massachusetts eight, Rhode-Island and Providence Plantations one, Connecticut five, New-York six, New-Jersey four, Pennsylvania eight, Delaware one, Maryland six, Virginia ten, North-Carolina five, South-Carolina five, and Georgia three.

When vacancies happen in the representation from any state, the executive authority thereof shall issue writs of election to fill such vacancies.

The House of Representatives shall chuse their Speaker and other officers; and shall have the sole power of impeachment.

Sect. 3. The Senate of the United States shall be composed of two Senators from each state, chosen by the legislature thereof, for six years; and each Senator shall have one vote.

Immediately after they shall be assembled in consequence of the first election, they shall be divided as equally as may be into three classes. The seats of the Senators of the first class shall be vacated at the expiration of the second year, of the second class at the expiration of the fourth year, and of the third class at the expiration of the sixth year, so that one-third may be chosen every second year; and if vacancies happen by resignation, or otherwise, during the recess of the legislature of any state, the executive thereof may make temporary appointments until the next meeting of the legislature, which shall then fill such vacancies.

No Person shall be a Senator who shall not have attained to the age of thirty years, and been nine years a citizen of the United States, and who shall not, when elected, be an inhabitant of that state for which he shall be chosen.

The Vice-President of the United States shall be President of the Senate, but shall have no vote, unless they be equally divided.

The Senate shall chuse their other officers, and also a President pro tempore, in the absence of the Vice-President, or when he shall exercise the office of President of the United States.

The Senate shall have the sole power to try all impeachments. When sitting for that purpose, they shall be on oath or affirmation. When the President of the United States is tried, the Chief Justice shall preside; And no person shall be convicted without the Concurrence of two-thirds of the members present.

Judgment in cases of impeachment shall not extend further than to removal from office, and disqualification to hold and enjoy any office of honor, trust or profit under the United States ; but the Party convicted shall nevertheless be liable and subject to indictment, trial, judgment and punishment, according to Law.

Sect. 4. The times, places and manner of holding elections for Senators and Representatives, shall be prescribed in each state by the legislature thereof ; But the Congress may at any time by law make or alter such regulations, except as to the places of chusing Senators.

The Congress shall assemble at least once in every Year, and such Meeting shall be on the first Monday in December, unless they shall by law appoint a different day.

Sect. 5. Each House shall be the judge of the elections, returns and qualifications of its own members, and a majority of each shall constitute a quorum to do business ; but a smaller number may adjourn from day to day, and may be authorized to compel the attendance of absent members, in such manner, and under such penalties as each House may provide.

Each House may determine the rules of its proceedings, punish its members for disorderly behaviour, and, with the concurrence of two thirds, expel a Member.

Each House shall keep a journal of its proceedings, and from time to time publish the same, excepting such Parts as may in their Judgment require Secrecy; and the Yeas and Nays of the Members of either House on any question shall, at the desire of one-fifth of those present, be entered on the journal.

Neither House, during the session of Congress, shall without the consent of the other, adjourn for more than three days, nor to any other place than that in which the two Houses shall be sitting.

Sect. 6. The Senators and Representatives shall receive a compensation for their services, to be ascertained by law, and paid out of the treasury of the United States. They shall in all cases, except treason, felony and breach of the peace, be privileged from arrest during their attendance at the session of their respective Houses, and in going to and returning from the same ; and for any speech or debate in either House, they shall not be questioned in any other place.

No Senator or Representative shall, during the time for which he was elected, be appointed to any civil office under the authority of the United States, which shall have been created, or the emoluments whereof shall have been encreased during such time ; and no person holding any office under the United States, shall be a member of either House during his continuance in office.

Sect. 7. All bills for raising revenue shall originate in the House of Representatives ; but the Senate may propose or concur with amendments as on other bills.

Every bill which shall have passed the House of Representatives and the Senate, shall, before it become a law, be presented to the President of the United States ; if he approve he shall sign it, but if not he shall return it, with his objections to that House in which it shall have originated, who shall enter the objections at large on their journal, and proceed to reconsider it. If after such reconsideration two-thirds of that House shall agree to pass the bill, it shall be sent, together with the objections, to the other House, by which it shall likewise be reconsidered, and if approved by two thirds of that House, it shall become a law. But in all such cases the votes of both Houses shall be determined by yeas and nays, and the names of the persons voting for and against the bill shall be entered on the journal of each House respectively. If any bill shall not be returned by the President within ten days (Sundays excepted) after it shall have been presented to him, the same shall be a law, in like manner as if he had signed it, unless the Congress by their adjournment prevent its return, in which case it shall not be a law.

Every order, resolution or vote to which the concurrence of the Senate and House of Representatives may be necessary (except on a question of adjournment) shall be presented to the President of the United States ; and before the same shall take effect, shall be approved by him, or being disapproved by him, shall be re-passed by two-thirds of the Senate and House of Representatives, according to the rules and limitations prescribed in the case of a bill.

2 1789

Sect. 8. The Congress shall have power—

To lay and collect taxes, duties, imposts and excises, to pay the debts and provide for the common defence and general welfare of the United States ; but all duties, imposts and excises shall be uniform throughout the United States :

To borrow money on the credit of the United States :

To regulate commerce with foreign nations, and among the several states, and with the Indian Tribes :

To establish an uniform rule of naturalization, and uniform laws on the subject of bankruptcies throughout the United States :

To coin money, regulate the value thereof, and of foreign coin, and fix the standard of weights and measures :

To provide for the punishment of counterfeiting the securities and current coin of the United States :

To establish post-offices and post-roads :

To promote the progress of science and useful arts, by securing for limited times to Authors and Inventors the exclusive Right to their respective Writings and Discoveries :

To constitute tribunals inferior to the Supreme Court :

To define and punish piracies and felonies committed on the high seas, and offences against the law of nations :

To declare war, grant Letters of marque and reprisal, and make rules concerning captures on land and water :

To raise and support armies, but no appropriation of money to that use shall be for a longer term than two years :

To provide and maintain a navy :

To make rules for the government and regulation of the land and naval forces :

To provide for calling forth the militia to execute the laws of the union, suppress insurrections and repel invasions :

To provide for organizing, arming, and disciplining the militia, and for governing such part of them as may be employed in the service of the United States, reserving to the States respectively, the appointment of the officers, and the authority of training the militia according to the discipline prescribed by Congress :

To exercise exclusive legislation in all Cases whatsoever, over such district (not exceeding ten miles square) as may, by cession of particular states, and the acceptance of Congress, become the seat of the government of the United States, and to exercise like authority over all places purchased by the consent of the legislature of the state in which the same shall be, for the erection of forts, magazines, arsenals, dock-yards, and other needful buildings :—And

To make all laws which shall be necessary and proper for carrying into execution the foregoing Powers, and all other Powers vested by this Constitution in the government of the United States, or in any department or officer thereof.

Sect. 9. The migration or importation of such persons as any of the states now existing shall think proper to admit, shall not be prohibited by the Congress prior to the year one thousand eight hundred and eight, but a tax or duty may be imposed on such importation, not exceeding ten dollars for each person.

The privilege of the writ of habeas corpus shall not be suspended, unless when in cases of rebellion or invasion the public safety may require it.

No bill of attainder or ex post facto law shall be passed.

No capitation, or other direct tax shall be laid, unless in proportion to the census or enumeration herein before directed to be taken.

No' tax or duty shall be laid on articles exported from any state. No preference shall be given by any regulation of commerce or revenue to the ports of one state over those of another ; nor shall vessels bound to, or from, one state, be obliged to enter, clear, or pay duties in another.

No money shall be drawn from the treasury, but in consequence of appropriations made by law ; and a regular statement and account of the receipts and expenditures of all public money shall be published from time to time.

No title of nobility shall be granted by the United States : And no person holding any office of profit or trust under them, shall, without the consent of the Congress, accept of any present, emolument, office, or title, of any kind whatever, from any king, prince, or foreign state.

Sect. 10. No state shall enter into any treaty, alliance, or confederation ; grant letters of marque and reprisal ; coin money ; emit bills of credit ; make any thing but gold and silver oin a tender in payment of debts ; pass any bill of attainder, ex post facto law, or law impairing the obligation of Contracts, or grant any title of nobility.

No state shall, without the consent of the Congress, lay any imposts or duties on imports or exports, except what may be absolutely necessary for executing its inspection laws : and the net produce of all duties and Imposts, laid by any state on imports or exports, shall be for the use of the treasury of the United States; and all such laws shall be subject to the revision and controul of the Congress. No state shall, without the consent of Congress, lay any duty of tonnage, keep troops, or ships of war in time of peace, enter into any agreement or compact with another state, or with a foreign power, or engage in war, unless actually invaded, or in such imminent danger as will not admit of delay.

ARTICLE II.

Sect. 1. The executive power shall be vested in a President of the United States of America. He shall hold his office during the term of four years, and, together with the Vice-President, chosen for the same term, be elected, as follows :

Each state shall appoint, in such manner as the legislature thereof may direct, a number of electors, equal to the whole number of Senators and Representatives to which the state may be entitled in the Congress: but no Senator or Representative, or person holding an office of trust or profit under the United States, shall be appointed an elector.

The electors shall meet in their respective states, and vote by ballot for two persons, of whom one at least shall not be an inhabitant of the same state with themselves. And they shall make a list of all the persons voted for, and of the number of votes for each; which list they shall sign and certify, and transmit sealed to the seat of the government of the United States, directed to the President of the Senate. The President of the Senate shall, in the presence of the Senate and House of Representatives, open all the certificates, and the votes shall then be counted. The person having the greatest number of votes shall be the President, if such number be a majority of the whole number of electors appointed ; and if there be more than one who have such majority, and have an equal number of votes, then the House of Representatives shall immediately chuse by ballot one of them for President; and if no person have a majority, then from the five highest on the list the said House shall in like manner chuse the President. But in chusing the President, the votes shall be taken by states, the representation from each state having one vote ; a quorum for this Purpose shall consist of a member or members from two- thirds of the States, and a Majority of all the States shall be necessary to a Choice. In every Case, after the Choice of the President, the Person having the greatest Number of Votes of the Electors shall be the Vice President. But if there should remain two or more who have equal Votes, the Senate shall chuse from them by Ballot the Vice President.

The Congress may determine the Time of chusing the Electors, and the Day on which they shall give their Votes; which Day shall be the same throughout the United States.

No Person except a natural born citizen, or a citizen of the United States, at the time of the adoption of this Constitution, shall be eligible to the Office of President; neither shall any person be eligible to that office who shall not have attained to the age of thirty-five years, and been fourteen years a resident within the United States.

In case of the removal of the President from office, or of his death, resignation, or inability to discharge the powers and duties of the said office, the same shall devolve on the Vice-President, and the Congress may by law provide for the case of removal, death, resignation, or inability, both of the President and Vice-President, declaring what officer shall then act as President, and such officer shall act accordingly, until the disability be removed, or a President shall be elected.

The President shall, at stated times, receive for his services, a compensation, which shall neither be encreased nor diminished during the Period for which he shall have been elected, and he shall not receive within that period any other emolument from the United States, or any of them.

Before he enter on the execution of his office, he shall take the following oath or affirmation:

"I do solemnly swear (or affirm) that I will faithfully execute the office of President of the United States, and will to the best of my ability, preserve, protect and defend the constitution of the United States."

Sect. 2. The President shall be commander in chief of the army and navy of the United States, and of the militia of the several states, when called into the actual service of the United States ; he may require the Opinion, in writing, of the principal officer in each of the executive departments, upon any subject relating to the duties of their respective offices, and he shall have power to grant reprieves and pardons for offences against the United States, except in cases of impeachment.

He shall have power, by and with the Advice and Consent of the Senate, to make treaties, provided two-thirds of the Senators present concur; and he shall nominate, and by and with the advice and consent of the Senate, shall appoint ambassadors, other public ministers and consuls, judges of the supreme Court, and all other officers of the United States, whose appointments are not herein otherwise provided for, and which shall be established by law. But the Congress may by law vest the appointment of such inferior officers, as they think proper, in the President alone, in the courts of law, or in the heads of departments.

The President shall have power to fill up all vacancies that may happen during the recess of the Senate, by granting Commissions which shall expire at the end of their next Session.

Sect. 3. He shall from time to time give to the Congress information of the state of the union, and recommend to their consideration such measures as he shall judge necessary and expedient; he may, on extraordinary occasions, convene both houses, or either of them, and in case of disagreement between them, with respect to the time of adjournment, he may adjourn them to such time as he shall think proper; he shall receive ambassadors and other public ministers; he shall take care that the laws be faithfully executed, and shall commission all the officers of the United States.

Sect. 4. The President, Vice President and all civil officers of the United States, shall be removed from office on impeachment for, and conviction of, treason, bribery, or other high crimes and misdemeanors.

ARTICLE III.

Sect. 1. The judicial power of the United States, shall be vested in one Supreme Court, and in such inferior courts as the Congress may from time to time ordain and establish. The judges, both of the supreme and inferior courts, shall hold their offices during good behaviour, and shall, at stated times, receive for their services, a compensation, which shall not be diminished during their continuance in office.

Sect. 2. The judicial power shall extend to all cases, in law and equity, arising under this constitution, the laws of the United States, and treaties made, or which shall be made, under their authority ; to all cases affecting ambassadors, other public ministers and consuls ; to all cases of admiralty and maritime jurisdiction ; to controversies to which the United States shall be a party ; to controversies between two or more states ; between a state and citizens of another state ; between citizens of different states ; between citizens of the same state claiming lands under grants of different states, and between a state, or the citizens thereof, and foreign states, citizens or subjects.

In all cases affecting ambassadors, other public ministers and consuls, and those in which a state shall be a party, the Supreme Court shall have original Jurisdiction. In all the other Cases before mentioned, the supreme Court shall have appellate jurisdiction, both as to law and fact, with such exceptions, and under such regulations as the Congress shall make.

The trial of all crimes, except in cases of impeachment, shall be by jury ; and such trial shall be held in the state where the said crimes shall have been committed ; but when not committed within any state, the trial shall be at such place or places as the Congress may by law have directed.

Sect. 3. Treason against the United States, shall consist only in levying war against them, or in adhering to their enemies, giving them aid and comfort. No person shall be convicted of treason unless on the testimony of two witnesses to the same overt act, or on confession in open court.

The Congress shall have power to declare the punishment of treason, but no attainder of treason shall work corruption of blood, or forfeiture except during the life of the person attainted.

ARTICLE IV.

Sect. 1. Full faith and credit shall be given in each state to the public acts, records, and judicial proceedings of every other state. And the Congress may by general laws prescribe the manner in which such acts, records and proceedings shall be proved, and the effect thereof.

Sect. 2. The citizens of each state shall be entitled to all privileges and immunities of citizens in the several states.

A person charged in any state with treason, felony, or other crime, who shall flee from justice, and be found in another state, shall on

demand of the executive authority of the state from which he fled, be delivered up, to be removed to the state having jurisdiction of the crime.
Sect. 3. New states may be admitted by the Congress into this union ; but no new state shall be formed or erected within the jurisdiction of any other state ; nor any state be formed by the junction of two or more states, or parts of states, without the consent of the legislatures of the states concerned as well as of the Congress.

The Congress shall have power to dispose of and make all needful rules and regulations respecting the territory or other property belonging to the United States ; and nothing in this constitution shall be so construed as to prejudice any claims of the United States, or of any particular state.
Sect. 4. The United States shall guarantee to every state in this union a republican form of government, and shall protect each of them against invasion ; and on application of the legislature, or of the executive (when the legislature cannot be convened), against domestic violence.

ARTICLE V.

The Congress, whenever two-thirds of both Houses shall deem it necessary, shall propose amendments to this constitution, or, on the application of the legislatures of two-thirds of the several states, shall call a convention for proposing amendments, which, in either case, shall be valid to all intents and purposes, as part of this constitution, when ratified by the legislatures of three-fourths of the several states, or by Conventions in three-fourths thereof, as the one or the other mode of ratification may be proposed by the Congress : Provided, that no amendment which may be made prior to the year one thousand eight hundred and eight shall in any Manner affect the first and fourth clauses in the ninth Section of the first article ; and that no state, without its consent, shall be deprived of its equal suffrage in the Senate.

ARTICLE VI.

All debts contracted and engagements entered into, before the adoption of this constitution, shall be as valid against the United States under this constitution, as under the confederation.

This constitution, and the laws of the United States which shall be made in pursuance thereof ; and all treaties made, or which shall be made, under the authority of the United States, shall be the supreme law of the land ; and the judges in every state shall be bound thereby, any thing in the constitution or laws of any state to the contrary notwithstanding.

The senators and representatives before mentioned, and the members of the several state legislatures, and all executive and judicial officers, both of the United States and of the several states, shall be bound by oath or affirmation, to support this constitution ; but no religious test shall ever be required as a qualification to any office or public trust under the United States.

ARTICLE VII.

The ratification of the conventions of nine States, shall be sufficient for the establishment of this constitution between the states so ratifying the same.

APPENDIX 2:

INSIDE THE DOZEN: THE BILL OF RIGHTS

The following text is a transcription of the preamble and original twelve articles sent to the states for ratification on October 2, 1789. Spelling and punctuation reflect the original. Author's notes in italics.[2]

Preamble: The Conventions of a number of the States, having at the time of their adopting the Constitution, expressed a desire, in order to prevent misconstruction or abuse of its powers, that further declaratory and restrictive clauses should be added: And as extending the ground of public confidence in the Government, will best ensure the beneficent ends of its institution.

Article the first. After the first enumeration required by the first article of the Constitution, there shall be one Representative for every thirty thousand, until the number shall amount to one hundred, after which the proportion shall be so regulated by Congress, that there shall be not less than one hundred Representatives, nor less than one Representative for every forty thousand persons, until the number of Representatives shall amount to two hundred ; after which the proportion shall be so regulated by Congress, that there shall not be less than two hundred Representatives, nor more than one Representative for every fifty thousand persons.

- *Approved by only ten state legislatures, this article did not become part of the Constitution.*

Article the second. No law, varying the compensation for the services of the Senators and Representatives, shall take effect, until an election of Representatives shall have intervened.

- *This Article was also rejected, but it had a second life. See note page 145.*

Article the third. Congress shall make no law respecting an establishment of religion, or prohibiting the free exercise thereof ; or abridging the freedom of speech, or of the press ; or the right of the people peaceably to assemble, and to petition the Government for a redress of grievances.

Article the fourth. A well regulated Militia, being necessary to the security of a free State, the right of the people to keep and bear Arms, shall not be infringed.

Article the fifth. No Soldier shall, in time of peace be quartered in any house, without the consent of the Owner, nor in time of war, but in a manner to be prescribed by law.

Article the sixth. The right of the people to be secure in their persons, houses, papers, and effects, against unreasonable searches and seizures, shall not be violated, and no Warrants shall issue, but upon probable cause, supported by Oath or affirmation, and particularly describing the place to be searched, and the persons or things to be seized.

Article the seventh. No person shall be held to answer for a capital, or otherwise infamous crime, unless on a presentment or indictment of a Grand Jury, except in cases arising in the land or naval forces, or in the Militia, when in actual service in time of War or public danger ; nor shall any person be subject for the same offence to be twice put in jeopardy of life or limb ; nor shall be compelled in any criminal case to be a witness against himself, nor be deprived of life, liberty, or property, without due process of law ; nor shall private property be taken for public use, without just compensation.

Article the eighth. In all criminal prosecutions, the accused shall enjoy the right to a speedy and public trial, by an impartial jury of the State and district wherein the crime shall have been committed, which district shall have been previously ascertained by law, and to be informed of the nature and cause of the accusation ; to be confronted with the witnesses against him ; to have compulsory process for obtaining witnesses in his favor, and to have the Assistance of Counsel for his defence.

Article the ninth. In suits at common law, where the value in controversy shall exceed twenty dollars, the right of trial by jury shall be preserved, and no fact tried by a jury, shall be otherwise re-examined in any Court of the United States, than according to the rules of the common law.

Article the tenth. Excessive bail shall not be required, nor excessive fines imposed, nor cruel and unusual punishments inflicted.

Article the eleventh. The enumeration in the Constitution, of certain rights, shall not be construed to deny or disparage others retained by the people.

Article the twelfth. The powers not delegated to the United States by the Constitution, nor prohibited by it to the States, are reserved to the States respectively, or to the people.

APPENDIX 3:

A TIMELINE OF THE FOUNDING OF
THE UNITED STATES AND
THE FEDERAL GOVERNMENT

1754

May: Lt. Col. George Washington of the Virginia Militia leads Virginia militiamen into territory claimed by the French. His defeat of a French patrol near today's Uniontown, Pennsylvania, is a prelude to the French and Indian War.

1756-1763

The French and Indian War—the North American portion of the world-spanning conflict known as the Seven Years War—pits Great Britain against France and Indians allied with France; Spain joins France in 1762. Britain – aided by American troops – defeat the French and secure vast new territories.

1763

February: Under the treaty ending the French and Indian War, Britain gets the Spanish colony of Florida and part of the French colony of Louisiana. The British form the territory into two colonies: East Florida and West Florida.

October: King George III restricts the movement of colonists by barring trade and settlement west of the Appalachian Mountains.

1764

April: The British Parliament, without consulting the colonies, imposes its first tax on them: a three-cent tax on refined sugar. The

Revenue Act also increases taxes on coffee, indigo, and some wines; it also bans the importation of rum and French wine. The British government views the taxes as a reasonable way to collect revenue in order to pay the costs of the French and Indian War, and to pay the costs of defending the American Colonists. The Americans resent any tax, no matter how modest, imposed without the consent of their representatives.

1765

March: Parliament, wishing to pay off Britain's massive national debt following the Seven Years War, passes the Stamp Act, which requires colonists to buy a stamp that is affixed to every piece of paper they use, including legal documents, licenses, newspapers, and playing cards.

May: Parliament passes the Quartering Act, which orders each colonial assembly to provide British soldiers in America with bedding, cooking utensils, firewood, beer or cider, and candles. A later amendment requires the colonial assemblies to find billeting for the soldiers. (It is this act which is the direct inspiration for the Third Amendment to the 1787 Constituion, which reads "No Soldier shall, in time of peace be quartered in any house, without the consent of the Owner, nor in time of war, but in a manner to be prescribed by law.")

1767

November: Parliament passes the Townshend Acts, raising new taxes on various items imported to the American colonies. Another law aids customs officials by authorizing blank search warrants called Writs of Assistance.

1768

February: Massachusetts House of Representatives sends a Circular Letter, written by Samuel Adams, to the legislature of the other colonies declaring that the Townshend Acts were unconstitutional because of a lack of representation in Parliament.

1770

March: In a confrontation with a Boston mob, British soldiers kill five people. Sons of Liberty leader Paul Revere produces a sensational color print and calls the incident "The Bloody Massacre." Reacting to the colonists' boycott of British goods, Parliament amends revenue laws, removing Townshend items except tea.

1772

November: John Adams proposes that the colonies establish a correspondence network to keep everyone informed of political activities.

1773

March: Virginia House of Burgesses creates a Committee of Correspondence and Inquiry that will keep in touch with other colonies about "affairs of this colony ... connected with those of Great Britain."

May: Parliament passes the Tea Act, which creates a monopoly. British officials pick Tories in Boston as the exclusive merchants.

December: Patriots in Boston dump tea from ships that Sons of Liberty had kept from unloading.

1774

March: Britain closes the port of Boston; other colonies come to the aid of Massachusetts.

September: The First Continental Congress convenes in Philadelphia in reaction to the closing of the port of Boston and other "Intolerable Acts": enlarging Quebec and granting religious freedom to Catholics living there; allowing royal governors to appoint all law officers and have the power to move trials to England; and a demand for expanded quartering of British troops.

1775

April: Firefights at Lexington and Concord pit Massachusetts Patriots against British troops. As news travels down the eastern seaboard, thousands of militiamen head for Cambridge, beginning the Continental Army.

May: The Continental Congress, with delegates from every state but Georgia, names George Washington of Virginia as commander in chief of the Continental Army. He heads for Cambridge.

June: Patriots inflict heavy casualties on British troops in what will be known as the Battle of Bunker Hill.

1776

January: Tom Paine's *Common Sense*, a call for independence, is published and becomes a best-seller.

March: The Continental Army takes control of Dorchester Heights and begins a siege of Boston, eventually forcing Gen. William Howe and his troops to evacuate.

July: The Second Continental Congress declares independence.

August: British drive Washington's Continental Army from Brooklyn.

October: British capture New York City.

December: George Washington crosses the Delaware River and attacks 1,400 Hessians at Trenton, New Jersey. He next takes Princeton. After the fighting, Alexander Hamilton, who has fought at both engagements, becomes an aide to Washington.

1777

September: Washington is defeated at Brandywine as British troops march on to take Philadelphia. Congress flees Philadelphia and reassembles in York, Pennsylvania.

October: Burgoyne surrenders to Gen. Horatio Gates at Saratoga, New York. The victory convinces France to support the Patriots.

November: The Second Continental Congress sends the Articles of Confederation to the various states for ratification, a drawn-out process that will takes much of the rest of the war to complete.

December: Washington's army goes into winter quarters at Valley Forge.

1778

February: Rhode Island allows the enlistment of "every able-bodied negro, mulatto, or Indian man slave" with the promise "every slave so enlisting shall, upon his passing muster . . . be immediately discharged from the service of his master or mistress, and be absolutely free." with the owners of enlisted slaves compensated at market value. Eighty-eight slaves enlisted in the next few months. They become part of the 1st Rhode Island Regiment – also known as the Black Regiment.

June: British troops evacuate Philadelphia, beginning a march to New York. Washington's army, well trained and better disciplined, emerges from Valley Forge and pursues the British. At Monmouth, New Jersey, the Continental Army mauls but does not defeat the British as they march to New York.

December: The British begin a southern campaign by taking Savannah, Georgia.

1779

October: A joint American-French attempt to retake Savannah ends with the French losing 635 men and the Patriots 457 while the British and Loyalist defenders saved the city at a cost of 55 lives.

1780

May: British take Charlestown (Charleston), South Carolina. Troops under Gen. Charles Cornwallis head to the interior on a campaign to conquer the South.

August: British rout Gen. Horatio Gates and his army at Camden, South Carolina.

September: Benedict Arnold, in command of the crucial Hudson River fort at West Point, meets with British Maj. John André, in a rendezvous set up by a prominent New York Tory. Arnold is exposed and escapes, but André is captured and later hanged.

1781

January: Newly commissioned a British general, Benedict Arnold leads an amphibious invasion of Virginia. The invaders raid Richmond and occupy Portsmouth.

March: Washington sends about 3,000 men under Marquis de Lafayette to Virginia. He prevents the British from capturing Richmond. At Guilford Courthouse, North Carolina, Gen. Nathanael Greene is defeated by Gen. Cornwallis but inflicts heavy casualties, continuing his strategy to wear down the British.

March 1: The Articles of Confederation, finally having been ratified by all thirteen states, come into effect, and almost immediately prove to be unsatisfactory. The Congress of the Confederation has no power to tax, and the States frequently fail to pay their contributions to the central government.

July: British troops evacuate Savannah.

September: A joint French and American army under Washington maneuvers to encircle and besiege Cornwallis, who holds Yorktown, Virginia, in anticipation of support from the Royal Navy via the York River. A French fleet in Chesapeake Bay defeats a British fleet, preventing a Royal Navy rescue of Cornwallis.

October: Cornwallis surrenders, ending the last major military engagement of the war.

1782

February: The British Parliament votes to end all offensive military operations in America.

March: British Prime Minister Frederick North, (Lord North) resigns.

April: American and British negotiators meet in Paris, seeking to end the war. The Dutch Republic recognizes the United States of America as a sovereign nation.

November: In the last battle of the war Americans forces attack a Shawnee village in the Ohio territory as retaliation against Tories and Indian actions.

November 30: British and American representatives sign preliminary peace articles.

1783

March: Washington addresses troops in Newburgh, New York, and in so doing quashes a nascent mutiny by disgruntled and unpaid troops.

June: About 400 Pennsylvania militia men and officers march on the State House (now Independence Hall) to demand back pay. They seek to confront, not the powerless Congress of the Confederation, but the state executive council. Nonetheless, members of Congress take note of the threatening situation, and decamp from Philadelphia to Princeton, New Jersey.

July: The Massachusetts Supreme Court bans slavery in that State.

September: The Treaty of Paris is signed by delegates from America, Britain, Spain, France, and the Netherlands.

October: Virginia's House of Burgesses grants freedom to slaves who served in the wartime army.

November: Washington delivers his farewell address to his troops. The last British soldiers are evacuated from New York City, along with about 30,000 Tories, who join the Loyalists already in Canada. November 25, Evacuation Day, will long be noted as a major holiday in New York.

December: Washington appears before Congress, then meeting in Annapolis, and takes an action unprecedented for a victorious army commander: he resigns his commission. For the first time – but not the last – he voluntarily, even gratefully, relinquishes a position of great power in order to return to private life, and at the same time gives greater strength to the American tradition of the military power being subordinate to the civilian.

1784

January 14: The Treaty of Paris is ratified by Congress, officially ending the Revolutionary War.

April: The Congress of the Confederation passes the Ordinance of 1784, creating the Northwest Territory out of land ceded by Britain in the Treaty of Paris.

1785

March: The Mount Vernon Conference, a meeting between representatives of Maryland and Virginia, convenes to negotiate rights of navigation on the Potomac River and other waterways. It is an early step that establishes the precedent of state governments coming together to deal with issues not dealt with under the Articles of Confederation. The resulting agreement comes to be known as the Mount Vernon Compact.

1786

January: The Virginia General Assembly urges that a convention be called for the purpose of resolving trade and other issues between the States.

September: Five States – Delegates from Virginia, Delaware, New Jersey, New York and Pennsylvania – meet in an Annapolis tavern in an attempt to improve commerce and establish uniform regulations. The other eight States either fail to send delegates, or failed to attend—including the host state of Maryland. The Annapolis Convention—formally the "Meeting of Commissioners to Remedy Defects of the Federal Government" —conveys to Congress a request to hold another convention the following May with a view to amending and improving the Articles of Confederation.

November- December: New Jersey, Virginia, and Pennsylvania elect delegates to the proposed convention.

1787

January: Protests against taxation culminate in an armed mob marching on government buildings in Massachusetts in what comes to be known as Shays' Rebellion. Militia fire cannon loaded with grapeshot and kill four Shayites, and the rebellion collapses – but not before demonstrating the dangers of a weak central government.

January to May: All the remaining States, except Rhode Island, elect delegates tp the Convention. In May, "Certain Citizens" of Rhode Island send a letter expressing their regrets that not every State will be involved.

May 25: After delays caused by the lack of a quorum, the delegates of the eleven participating States (the New Hampshire delegation not arriving until late July) set to work on their task of amending the Articles of Confederation, but in in short order instead elect to start from scratch and create an entirely new system of government embodied in a new Constitution of the United States. George Washington, a reluctant attendant, is elected president of the convention.

July 13: The Congress of the Confederation passes the Northwest Ordinance. This law establishes the groundwork for creating new States, rather than expanding the territory of the existing States, and makes clear the new States will be in all respects the co-equals of the existing States. It further bans slavery in the Northwest Territory, and in new States created out of that land, but also allows for fugitive slaves from outside the territory to be captured and returned to their owners.

September 17: The new Constitution is signed by 39 delegates from all the states but Rhode Island. In the following few days, it is published and delivered to the Congress of the Confederation, and from Congress to the States for ratification. It is agreed that the Constitution will go into effect only after nine States have ratified it.

September 27: The first "anti-Federalist" paper, signed by "Cato" is released, launching the months'-long pamphleteering debate over ratification. Many modern-day scholars believe that New York Governor George Clinton was behind the pseudonym, taken from the name of a Roman republican who opposed Julius Ceaser, but "Cato's" identity is still uncertain.

October 27: The First of the Federalist Papers is published. They are written by Alexander Hamilton, John Hay, and James Madison, under the pseudonym "Publius." Published between October 1787 and August 1788, they are the bedrock arguments in favor of ratifying the Constituion, and are much reprinted, both in newspapers and in book form. The identities of the authors are kept secret at the time, though many contemporaries rightly suspected the trio of Hamilton, Jay, and Madison. Federalist No. 10, written by Madison, argues in favor of a representative republic as opposed to direct democracy. Picking up from Federalist No, 9, it is entitled: "The Same Subject Continued: The Utility of the Union as a Safeguard Against Domestic Faction and Insurrection." Federalist No. 84 is notable for its opposition to including what later became the Bill of Rights. Penned by Hamilton, it argued that the enumeration of rights would lead to the presumption that the listed rights were the *only* rights retained by the people.

December: Delaware is the first State to ratify the Constitution, quickly followed by Pennsylvania and New Jersey.

1788

January: February: Georgia, Connecticut and Massachusetts ratify the Constitution.

March: Rhode Island calls for a popular referendum on the Constitution. It goes to a vote, and ratification is turned down on March 24.

April: Maryland ratifies the Constitution.

May: South Carolina ratifies the Constitution.

June 21: New Hampshire becomes the ninth State to ratify the Constitution, officially establishing the Constitution in those States that have approved it. New Hampshire requests twelve alterations to the Constitution.

June: Virginia becomes the tenth ratifying State—and requests twenty alterations to the document.

July 2: The Congress of the Confederation is informed that the necessary nine States have6 ratified the Constitution, and soon after sets to work on a plan for bringing the Constitution into effect.

July 26: New York ratifies the Constitution and requests thirty-three alterations.

July-August: North Carolina's legislature, seeking to add pressure for the inclusion of a bill of rights, approved a resolution saying the State does not reject or ratify the Constitution.

September 13: The Congress of the Confederation certifies that the Constitution has been ratified and sets the dates for the first presidential election and the first meeting of the new government.

December 15 1788 –January 10, 1789: The first presidential election, in the form of electors meeting in each State, takes place.

ACKNOWLEDGMENTS

As noted in the Bibliography, my main research source for this book were the volumes in the magnificent *Documentary History of the First Federal Congress, 1789–1791*; Founders Online, at the National Archives; and the Papers of George Washington, at the University of Virginia. At the Library of Congress, I was particularly helped and encouraged by Tom Mann, Abby Yochelson, and Jurretta Heckscher. In the Library's Newspaper & Current Periodicals Reading Room, I received help and advice from Erin Sidwell.

At Mount Vernon, Mary Thompson, Diana Cordray, Michele Lee, and Joan Stahl were of great help. I also made frequent use of the new and authoritative George Washington Digital Encyclopedia created at Mount Vernon: http://www.mountvernon.org/library/digitalhistory/digital-encyclopedia/

For definitions, I usually turned to https://www.merriam-webster.com/.

Alan Dorfman, formerly of the U.S. Bureau of Labor Statistics, is the friend and neighbor who converted eighteenth-century money to twenty-first century money [see note page 52]. Fellow writer and pal Paul Dickson was always at hand when I needed a boost.

My children Chris, Roger, and Connie, along with granddaughter Victoria of the American University Library, all provided me with their generation's knowledge of modern technical, literary, and digital research. Rog, a writer and publisher, responded to countless requests for editorial aid in straightening out manuscript quirks. And Victoria found on the AU campus a keen researcher, Kenya Roy, who was of great help at the beginning by helping to keep track of sources.

My wife, Scottie, and I spent many days in state archives from Virginia to Georgia because I believed that the archives might contain signs of the 1789 transformation from statehood to nationhood. What we found is that state legislatures had more documents and speeches and committees for running a state than the First Federal Congress did for running a new nation.

Thomas B. Allen
June, 2018
Bethesda, Maryland

Thomas B. Allen died at the age of 89 on December 11, 2018. The text of *1789: The Founders Create America* was complete at that time. Mr. Allen's son Roger worked to proofread the text, to confirm and update sources and citations, to finish up various editorial and technical tasks on the manuscript, to update the bibliography, to create the index, and to prepare the work for publication.

Notes

PROLOGUE: ELEVEN STATES CREATE A NATION

1. Madison, James *Madison Debates, September 17, 1797*, 1787.
2. Burnett, Edmond C. *Letters of Members of the Continental Congress*, 1921.
3. Library of Congress *Today In History -- April 19*, 2020.
4. Adams, John *VIII. To the Inhabitants of the Colony of Massachusetts-Bay, 13 March 1775*, 1775.
5. Ballagh, James C. *The Letters of Richard Henry Lee*, 1914, pp. Vol 1, 198.
6. McGaughy, J. Kent, 2016 *Richard Henry Lee (1732-1794)*.
7. Wills, Garry *Inventing America: Jefferson's Declaration of Independence*, 1979, p. 325.
8. Wills, Garry *Inventing America: Jefferson's Declaration of Independence*, 1979, p. 30.
9. "Secret Journals of the Acts and Proceedings of U.S. Congress," vol. 1, page 34. Cited in Tansill, Charles C. *Documents Illustrative of the Formation of the Union of the American States*, 1927, p. 18.
10. Wills, Garry *Inventing America: Jefferson's Declaration of Independence*, 1979, p. 325.
11. Adams, John, 1774 *From John Adams to William Tudor, September 29, 1774*.
12. Wills, Garry *Inventing America: Jefferson's Declaration of Independence*, 1979, p. 34
13. Wills, Garry *Inventing America: Jefferson's Declaration of Independence*, 1979, p. 377. Source quotes from Jefferson's "Notes of Proceedings," which included "the form of the declaration as originally reported."
14. National Archives, 2018 *The Declaration of Independence: A History*.
15. Kennedy, Frances H. *The American Revolution: A Historical Guidebook*, 2014, p. 103.

16. Allen, Thomas B. *Tories: Fighting for the King in America's First Civil War*, 2010, pp. 114-115, 277.

17. Allen, Thomas B. *Tories: Fighting for the King in America's First Civil War*, 2010, p. xiv Letter, Nathanael Greene to Colonel Alexander Hamilton, 1781, quoted on page xiv.

18. Debruyne, Nese F., 2019 *American War and Military Operations Casualties: Lists and Statistics*. p. 1

19. American Battlefield Trust, 2020 *American Revolution Facts*

20. Ramsay, David *The History of the American Revolution*, 1811, pp. vol. 2, 353

CHAPTER 1: THE GREAT CAUSE

1. Waymarkings.com, 2016 *David Humphreys -- Hartford CT*.

2. Humphreys, David *The Miscellaneous Works of David Humphreys*, 1804, p. 232. Connecticut also honors Humphreys for bringing the first merino sheep to America in 1803, after he had ended an ambassadorship to Spain.

3. Paine, Thomas *Thomas Paine, Rights of Man, Common Sense, and Other Political Writings*, 1995, p. 24

4. Humphreys, Frank L. *Life and Times of David Humphreys*, 1917, p. 1. 234.

5. Leepson, Marc *Lafayette: Lessons in Leadership for the Idealist General*, 2011, p. 114. Source quotes Lafayette letter to Jean-Frédéric Phélypeaux, count of Maurepas and the French secretary of state, October 20, 1781.

6. Fitzpatrick, John C. *The Writings of George Washington From the Original Manuscript Sources*, 1939, p. 352. The letter, dated November 18, 1781, was to Robert Hanson Harrison, a wartime aide-de-camp.

7. Braisted, Todd, 2017 *War Chronology*.

8. Polf, William A. *Garrison Town: The British Occupation of New York City. 1776-1783*, 1976, p. 31.

9. Washington's Headquarters State Historic Site *Mountaintop Beacons*. information on file at Washington Headquarters Museum, Newburgh, NY, reviewed on July 16, 2016. "Mountaintop Beacons," information on file at Washington Headquarters Museum, Newburgh, NY, reviewed July 16, 2016. See also Diamant, Lincoln *Chaining the Hudson: The Fight for the River in the American Revolution*, 2004, pp. 68-84.

10. Humphreys, Frank L. *Life and Times of David Humphreys*, 1917, pp. 259-260.

11. Humphreys, Frank L. *Life and Times of David Humphreys*, 1917, pp. 259-262.

12. Atterbury, William W. *Elias Boudinot: Reminiscences of the American Revolution*, 1894.

13. Haggard, Robert F. *The Nicola Affair: Lewis Nicola, George Washington, and American Military Discontent during the Revolutionary War*, June 2002, p. 148.

14. Bell, Jr., Whitfield J. *Patriot-Improvers: Biographical Sketches of Members of the American Philosophical Society Vol 2*, 1999, pp. 53-55.

15. Furr, Grover, 2007 *Col. Lewis Nicola's Letter to George Washington of May 22, 1782*. Grover Furr of Montclair State University has published a transcription of the original document with an interpretation: https://msuweb.montclair. edu/~furrg/gbi/docs/nicolatowashington.html.

16. Furr, Grover, 2007 *Col. Lewis Nicola's Letter to George Washington of May 22, 1782*.

17. Varnum, James M., 1782 *To George Washington from James Mitchell Varnum, June 23 1782*.

18. Fitzpatrick, John C. *The Writings of George Washington From the Original Manuscript Sources*, 1939, p. 24. 415.

19. Washington, George, 1786 *From George Washington to Benjamin Lincoln, February 6 1786,*).

20. Magazine of American History, The *The Historic Temple at New Windsor, 1783*, 1890. Republished at https://democraticthinker.wordpress.com/2010/01/03/ temple-of-virtue/ (accessed January 26, 2018.) See also https://archive.org/ stream/magazineofamericv24stev#page/282/mode/2up.

21. Hunt, Galliard *Journals of the Continental Congress 1774-1789*, 1922, pp. 291-93

22. Anon. *Journals of the American Congress from 1774 to 1788*, 1823. See also Washington, George, 1783 *From George Washington to Elias Boudinot, 12 March 1783*. The text of the "fellow soldier" letter is in Enclosure No. 2.

23. Chernow, Ron *Washington: A Life*, 2010, p. 390

24. Syrett, Harold C. *The Papers of Alexander Hamilton vol 2. 1779-1781*, 1961. See also the text of the letter: Washington, George, 1781 *From George Washington to Samuel Huntington, 23 January 1781*.

25. Thacher, James *A Military Journal during the American Revolutionary War, from 1775 to 1783*, 1854, p. 252.

26. Washington, George, 1781 *Circular Letter on Pennsylvania Line Mutiny, January 5, 1781*.

27. Washington, George, 1783 *From George Washington to Officers of the Army, March 15, 1783*.

28. Washington, George, 1783 *Newburgh Address: George Washington to Officers of the Army, March 15, 1783*. Three weeks earlier, Washington had written a

letter to David Rittenhouse of Philadelphia, America's best-known astronomer and instrument maker, thanking him for these spectacles, which Rittenhouse had made, saying they "magnify perfectly, and shew those letters very distinctly which at first [looked] like a mist" Washington, George, 1783 *From George Washington to David Rittenhouse, 16 February 1783*.

29. U.S. Army *Field Manual 1*, 2008, pp. 1-4.
30. Letter, George Washington to Theordorick Bland, April 4, 1783, quoted in Kenneth R. Bowling article: Bowling, Kenneth R. *New Light on the Philadelphia Mutiny of 1783: Federal-State Confrontation at the Close of the War for Independence*, 1977, pp. 419-50.
31. Bowling, Kenneth R. *New Light on the Philadelphia Mutiny of 1783: Federal-State Confrontation at the Close of the War for Independence*, 1977, pp. 419-50.
32. Supreme Executvie Council of Pennsylvania *Minutes of the Supreme Executive Council of Pennsylvania, from its organization to the termination of the Revolution. [Mar. 4, 1777 - Dec. 20, 1790]*, 1853, p. XIII. 656.
33. U.S. House of Representatives, 2015 *Chasing Congress Away*.
34. Bowling, Kenneth R. *New Light on the Philadelphia Mutiny of 1783: Federal-State Confrontation at the Close of the War for Independence*, 1977, pp. 419-50.
35. Founders Online, 1989 *From George Washington to the Society of the Cincinnati, 4 July 1789.* p. footnote.

CHAPTER 2: THE SPECTER OF A KING

1. Joyce, John S.G. *Story of Philadephia*, 1919, p. 179.
2. Quoted in Wharton, Francis *The Revolutionary Diplomatic Correspondence of the U.S.*, 1889, pp. 6. 292-293.
3. National Park Service, n.d. *Nathanael Greene (1742-1786).*Wayne plantation: Manuscripts Division, William L. Clements Library, University of Michigan, Anthony Wayne Family Papers, 1681-1913,
4. University of Michigan Clements Library, 1959 *Anthony Wayne Family Papers, (1681-1913)* https://quod.lib.umich.edu/c/clementsmss/umich-wcl-M-398way?view=text (accessed January 30, 2018).
5. Burgan, Michael *Thomas Paine: Great Writer of the Revolution*, 2005, p. 61.
6. Martin, Joseph P. *A Narrative of a Revolutionary Soldier*, 2001, pp. 239-40.
7. Martin, Joseph P. *A Narrative of a Revolutionary Soldier*, 2001, p. 243.
8. Martin, Joseph P. *A Narrative of a Revolutionary Soldier*, 2001, p. 205.
9. Encyclopædia Britannica, 1998 *Lucius Quinctius Cincinnatus*.

10. Jefferson in "Memorandum of a tour in Holland," written on March 16, 1788, mentions a meeting at a tavern in New York of Washington, Knox, Lee, and Adams, when Knox refers to wishing for "some ribbon to wear in his hat. . . . " The remark is contained in Society of the Cincinnati of Maryland *Register of the Society of the Cincinnati of Maryland Brought Down to February 22nd, 1897*, 1897, p. 2

11. Society of the Cincinatti, 2018 *Triennial Meetings*.

12. Society of the Cincinatti, n.d. *The Institution of the Society of the Cincinatti*.

13. Bowling, Kenneth R. *Peter Charles L'Enfant: Vision, Honor and Male Friendship in the Early American Republic*, 2002, p. 7.

14. Sawvel, Franklin B. *The Compete Anas of Thomas Jefferson*, 1903, p. 27.

15. Washington, H. A. *The Works of Thomas Jefferson*, 1884, vol . 10, p. 9, p. 89. The full title of the source is The Works of Thomas Jefferson: Being His Autobiography, Correspondence, Reports, Messages, Addresses, and Other Writings, Official and Private: Published by the Order of the Joint Committee of Congress on the Library, from the Original Manuscripts, Deposited in the Department of State, vol 10.

16. Bowling, Kenneth R. *Peter Charles L'Enfant: Vision, Honor and Male Friendship in the Early American Republic*, 2002, p. 8

17. Adams, John, 1785 *John Adams to Elbridge Gerry, April 25, 1785*.

18. Alexander, John *Samuel Adams: America's Revolutionary Politician*, 2002, p. 196.

19. Abbot, W. W. & Twohig, Dorothy *The Papers of George Washington: January-July 1784*, 1992, p. 144. Burke, Aedanus *Considerations on the Society or Order of Cincinnati*.

20. Burke, Aedanus *Considerations on the Society or Order of Cincinnati*. The Society of the Cincinnati, with more than 3,900 members descended from Revolutionary War officers, is now a nonprofit educational organization "devoted to the principles and ideals of its founders."

21. Society of the Cincinatti, 2018 *The Society and its Critics, 1784-1800*.

22. Randolph, Thomas J. *Memoirs, Correspondence and Private Papers of Thomas Jefferson*, 1829, vol. 4, pp. 454-455.

23. Winthrop Sargent, a delegate in 1784, copied Washington's words and encrypted them in a journal. In 1858, a decryption published by the journal keeper's grandson—a hereditary member also named Winthrop Sargent—revealed Washington's secret. He published the entire journal in the Memoirs of the

Historical Society of Pennsylvania Volume 6. Historical Society of Pennsylvania, 1858, pp. 57-115.

24. Letter, Benjamin Franklin to Sarah Bache, January 26, 1784, in The Works of Benjamin Franklin: Containing Several Political and Historical Tracts Not Included in Any Former Edition, and Many Letters Official and Private Not Hitherto Published: With Notes and a Life of the Author, ed. Jared Sparks. Short citation: Sparks, Jared *The Works of Benjamin Franklin*, 1844, p. 58.

25. State of Virginia *Laws of Virginia Relating to Fisheries of Tidal Water*, 1950, p. 110. Laws of Virginia Relating to Fisheries of Tidal Waters.

26. Maryland State Archives, 2007 *The Mt. Vernon Compact & the Annapolis Convention: Regional Cooperation: March 1785.*

27. Chernow, Ron *Alexander Hamilton*, 2004, p. 221.

28. Hamilton, Alexander, 2001 *Annapolis Convention. Address of the Annapolis Convention, [14 September 1786].*

29. Washington, George, 1786 *From George Washington to James Madison, November 5, 1786.*

30. Knox, Henry, 2002 *To George Washington from Henry Knox, 23 October 1786* Letter, "To George Washington from Henry Knox, 23 October 1786."

31. Washington, George, 1786 *From George Washington to David Humphreys, 22 October 1786.*

32. Knox, Henry, 2002 *To George Washington from Henry Knox, 23 October 1786.*

33. Fitch, William E. *Some Neglected History of North Carolina: Being an Account of the Revolution of the Regulators and of the Battle of Alamance, the First Battle of the American Revolution*, 1905, p. 110.

34. Bowen, Catherine D. *Miracle at Philadelphia*, 1968, p. 20.

35. Washington, George, 1786 *From George Washington to James Madison, 16 December 1786.*

36. Springfield Technical Community College, 2008 *A Bloody Encounter: "the body of the people assembled in arms".*

37. Letter, "Tobias Lear (1762–1816) to Henry Knox," Gilder Lehrman Collection. Lear, Tobias, 1787 *Lear, Tobias to Henry Knox*

38. Bowen, Catherine D. *Miracle at Philadelphia*, 1968, p. 20.

39. Ramsay, David *History of the United States, from Their First Settlement as English Colonies, in 1607, to the Year 1808*, 1818, p. 3. 49.

40. Worcester Magazine *Summary of Late Intelligence*, 1787, p. 238

41. Worcester Magazine *Summary of Late Intelligence*, 1787, p. 238

42. Society of the Cincinatti, 2018 *The Society and its Critics, 1784-1800*

43. Letter from Mercy Warren to Catharine Macaulay. See: *Mercy Warren* by Alice Brown. Brown, Alice *Mercy Warren*, 1896, p. 296.

44. Otto's remarks were written in New York on June 10, 1787 to Count de Montmorin, secretary of state for foreign affairs. The full text of the letter can be found in Giunta, Mary A. & Hartgrove, J. Dane *Documents of the Emerging Nation: U.S. Foreign Relations, 1775-1789*, 1998, pp. 255-59

45. U.S. Constitution, Article I, Section 2, Clause 3.

46. Quoted in Michael Nelson, Guide to the Presidency. (Nelson, Michael *Guide to the Presidency*, 2015, p. 14.

47. Farrand, Max *The Records of the Federal Convention of 1787*, 1911, p. 3. 479

48. Frost, David B. *Classified: A History of Secrecy in the United States Government*, 2017, p. 37.

49. Madison, James *Notes of Debates in the Federal Convention of 1787*, 1966 [1890].

50. Yates, Robert, 1886 *Notes of the Secret Debates of the Federal Convention of 1787, Taken by the Late Hon Robert Yates, Chief Justice of the State of New York, and One of the Delegates from That State to the Said Convention*

51. Mason quoted in "Debate in Virginia Ratifying Convention," for June 17, 1788, https://press-pubs.uchicago.edu/founders/print_documents/a2_1_1s16.html.

52. Quoted in Dunbar, Louise B. *A Study of "Monarchical" Tendencies in the United States from 1776 to 1801*, Vol X March 1922, p. 99

53. Federalist Papers, 1788 *Federalist Papers No 68* Federalist Papers No. 68, The Mode of Electing the President. From the New York Packet. Friday, March 14, 1788.

54. Chernow, Ron *Washington: A Life*, 2010, p. 538.

55. Quoted in Brookhiser, Richard *Founding Father: Rediscovering George Washington*, 1997, p. 66.

56. "Madison Debates, Tuesday, August 22, 1787," Madison, James, 1787 *Madison Debates August 22, 1787*

57. "George Mason's Objections to the Constitution," posted on the wall of Mason's home, now the Gunston Hall Mansion and Museum in Lorton, VA. See also Mason, George, n.d. *Objections to the Constitution*

58. Teaching American History, n.d. *The Six Stages of Ratification*.

59. David Ramsay, "An Address to the Freemen of South Carolina, on the Subject of the Federal Constitution," published in Ford, Paul L. *Pamphlets on the Constitution of the United States, published during its discussion by the people, 1787-1788*, 1888, pp. 373-79.

60. Washington, George, 1787 *From George Washington to Lafayette, 18 September 1787.*

61. U.S. Constitution, 2010 *New Hampshire's Ratification.*

62. Henry, Patrick, 2012 *Speech of Partrick Henry (June 5, 1788).*

63. Henry, Patrick, 2012 *Speech of Partrick Henry (June 5, 1788)*

64. Ramsay, David *History of the United States, from Their First Settlement as English Colonies, in 1607, to the Year 1808,* 1818, p. 2. 436.

65. Maier, Pauline *Ratification: The People Debate the Constitution, 1787-1788,* 2011, p. 432.

CHAPTER 3: THE RELUCTANT PRESIDENT

1. Fitzpatrick, John C. *The Writings of George Washington From the Original Manuscript Sources,* 1939, p. 30. 171 .

2. Kahler, Gerald E. *"Gentlemen of the family : General George Washington's aides-de-camp and military secretaries".* master's thesis, University of Richmond, 1997, 112–13.

3. Humphreys, David *Life of General Washington,* 2006, p. 7.

4. Stewart, David O. *The Summer of 1787: The Men Who Invented the Constitution,* 2002, p. 86.

5. Washington, George, 1789 *Undelivered First Inaugural Address: Fragments, 30 April 1789.* This fragment, in the De Coppet Collection at Princeton, was on page 24 of the 73-page speech that Washington sent to Madison.

6. Fitzpatrick, John C. *The Writings of George Washington From the Original Manuscript Sources,* 1939, p. 30. 176.

7. Sparks, Jared, 1827 *Jared Sparks to James Madison, 22 May 1827.*

8. See subsections of Collection Overview: "Biographical Information: Literary Career," in Harvard University Library Archives, n.d. *Papers of Jared Sparks, 1820-1861, 1866.* See also "History of the Diary Manuscripts," George Washington Papers, Library of Congress, Library of Congress, n.d. *History of the Diary Manuscripts.*

9. Washington, George, 1789 *Diary entry: 7 January 1789.*

10. U.S House of Representatives, n.d. *Electoral College & Indecisive Elections* "Electoral College & Indecisive Elections" The article quotes from a letter written by Morris on December 25, 1802. The whole text of the letter, in which he argues against a separate election for the Vice President, as per the Twelfth Amendment, can be found in Sparks, Jared *The life of Gouverneur*

Morris, with selections from his correspondence and miscellaneous papers, 1832, vol. 3, pp. 174.

11. National Archives, 2019 *What is the Electoral College*

12. Ratcliffe, Donald *The Right to Vote and the Rise of Democracy, 1787-1828.*, 2013, p. 224.

13. Ratcliffe, Donald *The Right to Vote and the Rise of Democracy, 1787-1828.*, 2013, p. 222.

14. Berggren, D. J., n.d. *Presidential Election of 1789*.

15. Anon. *Re: Washington-Blackburn*, 1998.

16. Maryland Journal *Maryland Journal, January 20, 1789.*, 1789.

17. Maier, Pauline *Ratification: The People Debate the Constitution, 1787-1788*, 2011, p. xiii.

18. DePauw, Linda G. *The Eleventh Pillar: New York State and the Federal Constitution*, 1966, p. 43.

19. Washington, George, 1789 *From George Washington to Lafayette, January 29, 1789*.

20. George Washington's Mount Vernon, n.d. *www.mountvernon.org/george-washington/real-estate*.

21. McCusker, John J. *A Historical Price Index*, 1992.

22. Washington, George, 1789 *From George Washington to Richard Conway, 6 March 1789*

23. Washington, George, 1786 *From George Washington to John Jay, 15 August 1786*.

24. "elective monarch," Hamilton: Ferling, John *Jefferson and Hamilton: The Rivalry that Forged A Nation*, 2014, p. 187; "elective monarch," Jefferson: Wood, Gordon S. *Empire of Liberty: A History of the Early Republic, 1789-1815*, 2009, p. 74; "foetus of monarchy," Randolph quoted in: Madison, James, 1787 *Debates in the Federal Convention of 1787*; "Rage for Monarchy," Letter: Thomas Tudor Tucker to St. George Tucker, May 13, 1789, Tucker-Coleman Papers, Swem Library, College of William and Mary, as quoted in Bickford, Charlene B. & Bowling, Kenneth R. *Birth of the Nation: The First Federal Congress 1789-1791*, 1989, p. 23.

25. Washington, George, 1789 *Undelivered First Inaugural Address: Fragments, 30 April 1789*.

CHAPTER 4: OUT WITH THE OLD

1. U.S. Congress, 1788 *Resolution of Congress, Dated July 2, 1788, Submitting Ratifications of the Constitution to a Committee.*
2. George Washington University, 2013 *New York as the Seat of Government* and George Washington University, 2013 *By the United States in Congress Assembled.*
3. Osborn, David, 2013 *Phillip Pell: Revolutionary War Leader, Last Member of the Continental Congress.* Pell is buried in St. Paul's cemetery.
4. Bickford, Charlene B. & Bowling, Kenneth R. *Birth of the Nation: The First Federal Congress 1789-1791*, 1989, p. 5.
5. Bickford, Charlene B. & Bowling, Kenneth R. *Birth of the Nation: The First Federal Congress 1789-1791*, 1989, p. 4.
6. A narrative of the case is found in "Crown v. John Peter Zenger" in Historical Society of the New York Courts, n.d. *Crown v. John Peter Zenger*
7. Bowling, Kenneth R. *Peter Charles L'Enfant: Vision, Honor and Male Friendship in the Early American Republic*, 2002, pp. 4-5.
8. Bowling, Kenneth R. *Peter Charles L'Enfant: Vision, Honor and Male Friendship in the Early American Republic*, 2002, p. 13.
9. Bowling, Kenneth R. *Peter Charles L'Enfant: Vision, Honor and Male Friendship in the Early American Republic*, 2002, pp. 12-15.
10. Early Republic, n.d. *Comte de Moustier to Comte de Montmorin Tuesday , 9 June 1789.* See also Letter, Comte de Moustier to Comte de Montmorin, Tuesday, June 9, 1789, in *DHFFC The Documentary History of the First Federal Congress: Vol. 9. The Diary of William Maclay and Other Notes on Senate Debates*, 1988, vol. 9, p. 9, Note 13.
11. Bowling, Kenneth R. *Peter Charles L'Enfant: Vision, Honor and Male Friendship in the Early American Republic*, 2002, p. 16.
12. Description adapted from "New York Friday, 24 April 1789"in U.S. Senate *Journal of the First Session of the Senate of the United States of America, Begun and Held at the City of New-York, March 4th, 1789, and in the Thirteenth Year of the Independence of the Said State*s, 1789
13. Bowling, Kenneth R. & Veit, Helen E. *The Diary of William Maclay and Other Notes on Senate Debates*, 1988. In 1812, the building was torn down and the four lots on which it stood were bought by individuals. The U.S. government later purchased three of the lots and built, in Greek Revival style, the New York Custom House. The site later became the Sub-Treasury, then the Federal Reserve Bank of New York. It is now designated the Federal Hall National Memorial. It is a National Historic Site and a National Memorial, open to visitors.

14. New York Society Library, 2020 *History of the Library*.

15. Description adapted from entry for "New York Friday, 24 April 1789" in U.S. Senate *Journal of the First Session of the Senate of the United States of America, Begun and Held at the City of New-York, March 4th, 1789, and in the Thirteenth Year of the Independence of the Said States*, 1789, p. 19.

16. New York Society Library, 2020 *History of the Library*. Two books were charged out to George Washington but were never returned. In 2010, representatives from Mount Vernon formally presented the Library with a copy of one of the missing books, *The Law of Nations* by Emer de Vattel. See http://library.nysoclib.org/record=b1243254.

17. Washington, George, 1776 *From George Washington to Lund Washington, 6 October 1776*.

18. Bickford, Charlene B. & Bowling, Kenneth R. *Birth of the Nation: The First Federal Congress 1789-1791*, 1989, p. 9.

19. Smith, Thomas E.V. *The City of New York in the Year of Washington's Inauguration, 1789*, 1889, p. 9.

20. Jones-Wilson, Faustine et al. *Encyclopedia of African-American Education*, 1996, p. 109.

21. New-York Daily Gazette, 1789 *1789 NY newspaper ABOLITION of SLAVERY Wm Wilberforce*.

22. Smith, Thomas E.V. *The City of New York in the Year of Washington's Inauguration, 1789*, 1889, p. 16.

23. Smith, Thomas E.V. *The City of New York in the Year of Washington's Inauguration, 1789*, 1889, p. 19

24. Bickford, Charlene B. & Bowling, Kenneth R. *Birth of the Nation: The First Federal Congress 1789-1791*, 1989, p. 7. The words come from Edwards Bangs, an essayist and orator from Worcester, Massachusetts, writing to Representative George Thatcher of the Maine District of Massachusetts.

CHAPTER 5: A NEW GOVERNMENT AWAKENS

1. Bickford, Charlene B. & Bowling, Kenneth R. *Birth of the Nation: The First Federal Congress 1789-1791*, 1989, p. 10. Bickford and Bowling report the writer was "probably" Thatcher.

2. Veit, Helen E. et al. *Creating the Bill of Rights: The Documentary Record from the First Federal Congress*, 1991, pp. 14-28. "Amendments Proposed by the States, June 8, 1789."

3. Mount Vernon Ladies' Association, n.d. *The Material Culture of the Presidency*.

4. Knox, Henry, 1789 *To George Washington from Henry Knox, 5 March 1789.*
5. Digital Maryland, n.d. *Maryland Colonial Currency - Enoch Pratt Free Library.*
6. Washington, George, 1789 *From George Washington to Richard Conway, 6 March 1789.*
7. U.S House of Representatives, n.d. *Historical Highlights: The first Speaker of the House, Frederick A.C. Muhlenberg of Pennsylvania.*
8. Sparks, Jared *The Writings of George Washington Vol 9*, 1847, p. 488.
9. U.S House of Representatives, n.d. *The Creation of the Formal House Rules and the House Rules Committee.*
10. U.S. Senate, n.d. *Senate History: Filibuster and Cloture.*
11. U.S. Congress *Rules for Conducting Business in the Senate of the United States*, 1849, pp. 3, 4.
12. Bordewich, Fergus M. *The First Congress: How James Madison, George Washington, and a Group of Extraordinary Men Invented the Government*, 2016, p. 32. Bordewich reports "on April 5, Richard Henry Lee arrived in New York to make a quorum in the Senate." He arrived on the fifth, but the quorum was achieved on the sixth.See also https://www.cop.senate.gov/artandhistory/history/minute/Senate_Doorkeeper.htm.
13. McCullough, David *John Adams*, 2001, pp. 393-394.
14. McCullough, David *John Adams*, 2001, p. 394.
15. Bell, Jr., Whitfield J. *Patriot-Improvers: Biographical Sketches of Members of the American Philosophical Society Vol 2*, 1999, pp. 192-193.
16. Bordewich, Fergus M. *The First Congress: How James Madison, George Washington, and a Group of Extraordinary Men Invented the Government*, 2016, p. 35.
17. Langdon, John, 1789 *To George Washington from John Langdon, 6 April 1789.*
18. Washington, George, 1789 *Address to Charles Thomson, 14 April 1789.*
19. Quoted in source: Bowling, Kenneth R. *Good-by "Charle": The Lee-Adams Interest and the Political Demise of Charles Thomson, Secretary of Congress, 1774-1789*, 1976, pp. 314-35.

CHAPTER 6: "NOW A KING"

1. Hirschfeld, Robert S. *The Power of the Presidency: Concepts and Controversy*, 1982, p. 26.
2. Hirschfeld, Robert S. *The Power of the Presidency: Concepts and Controversy*, 1982, pp. 28, 29

3. Joint Committee on Printing of the House and Senate *A Compilation of the Messages and Papers of the Presidents*, 1897, p. 1. 42.

4. Sparks, Jarad *The Writings of George Washington Vol 10*, 1847, p. 10. 461.

5. Fields, Joseph E. *'Worthy Partner': The Papers of Martha Washington*, 1994, p. 213.

6. Washington, George, 1789 *From George Washington to the Mayor, Corporation, and Citizens of Alexandria, 16 April 1789*.

7. Chernow, Ron *Washington: A Life*, 2010, pp. 562-63.

8. Lear, Tobias *President Washington in New York, 1789*, Vol. 32, No. 4 (1908), p. 500.

9. MacLeod, Jessie, n.d. *William (Billy) Lee*.

10. Breen, T. H. *George Washington's Journey: The President Forges a New Nation*, 2015, pp. 34-36, 38.

11. McHenry, James, 1789 *To George Washington from James McHenry, 29 March 1789*. McHenry served in the Continental Army as a physician and as an wartime aide, first to Washington, then to Lafayette. McHenry was also a delegate to the Continental Congress from 1783 to 1786.

12. Washington, George, 1789 *From George Washington to the Ladies of Trenton, 21 April 1789*.

13. Bartoloni-Tuazon, Kathleen *For Fear of an Elective King: George Washington and the Presidential Title Controversy of 1789*, 2014, p. 52.

14. Ellis, Joseph J. *His Excellency George Washington*, 2004, p. 185.

15. Smith, Thomas E.V. *The City of New York in the Year of Washington's Inauguration, 1789*, 1889, p. 223.

16. Lossing, Benson J. *The Home of Washington*, 1870, p. 215.

17. Boudinot, Elias, 1789 *To George Washington from Elias Boudinot, 22 April 1789*. p. n. 1.

18. Bowen, Clarence W. *History of the Centennial Celebration of the Inauguration of George Washington as First President of the United States*, 1892, p. 222.

19. Washington diary entry for April 23, 1789, as cited in notes in Boudinot, Elias, 1789 *To George Washington from Elias Boudinot, 22 April 1789*. p. n. 1.

20. Jefferson, Thomas, 1792 *From Thomas Jefferson to Thomas Mann Randolph, Jr., 16 March 1792*.

21. Herbert, Leila *"The First American: His Homes and His Households: Part III: In Philadelphia and Germantown*, 1899, p. 713.

22. Fleming, Thomas *The Perils of Peace: America's Struggles for Survival after Yorktown*, 2007, pp. 315-21.

23. DHFFC *The Documentary History of the First Federal Congress, Vol. 10. Debates in the House of Representatives, First Session, April-May 1789*, 1992, vol. 10, pp. 595-607.

24. Bartoloni-Tuazon, Kathleen *For Fear of an Elective King: George Washington and the Presidential Title Controversy of 1789*, 2014, p. 78. The author dismisses the "Mightiness" story as anecdotal (151).

25. Bartoloni-Tuazon, Kathleen *For Fear of an Elective King: George Washington and the Presidential Title Controversy of 1789*, 2014, p. 132.

26. Swanstrom, Roy *The United States Senate, 1787-1801: A dissertation on the first fourteen years of the upper legislative body*, 1988.

27. Bowling, Kenneth R. & Veit, Helen E. *The Diary of William Maclay and Other Notes on Senate Debates*, 1988, p. 67.

28. McCullough, David *John Adams*, 2001, p. 406.

29. Bowling, Kenneth R. & Veit, Helen E. *The Diary of William Maclay and Other Notes on Senate Debates*, 1988, pp. xiii-viii. The Bowling-Veit edition of the diary is the first to reveal it as he wrote it—and provides annotations that "help the reader understand the document."

30. Bowling, Kenneth R. & Veit, Helen E. *The Diary of William Maclay and Other Notes on Senate Debates*, 1988, p. 10.

31. Bowen, Catherine D. *Miracle at Philadelphia*, 1968, p. 257.

32. McGaughy, J. Kent *Richard Henry Lee of Virginia: A Portrait of an American Revolutionary*, 2004, p. 206.

33. Maclay, Edgar S. Journal of William Maclay, 1890, p. 7.

34. Bowling, Kenneth R. *Good-by "Charle": The Lee-Adams Interest and the Political Demise of Charles Thomson, Secretary of Congress, 1774-1789*, 1976.

35. Bowling, Kenneth R. *Good-by "Charle": The Lee-Adams Interest and the Political Demise of Charles Thomson, Secretary of Congress, 1774-1789*, 1976.

36. Smith, Thomas E.V. *The City of New York in the Year of Washington's Inauguration, 1789*, 1889, p. 226.

37. Beatty, Joseph M. *The Letters of Judge Henry Wynkoop, Representative from Pennsylvania to the First Congress of the United States*, 1914, p. 42.

38. Alexander, James C. *Off to a bad start: John Adams's tussle over titles*, 2008, p. 2.

39. Bowling, Kenneth R. & Veit, Helen E. *The Diary of William Maclay and Other Notes on Senate Debates*, 1988, p. 23.

40. All subsequent Maclay quotations are from Bowling, Kenneth R. & Veit, Helen E. *The Diary of William Maclay and Other Notes on Senate Debates*, 1988 pages 6, 16, 17.

41. Wood, Gordon S. *Empire of Liberty: A History of the Early Republic, 1789-1815,* 2009, p. 64.

42. Alden, John *Souvenir and Official Programme of the Centennial Celebration of the Inauguration of George Washington as President of the United States,* 1889, p. 270. See also a letter, Comte de Moustier to Comte de Montmorin, 9 June 1789, in DHFFC *The Documentary History of the First Federal Congress, Vol. 16, Correspondence: First Session, June-August 1789,* 2004, vol. 16, pp. 729-737.

43. National Park Service *George Washington Inaugural Bible,* 2015. The same Bible was used in the inaugurations of Presidents Warren G. Harding, Dwight D. Eisenhower, Jimmy Carter, and George H. W. Bush.

44. Duer, William A. *Description of the Inauguration,* 1867, pp. 68-70.

45. Jonassen, Frederick B. *Kiss the Book . . . You're President . . . : "So Help Me God" and Kissing the Book in the Presidential Oath of Office,* March 2012, pp. 854-951. This authoritative article covers issues ranging from atheists' and deists' litigation to varying opinions of historians.

46. Bowling, Kenneth R. & Veit, Helen E. *The Diary of William Maclay and Other Notes on Senate Debates,* 1988, p. 13.

47. Bowling, Kenneth R. & Veit, Helen E. *The Diary of William Maclay and Other Notes on Senate Debates,* 1988, p. 13.

48. DHFFC *The Documentary History of the First Federal Congress, Vol. 4, Legislative Histories: Amendments to the Constitution through Foreign Officers Bill [HR-1 16],* 1986, vol. 4, pp. 480-83.

49. National Archives, 1996 *Washington's Inaugural Address of 1789.*

50. Medhurst, Martin J. *From Duché to Provoost: The Birth of Inaugural Prayer,* 1982, pp. 573-88.

51. Mount Vernon's Ladies Association, n.d. *President Washington's Inauguration in New York City.*

CHAPTER 7: ETIQUETTE ADVICE FOR THE PRESIDENT

1. Washington, George, 1789 *To John Adams from George Washington, 17 May 1789.*

2. Adams, John, 1789 *To George Washington from John Adams, 17 May 1789.*

3. Adams, John, 1789 *To George Washington from John Adams, 17 May 1789.*

4. Hamilton, Alexander, 1789 *From Alexander Hamilton to George Washington, [5 May 1789].*

5. Hamilton, Alexander, 1789 *From Alexander Hamilton to George Washington, [5 May 1789]*.

6. Stuart, David *To George Washington from David Stuart, 2 June 1790*, 1790

7. Sparks, Jarad *The Writings of George Washington Vol 10*, 1847, p. 20

8. Thompson, Mary V., n.d. *Dining at Mount Vernon*.

9. Washington, H. A. *The Writings of Thomas Jefferson*, 1854, p. 132.

10. Letter, "David Stuart to George Washington 2 June 1790," in DHFFC *The Documentary History of The First Federal Congress, Vol. 19. Correspondence: Second Session, 15 March-June 1790*, 2012, vol. 19, pp. 1679-1682.

11. Washington, George, 1790 *From George Washington to David Stuart, 15 June 1790*.

12. Bowling, Kenneth R. & Veit, Helen E. *The Diary of William Maclay and Other Notes on Senate Debates*, 1988, p. 21.

13. Gazette of the United States *The President's Household*, 1789, pp. 3, col 2 bottom.

14. Griswold, Rufus W. *The Republican Court: Or, American Society in the Days of Washington*, 1854, p. 49.

15. American Art Association *The Important Collection of Baron Von Steuben Relics*, 1929, p. 24.

16. Bowling, Kenneth R. & Veit, Helen E. *The Diary of William Maclay and Other Notes on Senate Debates*, 1988, p. 121.

17. Bowling, Kenneth R. & Veit, Helen E. *The Diary of William Maclay and Other Notes on Senate Debates*, 1988, p. 160.

18. DHFFC *The Documentary History of the First Federal Congress: Vol. 15, Correspondence: First Session, March-May 1789*, 2004, vol. 15, p. 492.

19. Letter, "Erkuries Beatty to Josiah Harmar," in DHFFC *The Documentary History of the First Federal Congress: Vol. 15, Correspondence: First Session, March-May 1789*, 2004, vol. 15, pp. 618-19.

20. Letter: "Tobias Lear to George Augustine Washington, 3 May 1789," published as a footnote to Lear, Tobias, 1789 *From George Washington to John Adams, 10 May 1789*.

21. Smith, Thomas E.V. *The City of New York in the Year of Washington's Inauguration, 1789*, 1889, p. 239.

22. Smith, Thomas E.V. *The City of New York in the Year of Washington's Inauguration, 1789*, 1889, pp. 236-37.

23. Smith, Thomas E.V. *The City of New York in the Year of Washington's Inauguration, 1789*, 1889, pp. 236-37.

24. George Washinton's Mount Vernon & Center for History and New Media, n.d. *The 1790s* See alo Trenholm, Sandara, 2013 *Martha Washington: First Lady's grandchildren were her top priority*.

25. Adams, Abigail, 1789 *Abigail Adams to Mary Smith Cranch, 9 August 1789*.

26. Schroeder, John F. & Lossing, Benson J. *Life and Times of Washington*, 1903, p. 4. 1610.

27. Griswold, Rufus W. *The Republican Court: Or, American Society in the Days of Washington*, 1854, p. 168·

28. Washington, Mary B., 1788 *The Will of Mary Washington, as Registered in the Clerk's Office at Fredericksburg, Virginia*.

29. Chernow, Ron *Washington: A Life*, 2010, p. 589.

30. Bowling, Kenneth R. & Veit, Helen E. *The Diary of William Maclay and Other Notes on Senate Debates*, 1988, pp. 136-37.

31. Georgiana Cavendish, Duchess of Devonshire (1757–1806), a Whig partisan, canvassed for the parliamentary reelection of Charles James Fox in 1784. Jay's "Consatina" ("little conceit") about her is based on the general belief that she gave kisses in exchange for votes. His pun on the word *stone* was based on its vulgar usage.

32. Bowling, Kenneth R. & Veit, Helen E. *The Diary of William Maclay and Other Notes on Senate Debates*, 1988, p. 138.

33. Lyons, Maura *William Dunlap and the Construction of an American Art History*, 2005, p. 19.

34. Wharton, Anne H. *The Washingtons in Official Life*, 1896.

35. Dunlap, William *A History of the American Theatre*, 1832, p. 85.

36. Washington, Martha, n.d. *To George Washington from William Heth, 3 May 1789 (footnote)*

37. Griswold, Rufus W. *The Republican Court: Or, American Society in the Days of Washington*, 1854, pp. 201, 215-216.

38. Stone, William L. *The Centennial History of New York City: From the Discovery to the Present Day*, 1876, p. 185.

CHAPTER 8: "ALL IS BARE CREATION"

1. Reprinted in Christman, Margaret C.S. *The First Federal Congress 1789-1781*, 1989, p. 102. See also Gazette of the United States *NEW-YORK, June 24, 1789: Extract of a letter from Savanna, dated June 11*, 1789, pp. 3, col 3.

2. "Punishment of Crimes Bill {S-6}," in DHFFC *The Documentary History of the First Federal Congress: Vol. 6. Legislative Histories: Mitigation of Fines Bill*

[HR-38] through Resolution on Unclaimed Western Lands, 1986, vol. 6, pp. 1734-1752.

3. Madison, James, 1789 *To Thomas Jefferson from James Madison, June 30, 1789.*

4. Christman, Margaret C.S. *The First Federal Congress 1789-1781*, 1989, p. 95. Officially the number of men who served in the First Congress was twenty-six senators (because the senators of late-ratifying North Carolina and Rhode Island are counted) and sixty-five representatives; the total of ninety-five comes from replacements of a member who resigned and of two who replaced members who died.

5. Austin, James T. *The Life of Elbridge Gerry*, 1829, p. 99. Gerry, as governor of Massachusetts, in 1812 oversaw the creation of an election district favoring his party. Its weird boundaries inspired a cartoonist to draw it to look like a salamander, which was dubbed a "gerrymander." The word lived on to describe rigging of elective district boundaries to help or hinder candidates.

6. Bowling, Kenneth R. & Veit, Helen E. *The Diary of William Maclay and Other Notes on Senate Debates*, 1988, pp. 18, n. 2.

7. Wright, Jr., Robert K. & MacGregor, Jr., Morris J. *Soldier-Statesmen of the Constitution*, 1987, pp. 161-162.

8. Byrd, Robert C. *The Senate, 1789-1989*, 1988, p. 5.

9. U.S. Constitution, Article I, section 2, clause 3: "Representatives and direct Taxes shall be apportioned among the several States which may be included within this Union, according to their respective Numbers, which shall be determined by adding to the whole Number of free Persons, including those bound to Service for a Term of Years, and excluding Indians not taxed, three fifths of all other Persons [i.e., enslaved people]."

10. DHFFC *The Documentary History of the First Federal Congress, Vol. 14, Debates in the House of Representatives: Third Session, December 1790-March 1791*, 1996, vol. 14, pp. 922-23. See also Turnere, Orsamus *History of the Pioneer Settlement of Phelps and Gorham Purchase*, 1851, p. 136 and Maillard, Mary *A Map of Time and Blood*, 2014.

11. Austin, James T. *The Life of Elbridge Gerry*, 1829, p. 101.

12. Clement, Maud C. *The History of Pittsylvania County, Virginia*, 1999, pp. 201-02.

13. Ames, Fisher *The Works of Fisher Ames*, 1983, pp. 44-45.

14. Galloway, George B. *History of the House of Representatives*, 1968, p. 8.

15. Remini, Rovert V. *The House: The History of the House of Representatives*, 2006, p. 14.

16. Letter: "John Quincy Adams to James Bridge," (an old friend from Harvard), 21 September 1789 in DHFFC *The Documentary History of the First Federal Congress, Vol. 17, Correspondence: First Session, September-November 1789*, 2004, vol. 17, p. 1594.

17. "Members' Travel to New York City," in DHFFC *The Documentary History of the First Federal Congress: Vol. 15, Correspondence: First Session, March-May 1789*, 2004, vol. 15, pp. 19-22.

18. E. M. Stratton *Porte Pencil on Modes of Travel*, 1869, p. 36. Also cited in Vineyard, Ron, 2000 *Stage Waggons and Coachees*.

19. Kopper, Philip *Capitol Discovery*, 2003. A ledger stamped "Senators' Compensation and Mileage," begun in 1790 and ending in 1881, was one of sixty ledgers found in a storage room in the Capitol sub-basement during construction of the Capitol Visitor Center in 2002. The ledger is now in the archives of the Senate Historian and is expected to be put on the Senate website.

20. Christman, Margaret C.S. *The First Federal Congress 1789-1781*, 1989, p. 69.

21. Bickford, Charlene *Setting Precedent: The First Senate and President Washington Struggle to Define "Advice and Consent"*, 2014.

CHAPTER 9: THE CONSTITUTION AS BLUEPRINT

1. Bickford, Charlene B. & Bowling, Kenneth R. *Birth of the Nation: The First Federal Congress 1789-1791*, 1989, p. 28.

2. U.S. Senate *Journal of the First Session of the Senate of the United States of America*, 1820.

3. U.S. Senate, n.d. *James Mathers, Doorkeeper and Sergeant at Arms, 1789–1811*. Some sources report April 7, 1789 as the date of the first Senate quorum.

4. Wright, Jr., Robert K. & MacGregor, Jr., Morris J. *Soldier-Statesmen of the Constitution*, 1987, pp. 100-02.

5. U.S. Senate *Journal of the First Session of the Senate of the United States of America*, 1820, p. 41.

6. U.S. Senate *Senators Receive Class Assignments*, n.d. See also U.S. Senate *Journal of the Senate of the United States of America, 1789-1793; FRIDAY, MAY 15, 1789*, 1789.

7. U.S. Congress *American State Papers*, 1832, vol. 5, pp. 5-6.

8. Madison, James, 1789 *Import Duties, [28 April] 1789*. See also discussion in May 2, 1789, Gazette of the United States *New-York. Proceedings of Congress*, 1789, pp. 1-3.

9. *United States Statutes at Large,* vol. 1, 1st Congress, 1st Session, chap. 2. See United States *The Public Statutes of the United States of America / by Authority of Congress,* 1845, pp. 24-25.

10. Baldwin, Abraham, 1789 *Rep. Abraham Baldwin of Georgia to Governor Edward Telfair, June 17, 1789.*

11. "Jeremiah Wadsworth Representative from Connecticut," in DHFFC *The Documentary History of the First Federal Congress, Vol. 14, Debates in the House of Representatives: Third Session, December 1790-March 1791,* 1996, vol. 14, pp. 519-525.

12. U.S. Congress *Acts Passed At A Congress of the United States of America,* 1791, pp. 17-20.

13. "Tonnage Act [HR-5], July 20, 1789," in DHFFC *The Documentary History of the First Federal Congress: Vol. 6. Legislative Histories: Mitigation of Fines Bill [HR-38] through Resolution on Unclaimed Western Lands,* 1986, vol. 6, pp. 1947-1951.

14. Letter, "Comte de Moustier to Comte de Montmorin, October 3, 1789," in DHFFC *The Documentary History of the First Federal Congress, Vol. 17, Correspondence: First Session, September-November 1789,* 2004, vol. 17, pp. 1658-1665.

15. Bickford, Charlene B. & Bowling, Kenneth R. *Birth of the Nation: The First Federal Congress 1789-1791,* 1989, pp. 30, 31-33.

16. Stewart, Walter J. *The Lighthouses Act of 1789,* 1991.

17. U.S. Coast Guard *Coast Guard History,* n.d., pp. 1-2.

18. Bowling, Kenneth R. & Veit, Helen E. *The Diary of William Maclay and Other Notes on Senate Debates,* 1988, p. 117.

19. Madison, James, 1831 *James Madison to Nicholas P. Trist, December, 1831.* Trist, from a prominent Virginia family, had been a private secretary to President Andrew Jackson.

20. U. S. Marshals Service, n.d. *History -- Oldest Federal Law Enforcement Agency.*

21. Supreme-Court.Laws.com, 2019 *John Jay.*

22. Supreme-Court.Laws.com, 2019 *John Jay* and West v. Barnes, 2 U.S. 401 (1791) at U.S. Supreme Court, 1791 *West v. Barnes, 2 U.S. 401 (1791).*

23. Kent, William *Memoirs and letters of James Kent, LL.D.,* 1898, pp. 313-14.

24. "Introduction," in DHFFC *The Documentary History of the First Federal Congress: Vol. 13. Debates in the House of Representatives, Second Session, April-August, 1790,* 1995.

CHAPTER 10: COUNTING WE THE PEOPLE

1. Ellis, Joseph J., n.d. *The Early Republic*.
2. DHFFC *The Documentary History of the First Federal Congress, Vol. 4, Legislative Histories: Amendments to the Constitution through Foreign Officers Bill [HR-1 16]*, 1986, vol. 4, pp. 664-675.
3. Wilson, James G. & Fiske, John *Appleton's Cyclopedia of American Biography*, 1888, pp. 95-96.
4. Madison, James, 1784 *Bill Authorizing an Amendment in the Articles of Confederation, [21 June] 1784*.
5. Wright, Carroll D. *The history and growth of the United States census*, 1900, p. 12.
6. "The Congressional Register, 29 August 1789," in DHFFC *The Documentary History of the First Federal Congress, Vol. 11. Debates in the House of Representatives, First Session, June-September, 1789*, 1992, vol. 11, pp. 1366-1375.
7. U. S. Marshals Service, n.d. *History -- Oldest Federal Law Enforcement Agency*.
8. U. S. Marshals Service, n.d. *History -- The First Generation of United States Marshals*.
9. Wright, Carroll D. *The history and growth of the United States census*, 1900, p. 13.
10. U.S. Marshals, n.d. *Recognition of the Need for Federal Marshals*.
11. United States Census, 2019 *Census Instructions*.
12. An unincorporated territory is defined by the U.S. Department of the Interior as "a United States insular area in which the United States Congress has determined that only selected parts of the United States Constitution apply." See www.doi.gov/oia/islands/politicatypes U.S. Department of the Interior Office of Insular Affairs, n.d. *Definitions of Insular Area Political Organizations*.
13. U.S. Marshals Service, 2020 *History -- Roll Call*
14. U.S. Marshals Service, n.d. *History - Broad Range of Authority*.
15. "Fisher Ames to John Lowell, Tuesday, 28 July 1789," in DHFFC *The Documentary History of the First Federal Congress, Vol. 16, Correspondence: First Session, June-August 1789*, 2004, vol. 16, pp. 1155-59.
16. "The Congressional Register, 29 August 1789," in DHFFC *The Documentary History of the First Federal Congress, Vol. 11. Debates in the House of Representatives, First Session, June-September, 1789*, 1992, vol. 11, pp. 1366-75.
17. "An Act to Establish the Judicial Courts of the United States," The Judiciary Act; September 24, 1789, U.S. Congress, 1789 *An Act to Establish the Judicial Courts of the United States*.
18. United States Census Bureau *Heads of Families at the First Census of the United States*, 1907, pp. 3, 4.

19. United States Census Bureau *Heads of Families at the First Census of the United States*, 1907, pp. 3, 4.

20. United States Census Bureau *Heads of Families at the First Census of the United States*, 1907, p. 4.

21. "Enumeration Act," in DHFFC *The Documentary History of the First Federal Congress, Vol. 4, Legislative Histories: Amendments to the Constitution through Foreign Officers Bill [HR-1 16]*, 1986, vol. 4, pp. 664-675.

22. United States Census Bureau, 2019 *1790 Overview*.

23. United States Census Bureau, 1993 *Population: 1790 to 1990*.

24. Ellis, Joseph J., n.d. *The Early Republic*.

25. United States Census Bureau *A century of population growth from the first census of the United States to the twelfth 1790-1900*, 1909, pp. 54-55.

26. United States Census Bureau *A century of population growth from the first census of the United States to the twelfth 1790-1900*, 1909, p. 40.

27. Haines, Michael R. & Steckel, Richard H. *A Population History of North America*, 2000, p. 24

28. Wood, Gordon S. *Empire of Liberty: A History of the Early Republic, 1789-1815*, 2009, pp. 123-24.

29. Wood, Gordon S., 2012 *Lecture: The Making of the U.S. Constitution*.

30. "Naturalization Act, March 26, 1790," in DHFFC *The Documentary History of the First Federal Congress: Vol. 6. Legislative Histories: Mitigation of Fines Bill [HR-38] through Resolution on Unclaimed Western Lands*, 1986.

31. Wood, Gordon S., 2010 *Lecture: Gordon S. Wood, "The Articles of Confederation and the Constitution"*. The reference to British demographer Jim Potter is at approximately the 8:50 time mark.

32. Allen, Thomas B. *Tories: Fighting for the King in America's First Civil War*, 2010, pp. 116, 333.

33. Journal of a Lady of Quality. The journal's author is Janet Schaw, who in 1774 had sailed from Scotland to the West Indies and North Carolina. Andrews, Evangeline W. & Andrews, Charles M. *Journal of a Lady of Quality*, 1921, p. 198.

34. Allen, Thomas B. *Tories: Fighting for the King in America's First Civil War*, 2010, pp. 329-33.

35. Allen, Thomas B. *Tories: Fighting for the King in America's First Civil War*, 2010, p. 328.

36. Gilbert, George A. *The Connecticut Loyalists*, 1899, pp. 273-91.

37. Gilbert, George A. *The Connecticut Loyalists*, 1899, p. 291.

38. Gilbert, George A. *The Connecticut Loyalists*, 1899, p. 282.

39. Digital Encyclopedia of George Washington, n.d. *John Ramage*.

40. Constant Tiffany's handwritten manuscript was donated by his descendants to the Library of Congress, which cited it in 2003 for its information about Nathan Hale, the executed American spy. See "Nathan Hale Revisited: A Tory's Account of the Arrest of the First American Spy," in Hutson, James, 2003 *Nathan Hale Revisited : A Tory's Account of the Arrest of the First American Spy.*

41. Gilbert, George A. *The Connecticut Loyalists*, 1899, p. 277.

42. Episcopal Church, The *The Book of Common Prayer*, 2007, p. 820.

43. Royster, Charles *A Revolutionary People At War: The Continental Army and American Character, 1775-1783*, 2011, p. 106.

44. Gilder Lehrman Institute of American History, n.d. *History Resources: Loyalists and the British Evacuation of Philadelphia, 1778.*

45. Duffy, Shannon E., 2016 *Loyalists.*

46. "Second Letter from Phocion, [April 1784]" Hamilton, Alexander, 1784 *Second Letter from Phocion, [April 1784]* Alexander Hamilton wrote some letters under the pseudonym "Phocion." A brilliant general and statesman in ancient Athens, Phocion was hailed for his integrity and given the appellation "the good."

47. Hamilton, Alexander, 1784 *From Alexander Hamilton to Gouverneur Morris, 21 February 1784.*

CHAPTER 11: AMERICA'S "OTHER PERSONS"

1. Williams, George W. *History of the negro race in America from 1619 to 1880. Negroes as slaves, as soldiers, and as citizens*, 1885, p. 336.

2. Collins, Elizabeth M., 2013 *Black Soldiers in the Revolutionary War.*

3. Johnson, Richard, 2007 *Lord Dunmore's Ethiopian Regiment.*

4. Cashin, Edward J., 2005 *Revolutionary War in Georgia.*

5. Barnwell, Joseph W. *The Evacuation of Charleston by the British in 1782*, 1910, p. 26.

6. Srodes, James *Franklin: the Essential Founding Father*, 2002, p. 108.

7. Srodes, James *Franklin: the Essential Founding Father*, 2002, p. 107. See also Franklin, Benjamin, 1751 *Observations Concerning the Increase of Mankind* and "Observations Concerning the Increasing of Mankind, Peopling of Countries, &c.," in Franklin, Benjamin *The Complete Works of Dr. Benjamin Franklin*, 1806, vol. 2, p. 386. In the earlier version Franklin assumes enslaved persons will pilfer, "almost every Slave being by Nature a thief [.]" In the later versions, this is altered to read "almost every slave being, by the nature of slavery, a thief [.]" The 1806

edition also omits two closing paragraphs. The first opposes, in rather crude terms, the settlement of Germans in Pennsylvania. The second argues in flowery terms for "excluding all Blacks and Tawneys" in favor of "the lovely White and Red[.]"

8. Madison, James, 1810 *Annual Message to Congress, 5 December 1810.*

9. Madison, James, 1789 *James Madison, Memorandum on an African Colony for Freed Slaves.*

10. Mason, George, 2015 *George Mason Memorial* See also Mason, George *The Papers of George Mason, 1725-1792,* 1970, vol. 1, p. 173, n 7.

11. Washington, George, 1786 *From George Washington to Robert Morris, 12 April 1786.*

12. Mount Vernon Ladies' Association, n.d. *Slavery.*

13. Benjamin Franklin Historical Society, 2014 *Later Years and Death* See also, endnote to the National Humanities Center, "Death of Benjamin Franklin, Philadelphia, 17 April 1790," National Humanities Center, n.d. *On the Death of Benjamin Franklin.*

14. "Introduction," in DHFFC *The Documentary History of the First Federal Congress, Vol. 8, Petition Histories and Non-Legislative Official Documents,* 1998. See also "Nathanael Greene (1742–1786)," New Georgia Encyclopedia, Saba, Natalie D., 2004 *Nathanael Greene (1742-1786).*

15. "Lloyd's Notes, 12 February 1790," in DHFFC *The Documentary History of the First Federal Congress, Vol. 12. Debates in the House of Representatives, Second Session, January-March 1790,* 1995, vol. 12, pp. 295-301.

16. Lloyd's Notes adds a question mark after attributing the words to Thomas Tudor Tucker of South Carolina.

17. "Lloyd's Notes, 12 February 1790," in DHFFC, vol. 12 (95–301).

18. "Jonathan Trumbull, Jr. to Jeremiah Wadsworth, Sunday, 21 March 1790," in DHFFC *The Documentary History of The First Federal Congress, Vol. 19. Correspondence: Second Session, 15 March-June 1790,* 2012, vol. 19, pp. 958-959.

19. Toogood, Coxey, 2014 *U.S. Congress (1790-1800).*

20. Madison, James, 1790 *Slave Trade Petitions, [23 March] 1790.*

21. Stuart, David, 1790 *To George Washington from David Stuart, 15 March 1790.*

22. "From George Washington to David Stuart, 28 March 1790," Founders Online, National Archives, Washington, DC, https://founders.archives.gov/documents/Washington/05-05-02-0183. Accessed November 8, 2017.

23. "William Smith (S.C.) to Tench Cox, Wednesday, 14 April, 1790," in DHFFC *The Documentary History of The First Federal Congress, Vol. 19. Correspondence: Second Session, 15 March-June 1790*, 2012, vol. 19, pp. 598-99.

24. "William Smith (S.C.) to Edward Rutledge, Monday, 10 August 1789," in DHFFC *The Documentary History of the First Federal Congress, Vol. 16, Correspondence: First Session, June-August 1789*, 2004, vol. 16, pp. 1281-1285.

25. Excerpt from letter from William Smith to Edward Rutledge, 5 July 1789 in DHFFC *The Documentary History of the First Federal Congress, Vol. 16, Correspondence: First Session, June-August 1789*, 2004. Accessed February 14, 2018.

26. "James Madison to Benjamin Rush, Saturday, 20 March, 1790," in DHFFC *The Documentary History of The First Federal Congress, Vol. 19. Correspondence: Second Session, 15 March-June 1790*, 2012, vol. 19, pp. 933-934.

27. Rush, Benjamin Observations Intended to Favour a Supposition That the Black Color (As It Is Called) of the Negroes Is Derived from the Leprosy, *Transactions of the American Philosophical Society*, 1799, vol. IV, pp. 289-297.

28. Rush, Benjamin *An address to the inhabitants of the British settlements, on the slavery of the Negroes in America*, 1773, p. 2

29. DHFFC *The Documentary History of The First Federal Congress, Vol. 19. Correspondence: Second Session, 15 March-June 1790*, 2012, vol. 19, pp. 1157-1158.

30. "Voyage of the Sally," Brown University Brown Digital Repository, n.d. *Voyage of the Sally*.

31. Maier, Pauline *Ratification: The People Debate the Constitution, 1787-1788*, 2011, p. 458.

32. Wells, Colins *Poetry Wars: Verse and Politics in the American Revolution and Early Republic*, 2017, p. 118 The poem was attributed to the "Hartford Wits," who included presidential aide David Humphreys and poet Joel Barlow.

33. Maier, Pauline *Ratification: The People Debate the Constitution, 1787-1788*, 2011, p. 459.

34. Payne, Samanatha, 2015 *"Rogue Island": The last state to ratify the Constitution.*

35. Brown University Steering Committee on Slavery and Justice *Slavery and Justice: Report of the Brown University Steering Committee on Slavery and Justice*, 2006. Brown is one of more than a dozen universities that researched its ties to the slave trade. They include Harvard, Princeton, and Georgetown University,

founded in 1789 as the oldest Catholic and Jesuit institution of higher learning in the United States. See also "Digging into a Fraught History," by Jennifer Schuessler, New York Times, November 7, 2017, C1, C5, Schuessler, Jennifer *Princeton Digs Deep Into Its Fraught Racial History*, 2017.

36. Rappleye, Charles *Sons of Providence: The Brown Brothers, the Slave Trade, and the American Revolution*, 2006, p. 12.
37. Rappleye, Charles *Sons of Providence: The Brown Brothers, the Slave Trade, and the American Revolution*, 2006, p. 12.
38. Bartlett, John R. *Records of the Colony of Rhode Island and Providence Plantations, in New England*, 1861, p. 6. 416.
39. Brown University. *Slavery and Justice: Report of the Brown University Steering Committee on Slavery and Justice*, 2006, pp. 3, 12, 16.
40. Brown University. *Slavery and Justice: Report of the Brown University Steering Committee on Slavery and Justice*, 2006, p. 6.
41. Brown University. *Slavery and Justice: Report of the Brown University Steering Committee on Slavery and Justice*, 2006, p. 16
42. Brown University. *Slavery and Justice: Report of the Brown University Steering Committee on Slavery and Justice*, 2006, p. 17
43. Brown University Library, n.d. *Aftermath of the Voyage*. In 1804, the College of Rhode Island changed its name to Brown University in recognition of a gift from Nicholas's son, Nicholas Jr.
44. Awesome Stories, n.d. *The Famous Speech*. See also Wilberforce, William, 2007 *William Wilberforce's 1789 Abolition Speech* and an alteranate source at Wilberforce, William, n.d. *William Wilberforce's 1789 Abolition Speech*. There is no official text of the speech, and the quotation does not appear in all accounts of the speech. See https://brycchancarey.com/Carey_AOJ_2003.pdf for further discussion.
45. Klein, Martin A. *The A to Z of Slavery and Abolition*, 2014, p. 16.
46. Klein, Martin A. *The A to Z of Slavery and Abolition*, 2014, p. 9
47. Williams, William H. *Slavery and Freedom in Delaware, 1639-1865*, 2003, p. 171.
48. Johnson, Tim *Vermont's 1777 Slavery Ban Had a Complicated Reality*, 2014
49. Records of the Pennsylvania Department of State, 1789 *An Act for the Gradual Abolition of Slavery*.
50. Johnson, Matthew, n.d. *Timeline of Events Relating to the End of Slavery*.
51. Connecticut History, n.d. *Slavery and Abolition*.

52. Aaron, Lawrence *Confronting New Jersey's Slave Past*, 2006.

53. New-York Historical Society, n.d. *When Did Slavery End in New York State*.

CHAPTER 12: A TUB FULL OF RIGHTS

1. Madison, James, 1789 *Notes for Speech in Congress (June 8, 1789)*.

2. Double meaning of amendment: see Veit, Helen E. et al. *Creating the Bill of Rights: The Documentary Record from the First Federal Congress*, 1991, p. ix.

3. Bowling, Kenneth R. *'A Tub to the Whale': The Founding Fathers and Adoption of the Federal Bill of Rights*, 1988, p. 223.

4. Philadelphia Gazette *Under the heading NEW-YORK, July 8*, 1789

5. Rossum, Ralph A. *Federalism, the Supreme Court, and the Seventeenth Amendment: The Irony of Constitutional Democracy*, 2001, p. 88.

6. Wood, Gordon S. *Empire of Liberty: A History of the Early Republic, 1789-1815*, 2009, p. 69.

7. "Amendments Proposed by the States, June 8, 1789," in Veit, Helen E. et al. *Creating the Bill of Rights: The Documentary Record from the First Federal Congress*, 1991, pp. 14-28.

8. Bailyn, Bernard *To Begin the World Anew: The Genius and Ambiguities of the American Founders*, 2007, p. 48.

9. Letter, "'Pacificus' [Noah Webster] to Rep. James Madison, August 14, 1789," Papers of Madison 12: 334–35, as published in Bickford, Charlene B. & Bowling, Kenneth R. *Birth of the Nation: The First Federal Congress 1789-1791*, 1989, p. 51. See also Webster, Noah, 1789 *Pacificus [Noah Webster] to James Madison (August 14, 1789)*.

10. McMaster, John B. & Stone, Frederick D. *Pennsylvania and the Federal Constitution, 1787-1788*, 1888, pp. 457-58.

11. Coffman, Steve *Words of the Founder Fathers*, 2012, p. 302.

12. Bickford, Charlene B. & Bowling, Kenneth R. *Birth of the Nation: The First Federal Congress 1789-1791*, 1989, p. 51.

13. State of New Hampshire, 1788 *Ratification of the Constitution by the State of New Hampshire; June 21, 1788*.

14. "The Pennsylvania Packet 18 December 1790," in DHFFC *The Documentary History of the First Federal Congress, Vol. 14, Debates in the House of Representatives: Third Session, December 1790-March 1791*, 1996, vol. 14, pp. 54-66.

15. "Debates in the House of Representatives," in DHFFC *The Documentary History of the First Federal Congress, Vol. 11. Debates in the House of Representatives, First Session, June-September, 1789*, 1992, vol. 11, p. 821.

16. Letter, Louis Guillaume Otto to Comte de Montmorin, Tuesday, March 30, 1790 in DHFFC *The Documentary History of The First Federal Congress, Vol. 19. Correspondence: Second Session, 15 March-June 1790*, 2012, vol. 19, pp. 1045-1047.

17. Bordewich, Fergus M. *The First Congress: How James Madison, George Washington, and a Group of Extraordinary Men Invented the Government*, 2016, pp. 120-21.

18. Cogan, Neil E. *The Complete Bill of Rights: The Drafts, Debates, Sources, and Origins*, 2015, p. 1086.

19. Bowling, Kenneth R. *'A Tub to the Whale': The Founding Fathers and Adoption of the Federal Bill of Rights*, 1988, p. 244.

20. National Archives, 2019 *Bill of Rights*.

21. Bowling, Kenneth R. & Veit, Helen E. *The Diary of William Maclay and Other Notes on Senate Debates*, 1988, p. 133.

CHAPTER 13: "HE SHALL HAVE POWER"

1. Washington Papers, 2013 *Thanksgiving Proclamation*.

2. Washington Papers, 2013 *Thanksgiving Proclamation*.

3. Washington Papers, 2013 *Thanksgiving Proclamation*.

4. The book was printed by Francis Childs and John Swaine, Printers to the United States. The presidential copy annotated by George Washington was purchased by the Mount Vernon Ladies' Association at a Christie's auction in 2012 for $8.7 million, a record for an American book or historical document.

5. Amar, Akhil R. *Our Forgotten Constitution: A Bicentennial Comment*, 1987, pp. 281-98.

6. Maclay, Edgar S. *Journal of William Maclay*, 1890, p. 239.

7. Fitzgerald, Oscar P. *In Search of Joseph Nourse 1754-1841: America's First Civil Servant*, 1994.

8. Hunt, Gaillard *Calendar of Applications and Recommendations for Office during the Presidency of George Washington*, 1901, p. 74. At the time, the Department of State handled many domestic functions, including job requests sent to the president. Many were from jobholders hoping to be retained or men citing their "necessitous circumstances." The smallest number of applications came from candidates stressing their "political opinions."

9. Washington, George, 1789 *From George Washington to James Madison, 5 May 1789*.

10. Nutting, P. B. *"Tobias Lear, S.P.U.S.": First Secretary to the President*, Fall 1994, pp. 713-724.

11. Biographical Gazette in DHFFC *The Documentary History of the First Federal Congress: Vol. 2. Senate Executive Journal and Related Documents*, 1974, vol. 2, p. 491.

12. Decatur, Stephen, J. *Private Affairs of George Washington: From the Records and Accounts of Tobias Lear*, 1933, pp. 58-59.

13. Stegeman, John F. & Stegeman, Janet A. *Caty: a Biography of Catharine Littlefield*, 1977, p. 137.

14. Richardson, James D. *A Compilation of the Messages and Papers of the Presidents, 1789-1897, Volume 1*, 1897, vol. 1, pp. 50-51.

15. Sullivan, Buddy, 2002 *Lachlan McIntosh (1727-1806)*.

16. Massey, Gregory D., 2016 *Izard, Ralph*.

17. Bowling, Kenneth R. & Veit, Helen E. *The Diary of William Maclay and Other Notes on Senate Debates*, 1988, pp. 128-31.

18. Robbins, Alexander H. *Central Law Journal*, 1921, vol 93, p. 76.

19. Bowling, Kenneth R. & Veit, Helen E. *The Diary of William Maclay and Other Notes on Senate Debates*, 1988, p. 132.

20. Sparks, Jarad *The Writings of George Washington Vol 10*, 1847, vol. 10, p. 485. Also, see "Sentiments Expressed by the President to the Committee, Appointed to Confer with Him . . . Respecting Treaties and Nominations," United States Senate Committee, 1789 *Conference with a Committee of the United States Senate, 8 August 1789.*

21. Washington, George, 1790 *Letter to Catharine Macaulay Graham*.

22. Bickford, Charlene B. & Bowling, Kenneth R. *Birth of the Nation: The First Federal Congress 1789-1791*, 1989, p. 23. The remark appears in a letter written by Representative Thomas Tudor Tucker of South Carolina on May 13, 1789, to St. George Tucker, in Tucker-Coleman Papers, Swern Library, College of William and Mary.

23. The underlying animosity between Hamilton and Burke simmered for years, and Burke was a second for Aaron Burr in a 1799 duel with Alexander Hamilton's brother-in-law, John B. Church. Both antagonists survived. Church's pistols were used in the 1804 duel in which Burr killed Hamilton. "Introduction," in DHFFC *The Documentary History of the First Federal Congress, Vol. 8, Petition Histories and Non-Legislative Official Documents*, 1998. See also Napier, John L., 2016 *Burke, Aedanus*, and also Hamilton, Alexander & Burke, Aedanus, 1790

Search Results for Hamilton-Burke Correspondence, and also Fisher, David R., 1986 *CHURCH, John Barker (1748-1818), of Down Place, Berks.*

24. Elliot, Jonathan *The debates in the several state conventions on the adoption of the federal Constitution*, 1836, p. 4. 364.

25. Adams, John, 1789 *From John Adams to Benjamin Rush, June 9, 1789.*

CHAPTER 14: STRICKEN WASHINGTON, FEARFUL NATION

1. Jefferson, Thomas, 1787 *From Thomas Jefferson to James Madison, December 20, 1787.*

2. Martha Parke Custis and John Parke Custis, biographical information from Digital Encyclopedia of George Washington, n.d. *Martha Parke Custis* and Thompson, Mary V., n.d. *John Parke Custis.*

3. Marx, M.D., Rudolph *A Medical Profile of George Washington*, 1955.

4. Chernow, Ron *Alexander Hamilton*, 2004, p. 203.

5. Bell Jr., Whitfield J. *Patriot-Improvers: Biographical Sketches of Members of the American Philosophical Society Vol 1*, 1997, p. 375.

6. Guba, James E. & Chase, Philander D. *Anthrax and the President, 1789*, 2002.

7. Custis, George W.P. *Recollections and private memoirs of Washington*, 1861, p. footnote 398.

8. Custis, George W.P. *Recollections and private memoirs of Washington*, 1861, p. 398,

9. Madison, James, 1789 *From James Madison to Edmund Randolph, 24 June 1789.*

10. Jefferson, Thomas, 1790 *From Thomas Jefferson to William Short, 27 May 1790.*

11. Kaminski, John P. *Abigail Adams, An American Heroine*, 2007, p. 109.

12. *Founders Online, n.d. William Jackson to Clement Biddle, 2 May 1790 Editorial Note.*

13. Walsh, Jennifer, 2010 *Dr. James Fever Powder, circa 1746* Jennifer Welsh, Scientist, October 1, 2010.

14. "Peripneumony" was inflammation of the lungs, or pneumonia. Madison, James, 1790 *From James Madison to Edmund Randolph, 19 May 1790.*

15. Ballagh, James C. *The Letters of Richard Henry Lee*, 1912, pp. Vol II, 514-515

16. Letter, "William Maclay to Benjamin Rush, May 12, 1790," (accessed February 12, 2017). Note from manuscript preparer: The letter from Maclay is cited in footnote 4 of the Editoral Note discussed in the remainder of this citation is described as "Maclay to Benjamin Rush 7 May 1790," and reported to be in the Library of Congress, Benjamin Rush Papers. Owing to restrictions on access

to the Library of Congress due to the pandemic, I have been unable to confirm this citation. See also discussion in the Editorial Note re William Jackson
to Clement Biddle 2 May 1790 at https://founders.archives.gov/documents/
Washington/05-05-02-0253: Founders Online, n.d. *William Jackson to Clement
Biddle, 2 May 1790 Editorial Note.*

17. Richard Bland Lee to David Stuart, Clymer, and Sedgwick quoted in Founders
    Online, n.d. *William Jackson to Clement Biddle, 2 May 1790 Editorial Note.*
18. Letter, "John Page to St. George Tucker," in DHFFC *The Documentary History
    of The First Federal Congress, Vol. 19. Correspondence: Second Session, 15 March-
    June 1790,* 2012, vol. 19, pp. 1515-1516.
19. Letter, "Michael Jenifer Stone to Walter Stone, Saturday 22 May," in DHFFC
    *The Documentary History of The First Federal Congress, Vol. 19. Correspondence:
    Second Session, 15 March-June 1790,* 2012, vol. 19, pp. 1563-1564.
20. Letter, "Robert Morris to Mary Morris, April 28, 1790," in DHFFC *The
    Documentary History of The First Federal Congress, Vol. 19. Correspondence:
    Second Session, 15 March-June 1790,* 2012, vol. 19, p. 1357.
21. Buchan, William *Domestic Medicine, or the Family Physician,* 1769, title page.
22. Dunn, Peter M. *Dr William Buchan (1729-1805) and His Domestic Medicine,*
    2000, pp. 71-73.
23. Buchan, William *Domestic Medicine, or the Family Physician,* 1769, p. 576.
24. DHFFC *The Documentary History of the First Federal Congress, Vol. 18.
    Correspondence: Second Session, October 1789-14 March 1790,* 2012, vol. 18, pp.
    461-462.
25. DHFFC *The Documentary History of the First Federal Congress, Vol. 18.
    Correspondence: Second Session, October 1789-14 March 1790,* 2012, vol. 18, p.
    408.
26. Christman, Margaret C.S. *The First Federal Congress 1789-1781,* 1989, p. 118.
27. Price, Annie, 2020 *Asafoetida: The Ancient Roman Spice with Health Benefits.*
28. Pitman, John *Diary in the Manuscript Collection of the Rhode Island Historical
    Society,* 1785. John Pitman, Diary in the Manuscripts of the Rhode Island
    Historical Society, December 15, 1785.
29. Wood, Gordon S. *The Bleeding Founders.* Book review of Revolutionary
    Medicine: The Founding Fathers and Mothers in Sickness and in Health by
    Jeanne E. Abrams, 2013, NYU Press. Page 16 states GW, A, Adams, B Franklin
    supported bleeding, p. 26 and etc. re: Rush on bleeding. (re: books.google.com).
30. Percy M. Ashburn's A History of the Medical Department of the United States
    Army (Boston: Houghton Mifflin, 1929) is quoted in Rutkow, Ira *Seeking the*

Cure: A History of Medicine in America, 2010, p. 44. See also quotation from Ashburn in North, Robert L. *Benjamin Rush, MD: assassin or beloved healer?*, 2000, pp. 45-49.

31. Myrsiades, Linda S. *Law and Medicine in Revolutionary America: Dissecting the Rush v. Cobbett Trial, 1799*, 2012, p. 94. See also quotation from Cobbett in North, Robert L. *Benjamin Rush, MD: assassin or beloved healer?*, 2000, pp. 45-49.

CHAPTER 15: WASHINGTON GETS A BASTILLE KEY

1. Bahr, William J. *George Washington's Liberty Key*, 2016, pp. 85-88.
2. Bahr, William J. *George Washington's Liberty Key*, 2016, p. 87.
3. Digital Encyclopedia of George Washington, n.d. *Bastille Key*.
4. Jefferson, Thomas, 1789 *Thomas Jefferson to George Washington, May 10, 1789*.
5. Jefferson, Thomas, 1789 *Thomas Jefferson to George Washington, May 10, 1789*.
6. Washington, George, 1789 *From George Washington to Lafayette, 14 October 1789*.
7. Library of Congress, n.d. *Thomas Jefferson: A Revolutionary World*.
8. Thomas Jefferson Encyclopedia *Paris Residences*, n.d.
9. Washington, George, 1792 *Enclosure: George Washington to Gouverneur Morris, 28 January 1792*.
10. Morris, Gouverneur, 1792 *To George Washington from Gouverneur Morris, 6 April 1792*. Mention of his plotting with the royal family is in a footnote credited to his Diary, vol. 2, 465-66, 472-80 (all accessed December 21, 2017 and February 9, 2021.) Morris, Gouverneur *The Diary and Letters of Gouverneur Morris*, 1888.
11. Potter, Lee A. & Eder, Elizabeth K., 2009 *George Washington's Printed Draft of the Constitution and Mike Wilkins' "Preamble"*. Library of Congress, 2021 Pre.1.2 Preamble: Historical Background.
12. Teaching American History, n.d. *Scene of Gouverneur Morris' Accident*.
13. Wood, Gordon S. *Empire of Liberty: A History of the Early Republic, 1789-1815*, 2009, p. 175.
14. American History from Revolution to Reconstruction and Beyond, n.d. *A Biography of Thomas Paine (1737-1809)*. Hogeland, William, 2011 *Thomas Paine's Revolutionary Reckoning*.

15. The Brissotins, led by Jacques-Pierre Brissot de Warville, supported a constitutional monarchy. Nelson, Craig *Thomas Paine: Enlightenment, Revolution, and the Birth of Modern Nations*, 2008, p. 275.

16. "Thomas Paine, Brief Biography," UShistory.org, n.d. *Thomas Paine Brief Biography*.

17. Paine, Thomas, 1794 *Age of Reason Part 1*.

18. Lafayette College, n.d. *The Prisoner of Olmütz*. Exhibit at Lafayette Colllege, Easton, PA, https://sites.lafayette.edu/olmutz. Accessed December 20, 2017.

19. McPhee, Peter *The French Revolution 1788-1799*, 2002, p. 2.

CHAPTER 16: SEEING AMERICA'S FARMS AND FACTORIES

1. Washington, George, 1789 *October 1789*.

2. Washington, George, 1789 *Diary Entry 17 October 1789*.

3. Nutting, P. B. *"Tobias Lear, S.P.U.S.": First Secretary to the President*, Fall 1994, pp. 713-24.

4. Washington's route was mostly on the Boston Post Road, a postal system of three roads: Lower Post Road, along the shore and reaching Providence, Rhode Island (now much of U.S. 1); the Upper Post Road (roughly now U.S. 5 and U.S. 20), from New Haven, Connecticut, to Boston via Springfield, Massachusetts; and the Middle Post Road, running northeastward to Boston via Pomfret, Connecticut.

5. Breen, T. H. *George Washington's Journey: The President Forges a New Nation*, 2015, pp. 14-15

6. Breen, T. H. *George Washington's Journey: The President Forges a New Nation*, 2015, pp. 14-15

7. Chernow, Ron *Washington: A Life*, 2010, p. 608.

8. Howard, James L. *The Origin and Fortunes of Troop B. 1788, Governor's Independent Troop of Horse Guards, 1911, Troup Be Cavalry, Connecticut National Guard 1917*, 1921, p. 31

9. Lang, Joel, n.d. *Jeremiah Wadsworth, "foremost in every enterprise"* Although the source describes "machinery to spin broadcloth" it is in fact a woven material made from wool yarn.

10. Washington, George, 1789 *George Washington to Beverley Randolph, November 22, 1789*. See also Washington, George, 1789 *October 1789 (note 3 to Oct 20)*.

11. MacDonald, Kim, 2003 *Silk in Connecticut* Kim MacDonald, "Silk in Connecticut," in The Northampton Silk Project, proceedings, "Silk Unraveled,"

symposium, March 28–30, 2003, Smith College, Northampton, MA, www.smith.edu/hsc/silk/circa1840.html (accessed February 22, 2017). Note from manuscript preparer: this source no longer accessible as of May 14 2020 May 14. I found a copy of the page at https://web.archive.org/web/20180422184953/https://www.smith.edu/hsc/silk/papers/macdonald.html.

12. Lossing, Benson L.e. *The Diary of George Washington, from 1789 to 1791*, 1860, p. 29.
13. Chernow, Ron *Washington: A Life*, 2010, p. 611.
14. Fauci, Anthony S. & Morens, David M. *The Perpetual Challenge of Infectious Diseases*, 2012, pp. 454-61.
15. Black, Euphemia V. *History of Newburyport*, 1854, pp. 132-33. To hear the ode set to music, go to www.mountvernon.org/video/watch/he-comes-the-hero-comes.
16. White, George S. *Memoir of Samuel Slater. the Father of American Manufacures*, 1836, p. 38.
17. Lovett, Robert W. *The Beverly Cotton Manufactory: Or Some New Light on an Early Cotton Mill*, 1952, pp. 218-42.
18. Carding, long done by hand, separated entangled cotton fibers and assembled them into loose strands to make them easier to spin.
19. Washington, George, 1789 *Diary entry: 30 October 1789.*
20. Connors, Anothy J. *Ingenious Machinists: Two Inventive Lives from the American Industrial Revolution*, 2014, p. 18.
21. Lovett, Robert W. *The Beverly Cotton Manufactory: Or Some New Light on an Early Cotton Mill*, 1952, pp. 218-42.
22. Lovett, Robert W. *The Beverly Cotton Manufactory: Or Some New Light on an Early Cotton Mill*, 1952, pp. 218-42.
23. White, George S. *Memoir of Samuel Slater. the Father of American Manufacures*, 1836, p. 95.
24. Letter, "George Cabot to Benjamin Goodhue, Tuesday, 6 April 1790," in DHFFC *The Documentary History of The First Federal Congress, Vol. 19. Correspondence: Second Session, 15 March-June 1790*, 2012, vol. 19, pp. 366-372.
25. "Report of the Secretary of the Treasury, 12 April 1792," in DHFFC *The Documentary History of the First Federal Congress: Vol. 7, Petition Histories: Revolutionary War-related Claims*, 1997, vol. 7, pp. 55-56.
26. Cabot, George, 1791 *To Alexander Hamilton from George Cabot, 6 September 1791.*
27. Bowling, Kenneth R. *The Creation of Washington, D.C.: The Idea and Location of the American Capital*, 1991, p. ix.

28. "Seat of Government Location," DHFFC *The Documentary History of the First Federal Congress, Vol. 8, Petition Histories and Non-Legislative Official Documents*, 1998, vol. 8, pp. 448-449.

29. Philadelphia Independent Gazetteer *Letter from New York*, 1789 reprinted at Baltimore; Fredericksburg, Virginia; and Edenton, North Carolina. DHFFC *The Documentary History of the First Federal Congress, Vol. 17, Correspondence: First Session, September-November 1789*, 2004, vol 17, p. 1484.

30. Lawler, Jr., Edward *The President's House in Philadelphia*, 2010

31. U.S. House of Representatives, n.d. *The First Bank of the United States.*

32. Bowling, Kenneth R. *The Creation of Washington, D.C.: The Idea and Location of the American Capital*, 1991, pp. 218-19.

33. Breen, T. H. *George Washington's Journey: The President Forges a New Nation*, 2015, pp. 208-09.

34. Pennsylvania Magazine of History and Biography *Pennsylvania Weather Records, 1644-1835*, 1891. Papers of George Washington *George Washington Day By Day*, 2015.

35. Papers of George Washington *George Washington Day By Day*, 2015.

36. Columbia Historical Society *The Writings of George Washington Relating to the National Capital*, 1914, pp. 1-233.

37. Bedini, Silvio *The Life of Benjamin Banneker: The First African-American Man of Science*, 1999, pp. 24-25.

38. Lear, Tobias *Observations on the River Potomack, the Country Adjacent, and the City of Washington*, 1905, pp. 22, 127, 132

39. Papers of George Washington *George Washington Day By Day*, 2015

40. Breen, T. H. *George Washington's Journey: The President Forges a New Nation*, 2015, p. 251.

41. Jackson, Donald & Twohig, Dorothy *The Diaries of George Washington. Vol. 5. January-February 1789*, 1979, p. 6. 158.

42. Henderson, Archibald *Washington's Southern Tour, 1791*, 1923, p. 62.

43. Ford, Paul L. *The True George Washington*, 1896, p. 182.

44. Breen, T. H. *George Washington's Journey: The President Forges a New Nation*, 2015, p. 150

45. Henderson, Archibald *Washington's Southern Tour, 1791*, 1923, p. 254.

46. Lewis, Catherine H. *Horry County, South Carolina, 1730-1993*, 1988, p. 101.

47. See also Henderson, Archibald *Washington's Southern Tour, 1791*, 1923, pp. 15, 181, 195, 217, 230, 253.

48. Mount Vernon Ladies' Association, n.d. *Washington's Southern Tour: An Interview with Walter Bingham.*

49. Lear, Tobias, 1791 *To George Washington from Tobias Lear, 5 April 1791.*

50. Lear, Tobias, 1791 *From George Washington to Tobias Lear, 21 April 1791.*

51. Lear, Tobias, 1791 *From George Washington to Tobias Lear, 21 April 1791.*

52. Historic Germantown, 2013 *Oney Judge Staines: Washington's Runaway Slave.*

53. Mount Vernon Ladies' Association, n.d. *George Washington and Slavery: Key Events.* See also Runaway Advertisement for Oney Judge in The Pennsylvania Gazette, May 24, 1796, Encyclopedia Virginia, 2017 *Primary Resource Advertisement for the Capture of Oney Judge, Philadelphia Gazette (May 24, 1796)*

54. Comment by George Washington, recorded by David Humphreys or Humphries, in a manuscript biography of Washington, now in the Rosenbach Library in Philadelphia. Humphreys, David *Manuscript Biography of George Washington,* 1788 (This is not the same work as Humphrey's published *Life of General Washington* (Humphreys, David *Life of General Washington,* 2006). That 1991 book (reprinted 2006) was edited by Rosemarie Zagarri, who assembled manuscripts from three separate archives to "reconstruct" a text.) See also Hirschfeld, Fritz *George Washington and Slavery: A Documentary Portrayal,* 1997, pp. 213, note 5. See also the article derived from a talk by Mary V. Thompson (Thompson, Mary V., 1999 *"The Only Unavoidable Subject of Regret"*) and the book of the same name by the same author (Thompson, Mary V. *The Only Unavoidable Subject of Regret,* 2019).

CHAPTER 17: MANY PIRATES—AND NO NAVY

1. Vanhorn, Kellie M. *Eighteenth-Century Colonial American Merchant Ship Construction; MA Thesis,* 2004, pp. 2, 171-172.

2. Toll, Ian W. *Six Frigates: The Epic History of the Founding of the U.S. Navy,* 2006, p. 20.

3. Morgan, William J. *Naval Documents of the American Revolution,* 1972, p. vi.

4. Leiner, Frederick C. *Yes, Privateers Mattered,* 2014.

5. Toll, Ian W. *Six Frigates: The Epic History of the Founding of the U.S. Navy,* 2006, p. 16. See also Naval History and Heritage Command *Frigates, Brigs, Sloops, Schooners, and the Early Continental Navy's Struggle for Success,* 2014.

6. Historical Society of Pennsylvania, 2009 *The 'Barbary Wars' and Their Philadelphia Connections.* Many sources list O'Bryen under the spelling O'Brien. Richard O'Bryen himself signed his letters with multiple variations of the spell-

ing of his last name. Founders Online indexes his letters under O'Bryen, but he himself also used Obryen, O Bryen, O Brien and Obrien. Founders Online, n.d. *Search Results for O'Byren.*

7. Historical Society of Pennsylvania, 2009 *The 'Barbary Wars' and Their Philadelphia Connections.*

8. Historical Society of Pennsylvania, 2009 *The 'Barbary Wars' and Their Philadelphia Connections.*

9. Foss, John *A Journal of the Captivity and Sufferings of John Foss*, 1798, pp. 24-25.

10. "Report of Thomas Jefferson to the President, 28 December, 1790," in DHFFC *The Documentary History of the First Federal Congress: Vol. 2. Senate Executive Journal and Related Documents*, 1974, vol. 2, pp. 425-435,

11. "Report of Thomas Jefferson to the President, 28 December, 1790," in DHFFC *The Documentary History of the First Federal Congress: Vol. 2. Senate Executive Journal and Related Documents*, 1974, vol. 2, pp. 425-435.

12. Short, William, *To Thomas Jefferson from William Short, 7 July 1790*, 1790. Accessed December 21, 2017.

13. U.S. Congress *American State Papers : Documents, Legislative and Executive, of the Congress of the United States*, 1832, p. 103.

14. Jefferson, Thomas, 1790 *IV. Report on American Captives in Algiers, 28 December 1790.*

15. Jefferson, Thomas, 1790 *IV. Report on American Captives in Algiers, 28 December 1790*

16. Owens, Mackubin, n.d. *Navy Clause.*

17. Madison, James, 1787 *Madison Debates, June 29, 1787.*

18. Jefferson, Thomas, 1786 *From Thomas Jefferson to James Monroe, 11 August 1786*

19. Crawford, Michael J. & Hughes, Christine F. *The Reestablishment of the Navy, 1787-1801: Historical Overview and Select Bibliography*, 1995, p. 2.

20. Washington, George, 1793 *From George Washington to the United States Senate and House of Representatives, 3 December 1793.*

21. Virginia Places, n.d. *Norfolk Naval Shipyard.*

22. Crawford, Michael J. & Hughes, Christine F. *The Reestablishment of the Navy, 1787-1801: Historical Overview and Select Bibliography*, 1995, pp. 6-7.

23. Crawford, Michael J. & Hughes, Christine F. *The Reestablishment of the Navy, 1787-1801: Historical Overview and Select Bibliography*, 1995, p. 9.

24. Uva, Katie *Quasi War*, n.d.

25. Crawford, Michael J. & Hughes, Christine F. *The Reestablishment of the Navy, 1787-1801: Historical Overview and Select Bibliography*, 1995, p. 9.

26. U.S. Department of State Archive, n.d. *The XYZ Affair and the Quasi-War with France, 1798-1800*.

CHAPTER 18: THE SECOND SESSION: HOPE AND ANGST

1. Diary entry: 8 January 1790, Jackson, Donald & Twohig, Dorothy *The Diaries of George Washington, vol. 6, 1 January 1790–13 December 1799*, 1979.

2. Lossing, Benson J. *George Washington's Mount Vernon*, 1977, pp. 246-47. This 1977 edition is a facsimile of the original 1870 edition.

3. Griswold, Rufus W. *The Republican Court: Or, American Society in the Days of Washington*, 1854, p. 217.

4. *Journal of the Convention Held at Fayetteville November 1789*, North Carolina Archives, Raleigh. The Journal's many crossed-out sentences and paragraphs attest to the intensity of the debate over ratification.

5. Washington, George, 1790 *From George Washington to the United States Senate and House of Representatives, 8 January 1790*.

6. According to https://history.house.gov/Institution/SOTU/State-of-the-Union/ U.S. House of Representatives, n.d. *State of the Union Address*, the address was formally known as the Annual Message from 1790 to 1946. It began to be informally called the "state of the Union" message/address from 1942 to 1946. Since 1947 it has officially been known as the State of the Union Address.

7. *Washington, George, 1783 George Washington, Circular to the States [excerpt]*.

8. "Lloyd's Notes, 16 April 1790," in DHFFC *The Documentary History of the First Federal Congress: Vol. 13. Debates in the House of Representatives, Second Session, April-August, 1790*, 1995, vol. 13, pp. 1038-1053.

9. Washington, George, 1783 *George Washington, June 8, 1783, Circular to States on Farewell to the Army*. See also Washington, George, 1783 *From George Washington to The States, 8 June 1783*.

10. Irving, Washington *The Life and Times of Washington*, 1876, p. 271.

11. Irving, Washington *The Life and Times of Washington*, 1876, p. 271

12. "Louis Guillaume Otto to Comte de Montmorin, 12 January 1790" in DHFFC *The Documentary History of the First Federal Congress, Vol. 8, Petition Histories and Non-Legislative Official Documents*, 1998.

13. "Lloyd's Notes, 16 April 1790," in DHFFC *The Documentary History of the First Federal Congress: Vol. 13. Debates in the House of Representatives, Second Session, April-August, 1790*, 1995, vol. 13, pp. 1038-53.

14. Report of the Secretary of the Treasury on the Public Credit, January 14, 1790 in DHFFC *The Documentary History of the First Federal Congress: Vol. 5. Legislative Histories: Funding Act [HR-63] through Militia Bill [HR112]*, 1986, vol. 5, pp. 743-823.

15. Report of the Secretary of the Treasury on the Public Credit, January 14, 1790 in DHFFC *The Documentary History of the First Federal Congress: Vol. 5. Legislative Histories: Funding Act [HR-63] through Militia Bill [HR112]*, 1986, vol. 5, pp. 743-823.

16. Bickford, Charlene B. & Bowling, Kenneth R. *Birth of the Nation: The First Federal Congress 1789-1791*, 1989, pp. 64-65.

17. Wood, Gordon S. *Empire of Liberty: A History of the Early Republic, 1789-1815*, 2009, p. 141.

18. New York Daily Gazette, 1790 *New York Daily Gazette, April 27, 1790*. Note from manuscript preparer: I was unable to locate a fuller citation for this item.

19. Wood, Gordon S. *Empire of Liberty: A History of the Early Republic, 1789-1815*, 2009, p. 141.

20. A waxed thread ending in a bristle and inserted into a shoemaker's awl.

21. Bowling, Kenneth R. & Veit, Helen E. *The Diary of William Maclay and Other Notes on Senate Debates*, 1988, pp. 241-42.

22. Jefferson, Anas of Thomas Jefferson, 32, as noted by Chernow, Ron *Alexander Hamilton*, 2004, p. 326.

23. "Richard Bland Lee [to Charles Lee]" in DHFFC *The Documentary History of The First Federal Congress, Vol. 19. Correspondence: Second Session, 15 March-June 1790*, 2012, vol. 19, pp. 394-395. The letter was found "in the dwelling house of General [Jeb] Stuart, in Virginia," according to the Cincinnati Daily Commercial, 6 November 1862. [Charles Lee is the unnamed but almost certain recipient.]

24. Young, Edward *Special report on the customs-tariff legislation of the United States with appendixes*, 1877, p. XVII.

25. Chernow, Ron *Alexander Hamilton*, 2004, p. 327.

26. Bowling, Kenneth R. & Veit, Helen E. *The Diary of William Maclay and Other Notes on Senate Debates*, 1988, p. 292.

27. Bowling, Kenneth R. & Veit, Helen E. *The Diary of William Maclay and Other Notes on Senate Debates*, 1988, p. 292.

28. Bowling, Kenneth R. & Veit, Helen E. *The Diary of William Maclay and Other Notes on Senate Debates*, 1988, p. 297.

29. Anas is the plural of ana, meaning a collection of sayings, anecdotes, or information about a person or a place. For a detailed history of the compilation of Jefferson's Anas, see "Editorial Note: The 'Anas,'" Founders Online, National Archives, Washington, D.C. Founders Online, n.d. *Editorial Note: The "Anas"*

30. "Thomas Jefferson Memorandum on the Compromise of 1790," in Online Library of Liberty, 2004 *Liberty and Order: The First American Party Struggle [1787]*. pp. 64-65.

31. The letters have not been found.

32. Bowling, Kenneth R. *The Creation of Washington, D.C.: The Idea and Location of the American Capital*, 1991, p. 189.

33. Bowling, Kenneth R. *The Creation of Washington, D.C.: The Idea and Location of the American Capital*, 1991, pp. 189, 193.

34. Bowling, Kenneth R. *The Creation of Washington, D.C.: The Idea and Location of the American Capital*, 1991, p. 195.

35. Rogers, Horatio *Discourse before the Rhode Island Historical Society at its Centennial Celebration of Rhode Island's Adoption of the Federal Constitution*, 1890, pp. 24-38.

36. Van de Water, Frederic F. *The Reluctant Republic: Vermont, 1724-1791*, 1941, p. 337.

37. Congress of the United States *An Act for the Admission of the State of Vermont into this Union*, 1791.

38. Doyle, Bill *Vermont Joins the Union*, 2013

39. Maine Historical Society *The Missouri Compromise: A Moral Dilemma*, 2019

CHAPTER 19: ON THE FRONTIER, SPIES AND PLOTS

1. Drexler, Ken, 2020 *Northwest Ordinance: Primary Documents in American History*.

2. National Park Service, n.d. *National Register of Historic Places -- Nomination Form General Rufus Putnam House*.

3. Campus Martius Museum, n.d. *Campus Martius Museum*.

4. Toomey, Michaell, 2016 *State of Franklin*.

5. Ohio History Central, n.d. *Treaty of Fort Harmar (1789)*.

6. Hillhouse, William, 1789 *A dissertation By William Hillhouse, Jr., New Haven, Connecticut, January 12, 1789*.

7. Van Dusen, Albert E. *Connecticut*, 1961, p. 199. The Firelands are made up by the present-day Erie and Huron Counties, as well as a small portion of Ashland County, Ohio.

8.   Putnam, Rufus *The Memoirs of Rufus Putnam and Certain Official Papers and Correspondence*, 1903.

9.   Clymer, George, 1789 *Rep. George Clymer of Pennsylvania to Benjamin Rush*.

10. Washington, George, 1790 *May 1790 [diary]*.

11. Hildreth, Samuel P. *Pioneer History*, 1848, pp. 263-66.

12. Bowling, Kenneth R. & Veit, Helen E. *The Diary of William Maclay and Other Notes on Senate Debates*, 1988, p. 245.

13. Washington, George *Journal of George Washington written during an expedition along the Ohio and Kanwha Rivers*, 1770.

14. Burton, Clarence M. *John Connolly, A Tory of the Revolution*, 1909, pp. 85-90.

15. Innes, Harry, 1788 *To George Washington from Harry Innes, 18 December 1788*, note 1.

16. Burton, Clarence M. *John Connolly, A Tory of the Revolution*, 1909, pp. 71, 94. 99, 102.

17. Linklater, Andro *An Artist in Treason: The Extraordinary Double Life of General James Wilkinson*, 2009, pp. 72-75

18. "Wilkinson, James," Biographical Gazetteer in DHFFC *The Documentary History of the First Federal Congress, Vol. 17, Correspondence: First Session, September-November 1789*, 2004.

19. Marshall, Thomas, 1789 *To George Washington from Thomas Marshall, 12 February 1789*.

20. Shepherd, W.R. *Wilkinson and the Beginning of the Spanish Conspiracy*, 1904

21. Marshall, Thomas, 1789 *To George Washington from Thomas Marshall, 12 February 1789*.

22. Ockerman Jr., Foster *Celebrate Kentucky's statehood: it was a slog*, 2017

23. Harrison, Lowell H. & Klotter, James C. *A New History of Kentucky*, 1997, p. 61

24. Kleber, John E. *The Kentucky Encyclopedia*, 1997, p. 294.

25. Fitzpatrick, John C. *The Writings of George Washington from the Original Manuscript Sources 1745-1799*, 1934, p. 32. 115. Washington, George *From George Washington to Henry Knox, 13 August 1792*, 1792

26. Soodalter, Ron, 2018 *Untouchable Agent 13*. See also Linklater, Andro *An Artist in Treason: The Extraordinary Double Life of General James Wilkinson*, 2009, p. 5

27. Washington, George, 1783 *From George Washington to Officers of the Army, 15 March 1783*.

28. Washington, George, 1783 *From George Washington to James Duane, 7 September 1783*. Duane, first mayor of New York City 1784-1789, had been New York state Indian commissioner.

29. "Treaty of New York with the Creeks," in DHFFC *The Documentary History of the First Federal Congress: Vol. 20, Correspondence: Second Session, July-October 1790*, 2012, vol. 20, pp. 2411-2412. The first treaty ratified—but not negotiated—under the federal government had been concluded between territorial Governor Arthur St. Clair and various nations of the Northwest Territory at Fort Harmar on January 9, 1789.

30. "A letter dated 4th January 1789 from Alexander McGillivray," while United States in Congress assembled, August 7, 1786 in DHFFC *The Documentary History of the First Federal Congress: Vol. 5. Legislative Histories: Funding Act [HR-63] through Militia Bill [HR112]*, 1986, vol. 5, pp. 1010-1121.

31. Frank, Andrew K., 2002 *Alexander McGillivray (ca. 1750-1793)*.

32. Judith Sargent Murray to Winthrop Sargent and Judith Saunders Sargent (her parents), 3 July 1790," quoted in Murray, Judith S. & Smith, Bonnie H. From Gloucester to Philadelphia in 1790, 1998, pp. 256-257.

33. "Treaty of New York with the Creeks," in DHFFC *The Documentary History of the First Federal Congress: Vol. 20, Correspondence: Second Session, July-October 1790*, 2012, vol. 20, pp. 2411-2412.

34. Introduction to DHFFC *The Documentary History of the First Federal Congress, Vol. 14, Debates in the House of Representatives: Third Session, December 1790-March 1791*, 1996.

35. Bowling, Kenneth R. & Veit, Helen E. *The Diary of William Maclay and Other Notes on Senate Debates*, 1988, p. 357.

36. Kohn, Richard H. *Eagle and Sword: The Federalists and the Creation of the Military Establishment in America, 1783-1802*, 1975, p. 96.

37. Washington, George, 1790 *From George Washington to the United States Senate and House of Representatives, 8 January 1790*.

38. Bowling, Kenneth R. & Veit, Helen E. *The Diary of William Maclay and Other Notes on Senate Debates*, 1988, p. 245.

39. Academic Dictionaries and Encyclopedias *Harmar Campaign*, 2000-2019

40. Kohn, Richard H. *Eagle and Sword: The Federalists and the Creation of the Military Establishment in America, 1783-1802*, 1975, pp. 95, 104-107. Maass, John R. *Defending a New Nation*, 2013, pp. 19-27.

41. Ohio History Central, n.d. *Harmar's Defeat*.

42. Kohn, Richard H. *Eagle and Sword: The Federalists and the Creation of the Military Establishment in America, 1783-1802*, 1975, p. 109 The "overawe" quotation: Knox, Henry, 1791 *To George Washington From Henry Knox, 22 January 1791*.

43. Feng, Patrick, n.d. *The Battle of the Wabash: The Forgotten Disaster of the Indian Wars*.

44. Kohn, Richard H. *Eagle and Sword: The Federalists and the Creation of the Military Establishment in America, 1783-1802*, 126, 233.

45. Nelson, Paul D. *Anthony Wayne, Soldier of the Early Republic*, 1985, p. 227.

CHAPTER 20: TOWARD AN AMERICAN LANGUAGE

1.   Reef, Catherine *Noah Webster: Man of Many Words*, 2015, pp. 49-50.

2.   Dobbs, Christopher, n.d. *Noah Webster and the Dream of a Common Language*.

3.   McDavid, Raven I., 1998 *Noah Webster: American lexicographer*.

4.   Webster, Noah *Dissertations on the English Language*, 1789, p. 20.

5.   Webster, Noah *Dissertations on the English Language*, 1789, p. 82.

6.   Webster, Noah *Dissertations on the English Language*, 1789, p. 108.

7.   Bicknell, Arthur J. *From Noah Webster to Merriam-Webster*, 2006, p. 15.

8.   Bicknell, Arthur J. *From Noah Webster to Merriam-Webster*, 2006, p. 7.

9.   DHFFC *The Documentary History of the First Federal Congress, Vol. 4, Legislative Histories: Amendments to the Constitution through Foreign Officers Bill [HR-1 16]*, 1986, vol. 4, pp. 522-26.

10. Anon. *The American Museum, or Universal Magazine, "For the Year 1792, Part II. From July to December, 1792"*, 1792.

11. George Washington's Mount Vernon, n.d. *The American Museum, or, Universal Magazine*.

12. Sher, Richard B. *The Enlightenment and the Book*, 2008, p. 544.

13. Carey, Matthew *To George Washington from Mathew Carey, 21 April 1789*, 1789, note 1.

14. Richardson, Lyon R. *A History of Early American Magazines, 1741-1789*, 1931, pp. 334-35.

15. Judith Sargent Murray, On the Equality of the Sexes, originally published in *Massachusetts Magazine*.

16. Unger, Harlow G. *Noah Webster: The Life and Times of an American Patriot*, 1998, pp. 140-42.

17. Winton, Calhoun *The Theater and Drama*, 1977, p. 88.

18. Meranze, Michael *Laboratories of Virtue: Punishment, Revolution and Authority in Philadelphia, 1760-1835*, 2012, p. 160.

19. "Jeremiah Wadsworth to Samuel B. Webb," in DHFFC *The Documentary History of the First Federal Congress, Vol. 16, Correspondence: First Session, June-August 1789*, 2004, vol. 16, p. 694.

20. Levett, Karl, 2009 *Reviews -- The Contrast*.

21. Maine, officially the "Maine District of Massachusetts," often acted as if it were already a state.

22. "American Newspapers, 1787–1790," derived from Brigham, Clarence S. *History and Bibliography of American Newspapers, 1690-1820*, 1947. See also American Newspapers 1787-1790 in Jensen, Merrill *Constitutional documents and records, 1776-1787*, 1976.

23. Bickford, Charlene B. & Bowling, Kenneth R. *Birth of the Nation: The First Federal Congress 1789-1791*, 1989, p. 18. See also "The First Congress" in DHFFC *The Documentary History of the First Federal Congress: Vol. 1. Senate Legislative Journal*, 1972.

24. Chronicling America, n.d. *About Gazette of the United-States. [volume] (New-York [N.Y.]) 1789-1793*.

25. New-York Journal and Weekly Register *The New-York Journal and Weekly Register October 22, 1789*, 1789.

26. Wilmington Centinel *The Wilmington Centinel February 19, 1789*, 1789.

27. Library of Congress, Newspaper & Current Periodicals Reading Room, America's Historical Newspapers database, Herald of Freedom and the Federal Advertiser, January 27, 1789. Note from manuscript preparer: I have been unable to create a fuller citation for this item.

28. Rosenberg, Chaim M. *Yankee Colonies across America*, 2015, p. 195.

29. Daily Advertiser *The Daily Advertiser February 4, 1789*, 1789.

30. Brown, William H. *The Power of Sympathy or, The Triumph of Nature, Founded in Truth*, 1789. See also Brown, William H. *The Power of Sympathy*, 1969 edited by William S. Kable, for the full text of the book with scholarly notes.

31. New England Historical Society, n.d. *The 1788 Scandal of Fanny Apthorp Never Dies*.

32. New England Historical Society, n.d. *The 1788 Scandal of Fanny Apthorp Never Dies*.

33. New England Historical Society, n.d. *The 1788 Scandal of Fanny Apthorp Never Dies*.

34. History of American Women, n.d. *Sarah Wentworth Morton* "Sarah Wentworth Morton," History of American Women, www.womenhistoryblog.com/2012/08/sarah-wentworth-morton.html (accessed November 30, 2017). Note from manuscript preparer: When I went to confirm the citation, the original website was flagged as unsafe to visit due to some manner of hacking attack. A safer copy of the page can be found at https://web.archive.org/web/20200209091821/www.womenhistoryblog.com/2012/08/sarah-wentworth-morton.html

35. Well over a century after its publication, the belief was that the book's author was Sarah Wentworth Apthorp Morton, who wrote poetry under the pen name Philenia, and was of course sister to Fanny Apthorp. In 1894 William Hill Brown's still-living niece identified Brown as the author. In 1933, Milton Ellis assembled a detailed and circumstantial case arguing for Brown's authorship. Ellis, Milton *The Author of the First American Novel*, 1933, pp. 359-68. See the editor's introduction, by William S. Kable, in an edition of the book available at https://kb.osu.edu/handle/1811/6347 for further discussion of the author's identity, and for discussion of other candidates for "First American Novel." Brown, William H. *The Power of Sympathy*, 1969, pp. xi-xxxvi. See also *The Rise of the American Novel*, by Alexander Cowie, pages 1-10, for additional exploration on both subjects and endnote 37 to Chapter 1 of Cowie on the question of authorship. The full text of is available at https://archive.org/details/in.ernet.dli.2015.235748/. Cowie, Alexander *The Rise of the American Novel*, 1948, pp. 1-10.

36. Editors of Encycolpaedia Britannica, 1998 *William Hill Brown*.

37. Parramore, Thomas C., 1979 *Brown, William Hill*.

38. New England Historical Society, n.d. *The 1788 Scandal of Fanny Apthorp Never Dies*.

39. Metropolitan Museum of Art, n.d. *The Massachusetts Magazine, or, Monthly Museum of Knowledge and Rational Entertainment*.

40. Morse, Jedidiah *The American Geography*, 1792.

41. Moss, Richard J. *The Life of Jedidiah Morse: A Station of Peculiar Exposure*, 1995, p. 38.

42. Encyclopedia of World Biography, 2010 *Jedidiah Morse Facts*.

43. Morse, Jedidiah *The American Geography*, 1792, p. title page.

44. Morse, Jedidiah *The American Geography*, 1792, p. 390.

45. Morse, Jedidiah *The American Geography*, 1792, pp. 218-19.

46. Morse, Jedidiah *The American Geography*, 1792, p. 318.

47. Morse, Jedidiah *The American Geography*, 1792, p. 65.

48. Morse, Jedidiah *The American Geography*, 1792, p. 408.

49. Sprague, William B. *The Life of Jedidiah Morse, D.D.*, 1874, p. 219.

50. Sinclair, Donald A. *A guide to manuscript diaries and journals in the Special Collections Department, Rutgers University*, 1980, p. 7.

51. Martin, Joseph P. *A Narrative of a Revolutionary Soldier*, 2001, p. 88.

52. Shaw, John R. *A Narrative of the Life & Travels of John Robert Shaw, the Well-Digger, Now Resident in Lexington, Kentucky, Written By Himself*, 1807 and 1930, pp. 205, 206.

53. Boorstin, Daniel J. *From the Land to the Machine*, 1975, p. 24.

EPILOGUE: IN RISING GLORY

1. Washington, George, 1796 *Farewell Address* and Washington, George, 1796 *Farewell Address*. The first source, the Library of Congress digital collection, shows the handwritten text of the actual document. The Founders Online source, part of the website run by the National Archives, offers detailed footnotes and background information.

2. Kotowski, Peter, n.d. *Whiskey Rebellion* Accessed May 12, 2018.

3. Washington, George, 1784 *From George Washington to Lafayette, 1 February 1784*.

4. Overholser, Geneva & Jamieson, Kathleen H. *The Press*, 2005, p. 20.

5. National Postal Museum *Out of the Mail*, 2008

6. Lear, Tobias *Tobias Lear's Narrative Acccounts of the Death of George Washington*, 1799.

7. Washington, George *From George Washington to Alexander Hamilton, 12 December 1799*, 1799.

8. Washington, George *From Geoge Washington to John Adams, 13 July 1798*, 1798.

9. Washington, George *George Washington's Last Will and Testament, 9 July 1799*, 1799.

10. Mount Vernon Ladies' Association *10 Facts About Washington and Slaves*, n.d.

11. Washington, George George Washington's Last Will and Testament, 9 July 1799, 1799.

12. Mount Vernon Ladies' Association *10 Facts About Washington and Slaves*, n.d.

13. Mount Vernon Ladies' Association *Martha Washington as a Slaveowner*, n.d.

14. Stillwell, Margaret B. *Checklist of Eulogies and Funeral Orations on the Death of George Washington.*, 1916, pp. 404-05.

15. Masonic Geneology, n.d. *SAMUEL DUNN 1747-1815*.

16. Spragens, William C. *Popular Images of America Presidents*, 1988, p. 11.

APPENDICES

1. Bain, Henry *Errors in the Constitution—Typographical and Congressional*, 2012.
2. National Archives, 1789 *The Bill of Rights: A Transcription*.

BIBLIOGRAPHY

My main research source for this book were the volumes in the magnificent *Documentary History of the First Federal Congress, 1789–1791*, published by the Johns Hopkins University Press. Eight volumes contain the official congressional records. Six volumes preserve unofficially reported debates. Those debates would have been lost to posterity had they not been reported by the journalists who covered Congress and began America's grand tradition: Keep a vigilant journalist eye on Congress. There are also eight volumes of correspondence and other documents that reveal the thoughts of the members of Congress who began the political life of the nation.

Charlene Bangs Bickford is the director and coeditor of the *DHFFC*. Kenneth R. Bowling is the coeditor. Helen E. Veit and William Charles diGiacomantonio are the associate editors. The First Federal Congress Project is a research center that has been affiliated with the Department of History at George Washington University since 1966.

The volumes were digitized and made available for subscription. That is how I perused these treasures. I cite the sources with an abbreviation, including the volume and pages in the published version of the books, i.e., *DHFFC*, vol. 2, 134–36.*

---

*   Notes from manuscript preparer: For reasons related to managing the bibliography, and for the sake of clarity, citations to the volumes of the *DHFFC* have been changed to provide the full volume titles. Note also that the various volumes of the *DHFFC* are listed in the Bibliography in publication date order, rather than volume number order.

I also made much use of two other digitized sources: Founders Online, a product of the National Archives that contains the correspondence and other writings of George Washington, Benjamin Franklin, John Adams (and family), Thomas Jefferson, Alexander Hamilton, and James Madison. Many entries have additional information from the University of Virginia, which also provided a digitized version of the Papers of George Washington.

•••

BIBLIOGRAPHIC SOURCES

Aaron, Lawrence. *Confronting New Jersey's Slave Past. Bergen County Record*, 10 February 2006. pp. L-9. Available at: https://www.newspapers.com/image/504545947/?terms=confronting%20slave%20past&match=1. Subscription likely required to access listed URL.

Abbot, W. W. & Twohig, Dorothy 1992. *The Papers of George Washington: January-July 1784*. Edited by W. W. Abbot & Dororthy Twohig. Richmond, Virginia, United States of America: University of Virginia Press.

Academic Dictionaries and Encyclopedias, 2000-2019. *Harmar Campaign*. [Online] Available at: https://enacademic.com/dic.nsf/enwiki/11223976 [Accessed 20 June 2019].

Adams, Abigail, 1789. *Abigail Adams to Mary Smith Cranch, 9 August 1789*. [Online] National Archives Available at: https://founders.archives.gov/documents/Adams/04-08-02-0214 [Accessed 30 April 2020]. [Original source: The Adams Papers, Adams Family Correspondence, vol. 8, Mar 1787–Dec 1789, ed. C. J. Taylor, M. A. Hogan, J. M. Rodrique, G. L. Lint, H. Woodward, and M. T. Claffey. Cambridge, MA: Harvard University Press, 2007, pp 397-401.].

Adams, John, 1774. *From John Adams to William Tudor, September 29, 1774*. [Online] National Archives Available at: https://founders.archives.gov/documents/Adams/06-02-02-0052 [Accessed 16 April 2020]. Original source: The Adams Papers, Papers of John Adams, vol. 2, December 1773–April 1775, ed. Robert J. Taylor. Cambridge, MA: Harvard University Press, 1977, pp. 176–178.

————.1775. *VIII. To the Inhabitants of the Colony of Massachusetts-Bay, 13 March 1775*. [Online] Available at: https://founders.archives.gov/documents/Adams/06-02-02-0072-0009 [Accessed 16 April 2020]. Original source: The Adams Papers, Papers of John Adams, vol. 2, December 1773?–?April 1775, ed. Robert J. Taylor. Cambridge, MA: Harvard University Press, 1977, pp. 327–337.

————. 1785. *John Adams to Elbridge Gerry, April 25, 1785.* [Online] The University of Chicago Press Available at: http://press-pubs.uchicago.edu/founders/documents/v1ch15s30.html [Accessed 20 April 2020]. Founders' Const. Vol 1. Ch 15 Doc 30. The web page cites the following as the source for this material: Austin, James T. The Life of Elbridge Gerry. With Contemporary Letters. 2 vols. Boston, 1828--29.

————.1789. *From John Adams to Benjamin Rush, June 9, 1789.* [Online] National Archives Available at: https://founders.archives.gov/documents/Adams/99-02-02-0609 [Accessed 11 May 2020]. Note from web page: [This is an Early Access document from The Adams Papers. It is not an authoritative final version.].

————. 1789. *To George Washington from John Adams, 17 May 1789.* [Online] National Archives Available at: https://founders.archives.gov/documents/Washington/05-02-02-0228 [Accessed 29 April 2020]. [Original source: The Papers of George Washington, Presidential Series, vol. 2, 1 April 1789–15 June 1789, ed. Dorothy Twohig. Charlottesville: University Press of Virginia, 1987, pp. 312–314.].

Alden, John 1889. *Souvenir and Official Programme of the Centennial Celebration of the Inauguration of George Washington as President of the United States.* New York, New York, United States of America: Garnett & Gow. Available at: https://archive.org/details/souvenirofficial00alde/page/n15/mode/2up [accessed 29 April 2020].

Alexander, John 2002. *Samuel Adams: America's Revolutionary Politician.* Lanham, Maryland, United States of America: Rowman & Littlefield.

Alexander, James C., 2008. Off to a bad start: John Adams's tussle over titles. *Vanderbilt Undergraduate Research Journal,* 4(1), pp. 1-7. Available at: http://ejournals.library.vanderbilt.edu/index.php/vurj/article/view/2786.

Allen, Thomas B. 2010. *Tories: Fighting for the King in America's First Civil War.* New York: HarperCollins.

————. 2013. *A Gift for President Washington.* Kansas City, MO: Andrews McMeel.

Amar, Akhil R., 1987. Our Forgotten Constitution: A Bicentennial Comment. *Yale Law School Faculty Scholarship Series,* Available at: https://digitalcommons.law.yale.edu/cgi/viewcontent.cgi?article=2025&context=fss_papers [Accessed 11 May 2020].

American Art Association 1929. *The Important Collection of Baron Von Steuben Relics.* New York: American Art Association. Available at: https://archive.org/details/importantcollect00amer_1/page/n35/mode/2up [accessed 29 April 2020].

American Battlefield Trust, 2020. *American Revolution Facts*. [Online] Available at: https://www.battlefields.org/learn/articles/american-revolution-faqs [Accessed 2020 April 2020].

American History from Revolution to Reconstruction and Beyond, n.d. *A Biography of Thomas Paine (1737-1809)*. [Online] Available at: http://www.let.rug.nl/usa/biographies/thomas-paine/ [Accessed 13 May 2020].

Ames, Fisher 1983. *The Works of Fisher Ames*. Edited by Seth Ames. Indianapolis: Liberty Classics. Available at: https://archive.org/details/worksfisherames-s01kirkgoog/page/n68/mode/2up [accessed 26 February 2021]. Reprint of edition published in Boston by Little, Brown in 1854.

Andrews, Evangeline W. & Andrews, Charles M. 1921. *Journal of a Lady of Quality*. New Haven, Connecticut, United States of America: Yale University Press. Available at: https://archive.org/details/journalofladyofq00scha/page/n6/mode/2up. The journal's author is Janet Schaw, who in 1774 had sailed from Scotland to the West Indies and North Carolina.

Anon. 1792. *The American Museum, or Universal Magazine, "For the Year 1792, Part II. From July to December, 1792"*. Philadelphia, Pennsylvania, United States of America: M. Carey. Available at: https://babel.hathitrust.org/cgi/pt?id=osu.32435073185951;view=1up;seq=9 [accessed 20 May 2020].

Anon. 1823. *Journals of the American Congress from 1774 to 1788*. Washington: Way and Gideon.

Anon., 1998. *Re: Washington-Blackburn*. [Online] Available at: http://www.genealogy.com/forum/surnames/topics/washington/13/ [Accessed 23 April 2020].

Anon. *The Writings of George Washington Relating to the National Capital. Records of the Columbia Historical Society*, 1914. Available at: https://archive.org/details/jstor-40067048/page/n9/mode/2up [Accessed 14 May 2020].

Anonymous, 1789. Freeman's Journal. *Freeman's Journal*.

Atterbury, William W. 1894. *Elias Boudinot: Reminiscences of the American Revolution*. Privately Printed. Available at: https://books.google.com/books?id=BZVHAAAAYAAJ [accessed 17 April 2020]. No publication date shown, but a footnote indicates it was "Read Before the Huguenot Society, February 15, 1894."

Austin, James T. 1829. *The Life of Elbridge Gerry*. Boston. Austin, James T. The Life of Elbridge Gerry. Boston: Well and Lilly (1829): 99.

Awesome Stories, n.d. *The Famous Speech*. [Online] Available at: https://www.awesomestories.com/asset/view/THE-FAMOUS-SPEECH-Amazing-Grace [Accessed 7 May 2020].

Bahr, William J. 2016. *George Washington's Liberty Key*. Bloomingdale, Illinois, United States of America: IBEX Systems.

Bailyn, Bernard 2007. *To Begin the World Anew: The Genius and Ambiguities of the American Founders*. New York: Knopf Doubleday.

Bain, Henry, 2012. Errors in the Constitution -- Typographical and Congressional. *Prologue*, 44(2), Available at: https://www.archives.gov/publications/prologue/2012/fall/const-errors.html [Accessed 16 February 2021].

Baldwin, Abraham, 1789. *Rep. Abraham Baldwin of Georgia to Governor Edward Telfair, June 17, 1789*. [Online] George Washington University Available at: https://www2.gwu.edu/~ffcp/exhibit/p8/p8_4text.html [Accessed 2 May 2020]. Letter is credited courtesy of Duke University Library. See Telfair Papers, Duke University Library.

Ballagh, James C. 1912. *The Letters of Richard Henry Lee*. New York: The Macmillan Company. Available at: https://archive.org/details/lettersofrichard02leer/page/514/mode/2up [accessed 17 June 2020].

————. 1914. *The Letters of Richard Henry Lee*. New York: MacMillan. Available at: https://archive.org/details/lettersofrichard02leer/page/514/mode/2up.

Barnwell, Joseph W. *The Evacuation of Charleston by the British in 1782. The South Carolina Historical and Genealogical Magazine*, January 1910. Available at: https://archive.org/details/jstor-27575255/page/n1/mode/2up [Accessed 25 February 2021].

Bartlett, John R. 1861. *Records of the Colony of Rhode Island and Providence Plantations, in New England*. Providence, Rhode Island, United States of America: Knowles, Anthony & Co., State Printers. Available at: https://archive.org/details/recordsofcolony06rhod/page/416/mode/2up.

Bartoloni-Tuazon, Kathleen 2014. *For Fear of an Elective King: George Washington and the Presidential Title Controversy of 1789*. Ithaca, NY: Cornell University Press.

Beatty, Joseph M., 1914. The Letters of Judge Henry Wynkoop, Representative from Pennsylvania to the First Congress of the United States. *The Pennsylvania Magazine of History and Biography*, 38(1), pp. 39-64. The anecdote is in the introduction on page 42. Beatty cites Bucks County Historical Society Publications, vol III, p 156 as his source. Beatty's article is continued in Vol 38 Issue 2 of PMHB.

Bedini, Silvio 1999. *The Life of Benjamin Banneker: The First African-American Man of Science*. Baltimore: The Maryland Historical Society.

Bell Jr., Whitfield J. 1997. *Patriot-Improvers: Biographical Sketches of Members of the American Philosophical Society Vol 1*. Philadelphia: American Philosophical Society.

————.1999. *Patriot-Improvers: Biographical Sketches of Members of the American Philosophical Society Vol 2*. Philadelphia: American Philosophical Society.

Benjamin Franklin Historical Society, 2014. *Later Years and Death*. [Online]
   Available at: http://www.benjamin-franklin-history.org/later-years-and-death/
   [Accessed 6 May 2020].

Berggren, D. J., n.d. *Presidential Election of 1789*. [Online] Available at: https://
   www.mountvernon.org/library/digitalhistory/digital-encyclopedia/article/
   presidential-election-of-1789 [Accessed 23 April 2020].

Bernstein, Richard B., 1992. The Sleeper Awakes: the History and Legacy of the
   Twenty-seventh Amendment. *Fordham Law Review, Vol. 61, Issue 3.*

Bickford, Charlene. *Setting Precedent: The First Senate and President Washington
   Struggle to Define "Advice and Consent". Federal History Journal*, 4 April 2014.
   Available at: https://shfg.wildapricot.org/resources/Documents/FH%207%20
   (2015)%20Bickford.pdf [Accessed 30 April 2020]. Charlene Bickford (direc-
   tor, George Washington University First Federal Congress Project), presenting
   Roger R. Trask Award Lecture, April 4, 2014, Robert C. Byrd.

Bickford, Charlene B. & Bowling, Kenneth R. 1989. *Birth of the Nation: The First
   Federal Congress 1789-1791*. Madison, Wisconsin, United States of America:
   Madison House Publishers.

Bicknell, Arthur J. 2006. *From Noah Webster to Merriam-Webster*. Springfield:
   Merriam-Webster, Inc.

Black, Euphemia V., 1854. *History of Newburyport*. Newburyport: Damrell and
   Moore.

Boorstin, Daniel J., 1975. From the Land to the Machine. In Thomas B. Allen,
   ed. *We Americans*. Washington, D.C, United States of America: National
   Geographic Society.

Bordewich, Fergus M. 2016. *The First Congress: How James Madison, George
   Washington, and a Group of Extraordinary Men Invented the Government*. New
   York: Simon & Schuster.

Boudinot, Elias, 1789. *To George Washington from Elias Boudinot, 22 April 1789.*
   [Online] National Archives Available at: https://founders.archives.gov/
   documents/Washington/05-02-02-0100 [Accessed 25 April 2020]. [Original
   source: The Papers of George Washington, Presidential Series, vol. 2, 1 April
   1789–15 June 1789, ed. Dorothy Twohig. Charlottesville: University Press of
   Virginia, 1987, pp. 113–115.].

Bowen, Clarence W. 1892. *History of the Centennial Celebration of the Inauguration
   of George Washington as First President of the United States*. New York, New
   York, United States of America: Appleton.

Bowen, Catherine D. 1968. *Miracle at Philadelphia*. New York: Bantam. 1966
   Edition also used in preparation of the present book.

Bowling, Kenneth R., 1976. Good-by "Charle": The Lee-Adams Interest and the Political Demise of Charles Thomson, Secretary of Congress, 1774-1789. *The Pennsylvania Magazine of History and Biography*, 100(3), pp. 314-35. Available at: https://journals.psu.edu/pmhb/issue/view/2478.

————. *New Light on the Philadelphia Mutiny of 1783: Federal-State Confrontation at the Close of the War for Independence. Pennsylvania Magazine of History and Biography*, October 1977. pp. 419-50. Available at: https://journals.psu.edu/pmhb/article/view/43383/43104.

————. 1988. 'A Tub to the Whale': The Founding Fathers and Adoption of the Federal Bill of Rights. *Journal of the Early Republic*.

————. 1991. *The Creation of Washington, D.C.: The Idea and Location of the American Capital*. Fairfax, Virginia, United States of America: George Mason University Press.

————. 2002. *Peter Charles L'Enfant: Vision, Honor and Male Friendship in the Early American Republic*. Washington DC: Friends of The George Washington Universities Libraries.

Bowling, Kenneth R. & Veit, Helen E. 1988. *The Diary of William Maclay and Other Notes on Senate Debates*. Baltimore: Johns Hopkins University Press. This book is volume 9 of the series "Documentary history of the First Federal Congress of the United States of America, March 4, 1789-March 3, 1791".

Braisted, Todd, 2017. *War Chronology*. [Online] Available at: http://www.royalprovincial.com/index.htm [Accessed April September 2017].

Breen, T. H. 2015. *George Washington's Journey: The President Forges a New Nation*. New York: Simon & Schuster.

Brigham, Clarence S. 1947. *History and Bibliography of American Newspapers, 1690-1820*. Worcester: American Antiquarian Society.

Brookhiser, Richard 1997. *Founding Father: Rediscovering George Washington*. New York: Simon and Schuster. [Online] Available at: https://archive.org/details/foundingfatherre00broo/page/66/mode/2up.

Brown University Brown Digital Repository, n.d. *Voyage of the Sally*. [Online] Available at: https://repository.library.brown.edu/studio/collections/id_596/ [Accessed 6 May 2020].

Brown University Library, n.d. *Aftermath of the Voyage*. [Online] Available at: https://cds.library.brown.edu/projects/sally/narr_aftermath.html [Accessed 7 May 2020].

Brown University Steering Committee on Slavery and Justice 2006. *Slavery and Justice: Report of the Brown University Steering Committee on Slavery and Justice*. Providence, Rhode Island, United States of Americ: Brown Unversity. Available at: https://www.brown.edu/Research/Slavery_Justice/report. The report itself contains no publication data, such as publisher or publication date. See http://brown.edu/Research/Slavery_Justice/ for this information.

Brown, Alice 1896. *Mercy Warren*. New York: Charles Scribner's Sons. Available at: https://archive.org/details/mercywarren00browuoft/page/296/mode/2up.

Brown, William H. 1789. *The Power of Sympathy or, The Triumph of Nature, Founded in Truth*. Boston: Isaiah Thomas and Co. The work, which was published anonymously, but modern scholarship identifies Brown as the author.

———. 1969. *The Power of Sympathy*. Edited by William S. Kable. Ohio State University, Ohio, United States of America: Ohio State University. Available at: https://kb.osu.edu/handle/1811/6347. The complete book is available as a PDF file at the listed web address.

Buchan, William 1769. *Domestic Medicine, or the Family Physician*. Edinburgh: Balfour, Auld and Smellie. Available at: https://digital.ub.uni-duesseldorf.de/vester/content/titleinfo/4135894.

Burgan, Michael 2005. *Thomas Paine: Great Writer of the Revolution*. Minneapolis, Minnesota, United States of America: Compass Point Books.

Burke, Aedanus, Considerations on the Society or Order of Cincinnati. Philadelphia, Pennsylvania, United States of America: Robert Bell. Available at: https://quod.lib.umich.edu/e/evans/N14115.0001.001/1:1?rgn=div1;view=fulltext

Burnett, Edmond C. 1921. *Letters of Members of the Continental Congress*. Washington, DC, United States of America: Carnegie Institution. Letter, "John Adams to James Warren, July 6, 1775".

Burton, Clarence M. *John Connolly, A Tory of the Revolution. Proceedings of the American Antiquarian Society*, October 1909. Available at: https://www.americanantiquarian.org/proceedings/45647878.pdf.

Byrd, Robert C. 1988. *The Senate, 1789-1989*. Washington, D.C.: U.S. Government Printing Office.

Cabot, George, 1791. *To Alexander Hamilton from George Cabot, 6 September 1791*. [Online] National Archives Available at: https://founders.archives.gov/documents/Hamilton/01-09-02-0132 [Accessed 14 May 2020]. [Original source: The Papers of Alexander Hamilton, vol. 9, August 1791–December 1791, ed. Harold C. Syrett. New York: Columbia University Press, 1965, pp. 177–180.].

Campus Martius Museum, n.d. *Campus Martius Museum*. [Online] Available at: https://mariettamuseums.org/campus-martius/about-us/ [Accessed 26 February 2021].

Carey, Matthew, 1789. *To George Washington from Mathew Carey, 21 April 1789*. [Online] Available at: https://founders.archives.gov/documents/Washington/05-02-02-0088 [Accessed 20 May 2020]. [Original source: The

Papers of George Washington, Presidential Series, vol. 2, 1 April 1789–15 June 1789, ed. Dorothy Twohig. Charlottesville: University Press of Virginia, 1987, p. 99.].

Cashin, Edward J., 2005. *Revolutionary War in Georgia*. [Online] Available at: https://www.georgiaencyclopedia.org/articles/history-archaeology/revolutionary-war-georgia [Accessed 6 May 2020].

Chernow, Ron 2004. *Alexander Hamilton*. New York: Penguin.

———. 2010. *Washington: A Life*. New York: Penguin Press.

Christman, Margaret C.S. 1989. *The First Federal Congress 1789-1781*. Washington, D.C., United States of America: Smithsonian Institute Press.

Chronicling America, n.d. *About Gazette of the United-States. [volume] (New-York [N.Y.]) 1789-1793*. [Online] Library of Congress Available at: https://chroniclingamerica.loc.gov/lccn/sn83030483/ [Accessed 20 May 2020].

Clement, Maud C. 1999. *The History of Pittsylvania County, Virginia*. Baltimore.

Clymer, George, 1789. *Rep. George Clymer of Pennsylvania to Benjamin Rush*. [Online] Available at: https://www2.gwu.edu/~ffcp/exhibit/p10/p10_1text.html [Accessed 18 May 2020].

Coffman, Steve 2012. *Words of the Founder Fathers*. Jefferson, North Carolina, United States of America: McFarland & Company.

Cogan, Neil E. 2015. *The Complete Bill of Rights: The Drafts, Debates, Sources, and Origins*. New York, New York, United States of America: Oxford University Press.

Collins, Elizabeth M., 2013. *Black Soldiers in the Revolutionary War*. [Online] U.S. Army Available at: https://www.army.mil/article/97705/Black_Soldiers_in_the_Revolutionary_War/ [Accessed 6 May 2020].

Congress of the United States, 1791. *An Act for the Admission of the State of Vermont into this Union*. [Online] Available at: https://avalon.law.yale.edu/18th_century/vt03.asp [Accessed 5 September 2019].

Connecticut History, n.d. *Slavery and Abolition*. [Online] Available at: https://connecticuthistory.org/topics-page/slavery-and-abolition [Accessed 7 May 2020].

Connors, Anothy J. 2014. *Ingenious Machinists: Two Inventive Lives from the American Industrial Revolution*. Albany: State University of New York.

Cowie, Alexander 1948. *The Rise of the American Novel*. New York, New York, United States of America: American Book Company. Available at: https://archive.org/details/in.ernet.dli.2015.235748/.

Crawford, Michael J. & Hughes, Christine F. 1995. *The Reestablishment of the Navy, 1787-1801: Historical Overview and Select Bibliography*. Washington, D.C., United States of America: Naval Historical Center, Department of the Navy.

Available at: https://www.history.navy.mil/research/library/bibliographies/reestablishment-navy-1787-1801.html.

Custis, George W.P. 1861. *Recollections and private memoirs of Washington*. Philadelphia: J. W. Bradley.

Daily Advertiser. *The Daily Advertiser*, 4 February 1789. pp. 1-4. [Accessed 8 September 2022]. Viewed via microfilm, Newspaper & Current Periodical Reading Room, Library of Congress

Debruyne, Nese F., 2019. *American War and Military Operations Casualties: Lists and Statistics*. [Online] Available at: https://crsreports.congress.gov/product/pdf/RL/RL32492 [Accessed 2020 April 2020].

Decatur, Stephen, J. 1933. *Private Affairs of George Washington: From the Records and Accounts of Tobias Lear*. Boston: Houghton Mifflin.

DePauw, Linda G. 1966. *The Eleventh Pillar: New York State and the Federal Constitution*. Ithaca, New York, United States of America: Cornell University Press.

DHFFC 1972. *The Documentary History of the First Federal Congress: Vol. 1. Senate Legislative Journal*. Edited by Linda Grant DePauw, Charlene Bangs Bickford & Marlene LaVonne Siegel. Baltimore, Maryland, United States of America: Johns Hopkins University Press.

DHFFC 1974. *The Documentary History of the First Federal Congress: Vol. 2. Senate Executive Journal and Related Documents*. Edited by Linda Grant DePauw, Charlene Bangs Bickford & LaVonne Marlene Siegel. Baltimore, Maryland, United States of America: Johns Hopkins University Press.

DHFFC 1986. *The Documentary History of the First Federal Congress, Vol. 4, Legislative Histories: Amendments to the Constitution through Foreign Officers Bill [HR-1 16]*. Edited by Charlene Bangs Bickford & Helen E. Veit. Baltimore, Maryland, United States of America: Johns Hopkins University Press.

DHFFC 1986. *The Documentary History of the First Federal Congress: Vol. 5. Legislative Histories: Funding Act [HR-63] through Militia Bill [HR112]*. Edited by Charlene Bangs Bickford & Helen E. Veit. Baltimore, Maryland, United States of America: Johns Hopkins University Press.

DHFFC 1986. *The Documentary History of the First Federal Congress: Vol. 6. Legislative Histories: Mitigation of Fines Bill [HR-38] through Resolution on Unclaimed Western Lands*. Edited by Charlene Bangs Bickford & Helen E. Veit. Baltimore, Maryland, United States of America: Johns Hopkins University Press.

DHFFC 1988. *The Documentary History of the First Federal Congress: Vol. 9. The Diary of William Maclay and Other Notes on Senate Debates*. Edited by

Kenneth R. Bowling & Helen E. Veit. Baltimore, Maryland, United States of America: Johns Hopkins University Press.

DHFFC 1992. *The Documentary History of the First Federal Congress, Vol. 10. Debates in the House of Representatives, First Session, April-May 1789.* Edited by Charlene Bangs Bickform, Kenneth R. Bowling & Helen E. Veit. Baltimore, Maryland, United States of America: Johns Hopkins University Press.

DHFFC 1992. *The Documentary History of the First Federal Congress, Vol. 11. Debates in the House of Representatives, First Session, June-September, 1789.* Edited by Charlene Bangs Bickford, Kenneth R. Bowling & Helen E. Veit. Baltimore, Maryland, United States of America: Johns Hopkins University Press.

DHFFC 1995. *The Documentary History of the First Federal Congress, Vol. 12. Debates in the House of Representatives, Second Session, January-March 1790.* Edited by Charlene Bangs Bickford, Kenneth R. Bowling & William C. diGiacomantonio. Baltimore, Maryland, United States of America: Johns Hopkins University Press.

DHFFC 1995. *The Documentary History of the First Federal Congress: Vol. 13. Debates in the House of Representatives, Second Session, April-August, 1790.* Edited by Helen E. Veit, Charlene Bangs Bickford, Kenneth E. Bowling & William C. diGiacomantonio. Baltimore, Maryland, United States of America: Johns Hopkins University Press.

DHFFC 1996. *The Documentary History of the First Federal Congress, Vol. 14, Debates in the House of Representatives: Third Session, December 1790-March 1791.* Edited by William C. Giacomantonio, Kenneth R. Bowling, Charlene Bangs Bickford & Helen E. Veit. Baltimore, Maryland, United States of America: Johns Hopkins University Press.

DHFFC 1997. *The Documentary History of the First Federal Congress: Vol. 7, Petition Histories: Revolutionary War-related Claims.* Edited by Charlene Bangs Bickford, William C diGiacomantonio & Kenneth R. Bowling. Baltimore, Maryland, United States of America: Johns Hopkins University Press.

DHFFC 1998. *The Documentary History of the First Federal Congress, Vol. 8, Petition Histories and Non-Legislative Official Documents.* Edited by Charlene Bangs Bickford, Wlliam C. diGiacomantonio & Kenneth R. Bowling. Baltimore, Maryland, United States of America: Johns Hopkins University Press.

DHFFC 2004. *The Documentary History of the First Federal Congress, Vol. 16, Correspondence: First Session, June-August 1789.* Edited by Charlene Bangs Bickford, Kenneth R. Bowling, Helen E. Veit & William C. diGiacomantonio. Baltimore, Maryland, United States of America: Johns Hopkins University Press.

DHFFC 2004. *The Documentary History of the First Federal Congress, Vol. 17, Correspondence: First Session, September-November 1789*. Edited by Charlene Bangs Bickford, Kenneth R. Bowling, Helen E. Veit & William C. diGiacomantonio. Baltimore, Maryland, United States of America: Johns Hopkins University Press.

DHFFC 2004. *The Documentary History of the First Federal Congress: Vol. 15, Correspondence: First Session, March-May 1789*. Edited by Charlene Bangs Bickford, Kenneth R. Bowling, Helen E. Veit & William C. diGiacomantonio. Baltimore, Maryland, United States of America: Johns Hopkins University Press.

DHFFC 2012. *The Documentary History of the First Federal Congress, Vol. 18. Correspondence: Second Session, October 1789-14 March 1790*. Balitimore, Maryland, United States of America: The Johns Hopkins University Press.

DHFFC 2012. *The Documentary History of The First Federal Congress, Vol. 19. Correspondence: Second Session, 15 March-June 1790*. Edited by Charlene Bangs Bickford, Kenneth R. Bowling, Helen E. Veit & William C. diGiacomantonio. Baltimore, Maryland, United States of America: Johns Hopkins Unversity Press.

DHFFC 2012. *The Documentary History of the First Federal Congress: Vol. 20, Correspondence: Second Session, July-October 1790*. Edited by Charlene Bangs Bickford, Kenneth R. Bowling, Helen E. Veit & William C. diGiacomantonio. Baltimore, Marylad, United States of America: Johns Hopkins University Press.

Diamant, Lincoln 2004. *Chaining the Hudson: The Fight for the River in the American Revolution*. New York: Fordham University Press.

Digital Encyclopedia of George Washington, n.d. *Bastille Key*. [Online] Available at: https://www.mountvernon.org/library/digitalhistory/digital-encyclopedia/article/bastille-key/ [Accessed 13 May 2020].

———. n.d. *John Ramage*. [Online] Available at: https://www.mountvernon.org/library/digitalhistory/digital-encyclopedia/article/john-ramage/ [Accessed 5 May 2020].

———n.d. *Martha Parke Custis*. [Online] Available at: https://www.mountvernon.org/library/digitalhistory/digital-encyclopedia/article/martha-parke-custis [Accessed 12 May 2020].

Digital Maryland, n.d. *Maryland Colonial Currency - Enoch Pratt Free Library*. [Online] Available at: http://collections.digitalmaryland.org/cdm/landingpage/collection/mdoc [Accessed 14 March 2017].

Dobbs, Christopher, n.d. *Noah Webster and the Dream of a Common Language*. [Online] Available at: https://connecticuthistory.org/noah-webster-and-the-dream-of-a-common-language/ [Accessed 20 May 2020].

Doyle, Bill, 2013. *Vermont Joins the Union*. [Online] Available at: https://www.vt-world.com/vermont-joins-the-union.html [Accessed 5 September 2019].

Drexler, Ken, 2020. *Northwest Ordinance: Primary Documents in American History*. [Online] Available at: https://guides.loc.gov/northwest-ordinance [Accessed 18 May 2020].

Duer, William A., 1867. Description of the Inauguration. In *Reminiscences of an Old New Yorker*. New York: W. L. Andrews.

Duffy, Shannon E., 2016. *Loyalists*. [Online] Available at: https://philadelphi-aencyclopedia.org/archive/loyalists/ [Accessed 5 May 2020].

Dunbar, Louise B., Vol X March 1922. A Study of "Monarchical" Tendencies in the United States from 1776 to 1801. *University of Illinois Studies in the Social Sciences*.

Dunlap, William 1832. *A History of the American Theatre*. New York: J. & J. Harper.

Dunn, Peter M., 2000. Dr William Buchan (1729-1805) and His Domestic Medicine. *Archives of Disease in Childhood-Fetal and Neonatal*, Edition 83(1). See also http://fn.bmj.com/content/83/1/F71. Available at: https://fn.bmj.com/content/fetalneonatal/83/1/F71.full.pdf [Accessed 12 May 2020].

E. M. Stratton. *Porte Pencil on Modes of Travel. The New York Coach-Makers Magazine*, August 1869. Available at: https://archive.org/details/newyorkcoachmake11186stra/page/36/mode/2up.

Early Republic, The, n.d. *Comte de Moustier to Comte de Montmorin Tuesday , 9 June 1789*. [Online] Johns Hopkins University Press Available at: https://earlyrepublic.press.jhu.edu/about/index.html. Subscription required for access. Listed as also available in DHFFC Vol. 16, Correspondence.

Editors of Encycolpaedia Britannica, 1998. *William Hill Brown*. [Online] Available at: https://www.britannica.com/biography/William-Hill-Brown [Accessed 20 May 2020].

Elliot, Jonathan 1836. *The debates in the several state conventions on the adoption of the federal Constitution*. Washington: Printed by and for the Editor. Available at: https://archive.org/details/debatesofseveral04unse/page/364/mode/2up.

Ellis, Milton, 1933. The Author of the First American Novel. *American Literature*, pp. 359-68. Available at: https://www.enotes.com/topics/william-hill-brown/critical-essays/criticism [Accessed 12 February 2021].

Ellis, Joseph J. 2004. *His Excellency George Washington*. New York: Knopf.

———.n.d. *The Early Republic*. [Online] Available at: https://www.gilderleh-rman.org/history-now/early-republic [Accessed 18 November 2017]. A copy of the article can be found at http://lraushistory.weebly.com/uploads/2/9/9/9/29999639/the_early_republic_-_joseph_j._ellis.pdf.

Encyclopædia Britannica, 1998. *Lucius Quinctius Cincinnatus*. [Online] Available at: https://www.britannica.com/biography/Lucius-Quinctius-Cincinnatus [Accessed 19 April 2020].

Encyclopedia of World Biography, 2010. *Jedidiah Morse Facts*. [Online] Available at: http://biography.yourdictionary.com/jedidiah-morse#cdCX6Cop2pFg-7cOi.99 [Accessed 20 May 2020]. Entry credited to Encyclopedia of World Biography. Copyright 2010 The Gale Group, Inc. All rights reserved.

Encyclopedia Virginia, 2017. *Primary Resource Advertisement for the Capture of Oney Judge, Philadelphia Gazette (May 24, 1796)*. [Online] Available at: https://www.encyclopediavirginia.org/Advertisement_for_the_Capture_of_Oney_Judge_Philadelphia_Gazette_May_24_1796 [Accessed 15 May 2020].

Episcopal Church, The 2007. *The Book of Common Prayer*. New York: Church Publishing Incorporated. Available at: https://episcopalchurch.org/files/book_of_common_prayer.pdf [accessed 5 May 2020].

Farrand, Max 1911. *The Records of the Federal Convention of 1787*. New Haven, Connecticut, United States of America: Yale University Press.

Fauci, Anthony S. & Morens, David M., 2012. The Perpetual Challenge of Infectious Diseases. *New England Journal of Medicine*, 366(9), Available at: https://www.nejm.org/doi/full/10.1056/NEJMra1108296 [Accessed 14 May 2020].

Federalist Papers, 1788. *Federalist Papers No 68*. [Online] Available at: http://www.historycentral.com/elections/Federalist.html [Accessed 22 April 2020].

Feng, Patrick, n.d. *The Battle of the Wabash: The Forgotten Disaster of the Indian Wars*. [Online] Available at: https://armyhistory.org/the-battle-of-the-wabash-the-forgotten-disaster-of-the-indian-wars/ [Accessed 19 May 2020].

Ferling, John 2014. *Jefferson and Hamilton: The Rivalry that Forged A Nation*. New York: Bloomsbury.

Fields, Joseph E. 1994. *'Worthy Partner': The Papers of Martha Washington*. Westport, CT: Greenwood Press.

Fisher, David R., 1986. *CHURCH, John Barker (1748-1818), of Down Place, Berks*. [Online] The History of Parliment Trust Available at: http://www.historyofparliamentonline.org/volume/1790-1820/member/church-john-barker-1748-1818 [Accessed 11 May 2020].

Fitch, William E. 1905. *Some Neglected History of North Carolina: Being an Account of the Revolution of the Regulators and of the Battle of Alamance, the First Battle of the American Revolution*. New York: Neale Publishing.

Fitzgerald, Oscar P. 1994. *In Search of Joseph Nourse 1754-1841: America's First Civil Servant*. Washington: National Society of the Colonial Dames of America.

Fitzpatrick, John C. 1934. *The Writings of George Washington from the Original Manuscript Sources 1745-1799*. Washington: George Washington Bicentennial Commisison.

Fitzpatrick, John C. 1939. *The Writings of George Washington From the Original Manuscript Sources*. Washington: United States George Washington Bicentennial Commission.

Fleming, Thomas 2007. *The Perils of Peace: America's Struggles for Survival after Yorktown*. Washington, D.C., United States of America: Smithsonian Books.

Ford, Paul L. 1888. *Pamphlets on the Constitution of the United States, published during its discussion by the people, 1787-1788*. Brooklyn, New York, United States of America. Available at: https://archive.org/details/cu31924020874099/page/n387/mode/2up [accessed 18 June 2020].

Ford, Paul L. 1896. *The True George Washington*. Philadelphia, Pennsylvania, United States of America: J. B. Lippincott. Available at: https://archive.org/details/cu31924027041577/page/n211/mode/2up.

Foss, John 1798. *A Journal of the Captivity and Sufferings of John Foss*. Newburyport, Massachusetts, United States of America: Angier March. Available at: https://quod.lib.umich.edu/e/evans/N25429.0001.001/1:3?rgn=div1;view=fulltext [accessed 16 May 2020].

Founders' Constitution, 1888. *Debate in Virginia Ratifying Constitution*. [Online] Available at: http://press-pubs.uchicago.edu/founders/print_documents/a2_1_1s16.html. Source: Elliot, Jonathan, ed. *The Debates in the Several State Conventions on the Adoption of the Federal Constitution as Recommended by the General Convention at Philadelphia in 1787*. 5 vols. 2d ed. 1888. Reprint New York: Burt Franklin, n.d.

———. n.d., Rights, [Online] Available at: http://press-pubs.uchicago.edu/founders/documents/v1ch14s50.html. [Accessed 14 December 2016] The Founder's Constitution, Vol 1, Chap 15, Doc 50. Source: *Papers of James Madison*. Edited by W. T. Hutchinson et al. Chicago and London: University of Chicago Press, 1962--77 (vols. 1--10); Charlottesville: University Press of Virginia, 1977--(vols. 11--).

Founders Online, 1989. *From George Washington to the Society of the Cincinnati, 4 July 1789*. [Online] National Archives Available at: https://founders.archives.gov/documents/Washington/05-03-02-0055 [Accessed 17 April 2020]. [Original source: The Papers of George Washington, Presidential Series, vol. 3, 15 June 1789–5 September 1789, ed. Dorothy Twohig. Charlottesville: University Press of Virginia, 1989, pp. 114–116.].

———.n.d. *Editorial Note: The "Anas"*. [Online] National Archives Available at: https://founders.archives.gov/documents/Jefferson/01-22-02-1033-0001 [Accessed 17 May 2020]. [Original source: The Papers of Thomas Jefferson, vol. 22, 6 August 1791–31 December 1791, ed. Charles T. Cullen. Princeton: Princeton University Press, 1986, pp. 33–38.].

———.n.d. *Search Results for O'Byren.* [Online] Available at: https://founders. archives.gov/index.xqy?q=O%27Bryen&s=1111211111&sa=&r=1&sr= [Accessed 16 May 2020].

———. n.d. *William Jackson to Clement Biddle, 2 May 1790 Editorial Note.* [Online] National Archives Available at: https://founders.archives.gov/ documents/Washington/05-05-02-0253. Editorial Note footnote cites source. Letter, "William Maclay to Benjamin Rush, May 12, 1790," Founders Online, National Archives, Washington, DC, https://founders.archives.gov/ documents/Washington/05-05-02-0253#GEWN-05-05-02-0253-fn-0002.

Frank, Andrew K., 2002. *Alexander McGillivray (ca. 1750-1793).* [Online] Georgia Humanities Available at: https://www.georgiaencyclopedia.org/articles/histo-ry-archaeology/alexander-mcgillivray-ca-1750-1793 [Accessed 19 May 2020].

Franklin, Benjamin, 1751. *Observations Concerning the Increase of Mankind.* [Online] Available at: https://founders.archives.gov/documents/ Franklin/01-04-02-0080 [Accessed 6 May 2020]. See footnote 9 regarding alteration of text. [Original source: The Papers of Benjamin Franklin, vol. 4, July 1, 1750, through June 30, 1753, ed. Leonard W. Labaree. New Haven: Yale University Press, 1961, pp. 225–234.].

———.1806. *The Complete Works of Dr. Benjamin Franklin.* London, England, Great Britain: J. Johnson. Available at: https://archive.org/details/ completeworksin01frangoog/page/n418/mode/2up.

Frost, David B. 2017. *Classified: A History of Secrecy in the United States Government.* Jefferson, North Carilona, United States of America: McFarland & Co.

Furr, Grover, 2007. *Col. Lewis Nicola's Letter to George Washington of May 22, 1782.* [Online] Available at: https://msuweb.montclair.edu/~furrg/gbi/docs/nicola-towashington.html [Accessed 15 November 2016].

Galloway, George B. 1968. *History of the House of Representatives.* New York. Available at: https://archive.org/details/historyofhouseof00gall. Thomas Y. Crowell A revised edition of the book is available at https://archive.org/ details/historyofhouseof00gall.

Gazette of the United States. *NEW-YORK, June 24, 1789: Extract of a letter from Savanna, dated June 11. Gazette of the United States* , 24 June 1789. p. 4. Available at: https://chroniclingamerica.loc.gov/lccn/sn83030483/1789-06-24/ed-1/seq-3/ [Accessed 30 April 2020].

———. *New-York. Proceedings of Congress. Gazette of the United States*, 2 May 1789. p. 4. Available at: https://chroniclingamerica.loc.gov/lccn/ sn83030483/1789-05-02/ed-1/seq-1/.

———. *The President's Household. Gazette of the United States*, 6 May 1789. p. 4.

George Washington University, 2013. *By the United States in Congress Assembled.* [Online] Available at: https://www2.gwu.edu/~ffcp/exhibit/p2/p2_1.html [Accessed 24 April 2020].

———. 2013. *New York as the Seat of Government.* [Online] Available at: https://www2.gwu.edu/~ffcp/exhibit/p2/ [Accessed 24 April 2020].

George Washington's Mount Vernon, n.d. *The American Museum, or, Universal Magazine.* [Online] Available at: https://www.mountvernon.org/preservation/collections-holdings/browse-the-museum-collections/object/ml-207-w [Accessed 20 May 2020]. In February 2021 this web page was not available. A copy was available at http://www.mountvernon.org/preservation/collections-holdings/browse-the-museum-collections/object/ml-207-w/.

———. n.d. *www.mountvernon.org/george-washington/real-estate.* [Online] Available at: https://www.mountvernon.org/george-washington/real-estate [Accessed 23 April 2020].

George Washinton's Mount Vernon & Center for History and New Media, n.d. *The 1790s.* [Online] Available at: http://marthawashington.us/exhibits/show/martha-washington--a-life/the-1790s [Accessed 30 April 2020].

Gilbert, George A. *The Connecticut Loyalists. American Historical Review*, January 1899. Available at: https://archive.org/details/americanhistor_18981899jame/page/272/mode/2up.

Gilder Lehrman Institute of American History, n.d. *History Resources: Loyalists and the British Evacuation of Philadelphia, 1778.* [Online] Available at: https://www.gilderlehrman.org/history-resources/spotlight-primary-source/loyalists-and-british-evacuation-philadelphia-1778 [Accessed 5 May 2020].

Giunta, Mary A. & Hartgrove, J. Dane 1998. *Documents of the Emerging Nation: U.S. Foreign Relations, 1775-1789.* Wilmington, Delaware, United States of America: Scholarly Resources. Available at: https://openlibrary.org/books/OL695534M.

Griswold, Rufus W. 1854. *The Republican Court: Or, American Society in the Days of Washington.* New York: D. Appleton and Company.

Guba, James E. & Chase, Philander D., 2002. Anthrax and the President, 1789. *The Papers of George Washington Newsletter*, (Number 5), pp. 4-6. See also https://washingtonpapers.org/wp-content/uploads/2013/03/5.pdf. Available at: http://gwpapers.virginia.edu/anthrax-and-the-president-1789.

Haggard, Robert F., June 2002. The Nicola Affair: Lewis Nicola, George Washington, and American Military Discontent during the Revolutionary War. *Proceedings of ther American Philosophical Society*, p. 148.

Haines, Michael R. & Steckel, Richard H. 2000. *A Population History of North America*. Cambridge U.K & New York: Cambridge University Press. Available at: https://www.google.com/books/edition/A_Population_History_of_North_America/BPdgiysIVcgC

Hamilton, Alexander, 1784. *From Alexander Hamilton to Gouverneur Morris, 21 February 1784*. [Online] National Archives Available at: https://founders.archives.gov/documents/Hamilton/01-03-02-0331 [Accessed 5 May 2020]. [Original source: The Papers of Alexander Hamilton, vol. 3, 1782–1786, ed. Harold C. Syrett. New York: Columbia University Press, 1962, pp. 512–514.].

———.1784. *Second Letter from Phocion, [April 1784]*. [Online] National Archives Available at: https://founders.archives.gov/documents/Hamilton/01-03-02-0347 [Accessed 4 May 2020].

———.1789. *From Alexander Hamilton to George Washington, [5 May 1789]*. [Online] National Archives Available at: https://founders.archives.gov/documents/Hamilton/01-05-02-0128 [Accessed 29 April 2020]. [Original source: The Papers of Alexander Hamilton, vol. 5, June 1788–November 1789, ed. Harold C. Syrett. New York: Columbia University Press, 1962, pp. 335–337.

———.2001. *Annapolis Convention. Address of the Annapolis Convention, [14 September 1786]*. [Online] Available at: https://founders.archives.gov/documents/Hamilton/01-03-02-0556 [Accessed 21 April 2020].

Hamilton, Alexander & Burke, Aedanus, 1790. *Search Results for Hamilton-Burke Correspondence*. [Online] National Archives Available at: https://founders.archives.gov/search/Correspondent%3A%22Hamilton%2C%20Alexander%22%20Correspondent%3A%22Burke%2C%20%C3%86danus%22 [Accessed 11 May 2020].

Harrison, Lowell H. & Klotter, James C. 1997. *A New History of Kentucky*. Lexington, Kentucky, United States of America: University Press of Kentucky.

Harvard University Library Archives, n.d. *Papers of Jared Sparks, 1820-1861, 1866*. [Online] Harvard Library Available at: https://hollisarchives.lib.harvard.edu/repositories/4/resources/4151 [Accessed 23 April 2020].

Henderson, Archibald 1923. *Washington's Southern Tour, 1791*. Boston, Massachusetts, United States of America: Houghton Mifflin. Available at: https://archive.org/details/washingtonssouth00hend/page/62/mode/2up.

Henry, Patrick, 2012. *Speech of Partrick Henry (June 5, 1788)*. [Online] Available at: http://www.let.rug.nl/usa/documents/1786-1800/the-anti-federalist-papers/speech-of-patrick-henry-(june-5-1788).php [Accessed 22 April 2020].

Herald of Freedom and the Federal Advertiser. *The Herald of Freedom and the Federal Advertiser*, 30 January 1789. pp. 1-4. [Accessed 8 September 2022]. Viewed via microfilm, Newspaper & Current Periodical Reading Room, Library of Congress.

Herbert, Leila. *"The First American: His Homes and His Households: Part III: In Philadelphia and Germantown. Harper's Magazine*, Novemeber 1899.

Hildreth, Samuel P. 1848. *Pioneer History*. Cincinatti, Ohio, United States of America: H.W. Derby & Co. Available at: https://archive.org/details/pioneerhistorybe00hild/page/264/mode/2up.

Hillhouse, William, 1789. *A dissertation By William Hillhouse, Jr., New Haven, Connecticut, January 12, 1789*. [Online] Available at: https://ota.bodleian.ox.ac.uk/repository/xmlui/handle/20.500.12024/N16983 [Accessed 18 May 2020].

Hirschfeld, Fritz 1997. *George Washington and Slavery: A Documentary Portrayal*. Columbia, Missouri, United States of America: University of Missouri Press. Available at: https://books.google.com/books?id=4YX3czE0SGY-C&pg=PA213&lpg=PA213&dq=Humphries+%22The+Only+Unavoidable+Subject+of+Regret%22&source=bl&ots=BPA2LSivJY&sig=AC-fU3U3il7cbTxgxRwTgn6lb9MgN5AjNow&hl=en&sa=X&ved=2ahUKEwjRooDs7bbpAhXAg3IEHVCRBPEQ6AEwBHoECAkQAQ#v=on.

Hirschfield, Robert S. 1982. *The Power of the Presidency: Concepts and Controversy*. Florence, Kentucky, United States of America: Taylor & Francis Group.

Historic Germantown, 2013. *Oney Judge Staines: Washington's Runaway Slave*. [Online] Available at: https://freedomsbackyard.wordpress.com/2013/03/28/oney-judge-staines-washingtons-runaway-slave [Accessed 14 May 2020].

Historical Society of Pennsylvania, 1858. In *Memoirs of the Historical Society of Pennsylvania*.

——.2009. *The 'Barbary Wars' and Their Philadelphia Connections*. [Online] Available at: https://hsp.org/blogs/hidden-histories/the-barbary-wars-and-their-philadelphia-connections [Accessed 16 May 2020].

Historical Society of the New York Courts, n.d. *Crown v. John Peter Zenger*. [Online] Available at: https://history.nycourts.gov/case/crown-v-zenger/ [Accessed 24 April 2020].

History of American Women, n.d. *Sarah Wentworth Morton*. [Online] Available at: www.womenhistoryblog.com/2012/08/sarah-wentworth-morton.html [Accessed 2017 November 2017]. Website flagged as containing "Trojan" malware on 20 May 2020. A safer, older version of the page is available at https://web.archive.org/web/20200209091821/www.womenhistoryblog.com/2012/08/sarah-wentworth-morton.html.

Hogeland, William, 2011. *Thomas Paine's Revolutionary Reckoning*. [Online] Available at: https://www.historynet.com/thomas-paines-revolutionary-reckoning.htm [Accessed 13 May 2020]. Originally published in the June 2011 issue of American History.

Howard, James L. 1921. *The Origin and Fortunes of Troop B. 1788, Governor's Independent Troop of Horse Guards, 1911, Troup Be Cavalry, Connecticut National Guard 1917*. Hartford: Case, Lockwood & Brainard.

Humphreys, David 1788. *Manuscript Biography of George Washington*. Philadelphia, Pennsylvania, United States of America: American Manuscript Collection, Rosenbach Museum and Library. Available at: https://rosenbach.pastperfectonline.com/archive/7E4899C1-4AD8-4DF8-8711-722181101130. Catalog Number AMs 1079/6. Manuscript biography of George Washington, [1788] Portion of a draft of a biography of Washington. Also includes portions of several speeches by Washington. With additions and corrections in Washington's hand.

————. 1804. *The Miscellaneous Works of David Humphreys*. New York: T and J Swords.

————. 2006. *Life of General Washington*. Edited by Rosemarie Zagarri. Athens: University of Georgia Press.

Humphreys, Frank L. 1917. *Life and Times of David Humphreys*. New York: G. P. Putnam's Sons. Available at: https://archive.org/details/lifeandtimesdav01humpgoog/page/n280/mode/2up [accessed 21 February 2021].

Hunt, Gaillard 1901. *Calendar of Applications and Recommendations for Office during the Presidency of George Washington*. Washington: United States Government Printing Office.

————. 1922. *Journals of the Continental Congress 1774-1789*. Washington, D.C., United States of America : Library of Congress. Available at: https://memory.loc.gov/cgi-bin/ampage?collId=lljc&fileName=024/lljc024.db&recNum=298&itemLink=r%3Fammem%2Fhlaw%3A%40field%28DOCID%2B%40lit%28jc024126%29%29%230240299&linkText=1.

Hutson, James, 2003. *Nathan Hale Revisited : A Tory's Account of the Arrest of the First American Spy*. [Online] Available at: https://www.loc.gov/loc/lcib/0307-8/hale.html [Accessed 5 May 2020].

Innes, Harry, 1788. *To George Washington from Harry Innes, 18 December 1788*. [Online] National Archives Available at: https://founders.archives.gov/documents/Washington/05-01-02-0140 [Accessed 18 May 2020]. [Original source: The Papers of George Washington, Presidential Series, vol. 1, 24 September 1788–31 March 1789, ed. Dorothy Twohig. Charlottesville: University Press of Virginia, 1987, pp. 187–190.].

Irving, Washington 1876. *The Life and Times of Washington*. New York: G.P. Putnam.

Jackson, Donald & Twohig, Dorothy 1979. *The Diaries of George Washington, vol. 6, 1 January 1790–13 December 1799*. Charlottesville, Virginia, United States of

America: University Press of Virginia. Available at: https://founders.archives.gov/documents/Washington/01-06-02-0001-0001-0008.

———. 1979. *The Diaries of George Washington. Vol. 5. January-February 1789.* Charlottesville: University Press of Virginia. Available at: http://founders.archives.gov/documents/Washington/01-05-02-0004-0013 [accessed 1 June 2016].

Jefferson, Thomas, 1786. *From Thomas Jefferson to James Monroe, 11 August 1786.* [Online] National Archives Available at: https://founders.archives.gov/documents/Jefferson/01-10-02-0150 [Accessed 16 May 2020]. [Original source: The Papers of Thomas Jefferson, vol. 10, 22 June–31 December 1786, ed. Julian P. Boyd. Princeton: Princeton University Press, 1954, pp. 223–225.].

———. 1787. *From Thomas Jefferson to James Madison, December 20, 1787.* [Online] National Archives Available at: https://founders.archives.gov/documents/Jefferson/01-12-02-0454 [Accessed 12 May 2020]. [Original source: The Papers of Thomas Jefferson, vol. 12, 7 August 1787–31 March 1788, ed. Julian P. Boyd. Princeton: Princeton University Press, 1955, pp. 438–443.].

———. 1789. *Thomas Jefferson to George Washington, May 10, 1789.* [Online] Available at: https://memory.loc.gov/service/mss/mtj//mtj1/011/011_0318_0321.pdf [Accessed 13 May 2020]. from The Works of Thomas Jefferson in Twelve Volumes. Federal Edition. Collected and Edited by Paul Leicester Ford.

———. 1790. *From Thomas Jefferson to William Short, 27 May 1790.* [Online] National Archives Available at: https://founders.archives.gov/documents/Jefferson/01-16-02-0261 [Accessed 12 May 2020]. [Original source: The Papers of Thomas Jefferson, vol. 16, 30 November 1789–4 July 1790, ed. Julian P. Boyd. Princeton: Princeton University Press, 1961, pp. 443–445.].

———. 1790. *IV. Report on American Captives in Algiers, 28 December 1790.* [Online] National Archives Available at: https://founders.archives.gov/documents/Jefferson/01-18-02-0139-0005 [Accessed 16 May 2020].

———. 1792. *From Thomas Jefferson to Thomas Mann Randolph, Jr., 16 March 1792.* [Online] National Archives Available at: https://founders.archives.gov/documents/Jefferson/01-23-02-0247 [Accessed 26 April 2020]. [Original source: The Papers of Thomas Jefferson, vol. 23, 1 January–31 May 1792, ed. Charles T. Cullen. Princeton: Princeton University Press, 1990, p. 287.].

Jensen, Merrill 1976. *Constitutional documents and records, 1776-1787.* Madison: The State Historical Society of Wisconsin. Available at: http://digicoll.library.wisc.edu/cgi-bin/History/History-idx?type=article&did=History.DHRCv1.i0012&id=History.DHRCv1&isize=M. URL to cite for this work: http://digital.library.wisc.edu/1711.dl/History.DHRCv1.

Johnson, Matthew, n.d. *Timeline of Events Relating to the End of Slavery*. [Online] Massachusetts Historical Society Available at: http://www.masshist.org/teaching-history/loc-slavery/essay.php?entry_id=504 [Accessed 6 May 2020].

Johnson, Richard, 2007. *Lord Dunmore's Ethiopian Regiment*. [Online] Available at: https://www.blackpast.org/african-american-history/lord-dunmore-s-ethiopian-regiment/ [Accessed 6 May 2020].

Johnson, Tim. *Vermont's 1777 Slavery Ban Had a Complicated Reality. Burlington Free Press*, 4 April 2014. p. A3. Available at: https://www.usatoday.com/story/news/nation/2014/04/02/vermont-slavery-ban/7200493/. URL is for version of the article published by USA Today.

Joint Committee on Printing of the House and Senate 1897. *A Compilation of the Messages and Papers of the Presidents*. New York, New York, United States of America: Bureau of National Literature.

Jonassen, Frederick B., March 2012. Kiss the Book . . . You're President . . . : "So Help Me God" and Kissing the Book in the Presidential Oath of Office. *The William and Mary Bill of Rights Journal*, pp. 854-951. Available at: https://scholarship.law.wm.edu/cgi/viewcontent.cgi?article=1614&context=wmborj.

Jones-Wilson, Faustine et al. 1996. *Encyclopedia of African-American Education*. Westport, Connecticut, United States of America: Greenwood Press.

Joyce, John S.G. 1919. *Story of Philadephia*. Philadelphia, Pennsylvania, United States of America: Rex Print House.

Kahler, Gerald E. "Gentlemen of the family : General George Washington's aides-de-camp and military secretaries". master's thesis, University of Richmond, 1997, 112–13.

Kaminski, John P. 2007. *Abigail Adams, An American Heroine*. Madison, Wisconsin, United States of America: UW-Madison Libraries.

Kennedy, Frances H. 2014. *The American Revolution: A Historical Guidebook*. New York: Oxford University Press.

Kent, William 1898. *Memoirs and letters of James Kent, LL.D.* Boston, Little, Brown, and Company. Available at: https://archive.org/details/cu31924018816979/page/n333/mode/2up.

Kleber, John E. 1997. *The Kentucky Encyclopedia*. Lexington, Kentucky, United States of America: University Press of Kentucky.

Klein, Martin A. 2014. *The A to Z of Slavery and Abolition*. Lanham: Rowman & Littlefield.

Knox, Henry, 1789. *To George Washington from Henry Knox, 5 March 1789*. [Online] Available at: https://founders.archives.gov/documents/Washington/05-01-02-0276 [Accessed 23 April 2020]. [Original source: The Papers of George Washington, Presidential Series, vol. 1, 24 September

1788–31 March 1789, ed. Dorothy Twohig. Charlottesville: University Press of Virginia, 1987, pp. 365–366.].

————. 1791. *To George Washington From Henry Knox, 22 January 1791.* [Online] Nationa Archives Available at: https://founders.archives.gov/documents/Washington/05-07-02-0146 [Accessed 19 May 2020]. [Original source: The Papers of George Washington, Presidential Series, vol. 7, 1 December 1790–21 March 1791, ed. Jack D. Warren, Jr. Charlottesville: University Press of Virginia, 1998, pp. 262–271.].

————.2002. *To George Washington from Henry Knox, 23 October 1786.* [Online] Available at: https://founders.archives.gov/documents/Washington/04-04-02-0274 [Accessed 21 April 2020]. [Original source: The Papers of George Washington, Confederation Series, vol. 4, 2 April 1786–31 January 1787, ed. W. W. Abbot. Charlottesville: University Press of Virginia, 1995, pp. 299–302.].

Kohn, Richard H. 1975. *Eagle and Sword: The Federalists and the Creation of the Military Establishment in America, 1783-1802.* [Online] Available at https://archive.org/details/eagleswordfed00kohn/page/n9/mode/2up New York: The Free Press.

Kopper, Philip. *Capitol Discovery. Smithsonian Magazine*, June 2003.

Kotowski, Peter, n.d. *Whiskey Rebellion.* [Online] Available at: https://www.mountvernon.org/library/digitalhistory/digital-encyclopedia/article/whiskey-rebellion/ [Accessed 21 May 2020].

Lafayette College, n.d. *The Prisoner of Olmütz.* [Online] Lafayette College Available at: https://sites.lafayette.edu/olmutz/ [Accessed 13 May 2020].

Langdon, John, 1789. *To George Washington from John Langdon, 6 April 1789.* [Online] National Archives Available at: https://founders.archives.gov/documents/Washington/05-02-02-0028 [Accessed 24 April 2020]. [Original source: The Papers of George Washington, Presidential Series, vol. 2, 1 April 1789–15 June 1789, ed. Dorothy Twohig. Charlottesville: University Press of Virginia, 1987, p. 29.].

Lang, Joel, n.d. *Jeremiah Wadsworth, "foremost in every enterprise".* [Online] Available at: https://connecticuthistory.org/jeremiah-wadsworth/ [Accessed 21 January 2017].

Lawler, Jr., Edward, 2010. *The President's House in Philadelphia.* [Online] Available at: http://www.ushistory.org/presidentshouse/history/briefhistory.php [Accessed 17 June 2019].

Lear, Tobias, 1787. *Lear, Tobias to Henry Knox.* [Online] Available at: https://www.gilderlehrman.org/collection/glc0243703536 [Accessed 21 April 2020].

———. 1789. *From George Washington to John Adams, 10 May 1789*. [Online] National Archives Available at: https://founders.archives.gov/documents/Washington/05-02-02-0182 [Accessed 30 April 2020]. See footnote to GW's letter on website. GW's letter dated 10 May; Lear's to'GAW's dated 3 May. [Original source: The Papers of George Washington, Presidential Series, vol. 2, 1 April 1789–15 June 1789, ed. D. Twohig. Univ Press of Va 1987, pp 245-250.].

———. 1791. *From George Washington to Tobias Lear, 21 April 1791*. [Online] National Archives Available at: https://founders.archives.gov/documents/Washington/05-08-02-0099 [Accessed 15 May 2020]. [Original source: The Papers of George Washington, Presidential Series, vol. 8, 22 March 1791–22 September 1791, ed. Mark A. Mastromarino. Charlottesville: University Press of Virginia, 1999, pp. 124–125.].

———.1791. *To George Washington from Tobias Lear, 5 April 1791*. [Online] National Archives Available at: https://founders.archives.gov/documents/Washington/05-08-02-0050 [Accessed 15 May 2020]. [Original source: The Papers of George Washington, Presidential Series, vol. 8, 22 March 1791–22 September 1791, ed. Mark A. Mastromarino. Charlottesville: University Press of Virginia, 1999, pp. 67–68.].

———. 1799. *Tobias Lear's Narrative Acccounts of the Death of George Washington*. [Online] Available at: https://founders.archives.gov/ancestor/GEWN-06-04-02-0406 [Accessed 21 June 2019].

———. 1905. *Observations on the River Potomack, the Country Adjacent, and the City of Washington*. Washington: Historical Society of Washington, D.C. Available at: https://archive.org/details/jstor-40066903/page/n19/mode/2up/. Reprint of small book published anonymously but later attributed to TL, New-York, 1793, Samuael Loudon and Son.

———.Vol. 32, No. 4 (1908). President Washington in New York, 1789. *The Pennsylvania Magazine of History and Biography*, pp. 498-500. Available at: https://archive.org/details/pennsylvaniamaga32hist/page/n1029/mode/2up.

Leepson, Marc 2011. *Lafayette: Lessons in Leadership for the Idealist General*. New York: St. Martin's Press.

Leiner, Frederick C. *Yes, Privateers Mattered. Naval History Magazine*, March 2014.

Levett, Karl, 2009. *Reviews -- The Contrast*. [Online] Available at: http://www.metropolitanplayhouse.org/contrastreview [Accessed 20 May 2020].

Lewis, Catherine H. 1988. *Horry County, South Carolina, 1730-1993*. Columbia, South Carolina, United States of America: University of South Carolina Press. Available at: https://books.google.com/books?id=-dUfVeiy4yIC&q=cincinatti&f=false#v=snippet&q=cincinatti&f=false [accessed 15 May 2020].

Library of Congress, 2020. *Today In History -- April 19*. [Online] Available at: https://www.loc.gov/item/today-in-history/april-19 [Accessed 16 April 2020].

———. 2021. Pre.1.2 Preamble: Historical Background. [Online] Available at: https://constitution.congress.gov/browse/essay/pre-1-2/ALDE_00001234/ [Accessed 22 August 2021].

———. n.d. *History of the Diary Manuscripts*. [Online] Library of Congress Available at: https://www.loc.gov/collections/george-washington-papers/articles-and-essays/introduction-to-the-diaries-of-george-washington/history-of-the-diary-manuscripts [Accessed 23 April 2020].

———. n.d. *Thomas Jefferson: A Revolutionary World*. [Online] Available at: https://www.loc.gov/exhibits/jefferson/jeffworld.html [Accessed 13 May 2020].

Linklater, Andro 2009. *An Artist in Treason: The Extraordinary Double Life of General James Wilkinson*. New York: Walker Publishing Company.

Lossing, Benson L. 1860. *The Diary of George Washington, from 1789 to 1791*. Edited by Benson L. Lossing. New York, New York, United States of America: Charles B. Richardson & Co. Available at: https://archive.org/details/diaryofgeorgewas01wash/page/28/mode/2up.

Lossing, Benson J. 1870. *The Home of Washington*. Hartford, Connecticut, United States of America: A. S. Hale & Co. There were at least two 1870 editions of this work, from A. S. Hale & Co and From Virtue & Yorston of New York. Other editions appeared in later years, some under the title Mount Vernon: The Home of Washington.

———. 1977. *George Washington's Mount Vernon*. New York: Fairfax Press. This 1977 edition is a facsimile of the orignal 1870 edition.

Lovett, Robert W., 1952. The Beverly Cotton Manufactory: Or Some New Light on an Early Cotton Mill. *Bulletin of the Business Historical Society*, 26(4), pp. 218-42. Available at: https://www.jstor.org/stable/i356511 [Accessed 14 May 2020].

Lyons, Maura 2005. *William Dunlap and the Construction of an American Art History*. Boston: University of Massachusetts Press.

Maass, John R. 2013. *Defending a New Nation*. Washington: Center of Military History.

MacDonald, Kim, 2003. *Silk in Connecticut*. [Online] Available at: https://web.archive.org/web/20180422184953/https://www.smith.edu/hsc/silk/papers/macdonald.html. [Accessed 22 February 2017]. Website re Silk project no longer available at original page, https://www.smith.edu/hsc/silk/circa1840.html.

Maclay, Edgar S. 1890. *Journal of William Maclay*. New York, New York, United States of America: D. Appleton and Co. Available at: http://

memory.loc.gov/cgi-bin/ampage?collId=llmj&fileName=001/llmj001.
db&recNum=0&itemLink=r?ammem/hlaw:@field(DOCID+@
lit(mj0014))%230010008&linkText=1.

MacLeod, Jessie, n.d. *William (Billy) Lee.* [Online] Available at: http://www.
mountvernon.org/digital-encyclopedia/article/william-billy-lee/#1 [Accessed
15 March 2017].

Madison, James, 1784. *Bill Authorizing an Amendment in the Articles of
Confederation, [21 June] 1784.* [Online] National Archives Available at:
https://founders.archives.gov/documents/Madison/01-08-02-0044 [Accessed
3 May 2020]. [Original source: The Papers of James Madison, vol. 8, 10 March
1784–28 March 1786, ed. Robert A. Rutland and William M. E. Rachal.
Chicago: The University of Chicago Press, 1973, pp. 83–85.].

———.1787. *Debates in the Federal Convention of 1787.* [Online] Teaching
American History Available at: https://teachingamericanhistory.org/resourc-
es/convention/debates/preface/ [Accessed 23 April 2020]. See entry for 1 June
for Edmund Randolph on monarchy.

———.1787. *Madison Debates August 22, 1787.* [Online] Lillian Goldman Law
Library Yale Law School Available at: https://avalon.law.yale.edu/18th_centu-
ry/debates_822.asp [Accessed 22 April 2020].

———. 1787. *Madison Debates, June 29, 1787.* [Online] Available at: https://ava-
lon.law.yale.edu/18th_century/debates_629.asp [Accessed 16 May 2020].

———. 1787. *Madison Debates, September 17, 1797.* [Online] Available at: https://
avalon.law.yale.edu/18th_century/debates_917.asp [Accessed 16 April
2020]. Source: *The Debates in the Federal Convention of 1787, which framed
the Constitution of the United States of America, reported by James Madison, a
delegate from the state of Virginia.* Ed. by Gaillard Hund and James Brown Scott
Oxford Univ Press, 1920.

———. 1789. *From James Madison to Edmund Randolph, 24 June 1789.* [Online]
National Archives Available at: https://founders.archives.gov/documents/
Madison/01-12-02-0159 [Accessed 14 February 2017]. [Original source: The
Papers of James Madison, vol. 12, 2 March 1789–20 January 1790 and supple-
ment 24 October 1775–24 January 1789, ed. Charles F. Hobson and Robert
A. Rutland. Charlottesville: University Press of Virginia, 1979, p. 258.].

———. 1789. *Import Duties, [28 April] 1789.* [Online] National Archives
Available at: https://founders.archives.gov/documents/Madison/01-12-
02-0076#JSMN-01-12-02-0076-fn-0001 [Accessed 2 May 2020]. [Original
source: The Papers of James Madison, vol. 12, 2 March 1789–20 January 1790
and supplement 24 October 1775–24 January 1789, ed. Charles F. Hobson
and Robert A. Rutland. Charlottesville: University Press of Virginia, 1979, pp.
114–119.].

———. 1789. *James Madison, Memorandum on an African Colony for Freed Slaves.* [Online] Available at: http://press-pubs.uchicago.edu/founders/documents/v1ch15s43.html [Accessed 6 May 2020]. The Founders' Constitution, Volume 1, Chapter 15, Document 43. Source: *The Papers of James Madison.* Edited by William T. Hutchinson et al. Chicago and London: University of Chicago Press, 1962–77 (vols. 1–10); Charlottesville: University Press of Virginia, 1977–(vols. 11–).

———. 1789. *Notes for Speech in Congress (June 8, 1789).* [Online] Constitutional Sources Project Available at: https://www.consource.org/document/notes-for-speech-in-congress-1789-6-8/ [Accessed 8 May 2020].

———. 1789. *To Thomas Jefferson from James Madison, June 30, 1789.* [Online] National Archives Available at: http://founders.archives.gov/documents/Jefferson/01-15-02-0221 [Accessed 30 April 2020]. [Original source: The Papers of Thomas Jefferson, vol. 15, 27 March 1789–30 November 1789, ed. Julian P. Boyd. Princeton: Princeton University Press, 1958, pp. 224–229.].

———. 1790. *From James Madison to Edmund Randolph, 19 May 1790.* [Online] Available at: https://founders.archives.gov/documents/Madison/01-13-02-0149 [Accessed 12 May 2020]. [Original source: The Papers of James Madison, vol. 13, 20 January 1790–31 March 1791, ed. Charles F. Hobson and Robert A. Rutland. Charlottesville: University Press of Virginia, 1981, p. 222.].

———. 1790. *Slave Trade Petitions, [23 March] 1790.* [Online] National Archives Available at: https://founders.archives.gov/documents/Madison/01-13-02-0084 [Accessed 6 May 2020]. [Original source: The Papers of James Madison, vol. 13, 20 January 1790–31 March 1791, ed. Charles F. Hobson and Robert A. Rutland. Charlottesville: University Press of Virginia, 1981, pp. 116–118.].

———. 1810. *Annual Message to Congress, 5 December 1810.* [Online] National Archives Available at: https://founders.archives.gov/documents/Madison/03-03-02-0059 [Accessed 6 May 2020]. [Original source: The Papers of James Madison, Presidential Series, vol. 3, 3 November 1810–4 November 1811, ed. J. C. A. Stagg, Jeanne Kerr Cross, and Susan Holbrook Perdue. Charlottesville: University Press of Virginia, 1996, pp. 49–56.].

———. 1831. *James Madison to Nicholas P. Trist, December, 1831.* [Online] Available at: https://www.loc.gov/resource/mjm.23_0903_0911/ [Accessed 3 May 2020].

———. 1966 [1890]. *Notes of Debates in the Federal Convention of 1787.* New York: W. W. Norton.

Magazine of American History, The. *The Historic Temple at New Windsor, 1783. The Magazine of American History,* October 1890. p. 494. Available at: https://

archive.org/stream/magazineofamericv24stev#page/282/mode/2up [Accessed 17 April 2020].

Maier, Pauline 2011. *Ratification: The People Debate the Constitution, 1787-1788.* New York: Simon & Schuster.

Maillard, Mary 2014. *A Map of Time and Blood.* Skinner Family Papers. Available at: http://skinnerfamilypapers.com/?page_id=451.

Maine Historical Society, 2019. *The Missouri Compromise: A Moral Dilemma.* [Online] Available at: http://bicentennial.mainememory.net/page/4618/display.html [Accessed 5 September 2019].

Marshall, Thomas, 1789. *To George Washington from Thomas Marshall, 12 February 1789.* [Online] National Archives Available at: https://founders.archives.gov/documents/Washington/05-01-02-0217 [Accessed 18 May 2020]. [Original source: The Papers of George Washington, Presidential Series, vol. 1, 24 September 1788–31 March 1789, ed. Dorothy Twohig. Charlottesville: University Press of Virginia, 1987, pp. 291–298.].

Martin, Joseph P. 2001. *A Narrative of a Revolutionary Soldier.* New York: Signet Classics.

Marx, M.D., R. *A Medical Profile of George Washington. American Heritage*, August 1955.

Maryland Journal, 1789. Maryland Journal, January 20, 1789. *Maryland Journal.*

Maryland State Archives, 2007. *The Mt. Vernon Compact & the Annapolis Convention: Regional Cooperation: March 1785.* [Online] Available at: http://msa.maryland.gov/msa/mdstatehouse/html/compact_convention.html [Accessed 21 April 2020].

Mason, George 1970. *The Papers of George Mason, 1725-1792.* Edited by Robert A. Rutland. Chapel Hill, North Carolina, United States of America: University of North Carolina Press. Available at: https://archive.org/details/papersofgeorgema00maso/page/172/mode/2up.

———. 2015. *George Mason Memorial.* [Online] Available at: https://www.nps.gov/nama/planyourvisit/george-mason-memorial.htm [Accessed 6 May 2020].

Masonic Geneology, n.d. *SAMUEL DUNN 1747-1815.* [Online] Available at: http://masonicgenealogy.com/MediaWiki/index.php?title=GMDunn [Accessed 21 May 2020].

———. n.d. *Objections to the Constitution.* [Online] Available at: https://teachingamericanhistory.org/library/document/objections-to-the-constitution/ [Accessed 22 April 2020].

Massey, Gregory D., 2016. *Izard, Ralph.* [Online] University of South Carolina, Institute for Southern Studies Available at: http://www.scencyclopedia.org/sce/entries/izard-ralph/ [Accessed 11 May 2020].

McCullough, David 2001. *John Adams.* New York: Simon & Schuster Paperbacks.

McCusker, John J. 1992. *How Much is that In Real Money? A Historical Price Index.* Worcester: American Antiquarian Society. [Online] Available at: https://archive.org/details/howmuchisthatinr0101unse/page/n3/mode/2up

McDavid, Raven I., 1998. *Noah Webster: American lexicographer.* [Online] Available at: https://www.britannica.com/biography/Noah-Webster-American-lexicographer [Accessed 20 May 2020].

McGaughy, J. Kent 2004. *Richard Henry Lee of Virginia: A Portrait of an American Revolutionary.* Lanham, MD: Rowman & Littlefield.

———.2016. *Richard Henry Lee (1732-1794).* [Online] Available at: https://www.encyclopediavirginia.org/Lee_Richard_Henry_1732-1794#start_entry [Accessed 16 April 2020].

McHenry, James, 1789. *To George Washington from James McHenry, 29 March 1789.* [Online] National Archives Available at: https://founders.archives.gov/documents/Washington/05-01-02-0357 [Accessed 25 April 2020]. [Original source: The Papers of George Washington, Presidential Series, vol. 1, 24 September 1788–31 March 1789, ed. Dorothy Twohig. Charlottesville: University Press of Virginia, 1987, pp. 461–462.].

McMaster, John B. & Stone, Frederick D. 1888. *Pennsylvania and the Federal Constitution, 1787-1788.* Lancaster, Pennsylvania, United States of America: The Historical Society of Pennsylvania. Available at: https://archive.org/details/pennsylvaniafede00hist/page/456/mode/2up [accessed 8 May 2020].

McPhee, Peter 2002. *The French Revolution 1788-1799.* New York: Oxford University Press.

Medhurst, Martin J., 1982. From Duché to Provoost: The Birth of Inaugural Prayer. *Journal of Church and State,* 24(3), pp. 573-88. The citation page shows article dated as Autumn 1982 and 01 October 1982. Available at: https://doi.org/10.1093/jcs/24.3.573.

Meranze, Michael 2012. *Laboratories of Virtue: Punishment, Revolution and Authority in Philadelphia, 1760-1835.* Chapel Hill, North Carolina, United States of America: University of North Carolina Press.

Metropolitan Museum of Art, n.d. *The Massachusetts Magazine, or, Monthly Museum of Knowledge and Rational Entertainment.* [Online] Available at: https://www.metmuseum.org/art/collection/search/591868 [Accessed 20 May 2020].

Morgan, William J. 1972. *Naval Documents of the American Revolution.* Washington, D.C., United States of America: Naval History Division, Department of the Navy. Available at: https://www.history.navy.mil/research/

publications/publications-by-subject/naval-documents-of-the-american-revo-lution.html.

Morris, Gouverneur, 1792. *To George Washington from Gouverneur Morris, 6 April 1792*. [Online] Available at: https://founders.archives.gov/documents/Washington/05-10-02-0130 [Accessed 13 May 2020].

———. 1888. *The Diary and Letters of Gouverneur Morris*. Edited by Ann Cary Morris. New York, New York, United States of America: Charles Scribner's Sons. Available at: https://archive.org/details/diarylettersofgo02morr/page/480/mode/2up [accessed 9 February 2021].

Morse, Jedidiah 1792. *The American Geography*. London: John Stockdale, Piccadilly. Available at: https://ia802707.us.archive.org/20/items/americangeograph00mors/americangeograph00mors.pdf.

Moss, Richard J. 1995. *The Life of Jedidiah Morse: A Station of Peculiar Exposure*. Knoxville, Tennessee, United States of America: University of Tennessee Press. Available at: https://trace.tennessee.edu/cgi/viewcontent.cgi?article=1002&context=utk_early-american [accessed 21 May 2020].

Mount Vernon Ladies' Association, n.d. *10 Facts About Washington and Slaves*. [Online] Available at: https://www.mountvernon.org/george-washington/slavery/ten-facts-about-washington-slavery/ [Accessed 21 June 2019].

———. n.d. *George Washington and Slavery: Key Events*. [Online] Available at: http://www.mountvernon.org/george-washington/slavery/timeline-of-george-washington-and-slavery [Accessed 15 May 2020].

———. n.d. *Martha Washington as a Slaveowner*. [Online] Available at: https://www.mountvernon.org/george-washington/slavery/martha-washington-as-a-slaveowner/ [Accessed 21 June 2019].

———. n.d. *Slavery*. [Online] Available at: https://www.mountvernon.org/george-washington/slavery/ [Accessed 6 May 2020].

———. n.d. *The Material Culture of the Presidency*. [Online] Available at: https://www.mountvernon.org/preservation/collections-holdings/the-material-culture-of-the-presidency/#- [Accessed 24 April 2020].

———. n.d. *Washington's Southern Tour: An Interview with Walter Bingham*. [Online] Available at: https://www.mountvernon.org/george-washington/the-first-president/george-washingtons-1791-southern-tour/ [Accessed 15 May 2020].

———. n.d. *President Washington's Inauguration in New York City*. [Online] Available at: https://www.mountvernon.org/george-washington/the-first-president/inauguration/new-york [Accessed 29 April 2020].

Murray, Judith S., 1790. *On the Equality of the Sexes*. [Online] Digital Library, University of Pennsylvania Available at: http://digital.library.upenn.edu/women/murray/equality/equality.html [Accessed 20 May 2020].

Murray, Judith S. & Smith, Bonnie H. 1998. *From Gloucester to Philadelphia in 1790.* 1st ed. Cambridge, Massachusetts: HurdSmith Communications. Available at: https://archive.org/details/fromgloucesterto0000judi/mode/2up [accessed 7 February 2023].

Myrsiades, Linda S. 2012. *Law and Medicine in Revolutionary America: Dissecting the Rush v. Cobbett Trial, 1799.* Lanham, Maryland, United States of America: Rowman & Littlefield. Available at: https://www.google.com/books/edition/Law_and_Medicine_in_Revolutionary_Americ/nVwGxw8a6TYC.

Napier, John L., 2016. *Burke, Aedanus.* [Online] University of South Carolina, Institute for Southern Studies Available at: http://www.scencyclopedia.org/sce/entries/burke-aedanus/ [Accessed 11 May 2020].

National Archives, 1789. *The Bill of Rights: A Transcription.* [Online] Available at: https://www.archives.gov/founding-docs/bill-of-rights-transcript [Accessed 21 May 2020].

———. 1996. *Washington's Inaugural Address of 1789.* [Online] Available at: https://www.archives.gov/exhibits/american_originals/inaugtxt.html [Accessed 29 April 2020].

———.2018. *The Declaration of Independence: A History.* [Online] Available at: https://www.archives.gov/founding-docs/declaration-history [Accessed 2020 April 2020].

———. 2019. *Bill of Rights.* [Online] Available at: https://www.archives.gov/legis-lative/features/bor [Accessed 8 May 2020].

———. 2019. *What is the Electoral College.* [Online] Available at: www.archives.gov/federal-register/electoral-college/about.html [Accessed 23 April 2020].

National Humanities Center, n.d. *On the Death of Benjamin Franklin.* [Online] Available at: http://americainclass.org/sources/makingrevolution/constitu-tion/text7/deathoffranklin.pdf [Accessed 6 May 2020].

National Park Service, 2015. *George Washington Inaugural Bible.* [Online] Available at: https://www.nps.gov/feha/learn/historyculture/george-washington-inau-gural-bible.htm [Accessed 29 April 2020].

———. n.d. *Nathanael Greene (1742-1786).* [Online] Available at: https://www.nps.gov/people/nathanael-greene.htm [Accessed 19 April 2021].

———.n.d. *National Register of Historic Places -- Nomination Form General Rufus Putnam House.* [Online] Available at: https://npgallery.nps.gov/GetAsset?assetID=cc34111c-0bab-44ca-bfbb-479cfcad8f46 [Accessed 18 May 2020].

National Postal Museum, 2008. *Out of the Mail.* [Online] Available at: https://postalmuseum.si.edu/exhibition/out-of-the-mails-the-franking-privilege/george-washington-as-a-private-citizen [Accessed 27 Febraru 2021].

Naval History and Heritage Command, 2014. *Frigates,Brigs, Sloops, Schooners, and the Early Continental Navy's Struggle for Success.* [Online] Available at: https://www.navalhistory.org/2014/12/13/frigates-brigs-sloops-schooners-and-the-early-continental-navys-struggle-for-success [Accessed 17 June 2019].

Nelson, Paul D. 1985. *Anthony Wayne, Soldier of the Early Republic.* Bloomington: Indiana University Press.

Nelson, Craig 2008. *Thomas Paine: Enlightenment, Revolution, and the Birth of Modern Nations.* New York, New York, United States of America: Penguin.

Nelson, Michael 2015. *Guide to the Presidency.* New York: Routledge, Taylor & Francis Group.

New England Historical Society, n.d. *The 1788 Scandal of Fanny Apthorp Never Dies.* [Online] Available at: https://www.newenglandhistoricalsociety.com/1788-scandal-of-fanny-apthorp-never-dies/ [Accessed 20 May 2020].

New York Society Library, 2020. *History of the Library.* [Online] Available at: www.nysoclib.org/about/history-library [Accessed 28 April 2020].

New-York Daily Gazette, 1789. *1789 NY newspaper ABOLITION of SLAVERY Wm Wilberforce.* [Online] Available at: https://www.worthpoint.com/worthopedia/1789-ny-newspaper-abolition-slavery-78280926 [Accessed 28 April 2020]. The link is to an auction site offering a copy of the Gazette. The item description notes there are two columns of text by Wilberforce.

New-York Daily Gazette. 27 April 1790.

New-York Historical Society, n.d. *When Did Slavery End in New York State.* [Online] Available at: https://www.nyhistory.org/community/slavery-end-new-york-state [Accessed 7 May 2020].

New-York Journal and Weekly Register. *The New-York Journal and Weekly Register*, 22 October 1789. pp. 1-4. [Accessed 8 September 2022]. Viewed via microfilm, Newspaper & Current Periodical Reading Room, Library of Congress.

North, Robert L. *Benjamin Rush, MD: assassin or beloved healer?* Jan 2000. Available at: https://www.ncbi.nlm.nih.gov/pmc/articles/PMC1312212/.

Nutting, P. B., Fall 1994. "Tobias Lear, S.P.U.S.": First Secretary to the President. *Presidential Studies Quarterly, Vol. 24, No. 4.*, pp. 713-24.

Ockerman Jr., Foster. *Celebrate Kentucky's statehood: it was a slog. Lexington Herald-Leader*, 30 May 2017. Available at: https://www.kentucky.com/opinion/op-ed/article153360289.html [Accessed 5 September 2019].

Ohio History Central, n.d. *Harmar's Defeat.* [Online] Available at: http://www.ohiohistorycentral.org/w/Harmar's_Defeat?rec=505 [Accessed 19 May 2020].

————. n.d. *Treaty of Fort Harmar (1789).* [Online] Available at: https://ohiohistorycentral.org/w/Treaty_of_Fort_Harmar_(1789) [Accessed 18 May 2020].

Online Library of Liberty, 2004. *Liberty and Order: The First American Party Struggle [1787]*. [Online] Liberty Fund Available at: https://oll.liberty-fund.org/titles/banning-liberty-and-order-the-first-american-party-struggle [Accessed 17 May 2020].

Osborn, David, 2013. *Phillip Pell: Revolutionary War Leader, Last Member of the Continental Congress*. [Online] Available at: https://www.nps.gov/sapa/learn/historyculture/upload/Pell-updated.pdf [Accessed 24 April 2020].

Overholser, Geneva & Jamieson, Kathleen H. 2005. *The Press*. New York: Oxford University Press. Available at: https://books.google.com/books?id=M7L1d_XjwsoC&printsec=frontcover&source=gbs_ge_summary_r&cad=0#v=onepage&q&f=false [accessed 4 May 2020].

Owens, Mackubin, n.d. *Navy Clause*. [Online] Available at: https://www.heritage.org/constitution/#!/articles/1/essays/53/navy-clause [Accessed 16 May 2020].

Paine, Thomas, 1794. *Age of Reason Part 1*. [Online] Available at: https://www.ushistory.org/paine/reason/reason1.htm [Accessed 13 May 2020].

————.1995. *Thomas Paine, Rights of Man, Common Sense, and Other Political Writings*. Edited by Mark Philp. Oxford: Oxford University Press.

Papers of George Washington, 2015. *George Washington Day By Day*. [Online] Available at: http://daybyday.gwpapers.org/content/07-april-1791 [Accessed 21 February 2021]. There are individual pages for each day, broken out by period, year, and month. See also https://washingtonpapers.org.

Parramore, Thomas C., 1979. *Brown, William Hill*. [Online] North Carolina Government & Heritage Library Available at: https://www.ncpedia.org/biography/brown-william-hill [Accessed 20 May 2020]. Article is from the *Dictionary of North Carolina Biography*, six volumes, edited by William S. Powell. 1979-1996, University of North Carolina Press.

Payne, Samanatha, 2015. *"Rogue Island": The last state to ratify the Constitution*. [Online] Available at: https://prologue.blogs.archives.gov/2015/05/18/rogue-island-the-last-state-to-ratify-the-constitution/ [Accessed 7 May 2020].

Pennsylvania Magazine of History and Biography. *Pennsylvania Weather Records, 1644-1835*. *Pennsylvania Magazine of History and Biography*, 1891. Available at: https://archive.org/details/jstor-20083411/page/n1/mode/2up [Accessed 14 May 2020].

Philadelphia Gazette. *Under the heading NEW-YORK, July 8*. *Philadelphia Gazette*, 15 July 1789. p. 3. Available at: https://www.newspapers.com/image/41024376/?terms=frothy&match=1 [Accessed 25 February 2021]. Subscription likely required to access URL.

Philadelphia Independent Gazetteer. *Letter from New York*. *Philadelphia Independent Gazetteer*, 14 September 1789.

Pitman, John 1785. *Diary in the Manuscript Collection of the Rhode Island Historical Society*. Available at: https://rihs.minisisinc.com/RIHS/SCRIPTS/ MWIMAIN.DLL/118017025/1/1/2187?RECORD&UNION=Y. Incomplete citation. Likely Rev John Pitman Diaries. B 1751, D 1822. RI Historical Society MSS 622. See entry for date December 15, 1785.

Polf, William A. 1976. *Garrison Town: The British Occupation of New York City. 1776-1783*. Albany: New York State American Revolution Bicentennial Commission.

Potter, Lee A. & Eder, Elizabeth K., 2009. George Washington's Printed Draft of the Constitution and Mike Wilkins' "Preamble". [Online] National Council for the Social Studies. Available at: https://www.socialstudies.org/social-education/73/4/george-washingtons-printed-draft-constitution-and-mike-wilkinss-preamble [Accessed 22 August 2021].

Price, Annie, 2020. *Asafoetida: The Ancient Roman Spice with Health Benefits*. [Online] Available at: https://draxe.com/nutrition/asafoetida/ [Accessed 13 May 2020].

Putnam, Rufus 1903. *The Memoirs of Rufus Putnam and Certain Official Papers and Correspondence*. Edited by Rowena Buell. Boston and New York, United States of America: Houghton, Mifflin and Company. Available at: https://archive.org/details/memoirsofrufuspu00putnrich/page/234/mode/2up.

Ramsay, David 1811. *The History of the American Revolution*. Trenton, New Jersey: James J. Wilson.

———. 1818. *History of the United States, from Their First Settlement as English Colonies, in 1607, to the Year 1808*. Philadephia: M. Carey and Sons.

Randolph, Thomas J. 1829. *Memoirs, Correspondence and Private Papers of Thomas Jefferson*. London: Henry Colburn and Richard Bentley.

Rappleye, Charles 2006. *Sons of Providence: The Brown Brothers, the Slave Trade, and the American Revolution*. New York: Simon & Schuster.

Ratcliffe, Donald, 2013. The Right to Vote and the Rise of Democracy, 1787-1828. *Journal of the Early Republic*, 33(2). Subscription required to read full article. Available at: https://muse.jhu.edu/issue/27297.

Records of the Pennsylvania Department of State, 1789. *An Act for the Gradual Abolition of Slavery*. [Online] Available at: http://www.phmc.state.pa.us/portal/communities/documents/1776-1865/abolition-slavery.html [Accessed 7 May 2020].

Reef, Catherine 2015. *Noah Webster: Man of Many Words*. Boston: Houghton Mifflin Harcourt.

Remini, Rovert V. 2006. *The House: The History of the House of Representatives*. Washington: Smithsonian Books.

Richardson, James D. 1897. *A Compilation of the Messages and Papers of the Presidents, 1789-1897, Volume 1*. Washington, DC.: U. S. Congress. Available at: http://onlinebooks.library.upenn.edu/webbin/metabook?id=mppresidents [accessed 11 May 2020].

Richardson, Lyon R. 1931. *A History of Early American Magazines, 1741-1789*. New York: Thomas Nelson and Sons. Available at: https://archive.org/details/historyofearlyam0000rich_b9t5/page/334/mode/2up.

Robbins, Alexander H. 1921. *Central Law Journal*. St. Louis, Missouri, United States of America: Central Law Journal Company. Available at: https://www.google.com/books/edition/The_Central_Law_Journal/f71CAQAAMAA-J?hl=en&gbpv=1 [accessed 11 May 2020]. Article entitled The Senate and Our Foreign Relations dated August 5, 1921, starts on page 75.

Rogers, Horatio 1890. *Discourse before the Rhode Island Historical Society at its Centennial Celebration of Rhode Island's Adoption of the Federal Constitution*. Providence: Providence Press.

Rosenberg, Chaim M. 2015. *Yankee Colonies across America*. Lanham, Maryland, United States of America: Lexington Books, Rowman & Littlefield.

Rossum, Ralph A. 2001. *Federalism, the Supreme Court, and the Seventeenth Amendment: The Irony of Constitutional Democracy*. Lanham, Maryland, United States of America: Lexington Books.

Royster, Charles 2011. *A Revolutionary People At War: The Continental Army and American Character, 1775-1783*. University of North Carolina Press: University of North Carolina Press. Published in connection with the Omohundro Institute of Early American History and Culture.

Rush, Benjamin 1773. *An address to the inhabitants of the British settlements, on the slavery of the Negroes in America*. Philadelphia, Pennsylvania, United States of America: John Dunlap. Available at: https://quod.lib.umich.edu/e/evans/N10229.0001.001/1:2?rgn=div1;view=fulltext.

———.1799. Observations Intended to Favour a Supposition That the Black Color (As It Is Called) of the Negroes Is Derived from the Leprosy. *Transactions of the American Philosophical Society*, IV, pp. 289-97. Available at: https://www.biodiversitylibrary.org/item/44356#page/345/mode/1up.

Rutkow, Ira 2010. *Seeking the Cure: A History of Medicine in America*. New York: Simon & Schuster.

Saba, Natalie D., 2004. *Nathanael Greene (1742-1786)*. [Online] Available at: https://www.georgiaencyclopedia.org/articles/history-archaeology/nathanael-greene-1742-1786 [Accessed 6 May 2020].

Sawvel, Franklin B. 1903. *The Compete Anas of Thomas Jefferson*. New York: Round Table Press.

Schroeder, John F. & Lossing, Benson J. 1903. *Life and Times of Washington.* Albany, New York, United States of America: M. M. Belcher Publishing Co.

Schuessler, Jennifer. *Princeton Digs Deep Into Its Fraught Racial History. New York Times,* 7 November 2017. pp. C1, C5. Available at: https://www.nytimes. com/2017/11/06/arts/princeton-digs-deep-into-its-fraught-racial-history. html.

Shaw, John R. 1807 and 1930. *A Narrative of the Life & Travels of John Robert Shaw, the Well-Digger, Now Resident in Lexington, Kentucky, Written By Himself.* Lexington and Louisville: Daniel Bradford in 1807; George Fowlerin 1930. Available at: https://archive.org/details/in.ernet.dli.2015.88060/page/n10/ mode/2up. The edition in the URL listed here appears to be a 1930 near-facsimile of the 1807 edition, with a new introduction included. Both editions are cited as regards date, city, and publisher.

Shepherd, W.R. *Wilkinson and the Beginning of the Spanish Conspiracy. American Historical Review,* April 1904. Available at: https://archive.org/details/ jstor-1833472/page/n7/mode/2up [Accessed 18 May 2020]. See also https:// archive.org/details/americanhistori02assogoog/page/n525/mode/2up.

Sher, Richard B. 2008. *The Enlightenment and the Book.* Chicago: University of Chicago Press.

Short, William, 1790. *To Thomas Jefferson from William Short, 7 July 1790.* [Online] National Archives Available at: https://founders.archives.gov/documents/ Jefferson/01-17-02-0007#TSJN-01-17-0007-fn-00 [Accessed 25 April 2021. Source: The Papers of Thomas Jefferson, vol. 17, 6 July–3 November 1790, ed. Julian P. Boyd. Princeton: Princeton University Press, 1965, pp. 14–20.]

Sinclair, Donald A. 1980. *A guide to manuscript diaries and journals in the Special Collections Department, Rutgers University.* New Brunswick, New Jersey, United States of America: Rutgers University, Libraries, Special Collections. Available at: https://rucore.libraries.rutgers.edu/rutgers-lib/41138/.

Smith, Thomas E.V. 1889. *The City of New York in the Year of Washington's Inauguration, 1789.* New York: A. D. F. Randolph. Available at: https://archive.org/details/citynewyorkinye00smitgoog/page/n13/mode/2up.

Society of the Cincinatti, 2018. *The Society and its Critics, 1784-1800.* [Online] Available at: https://www.societyofthecincinnati.org/about/history/critics [Accessed 20 April 2020].

————. 2018. *Triennial Meetings.* [Online] Available at: https://www.societyofthecincinnati.org/about/history/triennial_meetings [Accessed 20 April 2020].

————. n.d. *The Institution of the Society of the Cincinatti.* [Online] Available at: www.societyofthecincinnati.org/pdf/SOTC_Institution.pdf [Accessed 20 April 2020].

Society of the Cincinnati of Maryland 1897. *Register of the Society of the Cincinnati of Maryland Brought Down to February 22nd, 1897*. Baltimore: Society of the Cincinnati of Maryland. Available at: https://archive.org/details/registerofsociet05soci/page/2/mode/2up [accessed 19 April 2020].

Soodalter, Ron, 2018. *Untouchable Agent 13*. [Online] Available at: https://www.historynet.com/untouchable-agent-13.htm [Accessed 19 May 2020].

Sparks, Jared, 1827. *Jared Sparks to James Madison, 22 May 1827*. [Online] Available at: https://founders.archives.gov/documents/Madison/99-02-02-1017 [Accessed 23 April 2020]. Notation on web page: [This is an Early Access document from The Papers of James Madison. It is not an authoritative final version.].

———. 1832. *The life of Gouverneur Morris, with selections from his correspondence and miscellaneous papers*. Boston, Massachusetts, United States of America: Gray & Bowen. Available at: https://archive.org/details/lifeofgouverneur03sparuoft/page/174/mode/2up. Full Title: The life of Gouverneur Morris, with selections from his correspondence and miscellaneous papers; detailing events in the American Revolution, the French Revolution, and in the political history of the United States.

———. 1844. *The Works of Benjamin Franklin*. Boston: Charles Tappan.

———. 1847. *The Writings of George Washington Vol 10*. New York: Harper & Brothers. Available at: https://archive.org/details/writingsofgeorge10washuoft/page/484/mode/2up.

———. 1847. *The Writings of George Washington Vol 9*. New York, New York, United States of America: Harper & Brothers. Available at: https://archive.org/details/writingsofgeorge09washuoft/page/488/mode/2up [accessed 24 April 2020]. Other edition from Boston: N. Hale and Gray and Bowen, 1829–1830 was cited with the letter at page 487.

Spragens, William C. 1988. *Popular Images of America Presidents*. Westport: Greenwood Publishing Group. Available at: https://books.google.com/books?id=vFXHb58t340C&printsec=frontcover#v=onepage&q&f=false [accessed 21 May 2020].

Sprague, William B. 1874. *The Life of Jedidiah Morse, D.D.* New York, New York, United States of America: Anson D.F. Randolph & Co. Available at: https://archive.org/details/lifejedidiahmor00spragoog/page/n7/mode/2up.

Springfield Technical Community College, 2008. *A Bloody Encounter: "the body of the people assembled in arms"*. [Online] Available at: http://shaysrebellion.stcc.edu/shaysapp/scenehtml.do?shortName=Arsenal [Accessed 21 April 2020].

Srodes, James 2002. *Franklin: the Essential Founding Father*. Washington, DC: Regnery.

State of New Hampshire, 1788. *Ratification of the Constitution by the State of New Hampshire; June 21, 1788*. [Online] Lillian Goldman Law Library Yale Law School Available at: https://avalon.law.yale.edu/18th_century/ratnh.asp [Accessed 8 May 2020].

State of Virginia 1950. *Laws of Virginia Relating to Fisheries of Tidal Water*. Charlottesville, Virginia, United States of America: Michie Co. LEXIS Law Publishing.

Stegeman, John F. & Stegeman, Janet A. 1977. *Caty: a Biography of Catharine Littlefield*. Athens, GA: University of Georgia Press.

Stewart, Walter J. 1991. *The Lighthouses Act of 1789*. Washington, D.C., United States of America: U.S. Senate Historical Office.

Stewart, David O. 2002. *The Summer of 1787: The Men Who Invented the Constitution*. New York: Simon and Schuster.

Stillwell, Margaret Bingham, 1916. Checklist of Eulogies and Funeral Orations on the Death of George Washington. [Online] Available at https://babel.hathitrust.org/cgi/pt?id=mdp.39015034784176&view=1up&seq=1 *Bulletin of the New York Pubic Library*, vol. 20, Issue 5.

Stone, William L. 1876. *The Centennial History of New York City: From the Discovery to the Present Day*. New York: R. D. Cooke. Available at: https://archive.org/details/centennialhistor00ston/page/184/mode/2up.

Stuart, David, 1790. *To George Washington from David Stuart, 15 March 1790*. [Online] National Archives Available at: https://founders.archives.gov/documents/Washington/05-05-02-0155 [Accessed 6 May 2020]. [Original source: The Papers of George Washington, Presidential Series, vol. 5, 16 January 1790–30 June 1790, ed. Dorothy Twohig, Mark A. Mastromarino, and Jack D. Warren. Charlottesville: University Press of Virginia, 1996, pp. 235–238.].

————. 1790. *To George Washington from David Stuart, 2 June 1790*. [Online] Available at: https://founders.archives.gov/documents/Washington/05-05-02-0288. [Original source: The Papers of George Washington vol. 5, ed. Dorothy Twohig, Mark A. Mastromarino, and Jack D. Warren. UVa Press 1966].

Sullivan, Buddy, 2002. *Lachlan McIntosh (1727-1806)*. [Online] Available at: http://www.ourgeorgiahistory.com/ogh/Lachlan_McIntosh [Accessed 11 May 2020].

Supreme Executvie Council of Pennsylvania 1853. *Minutes of the Supreme Executive Council of Pennsylvania, from its organization to the termination of the Revolution. [Mar. 4, 1777 - Dec. 20, 1790]*. Edited by Samuel Hazard. Harrisburg: Theo. Fenn & Co.

Supreme-Court.Laws.com, 2019. *John Jay*. [Online] Available at: https://su-preme-court.laws.com/john-jay [Accessed 3 May 2020].

Swanstrom, Roy 1988. *The United States Senate, 1787-1801: A dissertation on the first fourteen years of the upper legislative body*. Washington, D.C., United States of America: U.S. Senate. Available at: https://www.senate.gov/artandhistory/history/minute/The_Senate_Opens_Its_Doors.htm [accessed 26 April 2020]. Senate Document 100-31, 100th Cong., 1st sess., 1988.) Source of "The Senate Opens its Doors," https://www.senate.gov/artandhistory/history/minute/The_Senate_Opens_Its_Doors.htm.

Syrett, Harold C. 1961. *The Papers of Alexander Hamilton vol 2. 1779-1781*. New York: Columbia University Press.

Tansill, Charles C. 1927. *Documents Illustrative of the Formation of the Union of the American States*. Washington: Government Printing Office.

Teaching American History, n.d. *Scene of Gouverneur Morris' Accident*. [Online] Available at: http://teachingamericanhistory.org/static/convention/map/morrisaccident.html [Accessed 13 May 2020].

———. n.d. *The Six Stages of Ratification*. [Online] Available at: https://teachingamericanhistory.org/resources/ratification/stageone/ [Accessed 22 April 2020].

Thacher, James 1854. *A Military Journal during the American Revolutionary War, from 1775 to 1783*. Hartford, Connecticut, United States of America: Andrus and Son. There is also an 1823 edition from Richardson and Lord, Boston Massachusetts.

Thomas Jefferson Encyclopedia, n.d. *Paris Residences*. [Online] Available at: https://www.monticello.org/site/research-and-collections/paris-residences [Accessed 29 June 2019].

Thompson, Mary V., 1999. *"The Only Unavoidable Subject of Regret"*. [Online] Available at: https://www.mountvernon.org/george-washington/slavery/the-only-unavoidable-subject-of-regret/ [Accessed 15 May 2020].

———. 2019. *The Only Unavoidable Subject of Regret*. Charlottesville: University of Virginia Press.

———, n.d. *Dining at Mount Vernon*. [Online] Available at: http://www.mountvernon.org/digital-encyclopedia/article/smallpox/ [Accessed 29 April 2020].

———. n.d. *John Parke Custis*. [Online] Available at: https://www.mountvernon.org/library/digitalhistory/digital-encyclopedia/article/john-parke-custis [Accessed 12 May 2020].

Toll, Ian W. 2006. *Six Frigates: The Epic History of the Founding of the U.S. Navy*. New York: W.W. Norton.

Toogood, Coxey, 2014. *U.S. Congress (1790-1800)*. [Online] Available at: https://philadelphiaencyclopedia.org/archive/u-s-congress-1790-1800/ [Accessed 6 May 2020].

Toomey, Michaell, 2016. *State of Franklin*. [Online] Available at: http://northcarolinahistory.org/encyclopedia/state-of-franklin/ [Accessed 18 May 2020].

Trenholm, Sandara, 2013. *Martha Washington: First Lady's grandchildren were her top priority*. [Online] Available at: https://www.gilderlehrman.org/news/martha-washington-first-lady%E2%80%99s-grandchildren-were-her-top-priority [Accessed 30 April 2020].

Turnere, Orsamus 1851. *History of the Pioneer Settlement of Phelps and Gorham Purchase*. Rochester: Erastus Darrow.

U.S. Army, 2008. *Field Manual 1*. Washington: Department of the Army.

U.S. Coast Guard, n.d. *Coast Guard History*. Washington: U.S. Coast Guard Public Information Division. Available at: https://media.defense.gov/2017/Jun/26/2001769006/-1/-1/0/CG-213_USCG_HISTORY.PDF.

U.S. Congress, 1788. *Resolution of Congress, Dated July 2, 1788, Submitting Ratifications of the Constitution to a Committee*. [Online] Lillian Goldman Law Library Yale University Available at: https://avalon.law.yale.edu/18th_century/ressub03.asp [Accessed 24 April 2020].

———. 1789. *An Act to Establish the Judicial Courts of the United States*. [Online] Lillian Goldman Law School Yale Law School Available at: http://avalon.law.yale.edu/18th_century/judiciary_act.asp [Accessed 4 May 2020].

———. 1791. *Acts Passed At A Congress of the United States of America*. Philadelphia, Pennsylvania, United States of America: Francis Childs and John Swaine. Available at: https://archive.org/details/actspassedatfirs1791unit/mode/2up

———. 1832. *American State Papers*. Washington, D.C., United States of America: Gales and Seaton. Available at: http://memory.loc.gov/cgi-bin/ampage?collId=llsp&fileName=013/llsp013.db&recNum=4. There are 38 volumes, but numbering is complex. Volume 5 is the first volume concerning topic of Finance. See also http://memory.loc.gov/ammem/amlaw/lwsp.html.

———.1832. *American State Papers : Documents, Legislative and Executive, of the Congress of the United States*. Edited by Walter Lowrie & St. Claire Matthew Clarke. Washington: Gales and Seaton. Available at: https://archive.org/details/americanstatepap_c11unit/page/102/mode/2up/.

———.1849. *Rules for Conducting Business in the Senate of the United States*. Washington: Wm M. Belt.

U.S. Constitution, 2010. *New Hampshire's Ratification*. [Online] Available at: www.usconstitution.net/rat_nh.html [Accessed 22 April 2020].

U.S. Department of State Archive, n.d. *The XYZ Affair and the Quasi-War with France, 1798-1800*. [Online] U.S. Department of Stae Archive Available at: https://2001-2009.state.gov/r/pa/ho/time/nr/16318.htm [Accessed 16 May 2020].

U.S. Department of the Interior Office of Insular Affairs, n.d. *Definitions of Insular Area Political Organizations*. [Online] Available at: https://www.doi.gov/oia/islands/politicatypes [Accessed 4 May 2020].

U.S. House of Representatives, 2015. *Chasing Congress Away*. [Online] Available at: http://history.house.gov/Blog/2015/June/6-1-Chasing-Congress/ [Accessed 10 April 2017].

————.n.d. *State of the Union Address*. [Online] Available at: https://history.house.gov/Institution/SOTU/State-of-the-Union/ [Accessed 17 May 2020].

————. *The First Bank of the United States*. [Online] Available at: https://history.house.gov/Historical-Highlights/1700s/1791_First_Bank/ [Accessed 14 May 2020].

————.*Historical Highlights: The first Speaker of the House, Frederick A.C. Muhlenberg of Pennsylvania*. [Online] Available at: http://history.house.gov/HistoricalHighlight/Detail/36402 [Accessed 20 October 2016].

————.n.d. *The Creation of the Formal House Rules and the House Rules Committee*. [Online] Available at: https://history.house.gov/HistoricalHighlight/Detail/15032392020 [Accessed 24 April 2020].

————.n.d. *Electoral College & Indecisive Elections*. [Online] U.S House of Representatives Available at: https://history.house.gov/Institution/Origins-Development/Electoral-College/ [Accessed 23 APril 2020].

U.S. Marshals Service, 2020. *History -- Roll Call*. [Online] Available at: https://www.usmarshals.gov/history/roll_call.htm [Accessed 3 May 2020].

————. n.d. *History -- Broad Range of Authority*. [Online] Available at: www.usmarshals.gov/history/broad_range.htm [Accessed 4 May 2020].

————.n.d. *Recognition of the Need for Federal Marshals*. [Online] Available at: www.usmarshals.gov/history/judiciary/judiary_act_of_1789_7.htm [Accessed 4 May 2020].

————.n.d. *History -- Oldest Federal Law Enforcement Agency*. [Online] Available at: www.usmarshals.gov/history/oldest.htm [Accessed 3 May 2020].

————.n.d. *History -- The First Generation of United States Marshals*. [Online] Available at: https://www.usmarshals.gov/history/firstmarshals/marshals1.htm [Accessed 4 May 2020].

U.S. Senate 1789. *Journal of the First Session of the Senate of the United States of America, Begun and Held at the City of New-York, March 4th, 1789, and in the Thirteenth Year of the Independence of the Said States.* New York: Thomas Greenleaf. Available at: https://archive.org/details/journalfirstses00senagoog/page/n24/mode/2up.

————.*Journal of the Senate of the United States of America, 1789-1793; FRIDAY, MAY 15, 1789.* [Online] Available at: http://memory.loc.gov/cgi-bin/query/r?ammem/hlaw:@field(DOCID+@lit(sj00144)): [Accessed 2 May 2020].

————.1820. *Journal of the First Session of the Senate of the United States of America.* Washington: Gales & Seaton. Available at: http://memory.loc.gov/cgi-bin/query/r?ammem/hlaw:@field(DOCID+@lit(sj00112)): [accessed 19 June 2019].

————. n.d. *James Mathers, Doorkeeper and Sergeant at Arms, 1789–1811.* [Online] Available at: https://www.senate.gov/about/officers-staff/sergeant-at-arms/SAA-James-Mathers.htm [Accessed 2 May 2020].

————.n.d. *Senate History: Filibuster and Cloture.* [Online] Available at: https://www.senate.gov/about/powers-procedures/filibusters-cloture.htm [Accessed 27 February 2021].

————. n.d. *Senators Receive Class Assignments.* [Online] Available at: http://www.senate.gov/artandhistory/history/minute/Senatorial_Lottery.htm [Accessed 2 May 2020].

U.S. Supreme Court, 1791. *West v. Barnes, 2 U.S. 401 (1791).* [Online] Available at: http://scotus-cases.blogspot.com/2009/11/west-v-barnes-2-us-401-1791.html [Accessed 3 May 2020].

Unger, Harlow G. 1998. *Noah Webster: The Life and Times of an American Patriot.* New York: John Wiley and Sons.

United States Census Bureau 1907. *Heads of Families at the First Census of the United States.* Washington, D.C., United States of America: United States Government Printing Office. Available at: https://www.census.gov/library/publications/1907/dec/heads-of-families.html [accessed 4 May 2020].

————. 1909. *A century of population growth from the first census of the United States to the twelfth 1790-1900.* Washington, D.C., United States of America: United States Government Printing Office. Available at: https://archive.org/details/centuryofpopulat00unit/page/n12/mode/2up.

————.1993. *Population: 1790 to 1990.* [Online] Available at: https://www.census.gov/population/censusdata/table-16.pdf [Accessed 4 May 2020].

————.2019. *1790 Overview.* [Online] Available at: https://www.census.gov/history/www/through_the_decades/overview/1790.html [Accessed 4 May 2020].

————.2019. *Census Instructions.* [Online] Available at: https://www.gilderlehrman.org/history-now/early-republic [Accessed 4 May 2020].

United States Senate Committee, 1789. *Conference with a Committee of the United States Senate, 8 August 1789*. [Online] National Archives Available at: https://founders.archives.gov/documents/Washington/05-03-02-0239 [Accessed 11 May 2020]. [Original source: The Papers of George Washington, Presidential Series, vol. 3, 15 June 1789–5 September 1789, ed. Dorothy Twohig. Charlottesville: University Press of Virginia, 1989, pp. 400–403.].

United States 1845. *The Public Statutes of the United States of America / by Authority of Congress*. Boston, Massachusetts: Little, Brown.

University of Michigan Clements Library, 1959. *Anthony Wayne Family Papers, (1681-1913)*. [Online] Available at: https://quod.lib.umich.edu/c/clement-sead/umich-wcl-M-398way?view=text [Accessed 19 April 2019].

UShistory.org, n.d. *Thomas Paine Brief Biography*. [Online] Independence Hall Association Available at: https://www.ushistory.org/paine/.

Uva, Katie, n.d. *Quasi War*. [Online] Available at: https://www.mountvernon.org/library/digitalhistory/digital-encyclopedia/article/quasi-war/ [Accessed 19 June 2019].

Van de Water, Frederic F. 1941. *The Reluctant Republic: Vermont, 1724-1791*. New York: John Day Company.

Van Dusen, Albert E. 1961. *Connecticut*. New York, New York, United States of America: Random House. Available at: https://archive.org/details/connecticut00vand/page/198/mode/2up.

Vanhorn, Kellie M., 2004. *Eighteenth-Century Colonial American Merchant Ship Construction; MA Thesis*. MA Thesis. College Station: Texas A&M University.

Varnum, James M., 1782. *To George Washington from James Mitchell Varnum, June 23 1782*. [Online] Available at: https://founders.archives.gov/documents/Washington/99-01-02-08770 [Accessed 17 April 2020]. The online version had this notation: [This is an Early Access document from The Papers of George Washington. It is not an authoritative final version.].

Veit, Helen E. et al. 1991. *Creating the Bill of Rights: The Documentary Record from the First Federal Congress*. Baltimore, Maryland, United States of America: Johns Hopkins University Press.

Vineyard, Ron, 2000. *Stage Waggons and Coachees*. [Online] Williamsburg: Colonial Williamsburg Foundation Available at: https://research.colonial-williamsburg.org/DigitalLibrary/view/index.cfm?doc=ResearchReports\RR0380.xml&highlight=.

Virginia Places, n.d. *Norfolk Naval Shipyard*. [Online] Available at: www.virginia-places.org/military/norfolknavalshipyard.html [Accessed 16 May 2020].

Walsh, Jennifer, 2010. *Dr. James Fever Powder, circa 1746.* [Online] Available at: https://www.the-scientist.com/uncategorized/dr-james-fever-powder-circa-1746-43055 [Accessed 12 May 2020].

Washington Papers, 2013. *Thanksgiving Proclamation.* [Online] University of Virginia and the Mount Vernon Ladies' Association Available at: https://washingtonpapers.org/documents/thanksgiving-proclamation/ [Accessed 11 May 2020].

Washington, George, 1770. *Journal of George Washington written during an expedition along the Ohio and Kanwha Rivers.* [Online] Available at: http://www.wvculture.org/history/settlement/washingtonjournal1770.html [Accessed 20 June 2019]. extracted from The Writings of George Washington, by Jared Sparks, Volume II (Boston: Charles Tappan, 1846), pages 516-534.

———. 1776. *From George Washington to Lund Washington, 6 October 1776.* [Online] National Archives Available at: https://founders.archives.gov/documents/Washington/03-06-02-0379 [Accessed 28 April 2020]. [Original source: The Papers of George Washington, Revolutionary War Series, vol. 6, 13 August 1776–20 October 1776, ed. Philander D. Chase and Frank E. Grizzard, Jr. Charlottesville: University Press of Virginia, 1994, pp. 493–495.].

———. 1781. *Circular Letter on Pennsylvania Line Mutiny, January 5, 1781.* [Online] Library of Congress Available at: https://www.loc.gov/resource/mgw3c.004/?sp=61&st=text [Accessed 17 April 2020].

———. 1781. *From George Washington to Samuel Huntington, 23 January 1781.* [Online] National Archives Available at: https://founders.archives.gov/documents/Washington/99-01-02-04623 [Accessed 17 April 2020]. The online document included this note: [This is an Early Access document from The Papers of George Washington. It is not an authoritative final version.].

———. 1782. *From George Washington to Benjamin Lincoln, October 2, 1782.* [Online] Available at: https://founders.archives.gov/documents/Washington/99-01-02-09633 [Accessed 17 January 2017]. The source web page had this notation: [This is an Early Access document from The Papers of George Washington. It is not an authoritative final version.].

———. 1783. *From George Washington to David Rittenhouse, 16 February 1783.* [Online] Available at: https://founders.archives.gov/documents/Washington/99-01-02-10654 [Accessed 17 April 2020]. The web page included this note: [This is an Early Access document from The Papers of George Washington. It is not an authoritative final version.].

———. 1783. *From George Washington to Elias Boudinot, 12 March 1783.* [Online] National Archives Available at: https://founders.archives.gov/documents/Washington/99-01-02-10818 [Accessed 25 February 2021]. The full text of the "fellow soldier" letter is Enclosure No. 2 Note on web page: [This is

an Early Access document from The Papers of George Washington. It is not an
authoritative final version.].

———. 1783. *From George Washington to James Duane, 7 September 1783.*
[Online] Available at: https://founders.archives.gov/documents/
Washington/99-01-02-11798 [Accessed 19 May 2020].

———. 1783. *From George Washington to Officers of the Army, 15 March 1783.*
[Online] National Archives Available at: https://founders.archives.gov/doc-
uments/Washington/99-01-02-10840 [Accessed 19 May 2020]. [This is an
Early Access document from The Papers of George Washington. It is not an
authoritative final version.].

———. 1783. *From George Washington to Officers of the Army, March 15, 1783.*
[Online] National Archives Available at: https://founders.archives.gov/docu-
ments/Washington/99-01-02-10840 [Accessed 15 November 2016].

———. 1783. *From George Washington to The States, 8 June 1783.* [Online]
National Archives Available at: https://founders.archives.gov/documents/
Washington/99-01-02-11404 [Accessed 17 May 2020]. "From George
Washington to The States, 8 June 1783," Founders Online, National Archives,
https://founders.archives.gov/documents/Washington/99-01-02-11404.
[This is an Early Access document from The Papers of George Washington. It
is not an authoritative.

———. 1783. *George Washington, Circular to the States [excerpt].* [Online]
University of Chicago Press Available at: http://press-pubs.uchicago.edu/
founders/documents/v1ch7s5.html [Accessed 17 May 2020].

———. 1783. *George Washington, June 8, 1783, Circular to States on Farewell to the
Army.* [Online] Library of Congress Available at: https://www.loc.gov/item/
mgw434172/ [Accessed 17 May 2020]. George Washington Papers, Series 4,
General Correspondence: George Washington, June 8, Circular to States on
Farewell to the Army. June 8, 1783. Manuscript/Mixed Material. https://www.
loc.gov/item/mgw434172/.

———. 1783. *Newburgh Address: George Washington to Officers of the Army,
March 15, 1783.* [Online] Available at: https://www.mountvernon.org/educa-
tion/primary-sources-2/article/newburgh-address-george-washington-to-offi-
cers-of-the-army-march-15-1783 [Accessed 2020 April 2020].

———. 1784. *From George Washington to Lafayette, 1 February 1784.* [Online]
National Archives Available at: https://founders.archives.gov/documents/
Washington/04-01-02-0064 [Accessed 21 May 2020]. [Original source: The
Papers of George Washington, Confederation Series, vol. 1, 1 January 1784–17
July 1784, ed. W. W. Abbot. Charlottesville: University Press of Virginia,
1992, pp. 87–90.].

————. 1786. *From George Washington to Benjamin Lincoln, February 6 1786*. [Online] Available at: https://founders.archives.gov/documents/ Washington/04-03-02-0462 [Accessed 5 March 2017]. [Original source: The Papers of George Washington, Confederation Series, vol. 3, 19 May 1785–31 March 1786, ed. W. W. Abbot. Charlottesville: University Press of Virginia, 1994, pp. 547–548.].

————. 1786. *From George Washington to David Humphreys, 22 October 1786*. [Online] National Archives Available at: https://founders.archives.gov/documents/Washington/04-04-02-0272#GEWN-04-04-02-0272-fn-0002-ptr [Accessed 21 April 2020].

————. 1786. *From George Washington to James Madison, 16 December 1786*. [Online] Available at: https://founders.archives.gov/documents/ Washington/04-04-02-0395 [Accessed 21 April 2020]. [Original source: The Papers of George Washington, Confederation Series, vol. 4, 2 April 1786–31 January 1787, ed. W. W. Abbot. Charlottesville: University Press of Virginia, 1995, pp. 457–459.].

————. 1786. *From George Washington to James Madison, November 5, 1786*. [Online] National Archives Available at: http://founders.archives.gov/documents/Washington/04-04-02-0299 [Accessed 10 September 2016]. Original source: The Papers of George Washington, Confederation Series, vol. 4, 2 April 1786–31 January 1787, ed. W. W. Abbot. Charlottesville: University Press of Virginia, 1995, pp. 331–332.].

————. 1786. *From George Washington to John Jay, 15 August 1786*. [Online] Available at: https://founders.archives.gov/documents/ Washington/04-04-02-0199 [Accessed 23 April 2020].

————. 1786. *From George Washington to Robert Morris, 12 April 1786*. [Online] National Archives Available at: https://founders.archives.gov/documents/ Washington/04-04-02-0019 [Accessed 6 May 2020]. Original source: The Papers of George Washington, Confederation Series, vol. 4, 2 April 1786–31 January 1787, ed. W. W. Abbot. Charlottesville: University Press of Virginia, 1995, pp. 15–17.].

————. 1787. *From George Washington to Lafayette, 18 September 1787*. [Online] National Archives Available at: https://founders.archives.gov/documents/ Washington/04-05-02-0309 [Accessed 22 April 2020].

————. 1789. *Address to Charles Thomson, 14 April 1789*. [Online] Available at: https://founders.archives.gov/documents/Washington/05-02-02-0057 [Accessed 24 April 2020]. [Original source: The Papers of George Washington, Presidential Series, vol. 2, 1 April 1789–15 June 1789, ed. Dorothy Twohig. Charlottesville: University Press of Virginia, 1987, pp. 56–57.].

————. 1789. *Diary Entry 17 October 1789.* [Online] Available at: https://founders.archives.gov/documents/Washington/01-05-02-0005-0002-0017 [Accessed 14 May 2020]. [Original source: The Diaries of George Washington, vol. 5, 1 July 1786–31 December 1789, ed. Donald Jackson and Dorothy Twohig. Charlottesville: University Press of Virginia, 1979, pp. 463–466.].

————. 1789. *Diary entry: 30 October 1789.* [Online] Available at: https://founders.archives.gov/documents/Washington/01-05-02-0005-0002-0030 [Accessed 14 May 2020]. [Original source: The Diaries of George Washington, vol. 5, 1 July 1786–31 December 1789, ed. Donald Jackson and Dorothy Twohig. Charlottesville: University Press of Virginia, 1979, pp. 485–486.].

————. 1789. *Diary entry: 7 January 1789.* [Online] Available at: http://founders.archives.gov/documents/Washington/05-02-02-0130-0002 [Accessed 5 December 2016].

————. 1789. *From George Washington to James Madison, 5 May 1789.* [Online] Available at: https://founders.archives.gov/documents/Washington/05-02-02-0157 [Accessed 11 May 2020]. [Original source: The Papers of George Washington, Presidential Series, vol. 2, 1 April 1789–15 June 1789, ed. Dorothy Twohig. Charlottesville: University Press of Virginia, 1987, pp. 216–217.].

————. 1789. *From George Washington to Lafayette, 14 October 1789.* [Online] National Archives Available at: https://founders.archives.gov/documents/Washington/05-04-02-0129 [Accessed 13 May 2020]. [Original source: The Papers of George Washington, Presidential Series, vol. 4, 8 September 1789–15 January 1790, ed. Dorothy Twohig. Charlottesville: University Press of Virginia, 1993, pp. 191–192.].

————. 1789. *From George Washington to Lafayette, January 29, 1789.* [Online] Available at: https://founders.archives.gov/documents/Washington/05-01-02-0198. [Accessed 8 September 2016].

————. 1789. *From George Washington to Richard Conway, 6 March 1789.* [Online] Available at: https://founders.archives.gov/documents/Washington/05-01-02-0279 [Accessed 23 April 2020]. [Original source: The Papers of George Washington, Presidential Series, vol. 1, 24 September 1788–31 March 1789, ed. Dorothy Twohig. Charlottesville: University Press of Virginia, 1987, pp. 368–369.].

————. 1789. *From George Washington to the Ladies of Trenton, 21 April 1789.* [Online] Available at: http://founders.archives.gov/documents/Washington/05-02-02-0095 [Accessed 25 April 2020]. [Original source: The Papers of George Washington, Presidential Series, vol. 2, 1 April 1789–15 June

1789, ed. Dorothy Twohig. Charlottesville: University Press of Virginia, 1987, pp. 108–109.].

———. 1789. *From George Washington to the Mayor, Corporation, and Citizens of Alexandria, 16 April 1789.* [Online] National Archives Available at: https://founders.archives.gov/documents/Washington/05-02-02-0059 [Accessed 25 April 2020]. [Original source: The Papers of George Washington, Presidential Series, vol. 2, 1 April 1789–15 June 1789, ed. Dorothy Twohig. Charlottesville: University Press of Virginia, 1987, pp. 59–61.].

———. 1789. *George Washington to Beverley Randolph, November 22, 1789.* [Online] Available at: https://www.loc.gov/resource/mgw2.022/?sp=216&st=text [Accessed 14 May 2020].

———. 1789. *October 1789.* [Online] National Archives Available at: https://founders.archives.gov/documents/Washington/01-05-02-0005-0002#GEWN-01-05-02-pb-0452 [Accessed 14 May 2020]. [Original source: The Diaries of George Washington, vol. 5, 1 July 1786–31 December 1789, ed. Donald Jackson and Dorothy Twohig. Charlottesville: University Press of Virginia, 1979, pp. 448–488.].

———. 1789. *October 1789 (note 3 to Oct 20).* [Online] Available at: https://founders.archives.gov/documents/Washington/01-05-02-0005-0002#GEWN-01-05-02-0005-0002-0020-fn-0003-ptr [Accessed 14 May 2020]. [Original source: The Diaries of George Washington, vol. 5, 1 July 1786–31 December 1789, ed. Donald Jackson and Dorothy Twohig. Charlottesville: University Press of Virginia, 1979, pp. 448–488.].

———. 1789. *To John Adams from George Washington, 17 May 1789.* [Online] Available at: https://founders.archives.gov/documents/Adams/99-02-02-0562 [Accessed 29 April 2020]. [This is an Early Access document from The Adams Papers. It is not an authoritative final version.].

———. 1789. *Undelivered First Inaugural Address: Fragments, 30 April 1789.* [Online] Available at: http://founders.archives.gov/documents/Washington/05-02-02-0130-0002 [Accessed 5 December 2016].

———. 1790. *From George Washington to David Stuart, 15 June 1790.* [Online] Available at: https://founders.archives.gov/documents/Washington/05-05-02-0334 [Accessed 17 March 2017].

———. 1790. *From George Washington to the United States Senate and House of Representatives, 8 January 1790.* [Online] Available at: https://founders.archives.gov/documents/Washington/05-04-02-0361 [Accessed 9 February 2021].

———. 1790. *Letter to Catharine Macaulay Graham.* [Online] Available at: http://teachingamericanhistory.org/library/document/letter-to-catherine-macaulay-graham/ [Accessed 11 January 2017]. She was a British historian who visiited the Washingtons at Mount Vernon.

———. 1790. *May 1790 [diary]*. [Online] Available at: https://founders.archives.gov/documents/Washington/01-06-02-0001-0005 [Accessed 18 May 2020]. [Original source: The Diaries of George Washington, vol. 6, 1 January 1790–13 December 1799, ed. Donald Jackson and Dorothy Twohig. Charlottesville: University Press of Virginia, 1979, pp. 72–77.].

———. 1792. *Enclosure: George Washington to Gouverneur Morris, 28 January 1792*. [Online] National Archives Available at: https://founders.archives.gov/documents/Jefferson/01-23-02-0081#TSJN-01-23-0081-fn-0001 [Accessed 13 May 2020]. [Original source: The Papers of Thomas Jefferson, vol. 23, 1 January–31 May 1792, ed. Charles T. Cullen. Princeton: Princeton University Press, 1990, pp. 85–86.].

———. 1792. *From George Washington to Henry Knox, 13 August 1792*. [Online] Available at: https://founders.archives.gov/documents/Washington/05-10-02-0435 [Accessed 20 June 2019].

———. 1793. *From George Washington to the United States Senate and House of Representatives, 3 December 1793*. [Online] National Archives Available at: https://founders.archives.gov/documents/Washington/05-14-02-0306 [Accessed 15 May 2020]. [Original source: The Papers of George Washington, Presidential Series, vol. 14, 1 September–31 December 1793, ed. David R. Hoth. Charlottesville: University of Virginia Press, 2008, pp. 462–469.].

———. 1796. *Farewell Address*. [Online] Available at: https://www.loc.gov/resource/mgw2.024/?sp=229 [Accessed 21 May 2020].

———. 1796. *Farewell Address*. [Online] National Archives Available at: https://founders.archives.gov/documents/Washington/05-20-02-0440-0002 [Accessed 21 May 2020]. URL for this item described as "stable but nonpermanent link." Another notation: [This is an Early Access document from The Papers of George Washington. It is not an authoritative final version.].

———. 1798. *From Geoge Washington to John Adams, 13 July 1798*. [Online] Available at: https://founders.archives.gov/documents/Washington/06-02-02-0314#GEWN-06-02-02-0314-fn-0001 [Accessed 30 June 2019]. See note 1.

———. 1799. *From George Washington to Alexander Hamilton, 12 December 1799*. [Online] Available at: https://founders.archives.gov/documents/Washington/06-04-02-0402 [Accessed 21 December 2019].

———. 1799. *George Washington's Last Will and Testament, 9 July 1799*. [Online] Available at: https://founders.archives.gov/documents/Washington/06-04-02-0404-0001 [Accessed 2019 30 June]. [Original source: The Papers of George Washington, Retirement Series, vol. 4, 20 April 1799–13

December 1799, ed. W. W. Abbot. Charlottesville: University Press of Virginia, 1999, pp. 479–511.].

Washington, H. A. 1854. *The Writings of Thomas Jefferson*. Washington, D.C., United States: Taylor & Maury. Available at: https://archive.org/details/writingsthomasj01washgoog/page/n146 [accessed 7 June 2019]. Other editions: Cambridge Unversity Press, 1854. The author's full name is Henry Augustine Washington.

Washington, H. A. 1884. *The Works of Thomas Jefferson*. New York, New York, United States of America: Townsend Mac Co.

Washington, Martha, n.d. *The Gilder Lehrman Collection, The Gilder Lehrman Institute of American History*. [Online] Available at: https://www.gilderlehrman.org/collections/ac25df48-53c9-4c0f-ae85-368076307291 [Accessed 30 March 2017].

Washington, Martha, n.d. *To George Washington from William Heth, 3 May 1789 (footnote)*. [Online] National Archives Available at: https://founders.archives.gov/documents/Washington/05-02-02-0146. See footnote re undated letter from MW. [Original source: The Papers of George Washington, Presidential Series, vol. 2, 1 April 1789–15 June 1789, ed. Dorothy Twohig. Charlottesville: University Press of Virginia, 1987, pp. 204–206.].

Washington, Mary B., 1788. *The Will of Mary Washington, as Registered in the Clerk's Office at Fredericksburg, Virginia*. [Online] Available at: https://digitalcommons.wku.edu/dlsc_mss_fin_aid/2705/ [Accessed 27 February 2021]. A printed version of the one-page will is available for download at the web page listed.

Washington's Headquarters State Historic Site Mountaintop Beacons. information on file at Washington Headquarters Museum, Newburgh, NY, reviewed on July 16, 2016.

Waymarkings.com, 2016. *David Humphreys -- Hartford CT*. [Online] Available at: https://www.waymarking.com/waymarks/WMQAG1_David_Humphreys_Hartford_CT [Accessed 16 April 2020].

Webster, Noah 1789. *Dissertations on the English Language*. Boston, Massachusetts, United States of America: I. Thomas and Co. Available at: https://archive.org/details/dissertationsone00webs/page/18/mode/2up [accessed 20 May 2020].

———. 1789. *Pacificus [Noah Webster] to James Madison (August 14, 1789)*. [Online] Constitutional Sources Project Available at: https://www.consource.org/document/pacificus-noah-webster-to-james-madison-1789-8-14/ [Accessed 8 May 2020].

Wells, Colins 2017. *Poetry Wars: Verse and Politics in the American Revolution and Early Republic*. Philadelphia: University of Pennsylvania Press.

Wharton, Francis 1889. *The Revolutionary Diplomatic Correspondence of the U.S.* Washington, D.C., United States of America: Government Printing Office.

Wharton, Anne H. *The Washingtons in Official Life. Lippincott's Monthly Magazine*, 1896. Available at: https://babel.hathitrust.org/cgi/pt?id=pst.000020206147&view=1up&seq=880 [Accessed 30 April 2020].

White, George S. 1836. *Memoir of Samuel Slater. the Father of American Manufacures*. Philadelphia: A.M. Kelley.

Wilberforce, William, 2007. *William Wilberforce's 1789 Abolition Speech*. [Online] Available at: https://brycchancarey.com/abolition/wilberforce2.htm [Accessed 7 May 2020].

———.n.d. *William Wilberforce's 1789 Abolition Speech*. [Online] Available at: https://www.st-andrews-anglican-calgary.ca/downloads/WilberforceSpeech1789.pdf [Accessed 7 May 2020].

Williams, George W. 1885. *History of the negro race in America from 1619 to 1880. Negroes as slaves, as soldiers, and as citizens.* New York, New York, United States of America: G.P. Putman's sons. Available at: https://archive.org/details/historyofnegrora00willrich/page/n361/mode/2up.

Williams, William H. 2003. *Slavery and Freedom in Delaware, 1639-1865.* New York: Harper. Wilmington, DE: Scholarly Resources, 1996.

Willius, F. A. & Keys, T. E., 1942. The Medical History of George Washington (1732-1799) [Part II]. *Proceedings of the Staff Meetings of the Mayo Clinic*, pp. 107-12.

———.February 11, 1942. The Medical History of George Washington (1732-1799) I. *Proceedings of the Staff Meetings of the Mayo Clinic*, pp. 92-95.

Wills, Garry 1979. *Inventing America: Jefferson's Declaration of Independence.* New York: Vintage.

Wilmington Centinel, 1789. *The Wilmington Centinel February 19, 1789.* [Online] Available at: https://newspapers.digitalnc.org/lccn/sn83025833/1789-02-19/ed-1/seq-1/ [Accessed 20 June 2019].

Wilson, James G. & Fiske, John 1888. *Appleton's Cyclopedia of American Biography.* New York, New York, United States of America: D. Appleton and Company. Available at: https://archive.org/download/AppletonsCyclopediaOfAmericanBiographyVol.3.

Winton, Calhoun, 1977. The Theater and Drama. In E. Emerson, ed. *American Literature, 1764-1789: The Revolutionary Years.* Madison: University of Wisconsin Press.

Wood, Gordon S. 2009. *Empire of Liberty: A History of the Early Republic, 1789-1815.* New York: Oxford University Press.

————.2010. *Lecture: Gordon S. Wood, "The Articles of Confederation and the Constitution"*. [Online] Available at: https://www.humanitiestexas.org/news/articles/gordon-s-wood-articles-confederation-and-constitution [Accessed 4 May 2020]. The reference to British demographer Jim Potter is at approximately the 8:50 time mark.

————.2012. *Lecture: The Making of the U.S. Constitution*. [Online] San Antonio, United States of America Available at: https://www.youtube.com/watch?v=N-RnOAiCUfMM. See also http://www.humanitiestexas.org/archives/digital-repository/wood-making-us-constitution-2012 [Accessed 4 May 2020].

————. The Bleeding Founders. Book review of Revolutionary Medicine: The Founding Fathers and Mothers in Sickness and in Health by Jeanne E. Abrams, 2013, NYU Press. Page 16 states GW, A, Adams, B Franklin supported bleeding, p 26 and etc re Rush on bleeding. (Re books.google.com).

Worcester Magazine. *Summary of Late Intelligence. Worcester Magazine*, 1787. Available at: https://www.google.com/books/edition/Worcester_Magazine/omoAAAAAYAAJ?hl=en&gbpv=1&bsq=238 [Accessed 21 April 2020].

Wright, Jr., Robert K. & MacGregor, Jr., Morris J. 1987. *Soldier-Statesmen of the Constitution*. Washington, D.C., United States of America: U.S. Army Center of Military History. Available at: https://history.army.mil/books/RevWar/ss/johnson.htm. Cited from web site listed in URL.

Wright, Carroll D. 1900. *The history and growth of the United States census*. Washington, D.C., United States of America: United States Government Printing Office.

Yates, Robert, 1886. *Notes of the Secret Debates of the Federal Convention of 1787, Taken by the Late Hon Robert Yates, Chief Justice of the State of New York, and One of the Delegates from That State to the Said Convention*. [Online] Washington, United States of America: Lillian Goldman Law Library Yale Law School Available at: https://avalon.law.yale.edu/18th_century/yates.asp.

Young, Edward 1877. *Special report on the customs-tariff legislation of the United States with appendixes*. Washington, D.C., United States of America: United States Government Printing Office. Available at: https://archive.org/details/specialreportonc00youn/page/n21/mode/2up.

INDEX

Symbols

39-41 Broadway 76, 198. *See* also
Macomb House

A

abolition 127
gradual in Northern states. *See*
various state names
in New York 60
movement for in Britain 60
Quaker petitions for 129
Southern fear of 130
Act for Establishing the Temporary
and Permanent Seat of the
Government of the United
States 201
Act for the Encouragement of
Learning. *See* Copyright Law
Acts of Congress (book) 148
Act to Establish the Judicial Courts
112
Act to Regulate the Collection of the
Duties. *See* Tariff Act
Act to Regulate the Time and
Manner of Administering
Certain Oaths 106
Act to Restrict Trade with Rhode
Island 202
Adams, Abigail 93, 238
belief in bleeding as cure 161
death and stillbirth of children 157
fears for Washington's life 158
reports Washington treated with
James's Fever Powder 159
Adams, John 10, 12, 29, 51, 105, 156,
224, 232
and debates over presidential title 79,
80, 81

as president
establishes Department of Navy
188
names Washington Commander in
Chief 233
concerns about Society of the
Cincinnati 33
election as Vice President ratified 66
notified of his election 67
on presidential social activity 87
seeks in vain for guidance as to
behavior toward President 81
sworn in as Vice President before
President is sworn 68
takes oath of office as Vice President
107
Adams, John Quincy 102
Adams, Samuel
concerns about Society of the
Cincinnati 33
Addison, Joseph 96
African Chief, The (poem) 225
African Free School 60
Alexander, William 77
Algerian confrontations 184, 213
Algerian pirates 184
Algerian treatment of prisoners 185
Alien and Sedition Acts 232
Amendments. *See* also Constitution
of the United States of
America
arguments against attempting 138
proposed 137
The American Book of Common
Prayer. *See Book of Common
Prayer*
American Daily Advertiser 231
The American Geography (book) 225
American language
development of 218

American Magazine 220
The American Museum (magazine)
    135, 219
  endorsed by Washington 219
American Magazine and General
    Repository (magazine) 21
American Philosophical Society
The American Spelling Book 217
Ames, Fisher 85, 102, 118, 196, 204
Anas (book)
  account of assumption-residence deal
    in 198
  doubts over residence-debt account
    in 201
Anderson, James 234
Anglicans 124
Annapolis Convention 36
Annual Message to a Joint Session
    of Congress. *See* State of the
    Union
  Washington delivers 191
Anti-Federalist Party 52
Anti-slavery law
  in Pennsylvania 180
Anti-tax amendment proposed 143
The Apotheosis of George Washington,
    (allegorical painting) 244
The Apotheosis of Washington
    (engraving) 240
Apthorp, Fanny 224
Apthorp, Sarah 224
Apthorp, Sarah Wentworth 224
Architect of the Capitol 244
Arminian Magazine 220
Armstrong, John Jr.
  and "fellow soldier" letter 23
  membership in Society of the
    Cincinnati 32
  on Washington's arrival in New York
    75

Army Clause of U.S. Constitution.
    See also Constitution of the
    United States of America
army, fear of standing force 187
Article I of U.S. Constitution. *See*
    also Constitution of the
    United States of America
  taxing authority 108
Article II of U.S. Constitution 149,
    155
Article V of U.S. Constitution 139
  powers of Congress under 14
Article VI of U.S. Constitution 107,
    194
Articles of Confederation 10, 14, 35,
    116, 184
  no longer in effect 63
asafetida 161
Associated Press 221
assumption, federal, of state debts
    195
assumption of foreign debts
  accepted by Congress 197
Attorney General
  position created in Judiciary Act 113

B

balance maintained between
    northern and southern states
    202
Baldwin, Abraham 110
Bank of North America 170
Bank of the United States 175
Banneker, Benjamin 177
Bard, John 158
Bard, Samuel 157
Barr brothers (Scottish weavers) 173
Bastille
  storming of 163

Bastille Day 163
Bastille Key 163, 164
  displayed at Mount Vernon 164
Benson, Egbert 196
Beverly Cotton Manufactory 172
Beverly, Massachusetts 172
Bible used for First Inaugural 83
Bickford, Charlene 104
Bill of Rights 191. See also
        Constitution of the United
        States of America
  draft of transmitted from House to
        Senate 143
  House and Senate form Conference
        Committee to consider 144
  language covering freedom of religion
        142
  ratified by states 144
  rough draft in National Archives 143
Blackburn, Thomas 51
bleeding as cure 161
Blue-Backed Speller (book) 217
The Book of Common Prayer
  revision of 124
Boudinot, Elias 26, 74, 131, 196
Bourne, Sylvanus 67
Bowdoin, James 224
Bowling, Kenneth R.
  article on Philadelphia Mutiny 27
broadcloth
  woven for clothing for Inaugural
        events 65, 67, 110, 170
Brookes (slave ship) 134
Brown, John 133
Brown, Joseph 133
Brown, Moses 133
Brown, Nicholas 133
Brown, William Hill 223, 225
Brumidi, Constantino 244
Buchan's Domestic Medicine (book)
  160

Buchan, William 160
Burke, Aedanus 103, 118, 131, 143
  nearly duels with Hamilton 156
  opposes abolition 129
  opposes Federal Thanksgiving
        proclamation 147
  writes "Considerations on the Society
        or Order of Cincinnati" 33

C

Cabot, George 174
Campus Martius 204
Canada
  Loyalists move to 122
canvassing area in first Federal
        census. See U.S. Census
Capitol Building 243
Carey, Mathew 134, 219
Caribbean 183
Carroll, Charles 81
Carroll, Daniel 178
Cato (theatrical play) 96
Census. See U.S. Census
Ceracchi, Giuseppe 191
Charleston, South Carolina 127, 179
Chesapeake Bay 184
Children's Magazine 219
Christian's, Scholar's, and Farmer's
        Magazine 220
Church of England 124
cinchona tree bark 161
Cincinnati, Ohio 214
Cincinnati, Society of the. See
        Society of the Cincinnati
Cincinnatus, Lucius Quinctius 31
circular letter
  sent by Washington in 1783 192
citizenship 122
Clarkson, Thomas 134
classes
  to determine terms for U.S. Senators
        107

Clinton, George 67

Clymer, George 159, 196
  opposes migration to Northwest
    Territory 204

Coach
  Washington's 170, 191
  elaborate decoration of 191

Cobbett, William
  sued by Rush for libel re bleeding as
    cure 162

Coles, Isaac 101

Collection Act 111

Columbia, South Carolina 179

Columbian (magazine) 65

Committee of Style and Arrangement
  Constitutional Convention 42

Committee of the Whole in House of
  Representatives 66

Common Sense (book) 17, 166

Compact of 1785 35

Compromise of 1790 198

Confederation, Articles of. *See*
  Articles of Confederation

Confederation Congress 123,
    203. *See* Congress of the
    Confederation

Congress Hall 212
  description of 212

Congress of the Confederation 18,
    101, 150, 209
  abandons Philadelphia for Princeton
    26
  George Washington and 47
  last meeting of 55
  repeatedly moves from city to city 26

Connecticut 169, 226
  passes Gradual Abolition Act 135

Connolly, John 206
  attempts to recruit Wilkinson, tricks
    him into departing 209
  captured as Loyalist 206
  paroled, exchanged, recaptured,
    paroled, re-imprisoned 206

  travels to New York and England 207
  travels to Quebec and Louisville 207

*Considerations on the Society or Order of
    Cincinnati*
  pamphlet by Aedanus Burke 34

Constantia. *See* Morton, Sarah
    Wentworth

Constitutional Convention 9, 100,
    130, 140
  Committee of Style and Arrangement
    42
  compromise establishing House and
    Senate 55, 64
  debate on nature of "National
    Executive" 64
  debate on presidential powers 41
  debate over method of electing
    presidents 50
  opens on May 25 39
  proceeding kept secret 40

Constitution of the United States
    of America. *See* also
    Amendments
  Army Clause 187
  Article I
    taxing authority 108
  Article II
    executive powers 71
  Article V 139
  Article VI 107, 194
  Bill of Rights 99
  drafting text of Second Amendment
    141
  Madison notes reasons for
    amendments 137
  Naval Clause 187
  presidential oath in 83
  procedure for amending 139
  ratification of 44
  signing of 42
  slave clauses in 130
  Thirteenth Amendment bans slavery
    136

three-fifths clause 40, 101, 115
Twenty-seventh Amendment to 145
Continental Army 184
  officers petition Congress regarding
    pay 23
  soldiers furloughed 30
Continental Congress 101, 102, 107,
    183
Continental Navy 184
The Contrast (play) 221
Conway, Richard
  loans George Washington money 52
Copyright Act 219
Copyright law 220
Cornwallis, Charles 18
Corps of Invalids 21
Cortlandt, John Van 124
Cosby, William 56
Courier de Boston (magazine) 220
Coxe, Tench 198
Creek Nation 210
Cumberland Gap 206
Cumberland Gazette 221
Custis, Eleanor Calvert 51
Custis, Eleanor Parke 212
Custis, George Washington 234
Custis, George Washington Parke
    212
Custis, John Parke 51
  death from yellow fever 157
Custis, Martha Parke
  early death of 157

D

Daily Advertiser 222
Daily Gazette 196
Dalton, Tristram 107
Darby's Return (theatrical sketch) 96
Dauphin (ship) 185
debts, Revolutionary War 194
Declaration of Independence 12, 14
  deleted clause on slavery 12
  timeline of creation 12

Delaware
  bans slave trade but not slavery 135
Dickinson, John 25
Dissertations on the English Language
    (book) 217
Doorkeeper, Senate. *See* **also sergeant**
    at arms
  Mathers, James 106
dowry slaves 235
Duane, James 58, 60
Duer, Catherine Alexander 77
Dunlap, William 96
Dunmore, John Murray, 4th Earl of.
    See Dunmore, Lord
Dunmore, Lord
  offers slaves freedom in exchange for
    army service 127
Duties on imported goods 109

E

East Florida 127
Elections to First Federal Congress
  delays to 104
Electoral College 42
  as compromise solution 50
  original procedure for election 51
Elénor-François-Élie 57, 79, 111
Ellicott, Andrew 177
Ellsworth, Oliver 112
Episcopal Church 124
Ethiopian Regiment 127
Evacuation Day
  Boston 13

F

The Family Physician (book). *See*
    Buchan's Domestic Medicine
Farewell Address, Washington
  publishes 231
Farewell Address, Washington's 231
The Father or American Shandyism
    (theatrical play) 96
federal assumption of state debts 195

Federal bureaucracy
  beginning of 111
Federal Court System
  establishment of 113
Federal Hall 57, 114, 191, 211, 222
  construction of 58
  description of 58
  last official function in 212
  torn down in 1812 61
Federalist Papers 41
Federalist Party 52
Federalists
  opposition to constitutional
    amendments 138
"Fellow Soldier" letter 23
Fenno, John 221
Firelands 204
First Act of Congress
  Act to Regulate the Time and Manner
    of Administering Certain Oaths
    106
first American novel 223
First Continental Congress 10
first Federal Congress
  First session
    accomplishments of 99
First Federal Congress 59, 61, 71,
    100, 117, 129, 137, 190, 191,
    218. See Joint Congressional
    Committee on the
    Inauguration
  accomplishments of 61
  begins 63
  deadlocked over assumption 197
  elections to 56
  moves to Philadelphia 212
  second session 191, 192
  third session 212, 213
First ship to pay Federal impost
    duties
  Sally (ship) 110

Fishbourn, Benjamin
  abortive duel with James Gunn 153
  nomination refused by Senate 152
Fitzsimons, Thomas 188, 196, 212
foreign debts, assumption of
  accepted by Congress 197
Fort Harmar 214
Fort Washington 214
Foster, Abiel 104
Franklin, Benjamin 9, 18, 29
  as abolitionist 128
  as slave owner 127
  belief in bleeding as cure 161
  concerns about Society of the
    Cincinnati 34
  death and funeral of 128
  first writing about slavery 128
  petitions Congress to abolish slavery
    128
  suffering various illnesses 157
Franklin, Jesse 101
Franklin, Maria Bowne 76
Franklin (proposed state) 204
Franklin, Walter 76
Fraunces, Samuel 78, 92
Fraunces Tavern 55, 78
Freedom of religion
  language covering in Bill of Rights
    142
French fleet 184
French Revolution 163
  confused reports of its end 168
  news of delayed in America 165
frigates
  finally completed 188
  not completed 188
frigates for Continental Navy 184
frigates for U.S. Navy 188
frigates ordered sold by Congress
    187
Funding Act
  debt assumption added to 201

G

Gardoqui, Don Diego de 76
Gates, Horatio 75
 and "fellow soldier" letter 23
 membership in Society of the
  Cincinnati 32
Gazette of the State of Georgia 221
Gazette of the United States 99, 222
Genêt, Edmond-Charles
 Attempts to recruit American
  privateers 189
*Gentleman and Ladies Town and
 Country Magazine* 220
Geography Made Easy (book) 225
George III 10, 12, 13, 124, 159
George Washington (packet boat) 29
Georgia 213, 223, 226, 238
Georgia Gazette 99, 101
Gerry, Elbridge 100, 101, 131, 138,
 196
 refuses to sign Constitution 42
Gibbs, Henry 174
God Save the King (song)
 new lyrics to honor Washington 75
Goodhue, Benjamin 174
*A Grammatical Institute of the English
 Language* (book). *See* Blue-
 Backed Speller & *American
 Spelling Book*
Grand Banks 183
Grand Federal Procession 57
Greene, Nathanael 13, 153
Gunn, James 152
 abortive duel with Benjamin
  Fishbourn 153
Gwinnett, Button 153
 dies as result of duel with McIntosh
  153

H

Hagerstown 206
Halifax 127

Hamilton, Alexander 13, 53, 60, 67,
 233, 239
and Federalist Papers 105
calls for constitutional convention 36
deal over debt and residence 198, 199
defends Loyalists 125
membership in Society of the
 Cincinnati 32
nearly duels with Burke 156
on president's social activity 88
proposes furlough of soldiers 25
proposes National Bank 213
supports tax on distilled spirits 231
urges hands-off policy toward France
 165
writes report on public credit 194
Hamilton (barge) 74
Hamtramck, John F. 239
Hancock, John 67, 224, 132
 snubs Washington due to states rights
  172
Harmar, Josiah 214
Harmar's Defeat 214
Harriot, or the Domestic
 Reconciliation (short story)
 225
Harrison, Benjamin 116
Harrison, Robert 51
Harrison, Robert H. 67
Hartford Manufacturing Company
 110
Hartford Woolen Company 171
Hartley, David 29
Henry, Patrick 89
 as slave owner 127
 denounces proposed constitution 41,
  44
 distrustful of strong executive 71
*Herald of Freedom and the Federal
 Advertiser* 223
Hercules, enslaved chef to
 Washingtons 180

The History of the American Revolution, (book) 15, 37

A History of the Life and Death, Virtues and Exploits of General George Washington, (book) 240

Hopkins, Esek
commander of *Sally* 133

Hopkins, Stephen
owns slaves but writes against slavery 133

House and Senate rules 66

House of Representatives
debates anti-slavery petitions 129
public galleries of 114
resolution calling for naval force 188

Howe, Robert
suppresses mutiny at Pompton Camp 23

Humphreys, David 17, 72, 92, 155, 170, 191
and levees 89
calls for new general government 27
draft of Inaugural discarded 49
draft of inaugural with slavery reference rejected 48
warning to Washington regarding state of army 19
writes draft of first Inaugural 47
writes *Life of General Washington* (book) 48

Huntington, Samuel 171

I

Inaugural address
Washington delivers 84

Inauguration
plans for 78

Inauguration Day 1789 79, 81

Independence Hall 11

Indians. *See* Native Americans

Industrialization of Northern states 169

infant mortality 157

influenza epidemic 159

Innes, Harry 207

Ira and Isabella (play) 225

Irving, Washington
claims to witnesses Inauguration as a child 84

Izard, Ralph 79, 144
duel with Tucker 153

J

Jackson, Andrew 9

Jackson, James 103, 131

Jackson, William 170, 198

Jamaica 127

James's Fever Powder 159

Jay, John 29, 34, 51, 60, 67, 170
and Federalist Papers 105
nominated as chief justice 113

Jay Treaty 189

Jefferson, Thomas 9, 17, 18, 22, 89, 232
allows French revolutionaries to meet in his house 165
and French Revolution 164
as secretary of state 165, 186
concerned for Lafayette 164
concerns about Society of the Cincinnati 33
his concept of rights as protection against government 139
opposes tax on distilled spirits 231
presents report on Algerian prisoners to Washington 186
relates his version of assumption-residence deal 199
skeptical of first census result 119
urges support for France 165

Johnson, Thomas 178

Johnson, William Samuel 100

John Street Theatre 221

Joint Congressional Committee on the Inauguration 78

Jones, John Paul 183

Judge, Oney 180
  escapes from slavery 180
Judicial Supremacy 113
Judiciary Act 99, 112, 113, 116
  opposition to creation of federal
    judiciary 118

K

Kent, James 114
Kentucky 226
  admitted to Union 202, 210
  statehood conventions 209
Kentucky District of Virginia 205,
  206
Knox, Henry 64, 154, 214, 215
  and founding of Society of the
    Cincinnati 31
  warns of possible rebellion 36

L

Lafayette, Marquis de 18, 43, 52, 163,
  219
  arrested and imprisoned during
    French Revolution 168
  embroiled in French Revolution 164
  relationship with Washington 164
  released 168
Langdon, John 69, 106, 107, 144
  Administers oath of office to John
    Adams 107
Laurens, Henry 29, 133
Law, Elizabeth Parke Custis 238
Lear, Benjamin Lincoln 152
Lear, Tobias 38, 72, 77, 94, 152, 153,
  170, 191, 212, 233
  as chief of staff 151
  as secretary to the president 92
  schemes to keep Washington's slaves
    from freedom 180
  urges Washington to tour New
    England 169
Lee, Arthur 91
Lee, Billy (William) 73

arrives in New York 92
  freed in Washington's will 236
  unable to continue journey to New
    York 73
Lee, Charles 150
Lee, Francis Lightfoot 91
Lee, Henry
  eulogizes Washington 239
Lee, Richard Bland 159, 197
Lee, Richard Henry 80
  makes resolution for independence
    11
Legion of the United States 215
L'Enfant, Peter Charles 57. See also
  L'Enfant, Pierre
L'Enfant, Pierre. See also L'Enfant,
  Peter Charles
  commissioned to draw plans of new
    capital 177
  designs Cincinnati membership
    medal 32
levee 89
Lewis, Betty 65
Library of Congress 59
The Life and Travels of John Robert
  Shaw, (book) 228
life expectancy 157
Life of General Washington (book)
  by David Humphreys 48
Lighthouse Act 112
Lincoln, Abraham 240, 243
Livingston, Robert 77
Livingston, Robert R.
  administers oath of office to
    Washington 83
Livingston, Sarah 77
Lloyd, Thomas 221
Logan Act 189
Logan, George 189
Louisiana Territory 205
Louis XIV 57
Louis XVI 33
  executed 167
Loyalists 13, 122

arrested, property seized, and hanged 125

defended in court by Hamilton 125

in exile 123

mistreatment after Revolution 123

persecution of 30

remaining in U.S. 123

M

Maclay, William 79, 85, 107, 112, 144, 150, 159, 227

account of assumption-residence deal 197

and Washington's levees 90, 91, 94

disapproves Adams' reaction to Inaugural address 85, 86

journal as key source 80

journal's discovery and publication 80

on conspiracies in Kentucky 205

on creation of army 214

on Washington visiting Senate 154

purported cure for rheumatism 161

witnesses debt assumption vote 196

witnesses Inaugural address 84

Macomb House. *See also* 39-41 Broadway

Second presidential residence 77, 164

Madison, James 9, 70, 88, 100, 105, 131

and Federalist Papers 105

arranges release of Thomas Paine 167

assists Washington with First Inaugural Address 48

as slave owner 127

commenting on Washington's illness 158

keeps notes on Constitutional Convention 41

makes notes regarding constitutional amendments 137

on judicial supremacy 113

proposes Bill of Rights to House 140

proposes constitutional convention 37

proposes duties on many imported products 109

refers to Treaty of Paris 29

speaks against federal assumption of debt 196

writing against slavery 128

Maine 238

Maine District 118

Maria (schooner) 184

Marie Antoinette
executed 167

Marietta, Ohio 203
suffering of in 1790s 205

Marshall, Thomas 207
reports to Washington regarding Connolly 208

Martin, Joseph Plumb 228

Maryland Committee of Public Safety 206

Maryland Journal 131

Mason, George 41, 138

as slave owner 127

denounces slavery and calls for end to importation 42

refuses to sign constitution 42

writing against slavery 128

Masonic funeral rites
for Washington 237

Masons
mourn Washington 238

represented at Washington's funeral 239

Massachusetts 169

State Supreme Court rules slavery against State constitution 135

Massachusetts Magazine 220, 225

Massachusetts (Revenue Cutter) 112

Mathers, James
Doorkeeper to the Senate. *See* also sergeant at arms

Mathews, George 103

Maury, Fontaine 49
McGillivray, Alexander 211
McHenry, James 74
McIntosh, Lachlan
  nominated by Washington 153
  wounded in duel with Gwinnet 153
Miami village in Ohio 214
Miró, Esteban Rodríguez 208
mock funerals
  for Washington 238
Molasses
  duties on 110
  tariffs on 108
Monarchy
  continued desire for 53
Monroe, James 9, 41
Morris, Gouverneur 165
  appointed U.S. Minister
    Plenipotentiary to France 165
  author of Constitution's Preamble 42
  refuses to assist imprisoned Thomas
    Paine 167
Morris, Robert 63, 150, 154, 183, 197
Morse, Jedidiah 225
Morton, Perez 224
Morton, Sarah 224
Morton, Sarah Wentworth 225. See
  Sarah Apthorp
Mount Vernon 88, 232
  317 enslaved persons at 235
  Washington briefly returns in 1791
    178
Mount Vernon Ladies' Association
  164
Muhlenberg, Frederick Augustus
  Conrad 81
  first Speaker of the House 65
Murray, Judith Sargent 211, 220

N

Napoleon Bonaparte 189
A Narrative of a Revolutionary Soldier,
  (book) 228

National Bank 213
Native Americans
  not counted in U.S. Census 121
Natives Americans
  estimates of population 121
Naturalization Act 122
Naval Clause
  U.S. Constitution 187
Navy
  positive view of in Congress 187
Nelson, Thomas, Jr. 191
Newburyport, Massachusetts
  Washington's elaborate welcome at
    172
New Hampshire 104, 116, 141, 169,
  180
New Jersey 213
  begins slow abolition in 1804 135
New York 127, 213
  calls for convention to propose
    amendments 45
  legal system in 1780s 60
  passes Gradual Emancipation Act
    135
  ratifies Constitution 44
  slavery in 60
New York City
  city officials suppress anti-Washington
    cartoon 75
  condition of in 1789 59
New York Daily Gazette 60
New-York Journal and Weekly Register
  222
New York Society for the
  Encouragement of American
  Manufactures 222
New York Society for the
  Manumission of Slaves 60
New-York Society Library 59
New-York Theater 96
New-York Weekly Journal 56

Nicola, Lewis 20
  membership in Society of the
      Cincinnati 32
  writes Newburgh Letter 21
No. 1 Cherry Street 76, 77, 158
  as Washington's first house in New
      York 76
North Carolina 226
  ratifies Constitution 201
Northwest Territory 203, 204, 210
  1792 population estimate 121
  various state claims to 204
Notes of Debates in the Federal
      Convention of 1787 41
Nourse, Joseph
  career of 150
  "first federal worker" 150

O

O'Bryen, Richard 185
Ohio Company of Associates 203
Ohio River 115
Ohio Valley 213
Olive Branch Petition 10
Oney. See Judge, Oney
On the Equality of the Sexes. See
      Murray, Judith Sargent
Ordinance of 1784 203
Ordinance of 1787 203
Osgood, Samuel 76
Oswald, Richard 29
Otto, Louis-Guillaume 39, 194

P

Page, John 101, 160
Paine, Thomas 17, 166-167
  accepts Bastille Key 163
  arrested in France 167
  shunned for opposition to organized
      religion 167
Patriots 122
Paul, François Joseph 184
Pawtucket, Rhode Island 174

Peace Establishment 193
  instead of army 192
peaceful transfer of power 232
Peale, Charles Wilson 73
Pelham, New York 55
Pell, Philip 55
Pennsylvania 213, 226, 231
  law providing for slave to be freed
      after six months 180
  passes law of gradual abolition 135
Pennsylvania Gazette 127, 138
Pennsylvania Government
  arrests and executes Loyalists for
      treason 125
Pennsylvania Militia
  marches on State House 25
Pennsylvania Society for Promoting
      the Abolition of Slavery 128
Perkins, Thomas H. 223
Permanent Capital
  potential sites for 175
Peter, Martha Parke Custis 238
Philadelphia, Pennsylvania
  permits theatrical performance 221
Philenia. See Morton, Sarah
      Wentworth
pirates 184
population growth
  caused by optimism 122
Potomac River
  conference regulating use of 35
The Power of Sympathy (novel) 223
power to dismiss officials
  presidential 156
precedent
  Washington on establishing 155
precedents
  establishment of 151
Prescott, Martha 174
President
  debates over titles or form of address
      for 79, 80

executive power of 156
power to dismiss officials 156
presidential oath
in Constitution 83
Presidential Oath of Office 72
to be administered in public 72
President's House
in Philadelphia 176
prisoners in Algiers
ransom negotiations 186
privateers 184
Protestant Episcopal Church of the
United States. *See* Episcopal
Church
Punishment of Crimes Act 99
Puritan bans on theater fade away
220
Putnam, Rufus 203

Q

Quaker anti-slavery petitions 129
Quasi War 189, 232
Quebec 205

R

Ramage, John 124
Ramsay, David 14, 39
on debate about ratification 43
Randolph, Beverley 89, 171
Randolph, Edmund 53
refuses to sign Constitution 42
warns Martha Washington about
anti-slavery law 179
Randolph, Edmund Jennings 158
ransom
awarded in treaty with Algiers 188
ransom negotiations, Algerian 185,
186
Rawlins, Albin 235
Report of the Secretary of the
Treasury on the Public Credit
194

Residence Act 175
Revelations (Book of New Testament)
quoted in reference to George
Washington 74
revenue cutters 187
Revenue Marine. *See* Coast Guard
Revolutionary War
casualties in 14
Revolutionary War debts 194
Rhode Island
boycotts Constitutional Convention
132
gradual Abolition Act 135
involvement in slave trade 132. *See*
Triangle Trade
offers slaves freedom in exchange for
army service 127
ratifies Constitution 202
textile industry of 173
treated as foreign territory before
joining Union 111
Washington avoids on tour of North
169
Rights of Man (book) 166
Rogue Island
Insulting name for Rhode Island 132
Royal Navy 183
Rules of House and Senate 66
Rush, Benjamin 131, 156, 159, 222
belief in bleeding as cure 161
medical arguments against slavery
131
Rutledge, Edward 131
Rutledge, John 51, 67
Rutledge, John Jr. 163

S

Salem Mercury 223
Sally (ship)
first ship to pay Federal impost duties
110
Sally (slave ship) 133
disastrous voyage of 133

Savannah, Georgia 179
Schuyler, Elizabeth 105
Scott, Thomas 131
Seat of the Government of the
        United States. *See* permanent
        capital
Second Amendment
    drafting text of. *See* Constitution of
        the United States of America
Second Continental Congress 10
Secretary of the First Continental
        Congress
    Charles, Thomson 68
Sedgwick, Theodore 104, 160, 196
sergeant at arms 106
Shaw, John Robert 228
Shays' Rebellion 37, 38
Sherman, Roger 161, 174
    establishes precedents for form of
        Amendments 142
ships, design of American merchant
        183
Short, William 186
silk manufacturing 171
Slater, Samuel 173
slave clauses. *See* Constitution of the
        United States of America
    in U.S. Constitution 130
slave, runaway
    advertisement concerning 222
slavery
    gradual abolition in northern states.
        See various state names
    in New York 60
slavery economics 178
slaves
    accompany Washington on Northern
        tour 170
    account of cruelty toward 222
    as fraction of U.S. population 115
    counted in 1790 U.S. Census 121
    depart U.S. during Revolution 127
slave trade
    ends in Britain 134

Smith, William Loughton 131
Society of the Cincinnati 152, 153,
        240
    founding 31
    represented at Washington's funeral
        239
    senators and representatives as
        members of 100
    supposed support for monarchy
        during Constitutional
        Convention 39
    suspicions concerning 32
Soldier lands 31
South Carolina 226
Southwest Territory 204
Sparks, Jared 49
stagecoaches 102
standing army, fear of 187
State of Franklin 204
State of the Union Address 42, 192,
        213, 256. *See also* Annual
        Message to a Joint Session of
        Congress
St. Clair, Arthur 204, 214
    suspects Connolly is British agent
        207
St. Clair's Defeat 215
Steuben, Frederick William Von
        [Friedrich Wilhelm Von] 57,
        91
    membership in Society of the
        Cincinnati 31
St. Lucia 127
Stone, Michael Jenifer 160
Stuart, David 51, 88, 89, 159, 178
Sufferers' Land 204
Supreme Council of Pennsylvania.
        See Pennsylvania
Supreme Court of the United States
        99, 112
    first opinion of 114
    first session of 113
Symmes, John Cleves 213

T

A Tale of a Tub, (book) 138
Talleyrand 189
Tariff Act 150
Tariffs. *See* Duties on imported
    goods
  on Wheeled vehicles 110
Tax upon spirits distilled within the
    United States 231
Temple of Virtue 24
Tennessee 204
textile industry 174
Thatcher, George 109
theatrical performances
  in multiple cities 221
  permitted in Philadelphia 221
Thirteenth Amendment
  Bans slavery. *See* Constitution of the
    United States of America
Thompson, Catherine 101
Thomson, Charles 68, 72
  pushed out by Lee and Adams 80
  secretary of the First Continental
    Congress 68
  stripped of position 70
Three-fifths clause
  of U.S. Constitution 115, 116
  source of proposal 116
Tiffany, Constant 124
Tonnage Act 111
Tories. *See* Loyalists
travel 102, 103
treason laws proposed 124
Treaty of New York 210
Treaty of Paris
  ends Revolutionary War 203
  ratification of by Congress 30
  terms of 29
Triangle Trade 108
Trumbull, Jonathan Jr. 129
Tucker, Thomas Tudor 53, 103
  duel with Izard 153
  opposes Federal Thanksgiving
    proclamation 147
  proposes anti-tax amendment 143
Twenty-seventh Amendment
  to the U.S. Constitution 145
Tyler, Royall 221

U

Upper Canada 205
U.S. Census 115
  conduct of first in 1790 118
  Indians not counted 121
  modern analysis of 1790 data 121
  no count in Northwest Territory in
    1790 121
  result of 1790 count 119
  slaves counted in 1790 121
U.S. Coast Guard 112
U.S. Congress
  declares period of mourning for
    Washington 238
  rescinds treaties with France 233
U.S. Constitution. *See* Constitution
    of the United States of
    America
U.S. House and Senate
  joint session accepts electors
    certificates 67
U.S. House of Representatives
  establishes first quorum April 1, 1789
    65
U.S. Marshals Service 117
  establishment of 113, 117
  ordered to conduct census 117
U.S. Navy
  battles France in Quasi War 189
U.S. Senate
  debates kept secret 79
  establishes first quorum April 6, 1789
    66, 106
  lottery to determine classes 107
  Washington visits 152

V

Varnum, James Mitchell
  membership in Society of the
      Cincinnati 32
  urges monarchy or military state 22
Vermont
  admitted to Union 202
  bans slavery 135
  slaves mistakenly counted in 1790
      census 119
Vining, John 131
Virginia 213, 226
  most populous state in 1790 121
  ratifies Constitution 44
Virginia Declaration of Rights 138
Virginia General Assembly 209
Virginia Plan 105
Voting
  varying qualifications for 50

W

Wadsworth, Jeremiah 110, 170, 171,
    175, 196, 221
Warren, Mercy Otis 97
Washington, Bushrod 51
Washington, George 87, 228
  agrees to attend constitutional
      convention 38
  and first levees as president 89
  and image of monarchy 156
  and Society of the Cincinnati 34
  appoints first revenue officials 111
  appreciation for "the ladies" on
      Southern tour 178
  as diarist 227
  as host at Mount Vernon 88
  asks to be bled 235
  as lover of theater 95
  at Newburgh, New York 19
  attends opening of second session of
      Congress 191
  attends the play Darby's Return 96
  authorizes construction of naval
      frigates 188
  avoids Rhode Island on tour of North
      169
  bans slaves from Continental Army,
      then changes mind 127
  belief in bleeding as cure 162
  bled of more than five pints of blood
      235
  borrows money 52, 65
  calls for establishing navy 187
  carbuncle on thigh 158
  chosen as president of Constitutional
      Convention 39
  coach, horse-drawn 191
  concerns after victory at Yorktown 18
  death of 236
  declares neutrality in French-British
      war 188
  delivers Annual Message to a Joint
      Session of Congress 191, 192
  delivers Inaugural Address 84
  departs Mount Vernon for New York
      for Inauguration 72
  departs on Northern tour 170
  departs on tour of Southern states
      176
  diary during northern tour 171
  diary entry on Beverly manufacturing
      173
  diary entry prior to death 233
  does not stay in private homes on
      northern tour 171
  doubts about becoming president 47
  elected President 53
  election as President ratified 66
  endorses magazine The American
      Museum 219
  establishes precedent of peaceful
      transfer of power 232
  establishing precedents 151, 155
  eulogies and orations at death of 238
  Farewell Address 231

fear of being buried alive 236
first house in New York. *See* No. 1
    Cherry Street
frees one slave in will 236
general assumption he would be first
    President 70
issues Thanksgiving proclamation,
    1789 147
Last Will and Testament of 235
life expectancy 157
low opinion of militias 193
mock funerals held for 238
mode of travel on Northern tour 170,
    172
mode of travel on Southern tour 178
named commander in chief by
    President Adams 189
nominates persons for Federal jobs
    150
notates book Acts of Congress 148
notified of his election 69
official public funeral for 239
orders homespun suit of clothes for
    inauguration 52
orders in will for slaves to be freed
    after Martha's death 236
plans tour of "Eastern States" 169
private funeral rites at Mount Vernon
    237
proposes militia in 1783 193
publishes Farewell Address 231
reconsiders slavery 181
relationship with Lafayette 164
resigns as commander-in-chief 47, 78
responds to "fellow soldier" letter 24
responds to Newburgh Letter 21
responds to Varnum letter 22
retires to Mount Vernon 232
seeks peace with Indians through
    treaties 210
sees mother for last time 65
sees Northwest Territory as path to
    "rising Empire" 210

selects associate justices with eye to
    geographic balance 113
selects commissioners for choosing
    permanent capital site 175, 178
selects one will and destroys other
    235
sends 1783 circular letter 192
serious illness in 1789 157
signs bill for National Bank 176
signs Bill of Rights 144
skeptical of first census result 119
slaves accompany him on Northern
    tour 170
state coach 94
suffering pneumonia 158
suffers influenza 1790 159
supporting domestic manufacturing
    174
supports stronger federal government
    36
suppresses Whiskey Rebellion 231
surgery performed upon 158
swears never to visit Senate again 155
takes oath of office 83
takes the power to appoint marshals
    117
visits the Senate 152, 154
votes for Elector 50
wears suit made of American-made
    cloth for Inauguration 82
writes 1781 circular letter to
    governors and Congress 24
writing against slavery 128
Washington Influenza 172
Washington, John A. III 164
Washington, Martha 73, 212, 234
    arrives in New York 92
    burns letters exchanged with
        Washington 237
    enters mourning 237
    frees her slaves in interest of her own
        safety 238
    Friday-night levees 97

social obligations as wife of president
    93
takes slave out of state to avoid
    triggering freedom 180
Washington, Mary Ball 65
    death of 94
    slaves left to relatives in will 94
Washington's Strolling Players 95
Wayne, Anthony 215
    Endorses Fishbourn 152
Webster, Noah 217
    launches *American Magazine* 220
    on need for American language 217
    opposed Bill of Rights 140
    support state-by-state copyright laws
        219
Weems, Mason Locke 240
West, Benjamin 104
West Indies 183
Wethersfield, Connecticut 170
Wheeled vehicles
    tariffs on 110
Whiskey Rebellion 231
White, Alexander
    complains of indifference to
        Northwest Territory 205
White, James 211

Wilberforce, William 60
    Anti-slavery speech of 134
Wilkinson, James 208
    as Spanish Secret Agent 13 208
    commands U.S. Army whilst secret
        agent of Spain 210
    proposes Kentucky become Spanish
        colony 208
    treachery of not proved until after his
        death 210
    votes to declare Kentucky
        independent of Virginia 209
Wilmington Centinel 222
Wingate, Paine 107
Wood, Gordon S. 121
Wynkoop, Henry 81

Y

Yates, Robert
    notes on Constitutional Convention
        41
Yorktown, Battle of 18, 184

Z

Zenger, John Peter
    arrested for sedition 56

ABOUT THE AUTHOR

*T*homas B. Allen was born in Bridgeport, Connecticut, in 1929. The author of numerous history books, he was a frequent contributor to *Smithsonian Magazine, National Geographic, Military History Quarterly, Military History, Naval History,* the U.S. Naval Institute's *Proceedings,* and other publications.

Photo by Edith Allen

Tom began his professional career as a general assignment reporter for the Bridgeport *Herald* while still in his teens. He served in the U.S. Navy in the early 1950s, then returned to work as a reporter in Connecticut. In 1957, Tom became a feature writer for the New York *Daily News.* He began his book-writing career as the co-author of *Shadows in the Sea: The Sharks, Skates and Rays,* 1963. His first solo book was *The Quest,* 1965, an account of the search for extraterrestrial life.

He worked as an editor for Chilton Books of Philadelphia. In 1965, he became an editor for the National Geographic Society Book Service, and was named Associate Chief Editor in 1974. Prominent among the works he wrote and edited for the Society was the social history *We Americans.* Tom published his first novel, *The Last Inmate,* in 1973.

Tom became a full-time freelancer in 1981. He wrote major articles for the *National Geographic Magazine,* including pieces on D-Day, the air war in Europe, Turkey, Mongolia, the U.S.S. *Maine,* Pearl Harbor, and his home state of Connecticut. He traveled for his work from New Zealand to Europe, China and Japan, and throughout the world. As a freelancer, he wrote the National Geographic's Civil War book *The Blue and The Grey.*

His book *Possessed* is an account of the harrowing real-life events that inspired *The Exorcist. Possessed* was adapted for a Showtime movie of the same name.

Tom's 2010 book *Tories: Fighting for the King in America's First Civil War* is a narrative history of Loyalists in the American Revolution. The *Economist* called it "an original and copiously sourced history of the war's losers." The New York *Times* said Tories is "not for the faint of heart or for those who prefer revolutions in ideas."

His books include highly acclaimed non-fiction titles for younger readers, including *Remember Valley Forge*; and *Remember Pearl Harbor*, selected as one of the Notable Books of 2001 by the American Library Association. Two of Tom's other titles for young readers, *George Washington, Spymaster* and the highly acclaimed *Harriet Tubman, Secret Agent,* were named to many prominent book lists. *Mr. Lincoln's High-Tech War*, written with his son Roger, was selected by ALA as one of the best non-fiction young adult books of 2009.

He was the co-author, with Norman Polmar, of *World War II, 1941-1945*, an encyclopedia of the war; *Spy Book, The Encyclopedia of Espionage*; an account of the plan to invade Japan entitled *Code-name Downfall;* the biography *Rickover, Controversy and Genius*; and *Merchants of Treason*, a study of spies of the 1980s. The two also collaborated on the novel *Ship of Gold*. Tom was co-author, with Paul Dickson, of *The Bonus Army: An American Epic,* the story of the ill-fated World War I veterans who marched on Washington in 1932. *The New York Review of Books* said the book "recalls the subliminal force of *Let Us Now Praise Famous Men* with gaunt stories of character at the limits of dignity."

Tom wrote frequently on military and intelligence subjects. He was named by the U.S. Naval Institute as 2004 Naval History Author of the Year "for the sustained high quality of his literary contributions to Naval History magazine."

Tom was also a teacher of writing and of historical subjects, speaking and lecturing on many subjects over the years. He edited, guided, and encouraged many other writers throughout his career.

Tom died in December, 2018 at the age of 89, and was survived by his wife Scottie, his three children Chris, Connie, and Roger, and eight grandchildren.

Visit www.tballen.com to learn more about Tom and his work.